African
KAISER

African
KAISER

GENERAL PAUL VON LETTOW-VORBECK
AND THE GREAT WAR IN AFRICA, 1914-1918

Robert Gaudi

CALIBER
NEW YORK

CALIBER
Published by Berkley
An imprint of Penguin Random House LLC
375 Hudson Street, New York, New York 10014

Copyright © 2017 by Robert Gaudi
Penguin Random House supports copyright. Copyright fuels creativity, encourages diverse voices,
promotes free speech, and creates a vibrant culture. Thank you for buying an authorized edition of
this book and for complying with copyright laws by not reproducing, scanning, or distributing
any part of it in any form without permission. You are supporting writers and allowing
Penguin Random House to continue to publish books for every reader.

CALIBER and its colophon are trademarks of Penguin Random House LLC.

Library of Congress Cataloging-in-Publication Data

Names: Gaudi, Robert, author.
Title: African Kaiser: General Paul von Lettow-Vorbeck and the Great War in
Africa, 1914–1918 / Robert Gaudi.
Description: First edition. | New York: Caliber, published by Berkley, 2017.
Identifiers: LCCN 2016039912 (print) | LCCN 2016040742 (ebook) | ISBN
9780425283714 | ISBN 9780698411524 (ebook)
Subjects: LCSH: Lettow-Vorbeck, General von (Paul Emil), 1870–1964. | World
War, 1914–1918—Campaigns—German East Africa. | World War,
1914–1918—Aerial operations, German. | Germany. Heer. Schutztruppen. |
Germany—Armed Forces—Colonial forces.
Classification: LCC D576.G3 G38 2017 (print) | LCC D576.G3 (ebook) | DDC
940.416—dc23
LC record available at https://lccn.loc.gov/2016039912

First Edition: January 2017

Printed in the United States of America
1   3   5   7   9   10   8   6   4   2

Jacket photographs: Front: Zeppelin by Luftschiffbau Zeppelin; Soldiers by bpl, Berlin/Art Resource, NY.
Spine: German propaganda poster art by Galerie Bilderwelt/Hulton Archive/Getty Images.
Back: Paul Emil von Lettow-Vorbeck by Pictorial Press Ltd/Alamy Stock Photo.
Jacket design by Emily Osborne
Book design by Laura K. Corless

While the author has made every effort to provide accurate telephone numbers,
Internet addresses and other contact information at the time of publication, neither the publisher
nor the author assumes any responsibility for errors, or for changes that occur after publication.
Further, publisher does not have any control over and does not assume any responsibility
for author or third-party Web sites or their content.

For Gregor von Bismarck, whose idea it was . . .
and of course for my children

Contents

The Commander stands for the virtues of wisdom,
sincerity, benevolence, courage, and strictness.

—SUN-TZU, *Art of War*

Father, I call on you.
I am surrounded by smoke from the cannon.

—KÖRNER

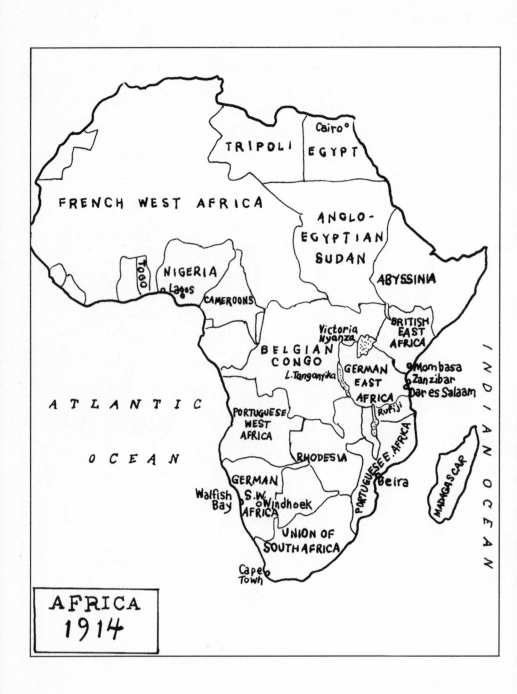

TRIPOLI

Cairo°

EGYPT

FRENCH WEST AFRICA

ANGLO-EGYPTIAN SUDAN

TOGO

NIGERIA

°Lagos

CAMEROONS

ABYSSINIA

BELGIAN CONGO

Victoria Nyanza

L. Tanganyika

BRITISH EAST AFRICA

GERMAN EAST AFRICA

°Mombasa
Zanzibar
Dar es Salaam

ATLANTIC

PORTUGUESE WEST AFRICA

OCEAN

Rufiji

RHODESIA

PORTUGUESE E. AFRICA

Beira

GERMAN S.W. AFRICA

Walfish Bay

°Windhoek

MADAGASCAR

UNION OF SOUTH AFRICA

INDIAN OCEAN

Cape° Town

AFRICA
1914

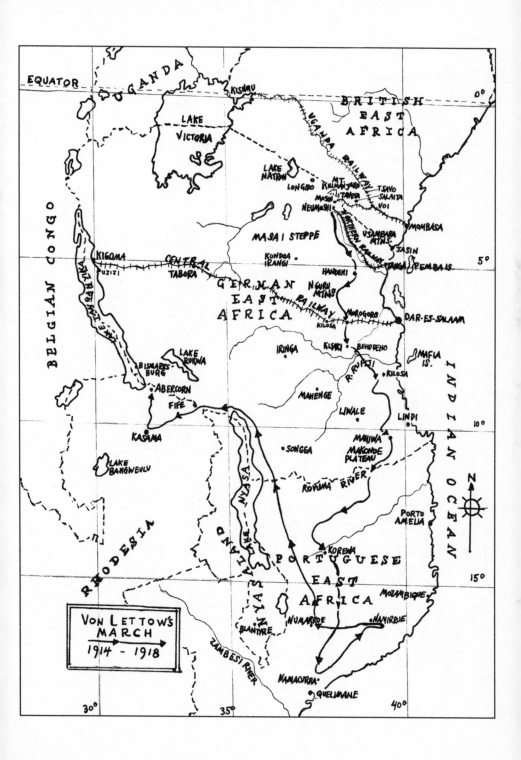

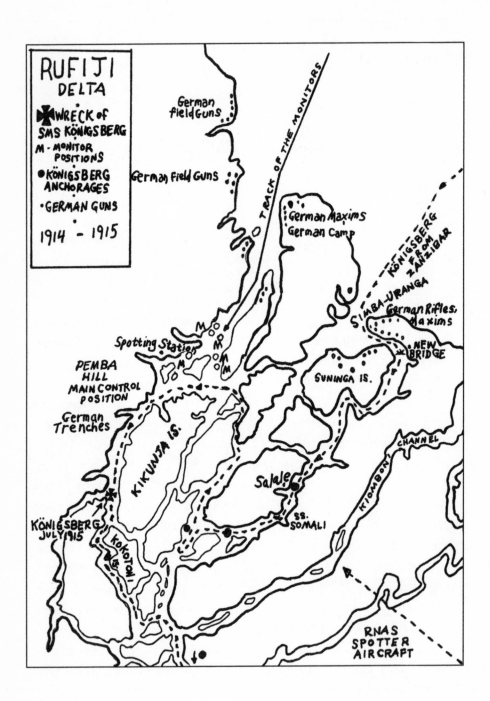

BLACK HEROES OF THE FATHERLAND

At the pinnacle of the Great Pyramid at Giza, in place of the long-vanished solid gold capstone of the pharaohs, stood a wireless receiving tower, its tall antennae bolted to the ancient pitted stone. Installed by British Naval Intelligence in 1915, this listening post was part of a secret network of many such posts all over Africa—a network designed to trap all the coded German messages rattling uncaught around the ether and send them on to cryptographers at the Admiralty back in London.

Meanwhile, 2,000 miles away, five degrees south of the equator, the "Black Heroes of the Fatherland" fought on against overwhelming odds. Cut off from the world by the British blockade in what remained of Germany's last colony, fed false information from British wireless towers like the one atop the Great Pyramid, they marched through bush and jungle and swamp and thorn scrub *pori*. They clambered up mountains and across arid, rocky plateaus, mostly without shoes. Their rifles were ancient or captured from the enemy; their artillery a few naval guns scavenged off a gutted battleship wrecked in the fetid sluice of the Rufiji. They attacked, retreated, advanced, attacked, retreated to fight again. And though vastly outnumbered by British, South African, Belgian, and Portuguese armies, they could not be caught or beaten.

This was German East Africa's small, redoubtable Schutztruppe—a "protection force" originally mustered in 1889 to help tame what was then Germany's newest colonial acquisition in Africa. Led in the early days by German adventurers, its ranks had embraced renegade Zulu warriors and

Sudanese soldiers demobbed from the Anglo-Sudanese Army. After 1905, it evolved into an armed police force run by military professionals commanding local East African *askaris* (the Swahili word for "soldier") skilled in bush warfare. In the last, uneasy years before World War One, only the Schutztruppe stood between German settlers and the persistent threat of native uprisings.

But led by an obscure, brilliant German officer, Oberstleutnant (Lieutenant Colonel) Paul von Lettow-Vorbeck, "one of the most successful guerrilla leaders in world history," GEA's Schutztruppe had been radically reinvented: Since the outbreak of "Universal Conflict"—von Lettow's memorable phrase—by August 1914, he had forged it into a highly efficient mobile fighting force, aggressive and completely self-supporting. Now its fanatically loyal *askaris* were led by a cadre of indomitable black NCOs and officered by seasoned German soldiers, marines, and sailors, many trained at the famous military academy at Kassel. Both through necessity and by design, the Schutztruppe had become the first racially integrated army in modern history. "Here in Africa we are all equal," von Lettow famously said. "The better man will always outwit the inferior and the color of his skin does not matter."

Ammunition dwindling, food down to starvation rations, critical quinine stores nearly exhausted, wireless sets kaput, the Schutztruppe, always on the verge of capitulation—at least according to the British General Staff in Nairobi—somehow always won the next fight. Victorious in a handful of dramatic pitched battles and countless skirmishes, they would hold out until Germany triumphed over her enemies in Europe or all were dead. And as long as they kept the Kaiser's flag flying somewhere in the bush—so von Lettow told his men—German East Africa remained undefeated.

Chapter 1

ZEPPELINS OF THE CHINA SHOW

A thick, billowing fog bank concealed the rocky shore of the Baltic island of Odensholm off the Estonian coast before dawn in the early morning of August 26, 1914. Odensholm—desolate, beautiful home to a small ethnic Swedish population of farmers and fishermen since Viking times—was also, according to legend, the final resting place of Odin, chief god of the Norse pantheon, patron of death, battles, frenzy, poetry, and a few other things. No one on Odensholm could say exactly where the god was buried, whether beneath this barrow or that mound; some insisted the island itself was his tomb, its cliffs and stony beaches the monument raised above his massive divine corpse.

But such mythological nonsense did not figure among the matters weighing on the mind of Korvettenkapitan Richard Habenicht of SMS *Magdeburg* as he threaded his warship through the shallow waters at the mouth of the Gulf of Finland in the last dark hours of the night. *Magdeburg*, one of the newest and fastest cruisers in the Kaiserlich Marine, 455 feet long, propelled by two powerful AEG Vulcan steam turbines, could make 27.5 knots fully loaded with all arms and ordnance and carrying its complement of 355 officers and men. Her twelve 10.5cm guns could blast an enemy vessel out of the water from 41,700 feet—nearly eight miles—away, as long as atmospheric conditions permitted lookouts to see that far. Part of the Kaiser's newly constituted Baltic Squadron under the command of Rear Admiral Behring, *Magdeburg* had been sent to harass Russian naval bases and warships in the Gulf of Finland. She had participated, along with

SMS *Augsburg*, three destroyers, and the minelayer *Deutschland*, in the bombardment of the Russian port of Libau on August 2, the opening naval action of the Baltic Campaign.

Then, on the morning of August 17, these German warships came into contact with a more powerful Russian squadron, including the *Admiral Makaroff, Gumboi, Bogatyr*, and *Pallada*. In naval warfare of the era, the captain of an outgunned ship presented with the choice between fight or flight would automatically choose the latter. Korvettenkapitan Habenicht ordered evasive maneuvers and soon put the slower, heavily armed Russians in his wake. A week later, skimming the Estonian coast on reconnaissance duty, *Magdeburg* came into contact with *Bogatyr* and *Pallada* for the second time. Still outgunned, she again showed them her stern; this time the Russian warships gave chase.

Night fell. SMS *Magdeburg*, with *Bogatyr* and *Pallada* somewhere close behind, ran into the fog bank near Odensholm at fifteen knots. Suddenly, a deep shudder ran the length of the ship, followed by a metallic shrieking sound. Every man aboard, from captain to cook, knew the worst had happened: *Magdeburg* had run aground. Korvettenkapitan Habenicht immediately ordered "full stop," but for a long minute the massive turbines throbbed forward, driving the ship farther out of the water. He then ordered "full speed reverse." No use. The metallic shrieking only intensified and *Magdeburg* wouldn't budge. "Full stop" again. *Magdeburg*, the Kaiser's fastest ship, was stuck hard on the rocks beneath Lighthouse Cliff at the northeast tip of Odensholm; she had been called by Odin's ghost to her doom.

Presently, *Magdeburg*'s escort destroyer, known only by its call letters, V.26, approached gingerly through the fog. Tow cables fixed, she attempted to pull the larger ship free, to no avail. *Magdeburg* was stuck for good, with the Russians lurking somewhere just over the edge of the horizon. Korvettenkapitan Habenicht then gave the order to abandon ship, two words that would haunt him for the rest of his life. The fog complicated matters, but V.26 managed to evacuate most of *Magdeburg*'s crew. A remnant, including the captain, remained aboard to perform a few last duties—most important, the destruction of the codebooks and cipher keys known as the *Signalbuch der Kaiserlichen Marine* (SKM), of which *Magdeburg* had been issued several copies. These critical documents allowed the Germans—heavily reliant on radio communication—to talk to one another without the enemy being able to eavesdrop.

Signal books destroyed, the unfortunate cruiser would be scuttled by charges set in the forward magazine. This sort of operation—fogbound, at night, in choppy seas, beneath a rocky cliff—dangerous at best, was doubly dangerous in wartime. A sailor fell into the cold waters of the Baltic and drowned as the scuttling charges were hastily set; several more died a few minutes later when they detonated prematurely.

At last, the fog lifted and morning sun lit the scene of Korvettenkapitan Habenicht's nightmare: There, between the bright Estonian coast seven miles off and Odensholm's stony cliff, stood *Bogatyr* and *Pallada*. The Russian ships began firing immediately, their big guns booming across the gulf. A dozen sailors died in the bombardment, vaporized by exploding shells. Forty-five more, still aboard *Magdeburg*, saved themselves by jumping overboard and swimming to the island. The bombardment quickly came to an end; *Magdeburg*, unable to offer any resistance, was a dead ship.

Korvettenkapitan Habenicht retired to his cabin, determined not to outlast the destruction of the ship he'd stupidly run aground on Odensholm. What had happened? A navigational error, a mistake in dead reckoning in a fog bank at night, had put them closer to the island than he'd suspected. One could blame the navigator, but ultimately the responsibility rested with the captain alone. He sat down behind his desk and tried not to think about the pistol in the drawer. An hour later, a Russian naval officer of English extraction, Lieutenant M. Hamilton, found Korvettenkapitan Habenicht still sitting there, head in his hands.

The captain looked up, all fight gone from his pale blue eyes, as Hamilton entered the cabin. The Russian gestured out the porthole to his torpedo boat, the *Boukaroff*, just come alongside. He tried Russian, French, and English, but Korvettenkapitan Habenicht didn't understand these languages. Then, in halting German, Hamilton managed, *"Wollen sie nach torpedo gehen?"* and again gestured to the *Boukaroff*. At last, the captain nodded.

He rose and strode about the cabin, agitated, picked up a few personal items, put them down, opened his desk drawer, closed it. In the end, he took nothing—then his eyes fell upon his sword hanging on a hook on the wall. He took it down and offered it to Lieutenant Hamilton, who refused politely and handed it back. It was not right, Hamilton later said, to take a captain's sword aboard his own ship. Korvettenkapitan Habenicht, overwhelmed by this small kindness, shook the young officer's hand and with that gesture became a prisoner of the tsar. He would remain so until his escape during the turmoil of the Russian Revolution in 1918.

The wreck of his ship, the SMS *Magdeburg*, scrapped by the Russians and still visible at low tide off Lighthouse Cliff on Odensholm, is today a popular spot for Baltic Sea sport divers.

———————

The fate of a single German cruiser and the capture of her captain, no matter how keenly felt at the time, remain minor incidents in a major war and would be all but forgotten now except for a single significant oversight: Unfortunately for the German war effort, the destruction of the *Magdeburg*'s naval codebooks had been interrupted by the premature explosion of the scuttling charges, then overlooked during the tumult of evacuation and bombardment.

The Russians, upon searching the ship, discovered two copies of the codebooks, one at the bottom of a storage locker aft, another—along with the cipher key and secret charts of the Baltic—in the wheelhouse. A third copy, dredged up by Russian divers from the rocky seabed, had been weighted with lead and tossed overboard. This copy, SKM 151, was offered by the Russians to their British allies. The Admiralty dispatched HMS *Theseus* to Alexandrovsk on the Arctic Circle to fetch SKM 151 to London; First Sea Lord Winston Churchill examined it in his office on October 30, 1914.

"At the beginning of September 1914, the German light cruiser *Magdeburg* was wrecked in the Baltic," recalled Churchill, getting his dates wrong and, characteristically, sacrificing accuracy for drama. "The body of a drowned German under-officer was picked up by the Russians a few hours later. Clasped in his bosom by arms rigid in death were the cipher and signal books of the German Navy. . . .

"Late on an October afternoon . . . I received from the hands of our loyal allies these sea-stained, priceless documents. We set on foot at once an organization for the study of the German wireless and for the translating of the messages taken in. The work was of great complexity as, of course, the cipher is only one element in the means of preserving a message. But gradually our officers succeeded in translating intelligible portions of various German naval messages."

The organization Churchill and others set afoot became the legendary Room 40, a secret cabal of cryptographers, mathematicians, philosophers, linguists, scholars, and similar useless types—the "best brains in the country." These eccentrics worked in a hidden warren of rooms at the Admiralty in the Old Building, then, as now, presided over by the statue of Nelson in his whitewashed niche. Twice a day, a superannuated functionary called simply Old Maskell, like a character out of Dickens, carried a black box containing deciphered German military communications from Room 40's puzzle-solvers to the strategic thinkers at British Naval Intelligence. These intercepted messages came in from every corner of the empire and from every front where Britain and her allies fought Kaiser Wilhelm II and his "Huns."

All through the first years of the war, the most eagerly awaited—and dreaded—German messages received in Room 40 pertained to the deadly Zeppelin raids on London. During this period, the great city endured her first "blitz"—a relentless series of air attacks perpetrated on civilian targets by the massive, unwieldy airships, attacks lent an extra punch by their very newness: For the first time in history, a civilian population was being bombed from the skies. The Kaiser, Germany's ultimate "War Chief," initially opposed the Zeppelin raids as unsportsmanlike. He also didn't want to bomb his royal cousins in Buckingham Palace. But as the British naval blockade tightened its grip on Germany and the German people felt the hunger pangs of food shortages, his resistance weakened and the Zeppelins began their reign of terror.

"People stand gazing into the sky from the darkened streets," wrote American journalist William Shepherd, describing an early Zeppelin attack on the British capital. "Among the autumn stars floats a long, gaunt Zeppelin;

it is dull yellow, the color of a harvest moon. . . . Great booming sounds shake the city. They are Zeppelin bombs—falling—killing—burning. . . . Suddenly, you realize the biggest city in the world has become the night battlefield on which seven million harmless men, women, and children live."

It's hard for us now, living in the faint afterglow of the Apollo missions, to understand the visceral impact of the Zeppelin *Luftschiff* (airship) on the world of 1914. They had been developed over several decades and through many spectacular disasters by the eccentric, monomaniacal Saxon count Ferdinand von Zeppelin—inspired after going aloft in a Union Army observation balloon at Fort Snelling, Minnesota, during the American Civil War.

The latest iterations, cigar-shaped and long as ocean liners, were ultra-combustible monsters, kept aloft by canvas bags full of a highly explosive hydrogen/oxygen mixture fixed to a rigid duralumin frame covered by a weatherproofed canvas skin. Five aviation engines suspended from aluminum scaffolding beneath their vast bellies provided forward push; a complex system of wheels, weights, and cables in two separate gondolas allowed for directional control. Their capacious, largely empty interiors, crisscrossed by catwalks and cargo platforms, could carry a payload of thousands of tons of bombs.

Once airborne, the Zeppelin emitted a steady drone, like the buzzing of some giant, destructive insect. In 1915, London Air Defense, casting about for a Zeppelin early-warning detection system, recruited blind volunteers to listen for this drone. Deprived of sight, the hearing of the blind must be that much more acute—so Air Defense reasoned. They thought the blind would be able to hear the Zeppelins coming before anyone else, thus allowing squadrons of B.E.2c fighters more time to scramble from aerodromes hidden around the city. (It took one of these slow, rickety planes an hour to screw up to the Zeppelin cruising altitude, above 10,000 feet.) And so dozens of blind volunteers stood with their ears pressed to giant sound amplification cones all through the London nights they could not see, as if listening for the voice of God. This system, despite its unintended poetry, didn't work very well; apparently the blind hear no better than anyone else.

"England is no longer an island," crowed the editorial writers of Leipzig's *Neueste Nachrichten*. "The city of London, the heart which pumps the life blood into the arteries of the brutal huckster nation, has been sown with bombs by German airships. . . . At last, the long yearned for punishment has fallen on England, this people of liars and hypocrites—their punishment for the overflowing measure of sins of years past. . . ."

Etc.

Less than eighteen months later, the Zeppelins had become a military redundancy. They exploded into flowers of flame with sickening, predictable regularity in the night skies over London. They fell slowly, dripping bright, fiery tendrils into the black water of the English Channel. To save weight and increase bomb-carrying capacity, Zeppelin crews were not allowed parachutes and so plummeted in their hundreds to the darkened earth and destruction. Once feared airborne predators, the Zeppelins had now become slow, lumbering prey—ridiculed by a no longer fearful British public as harmless airborne "gas bags." They had been rendered obsolete for offensive purposes by the invention of incendiary bullets that could ignite hydrogen gas with ease, by an increasingly efficient early-warning system that had nothing to do with superhearing blind people and was instead based on Room 40's deciphered messages, and by advances in aircraft design that allowed fighters to reach ever-higher altitudes. British pilots could now attain those rarefied stratums of the atmosphere where, like giant defecating birds, the Zeppelins did their business.

But, in the fall of 1916, Room 40's puzzle-solvers caught wind of something new and ominous—the faint echoes of an emerging threat, referred to in German coded messages as "China Show." The only thing they knew for sure about China Show was that it had to do with Zeppelins. Did this mean the Germans had developed more powerful airships, somehow impervious to incendiary bullets? Or larger and more destructive bombs for the Zeppelins to drop on London? Or were they planning a new offensive to recover their lost territories in the Far East? Oddly, several of the messages referring to China Show had been intercepted by the listening post atop the Great Pyramid in British-held Egypt.

Edwin T. Woodhall, in *Spies of the Great War*—an often fanciful survey of wartime espionage—credited old-fashioned human intelligence and not Room 40's eggheads with uncovering the secret meaning behind China

Show. Woodhall's dramatic tale, lent at least some plausibility by his record as one of England's top wartime spies and by a subsequent distinguished career at Scotland Yard, begins with a shadowy British agent known only as Mortimer. According to Woodhall, Mortimer parachuted behind enemy lines near Brod in southern Austria in late October 1916. From Brod, he reached Vienna and there checked into a shabby hotel for a prearranged clandestine meeting with an even more shadowy figure, an unnamed American of Bulgarian ancestry working for the British Secret Service in Bulgaria. Formerly neutral, Bulgaria had recently joined the Central Powers—Germany and Austro-Hungary—in its war against the Allies—Britain, France, Italy, Portugal, and later the United States. The unnamed Bulgarian-American-British agent, naturally fluent in Bulgarian, regularly brought intelligence gathered in Bulgaria to Vienna, where he briefed British agents infiltrated from London.

After an introduction that required the exchange of certain cryptic passwords, Mortimer and the unnamed agent settled down to their secret conversation: This time, the unnamed agent brought news of two "super Zeppelins," *L57* and *L59*, just built at the *Luftschiff* mother base at Friedrichshafen, in Germany. *L57*, constructed in detachable sections, would soon be shipped by train to a forward *Luftschiff* base at Jamboli in Bulgaria for reassembly. From there, loaded down with munitions and supplies, she would be sent on an ultrasecret mission—a complex operation code-named "China Show."

The new class of super Zeppelins—*L57* and *L59* being the latest examples—much improved over the early generations of *Luftschiff*, could reach altitudes of 18,000 feet, far above the combat ceiling of any attack plane. There they might remain aloft for days, with a posited range of 10,000 miles. Theoretically, a super Zeppelin leaving the safety of her shed in Germany with a huge payload of bombs could drop them three days later on Chicago. In practice these freakishly oversize Zeppelins—to this day, the largest man-made objects ever to rise above the earth—proved difficult to handle on the ground, unwieldy in the air, and prone to spectacular disasters:

On October 7 at the *Luftschiff* mother base in Friedrichshafen—so the unnamed agent told Mortimer—*L57* had been hauled from her shed for a test flight by a ground crew of 300. Hands cold on the guide ropes, the men of the ground crew waited anxiously for two words—Up ship!—from Korvettenkapitan Ludwig Bockholt of the Kaiserlich Marine's Naval Airship Service, the officer in command of *L57*. The vast airship, brand-new, still smelled of dope, the yellowish mixture of glue and varnish used to weatherproof her taut canvas hide. Suddenly, a squall moved in, bringing gale-force winds. Violent crosscurrents along the ground nearly smashed *L57*'s vulnerable nose cone—about as large around as one of the rings of a three-ring circus—into the corrugated metal door of her shed.

The prudent move at this point might have been to return *L57* to her berth. But Bockholt, determined to prove his super Zeppelin could fly in all weathers, ordered her aloft. Not one of the most skilled Zeppelin captains, Bockholt was nevertheless renowned for his daring and impossible exploits. While commanding *L23* in June 1916, he had captured the Norwegian schooner *Royal* carrying mining timbers to England. In a scene out of Jules Verne, he lowered a prize crew on rope ladders onto the pitching deck of the ship, which was then sailed to the nearest German port. The capture of the *Royal* would remain a unique occurrence, the first and only time a Zeppelin captured a ship at sea.

Now at Friedrichshafen, *L57*'s hold had just been loaded with eighty-five cases of medical supplies and hundreds of cases of ammunition. Perhaps Bockholt wanted to see how she would perform thus laden. But the winds grew stronger; *L57*, blown like a scrap of paper in this gale, could not be returned to her waiting shed. Three hundred extra handlers raced to assist the ground crew—to no avail. Korvettenkapitan Bockholt released enough water ballast to take *L57* up again. Like seagoing vessels during a hurricane, safest on the open ocean, Zeppelins were better off aloft, in the atmosphere, no matter how turbulent.

Bockholt decided he would take advantage of the prevailing winds and make for his interim destination, the *Luftschiff* base at Jamboli, Bulgaria. But he hesitated, waiting for additional food and supplies to be loaded. As he hovered fifty feet above the ground, the storm grew even worse and a sudden gust sent the 500 men below, still clinging to the guide ropes, sailing across the landing field. Entire ground crews had been lifted into the air by rogue Zeppelins before; they hung on until they couldn't anymore and fell to their deaths.

L57 rolled dangerously in the wind. The storm had the Zeppelin and wouldn't let go. A sudden blast whipped her around; the rear gondola tore loose. Completely out of control now, *L57* blew across the field and into the teeth of a tall metal fence. Korvettenkapitan Bockholt chose this moment to abandon ship. The captain and a dozen airmen jumped for safety. They were followed, not a moment too soon, by a certain Professor Dr. Max Zupitza, a zoologist and medical doctor who had been chief medical officer in German South West Africa during the dreadful Herero and Hottentot Rebellions in that restless colony a decade earlier. Zupitza was the rumored architect of China Show.

Then something—a spark from the atmosphere, the scrape of metal on metal—ignited the volatile hydrogen gas. There came a quick moment of breathlessness and the peculiar sucking sound of gas exploding and a few minutes later the crackle and pop of the overheated ammunition in her hold going off. Rifle cartridges and machine gun shells continued to explode all night long in a merry fusillade. Morning light revealed the blackened, twisted skeleton of a great airship—the apparent ignominious end of the mysterious China Show.

But once something had been ordered by the Kaiser, it must come to pass. And China Show had the Kaiser's special stamp of approval. According to Mortimer's unnamed agent—who had talked to eyewitnesses of the *L57* disaster—another brand-new super Zeppelin, the *L59*, had almost immediately arisen from the ashes. Amazingly, *Luftschiff* Command made her available to China Show within two weeks. China Show was clearly a very big deal.

The day after his secret meeting in Vienna, Mortimer escaped through neutral Switzerland to France. In Paris, Woodhall concludes, Mortimer "reported to the chiefs of Allied Intelligence the result of his mission." This was the first inkling anyone on the British side had of China Show. Mortimer himself disappeared from the record after his Paris debriefing. Woodhall tells us he was later killed in the trenches in France, in the last hours of the war.

The rest of the story comes—more reliably, perhaps—from official German naval airship records, the *Tambach Archive*, captured in the aftermath of World War Two, now in the joint custody of the British Admiralty and the U.S. Department of the Navy:

L59, lengthened and strengthened around the middle, could now carry additional cargo. At just over 750 feet long and 80 feet in diameter, she was both longer and broader than the unfortunate *L57* and displaced a volume of 2.5 million cubic feet. Five Maybach HSL engines produced more than 1,200 horsepower and allowed a top cruising speed of more than 60 miles per hour. Her cavernous interior, emptied of bombs and related material, was now filled with enough supplies and munitions to equip a small army: Military hardware included 311,100 rounds of rifle ammunition, 230 machine gun belts with 57,500 .50-caliber shells, 54 machine gun ammunition boxes containing an additional 13,500 cartridges, 30 guns, rifles for the Zeppelin's 22-man crew, 9 spare machine gun barrels, 61 sacks of medical supplies including enough quinine to last for a year or more in the tropics, rifle bolts, binoculars, fighting knives, spare radio parts, sewing kits for making new uniforms, and a case of wine to celebrate *L59*'s arrival at her destination should she ever make it there. All this amounted to a total cargo of more than 15 tons.

Though *L59* epitomized German ingenuity circa 1917, she had not been designed for a return journey. Rather, once on the ground, she would be disassembled and cannibalized, with every component intended for a specific earthbound purpose: The muslin envelopes of her gas bags could be turned into bandages and sleeping bags, the canvas sheathing over her duralumin frame used for tents and clothing, the duralumin frame itself turned into wireless masts, and the structural skeleton into load-bearing supports for temporary housing. Even the leather treads laid down on her interior catwalks were to be used in the manufacture of boots and belts. But *L59*'s most precious cargo was not quite tangible: news from the Fatherland, carried in a single thick mailbag, destined for troops who had not heard from family or friends in over two years of hard fighting.

On the way to Jamboli from Staaken in Germany, as if cursed by the ghost of *L57*, *L59* ran into a series of violent storms. Steering cables connected to the main and reverse rudders snapped and for a while the massive airship flew blind, muffled in a dense, sinister fog. Still, Bockholt—tenacious, determined—reached Jamboli in 28 hours and immediately began final preparations for the very long journey ahead. Bockholt was a big man, physically imposing, with a square head and small, pale eyes, afraid of nothing. He recognized the likelihood of failure; no Zeppelin had ever attempted such a distance, let alone over hostile latitudes. Two aborted attempts ensued. On the third, Bockholt, the mysterious Zupitza, and a twenty-man crew boarded *L59* just before dawn and settled in for an epic journey. The Zeppelin rose without incident, but more bad luck lay ahead: As *L59* passed over Smyrna, she was fired upon by Turkish troops. They had never seen such a thing! A floating sausage-shaped monstrosity so large it blotted out the sun. Surely, the Prophet—peace be upon him—had not intended men to fly! Despite the insistence of Turkish officers that this flying machine belonged to their allies the Germans, the Turks fired away. Bockholt immediately dropped ballast and *L59* soared far beyond the range of puny Turkish rifle fire.

The real peril came over the Mediterranean. Violent weather closed in, driving the heavily laden Zeppelin to within feet of the wine-dark, devouring sea. Bockholt jettisoned a ton of supplies, barely escaping a disastrous water landing, aborted the mission, and returned to Jamboli for repairs and to await better weather. For a week, he paced and fretted and consulted with Zupitza: Time was of the essence for China Show to come off as planned! Zupitza insisted another attempt must be made as soon as possible. One can imagine Korvettenkapitan Bockholt walking the Zeppelin sheds, hands behind his back, poised on the edge of history, as rain lashed the corrugated iron and the pines beyond the shed doors drooped in the rain.

At last, on November 20, 1917, the weather cleared and Bockholt readied his Zeppelin for a third attempt. The ground crew cheered as *L59* "walked" cleanly from her shed and rose unencumbered into the brightening sky. A cruising altitude of 10,000 feet was quickly achieved. Her nose cone aimed at an oblique angle to the rising sun, her mission *streng geheim*—top secret—*L59* sailed off south, toward a distant rendezvous somewhere in the heart of Africa.

Chapter 2

AT WAR IN BUSH AND DESERT

In the Namib Desert in German South West Africa on the morning of March 8, 1915, temperatures reached 132 degrees by ten a.m. Scalding winds blew down the bivouacs of the British Imperial troops. The Namib is one of the most fearsome places on earth, a parched, empty wasteland that receives an average of 0.55 inches of water per year.

As the sun rose and the extreme heat broiled and shimmered in the distance, horrified South African soldiers watched the desert floor crack and heave, and all at once millions of beetles emerged from cavities hidden deep underground, called to brief life by the hot, relentless winds. These dreadful burrowing insects, *Stenocara gracilipes*, the fogstand beetle, are scary-looking things, black and white with long spiderlike legs. All through late winter and early spring, in the Namib, they squat on these long appendages, angled at forty-five degrees to the ground fog, waiting for the seasonal winds to blow condensation down their waxy exoskeletons and into their open mandibles. They are a fascinating example of adaptability in an extreme environment, beloved by entomologists, and, despite their looks, essentially harmless. But to the men of General Botha's Northern Army chasing the retreating Germans through the desert and crunching across endless carpets of beetles in forced marches, this plague of *Stenocara gracilipes* must have seemed a vision from hell.

"It was one of the most awful scenes of desolation to be found on the face of the globe," said Major H. F. Trew, who served as one of General Botha's security officers during the campaign. "For miles and miles, the desert stretches, an expanse of grey plain with a thin, sandy crust covered with small pebbles."

And beetles, he might have added. Millions of them.

———————

Generals Louis Botha and Jan Smuts, both vigorous South African Boers, had fought hard against the British during the brutal Second Boer War of 1899–1902, but changed sides for the war against Germany just twelve years later. They had beaten back a fratricidal revolt of anti-British Boers—among whose ranks fought friends and family members—and joined themselves once and for all to the British cause. Now they led a raffish mixture of South Africans, British regular army troops, Rhodesian commandos, soldiers of fortune, Australians, and adventurers from every corner of the empire, all in the service of the king. As a captured German Baroness later commented, casting a gimlet eye on this heterogeneous force: "We Germans seem to be fighting the whole damn world."

The opposing Germans, under Colonel Victor Franke, didn't put up much of a resistance. Franke, known as the "Hero of Omaruru" for a bygone exploit during the colony's dreadful Herero Rebellion of 1904–05, was now probably a morphine addict—as suggested by clues in his war diaries. Alternately befuddled and brave to the point of self-annihilation, but indecisive as a commander, Franke had long ago lost the will to prevail in a hard fight.

German South West Africa—modern-day Namibia—while not Germany's largest African colony and arguably its least beautiful, was nonetheless the most populous, prized, and dearly won. GSWA's flat brown, wide-open spaces were well suited to cattle ranching. About 12,000 German colonizers lived a kind of Texas life on isolated ranches, in cow towns and small cities with names like Swakopmund, Grootfontein, and Windhoek, the colonial capital, which boasted substantial half-timbered German-style buildings, beer halls, modern sanitation, electric lights. Windhoek's powerful Telefunken wireless transmitter facility, which enabled High Command in Berlin to communicate with their commerce raiders and U-boats at sea, was the main British strategic objective in the war in GSWA.

"Coming out of the desert, Windhoek was a revelation, and a great tribute to German colonization," commented Major Trew, when Windhoek was taken. "The government buildings are most ornate and would have done credit to any city in the world." The town itself was dominated by an absurd replica of a traditional German castle.

Victorious British Imperial troops also found comfort in the arms of the lonely German women of Windhoek—after the manner of conquering armies from time immemorial. A charming, *susslich* Viennese beauty known only as Regina ran a private club for officers of the German General Staff that now, suddenly, catered to their British counterparts: Regina remained a German patriot, she insisted—never mind the fortunes of war that at the moment dictated otherwise. And she invited a bevy of similarly patriotic friends for evening dances with British officers to the music of a gramophone. They tangoed, they waltzed. Whatever else they did remains unmentioned. In exchange, Regina and her friends enjoyed the dubious benefits of British military rations and polished off their regimental champagne reserves.

After the fall of Windhoek, the rest of German South West Africa quickly succumbed to a fast-moving campaign described by the *Cambridge Military History of World War One* as "one of the neatest and most successful . . . of the Great War." The Germans experienced GSWA's loss as a painful diminishment of national pride: First because, as historian Edward Paice puts it in his monumental study, *World War I: The African Front*, "Africa *mattered* to the European powers at the beginning of the twentieth century." And second, the British victory rendered worthless the colony's vicious and hard-won pacification by German forces less than a decade earlier. The high cost of that pacification had been spiritual as well as physical: General Lothar von Trotha's merciless suppression of the native Hereros would be labeled genocide by later generations—the first such charge laid at the feet of the German people in the bloody century just dawning.

Abandoned German settlements, half buried in sand, their thick plaster and brick walls pockmarked with bullet holes, can be seen in Namibia to this day, bizarrely preserved by the super-arid climate. At Riet and Pforte, Jakkalswater and Trekhopf, rust-free relics of the battles of more than 100 years ago still lie strewn across the brittle surface of the desert.

The German defeat in GSWA in 1915 had followed hard on the heels of lesser but equally painful disasters in German Togoland and the Cameroons.

In those places, malarial hellholes of steaming jungle and equatorial swamp, valued strategically only for their wireless transmission towers, British and French victories came with a comparatively low "butcher's bill." In the Cameroons, for example, the British lost 1,668 men, the French 2,567—in both cases almost all from tropical diseases. As always, the Carrier Corps suffered the heaviest losses. These were the native porters impressed into service by both sides to haul supplies and munitions through the bush. Without them, no war could be fought in Africa, where roads were nonexistent and pack animals—vulnerable to the tse-tse fly, which could kill a strong horse or mule within days—could not survive.

Here, as elsewhere, during all the campaigns in Africa, Carrier Corps deaths were not deemed worth recording.

———

Today, a bronze historical marker in Belgium memorializes the first British shot of World War One and the first death in battle involving British troops. According to this marker, the opening round of uncountable millions was fired by Corporal Ernest Thomas of C Squadron, 4th Royal Irish Dragoons on August 22, 1914, in a cavalry action near the town of Casteau, Belgium. The first combatant killed, a German uhlan (mounted infantryman), is credited to Captain Charles B. Hornby in that same action. Captain Hornby pierced the unfortunate uhlan's heart by saber thrust—an ironically old-fashioned death (on horseback, with a sword) in what was to become a decidedly modern war (mechanized, faceless), its human toll exceeding 14,000,000. But the markers' assertions do not stand historical scrutiny; their authors disregard earlier campaigns in far-off Africa.

The first British shot of the war actually occurred on August 5, fired off by Regimental Sergeant Major Alhaji Grunshi, a black African soldier serving with British Imperial forces a few miles north of Lomé, in German Togoland. The first recorded British death in battle, one Lieutenant G. M. Thompson of the Gold Coast Regiment, took place sometime over the night of August 21–22, also in Togoland: Lieutenant Thompson, given command of a company of Senegalese *Tirailleurs*, fought it out with German *askaris* in a confused action in the thick bush on the banks of the river Chra. His comrades found him in the morning, lying dead and covered with insects in the midst of his slaughtered command. They buried them that way; the Senegalese arranged around Lieutenant Thompson's grave like a loyal pack of hounds around the tomb of a Paleolithic chief.

After less than a year of war, the German Overseas Empire—one of the main catalysts for the war in the first place—seemed nearly at an end.

In China, on the other side of the globe, the small German garrison holding the Kiao-Chow Concession found itself besieged by a Japanese Army 23,000 strong, supported by a small contingent of the 2nd Battalion of South Wales Borderers. The Concession—a 400-square-mile territory centered in the fortified port city of Tsingtao on the Yellow Sea—had been ceded to Germany in 1897 as compensation for the murder of two German Catholic priests by anti-Christian Chinese mobs. Tsingtao's commandant, Kapitän zur See Meyer-Waldeck, held out against the siege behind the city's thick walls for two months, under continual bombardment from land and sea as Japanese Infantry assault trenches pushed relentlessly forward. Realizing the pointlessness of further struggle against the combined might of the Japanese Army and Navy, Meyer-Waldeck surrendered his garrison of 3,000 German marines and sundry volunteers at last on November 16, 1914. It came as a surprise to him that the Japanese and the British were fighting together against Germany—they had signed a secret mutual defense treaty in 1902, only now bearing fruit.

Meanwhile, Australian, New Zealand, and Japanese forces easily captured German possessions in the South Pacific. These included the Bismarck Archipelago, the Caroline Islands, the Marshall Islands, the Marianas, Palau, New Caledonia, and Samoa—where the Kaiser's barefoot native soldiers sported fetching red sarongs beneath their formal German military tunics—and Kaiser-Wilhelmsland, now the northeastern part of Papua New Guinea. Here one intrepid German officer, a certain Hauptmann Herman Detzner, who had been off exploring the unknown interior with a contingent of native police, refused to surrender and remained on the loose in the wilderness for the duration of the war. He turned himself in to the occupying Australians on January 5, 1919, wearing his carefully preserved and outdated Imperial German uniform—a kind of German Rip van Winkle who had been asleep in the jungle while the world changed irrevocably around him.

By July 1915, of Germany's prewar colonial possessions, only German East Africa remained.

Chapter 3

A PHOTOGRAPH

The black-and-white photograph taken at Neu Moshi, German East Africa, just before the war, later captured by British forces and now part of the collection of World War One photographs at the Imperial War Museum in London, shows five German colonials seated around a table in the aftermath of lunch on the veranda of a planter's house.

The Germans look pleased with themselves. Unseen servants have cleared the food, no doubt heavy fare—pork chops and *Weiner schnitzel*, albeit made from African ostrich meat—Germanic and unsuitable for the intense tropical heat ablaze just beyond the edge of the veranda. Coffee has been set out in dainty Dresden cups; cordial glasses gleam. In an obvious bit of foreshadowing, a fat bottle of Bols Dutch gin and a bottle of Italian sweet vermouth of the same caliber menace the center spread like naval cannons trained on an alien shore.

Of the five Germans, three are officers in tropical white uniforms, their heads shaved close in the Prussian style. An unidentified civilian might be the planter husband of the slightly crazed-looking pale-eyed *frau* wearing a white dress seated across the table. The Universal Conflict and all its strenuous horrors are weeks away. Most hope it might yet be avoided by the diplomats in Europe; not a few long for it in their secret hearts:

"The spirit of those days will always embody a culminating point," wrote Ernst Junger, author of *In Stahlgewittern (Storm of Steel)*, the great, oddly lyrical memoir of trench fighting on the Western Front. "We had seen the generation before us grow old in security, and it seemed a wonderful dream to be permitted to fight as soldiers for our country's greatness, ready to give everything we had. . . . There is no good asking 'What was the use of it all?' for we stood on the threshold of a realm that surpassed the limits within which a practical purpose can exist."

Such existential musings seem far from the thoughts of the Germans on the veranda. No doubt, in the moments after the box camera's shutter snapped, one of them reached for the vermouth and filled the cordial glasses. Italian sweet vermouth was thought in those days to offer protection against malaria, which remained European colonists' most deadly scourge. Modern specialists tell us only quinine and various antimalarial synthetics are effective in fighting the disease, but perhaps the anopheles mosquito also can't abide the sticky-sugary taste of Italian sweet vermouth thick in the blood of its prey. The soldiers and engineers of the Anglo-German Border Commission brought along a huge supply of the stuff when they surveyed the demarcation between British East and German East Africa in 1890. The line they drew could be traced, so it was said, by following a trail of empty vermouth bottles as if by a dotted line on a map. Eventually nailed in place by international agreement, the border cut more or less straight from Wanga on the Swahili Coast to Shirati on the eastern shore of Lake Victoria Nyanza, but did a weird zigzag around Mount Kilimanjaro—allotting Africa's tallest peak to the Kaiser. His grandmother, Queen Victoria, had the Hindu Kush and the Himalayas and any number of other big mountains; the Kaiser had none and wanted a big mountain of his own.

On the whitewashed exterior wall of the plantation house in the photograph, just beneath the seated Germans, hang the skulls of more than a dozen elands—a muscular sort of antelope. These are trophies of the hunt, their vicious-looking black antlers like the horns of cartoon demons twisting defiantly toward heaven. All the colonials in German East Africa were crazy for hunting, as were their British counterparts just a few miles to the northeast. Big game—rhinoceros, giraffe, hippopotamus, water buffalo, elephant—not to mention the predatory cats—were one of the greatest draws of the region. The ex-American president Theodore Roosevelt had come on safari in 1909, guided by the famous English elephant hunter, naturalist, and author F. C. Selous. Many European aristocrats soon followed; a turn in the African bush quickly became part of the latest version of the

Grand Tour. Perhaps East Africa's abundant game and varied subject populations reminded them of the feudal world of their medieval ancestors: both big cats and serfs being in short supply in Europe circa 1914.

Also, there was the weather. Or more precisely, the *atmosphere* of almost unbearable physical beauty and primordial lushness. The air itself streamed "alive over the land, like a flame burning," wrote the Danish Baroness Karen von Blixen, who had a coffee farm in the Ngong Hills not far from Kilimanjaro. "It scintillated, waved, and shone like running water. . . . Up in this high air, you breathed easily, drawing in a vital assurance and lightness of heart." She would later immortalize the place and time in her famous memoir, written under another name.

But one of the Germans at the table in the photograph—though himself an avid hunter since early youth—has come for another sort of hunting entirely and has definitely not come just to breathe the air. He is seated second from right, the hot blaze of Africa behind him forming a fiery crown around his balding, cannonball head. This is Oberstleutnant Paul von Lettow-Vorbeck, newly appointed commander of the German East African Schutztruppe. His presence here has plucked this photograph from among the 1,000 or so pertaining to the African War, 1914–18, in the archives of the Imperial War Museum in London and turned it into a rare, nearly singular record: Here we have one of the few known images of von Lettow in Africa taken before the outbreak of his Universal Conflict.

Von Lettow was forty-five years old at this sitting, an officer of solid achievements though relatively unknown and underappreciated by many of his superiors at the German General Staff in Berlin. Like every man of talent, he had his many detractors among the mediocre. In the photograph his nose, sharp and beaklike, dominates a light mustachio and the hard, firm line of his mouth. Over six feet, tall for the era, he possesses a tall man's confidence. Everyone else smiles at the unseen photographer; the expression on von Lettow's face is wary and serious. He's got the face of a gambler or a gunman, the face of a man willing to wager other men's lives to achieve his ends. A soldier's face. He stares straight at the camera, waiting for something to begin.

Von Lettow was "spare, square-shouldered," according to British general C. P. Fendall, one of the 137 of that rank who fought against him over the course of the war. He had "close-cropped grey hair and . . . the bearing of a Prussian Guardsman, but with none of the bluster usually attributed to such. His manner was just what it should have been, courteous and polite." Von Lettow was also known for the strict, Prussian-style discipline he imposed on his small army—a strictness, however, mediated by a scrupulous sense of honor, the appreciation of a good joke, and a genuine affection for his men. And he was already famous—infamous in certain quarters—for having a bottomless respect for the fighting qualities of black African troops: "One of his great abilities was to take the African precisely as he found him, without any transfer of European mores," concluded General Fendall.

Looking closely at the photograph with a magnifying glass, you can see there's something wrong with one of von Lettow's eyes—the left one— which gives his gaze a slightly ethereal quality. The eye is rumored to be glass. He had sustained a serious facial injury during an action against the Hottentots in German South West Africa in 1905.

A story told involving the disputed glass eye is perhaps apocryphal: In 1917, during a fight in the East African bush, one of von Lettow's German *askaris* found it lying beneath some leaves in the undergrowth. The eye had been knocked out of the *Oberstleutnant*'s head by the concussion of an exploding British shell, rolled off, and was lost. Von Lettow accepted the return of his missing eye from the *askari* with obvious irritation. The lost eye hadn't really been lost at all, he explained curtly. He'd carefully placed it exactly where it had been found to keep watch over the conduct of his troops during the battle.

Chapter 4

ANCESTORS

In his *Peloponnesian Wars*, Thucydides records the exploits of Gylippus, the Spartan general who came to the aid of Syracuse during the Athenian siege of 414 BC. The Syracusans, surrounded by their enemies and blockaded by the Athenian fleet, facing starvation and death on one hand, surrender and rapine on the other, called to their allies in distant Sparta for help. The Spartans, themselves hard-pressed, could spare only one man, a certain General Gylippus who some said was only half Spartan, his mother having been a Helot slave. Expecting an army of tough, warlike Spartans, the Syracusans were disappointed. But Gylippus, by sheer force of personality and military skill, reorganized the city's defenses, submitted the pleasure-loving Syracusans to rigorous military discipline and, choosing the right moment to attack, turned the tide of the war against the Athenians.

To von Lettow's contemporaries, there was something classical—indeed Gylippian—about the man. At war, he showed himself to be stoical, resourceful, utterly driven, and completely ruthless. And, rare quality in a soldier, prepared for either victory or defeat:

"How did it feel," Baroness von Blixen once asked him, "to fight against a force so superior that the result is given in advance, and one has no hope of victory?"

"Well, that is not easy to explain," von Lettow replied thoughtfully. "Perhaps one should say that in such a certainty, there may lie as great an inspiration as in any faith in victory."

———————

The soldier who uttered these words came from a long line of soldiers, a thousand generations of men whose hands, to paraphrase the poet W. B. Yeats, never tired of reaching for the sword.

The name von Lettow perhaps indicates an origin in the Moravian town of Lettowitz. It is written with two Germanic runes (law and Tyr), which sound out the syllables of the name but also when put together resemble an anchor with bits missing. This sign, illustrated on a shield, hung from the beam of one of the fortified homes of a von Lettow ancestor somewhere in the north German borderlands; in the guise of a broken anchor it was adopted as a coat of arms by another ancestor who survived a monstrous storm, apparently through the intervention of several angels, during a crusading voyage to Lithuania.

In von Lettow's autobiography, *Mein Leben*, written in the spare workmanlike prose of a career military man—though leavened with humor and occasional poetry—he discredits this possibility. He regarded the von Lettow rune, he said, as no more than a kind of monogram "such as people embroider on underwear, hats, and gloves." He was also a bit skeptical that angels would intervene on his ancestor's behalf.

Paul von Lettow-Vorbeck's ancestors most likely migrated to Pomerania, which is to say northwestern Prussia, with the religious-military order known as the Teutonic Knights in the early 1200s. The shield device borne by these aristocratic warriors (black cross on white ground) would later be adopted by the German armies of wars to come. The Teutonic Knights were the last of the Crusading orders—like the Templars and the Knights of St. John before them—to join the attempt to wrest Jerusalem and the Holy Land from the Muslim conquerors. They were also the last to leave, clinging to the Crusader citadel at Acre until the great siege engines of Caliph al-Ashraf smashed the walls and drove European Christians from the Middle East. From Acre, the Teutonic Knights went to Venice. Then, at the behest of Pope Honorius, they founded a new citadel at Marienwerder on the Liwa River, in what is now Poland. There they would participate in a long series of ferocious wars against the "Old Prussians" and other pagan tribes of the Baltic. Bloody fighting between the knights and the Old Prussians continued for generations. According to the *Chronicles of the Teutonic Order*, knights captured by the Old Prussians would be "roasted alive in their armor, like chestnuts, before the shrine of a local god."

This dark, confused, centuries-long conflict known as the Northern Crusades is beyond our scope here and indeed practically eludes modern understanding. Suffice it to say that in the remote Baltic borderlands, the native peoples (Balts, Slavs, Estonians, Livonians, Lithuanians, Old Prussians, and others) had rejected early Christian attempts at conversion, martyred the missionaries, and clung tenaciously to their ancient gods and goddesses of woods and wind and animals, birth and fecundity, destiny and war. Obstinate in their worship of these elemental deities, isolated in the fastness of their forests, they held out against the Christian age for more than 1,000 years: The Roman emperor Constantine the Great painted the Chi-Rho symbol of Christ on his standard the night before the Battle of the Milvian Bridge on October 28, AD 312, inspired by a prophetic vision in which he saw a burning cross in the sky inscribed with the words *In hoc signo vinces* (By this sign, you shall conquer); yet there still existed unconquered congregations of pagans practicing their ancient Nordic religions in rural areas of Lithuania as late as the sixteenth century.

In 1263, Pope Honorius called for the Teutonic Knights to establish a bulwark of fortresses along the river Niemen. These utilitarian structures were not what we might imagine—castles of mortar and stone—but log redoubts, more like the forts of our own Western Frontier during the Indian Wars. It is likely that the von Lettows helped construct and defend this Crusader bulwark.

Centuries passed. Old Prussia became Christian at last by force of arms, intermarriage, and assimilation—though it is to be supposed, given later German history, that some seeds of the old knight-roasting pagan savagery remained buried deep in Prussian hearts. The von Lettows, having merged with the Prussian Vorbecks along the way, acquired property and estates in the vicinity of Rummelsberg in eastern Pomerania. There they fought for the dukes of Pomerania who became electors of Brandenburg, and at last kings of Prussia.

In the Thirty Years' War (1618–48) the von Lettow-Vorbecks lost almost all their property. This man-made cataclysm, as destructive of human life as any volcano, devastated much of Central Europe, rendering entire fat principalities into wasteland and forcing a significant number of starving, displaced Germans to the dreadful expediency of cannibalism. That the ruin wrought on Germany in this multigenerational conflict resembled the ruin experienced by East African tribes during the 1914–18 war is an irony certainly not lost on the acute von Lettow: The Thirty Years' War was known for the "wolf strategy" of its combatants—this apt expression describes a mode of warfare in which "armies of both sides plundered as they marched, leaving cities, towns, villages, and farms ravaged." The Schutztruppe practiced a modernized version of this strategy in German East Africa 300 years later.

But cataclysm often spurs new growth, another example of history's many ironies: The more severe the eruption, the lusher the harvest when planting begins again in mineral-rich volcanic soil. Thus, the horrors of the seventeenth century gave way to the European Enlightenment of the eighteenth.

In Prussia, this age belonged to Frederick II, the quirky, brilliant homosexual king and military strategist, chief architect of the modern German state and the father of its professional standing army. Witty, cynical, prey to dark humors—the very type of the enlightened despot—warlike Frederick also hungered for an intellectual life. He hosted Voltaire and other "philosophes" of the day at his countryseat, Sanssouci. Witty dinner-table conversation was the only compensation required for his kingly hospitality. He welcomed opposing views and could tolerate dissent—to a point. (Voltaire, arrested over some stray impertinent comment, was quickly deported.) Through land grants and royal patronage, successive generations of Prussian kings had done much to revive the minor aristocracy—that landowning class of soldierly gentleman farmers called "Junkers." The officers of Frederick II's victorious armies were drawn from among their ranks, including the von Lettow-Vorbecks and the von Bismarcks to whom they were closely related.

Perhaps as a counterweight to a deep-seated personal gloom, Frederick II loved a clown: Paul von Lettow-Vorbeck's great-great-granduncle, General Heinrich Wilhelm von Lettow-Vorbeck, both brave and funny, became one of Frederick's favorites, a part of his inner circle of friends and confidants. He was remembered by his great-great-grandnephew Paul for his heroism on the battlefield and also for his clownishness: Heinrich Wilhelm was the author of certain satirical stanzas mocking his royal patron ever so gently—a greater hazard, perhaps, than facing the massed cannons of the enemy. Heinrich Wilhelm served for several years as a mercenary with the King of Poland until recalled to fight Prussia's wars against Austria and France. In these conflicts, he fought alongside other members of his family; the von Lettow-Vorbecks paid a high price for Frederick II's royal patronage:

"Seventeen members of the family were killed in action during the wars of the Great King," Paul von Lettow-Vorbeck records, "six at the Battle of Leuthen alone. This example of the sacrifice and suffering of our old military families occurred during a period when battlefield casualties were generally very much less than today." The tradition of dying for the Fatherland would also mark the von Lettow-Vorbecks of Germany's future wars: Six of the twelve who served in World War One were killed, as were six of the nine who served in World War Two. Heinrich Wilhelm, however, survived and was awarded the Pour le Mérite—Prussia's highest military honor, newly instituted by Frederick II—for his valiant service. Severely wounded in action, he retired in 1771 and died childless.

His estates, much enhanced by the king, passed to his brother, Paul von Lettow-Vorbeck. This man's son, Karl Wilhelm, joined the army at fourteen and fought in the Napoleonic Wars that, following the battles of Jena and Auerstädt, once again ruined Prussia. History's endless returning cycles are played out in the lives of the people; we take it in with each breath and expel it again anew, but it's the same old air: The von Lettow-Vorbecks emerged from their nation's twenty years' struggle with the "Corsican upstart" again impoverished. Karl Wilhelm's twelve children—among them Paul von Lettow's father, Paul Karl—were raised in "Spartan simplicity with only a piece of dry bread and an apple for breakfast." "Butter was a luxury," for them, Paul von Lettow explains in *Mein Leben*. But "real piety and unconditional loyalty to King and Fatherland," he adds, "characteristic of life in our region," sustained them in the lean years.

"In Prussia during the latter part of the nineteenth century, military service was regarded as an essential experience. The officer class was an elite. . . . The education and training these men received was among the best obtainable. . . . Prussian officers were not only extremely competent professionals, they were expected to . . . move in the highest levels of society as educated gentlemen."

These words, written about Paul von Lettow-Vorbeck by his American translator, might just as easily be applied to his father, who joined the Prussian Cadet Corps in 1850. Hardworking and severe, the product of a kind of stern, aristocratic deprivation, Paul Karl rose quickly in the ranks, became a staff officer under General Steinmetz, and later commanded a company in Saarlouis, a dull but strategically important garrison town not far from the French border. His house there still stands, a modest structure on a commercial street, now as then with shops on the ground floor and apartments above. Here his first surviving son, Paul Emil, was born there on March 20, 1870, four months before the outbreak of the Franco-Prussian War.

Paul's mother, Marie von Eisenhart-Rothe, the oldest of nine children, also came from a venerable Pomeranian Junker family, of the same class and distinguished military background as the von Lettows. Her great-grandfather, General von Eisenhart-Rothe, had been an adjutant to the famous, half-mad Field Marshal von Blücher, whose cavalry, arriving late but at the exactly appropriate moment, turned the tide against Napoleon at Waterloo. Though brilliant on horseback, von Blücher was something of a simpleton afoot: Once, Napoleon himself summoned von Blücher for an interview at Finkenstein Castle in Danzig. The rough, powerful six-foot-tall cavalry officer stood before the diminutive, impassioned emperor who himself stood with his back to an open window high up in the battlements. Napoleon harangued von Blücher for an hour about the inevitability of French victory—at one point the two of them were alone in the room—then released him.

Later, General von Eisenhart-Rothe questioned von Blücher about the meeting, astonished that the latter hadn't taken advantage of the opportunity and pushed Napoleon out the window to his death and thus changed the course of history. Blücher's jaw dropped at the thought. The idea of killing Napoleon had somehow not occurred to him, perhaps because his intellect couldn't encompass the possibility, or perhaps because it simply wouldn't have been sporting. This incident echoes down the years to a similar incident in the African bush in 1917—as we shall see.

The Eisenhart-Rothe family, though Junkers like the von Lettows, were of a markedly different temperament, more "gentlemanly" and artistic. From them, perhaps, derived Paul von Lettow-Vorbeck's sense of fair play— and certainly his abiding interest in the arts: His maternal grandfather, a virtuoso on the piano, wrote plays and music and loved to dance; his maternal grandmother played the accordion like a Gypsy. The pair would give impromptu concerts together under the linden tree in the front yard of their house in Lietzow all through the spring and summer, and neighbors and villagers would come to dance.

"My mother was very clever," von Lettow later said. "She had a strong character and was very helpful." She was also deeply religious, and though her son resembled her in many ways, religiosity was not one of them. His only god, in the end, was the God of Battles. The hard, warlike God of his distant ancestors—those unnamed, forgotten men who had ridden into the darkness of the pagan forests with the Teutonic Knights 600 years before his birth.

Chapter 5

YOUTH

As German armies mobilized for the invasion of France in June 1870, Marie von Lettow-Vorbeck sought to return to her parents' home in Pomerania with her infant son, Paul. There mother and son might wait out the war in comparative safety. But the massive flow of troops and ordnance to the front made travel impossible. No place could be found on the military trains for women and children. Stranded on the platform, Marie was at last compelled to bribe an official for a narrow berth. As she fled the Franco-German frontier, infant in her arms, in the background from the direction of France came the rumble of heavy artillery. History is full of sympathetic vibrations: 100 years before Marie's troubled journey, Letizia Bonaparte, pregnant with the future Napoleon I, escaped Ajaccio to the hills as musket fire rattled in the streets below.

The Franco-Prussian War came as a severe shock to the body of Europe. German armies led by Prussia crushed and swept away the last vestiges of Imperial France—a victory of military professionalism over the famous French élan, or fighting spirit.

The war itself lasted barely a year, but much of von Lettow's life was spent in its shadow. Germany's smashing victory sealed a sense of superiority in the German *Volk*. It engendered a new and vigorous national pride and, on January 18, 1871, brought about the final unification of Germany—until then divided into a motley collection of small states and principalities, often at odds with each other. Germany had suddenly become the largest nation in Europe, both in terms of population and terrain: a European empire under the rule of the Prussian king, Wilhelm I, now elevated to the dignity of a caesar—literally, "Kaiser." Marxist historians will cite economic factors and intractable class struggles as the prime motivators for armed conflict, indeed as the dark matter behind all human experience. But there is another motivation, simple yet profoundly complex: pride. And pride, in its nationalistic manifestation, more than any other factor, would lead millions to grief in 1914–18.

The German victory of 1870–71 also taught an invaluable military lesson to the next generation of German officers—among whom von Lettow was one of the most brilliant—namely the overwhelming value of "independence and self-reliance" in battle. This idea of operational independence created an officer class "who could act with the strongest conviction and responsibility" on the battlefield in the absence of orders from above, he later wrote. The hidebound military structure of the Imperial French armies, their lack of initiative in command and their overreliance on preset battle plans in fluid situations, von Lettow believed, accounted for the devastating defeat of the French at Sedan, September 4, 1870.

In battle, "a situation can emerge that is unforeseeable," and to educate young officers who could deal with the unforeseen, von Lettow saw as "the army's educational task. The battlefield is constantly in flux; the commander who can react quickly to changing circumstances and act with confidence on his own initiative is usually victorious. Leadership in war was and remains an art."

Paul von Lettow's father, Paul Karl, decorated for bravery during the Franco-Prussian War, took part in the decisive battles of Amiens and Metz and later served as a battalion commander during the occupation of France. Paul's early childhood was spent in France at various garrison towns. His first language, a mishmash of German and French, pointed the way to a linguistic facility that served him well in later years and helped him quickly acquire fluency in a variety of African languages.

Military childhoods are similar in all times and places. The "army brat" phenomenon of the "American Century" decades following World War Two would have been recognizable to the Paul von Lettow-Vorbeck of 1875. After occupation duty, the elder von Lettow, now a general, was sent to Brandenburg on the Havel, where he lived with his family in the forecourt of the cathedral opposite the riding academy, near the apartments reserved for the sorrowing young widows of German officers killed in the war—in other words, within sight of war's inevitable cost.

They were then transferred to Königsberg, the seat of power of ancient Prussian kings. In 1878, General von Lettow-Vorbeck, appointed commander of the Defense District of Berlin, moved his family to the capital. Here Paul ran a bit wild, joining a gang of neighborhood kids perpetually at war with a similar gang on the opposing block; they battled over turf in the nearby zoological park. Paul's gang kept a secret hideout there in the thick bushes, from which they launched raids on their enemies and on strolling policemen—not so different from the tactics he employed on the slopes of Kilimanjaro in Africa forty years later.

In Berlin Paul attended the French school where the main lessons were taught in that language, improving his early facility into fluency. At home, Paul's father the general—stern, forbidding, punctilious—kept his children in a state of awe bordering on terror. A disciplinarian and taskmaster with both his family and in military life, he was known to his superiors for his ability to restructure troubled regiments. "The task of reestablishing strict discipline was entirely my father's responsibility," Paul later wrote with grudging admiration. Regarding this precious matter, "he was gruff, even to his superiors."

An old-fashioned reticence regarding family matters inhibits the son from describing what it was like living with such a father in *Mein Leben*. Though from a stray comment or two, and reading between the lines, one can discern the vague outline of a serious clash of wills and some familial unhappiness. Still, Paul grew into a likable youth, affable, charming, but with a core of steel. At last, as his father had done thirty-one years earlier, he entered the cadet corps at Potsdam. Here began the future guerrilla fighter's formal military education, first in the famous military academy at Kassel, then in the main cadet training facility at Gross-Lichterfelde, near Berlin. The education to be had in these places ranked among the best in the world. The cadets studied the classics, mathematics, engineering, the latest sciences, philosophy. Young Cadet von Lettow was particularly fond of Plato, Kant, and Schopenhauer.

"The cadet institutions were a blessing for the officer families," von Lettow commented. "They protected their sons from the frequent changes of school associated with transfers among the different garrisons. . . . The secondary school curriculum was in no sense narrow. We were also exposed to the important developments of the day. Schliemann had at that time carried out his successful excavations at Mycenae and Troy, and had proven that the Greek mythological world rested on fact."

Later, at the academy at Kassel, Paul von Lettow met Tom von Prince, who would become one of his greatest friends, a friendship preserved over great distances and long decades and renewed in Africa on the eve of world war. The two boys were the exact opposite in temperament, which perhaps accounted for their lasting relationship. In his years at Kassel, von Lettow— the product of a general and a general's daughter—was a dedicated student, a rule follower, a young man with a family reputation to uphold. Von Prince adhered to none of the above. Burly and bearded even in those days, he was known for his temper, his combativeness, and his resistance to authority, and was eventually expelled. But von Prince's main personality trait—an outrageous pugnacity—made him well suited for a life of violence and adventure in Africa, for which he departed at an early age.

Meanwhile, Paul von Lettow-Vorbeck passed his academic exams with honors and a commendation from the Kaiser. Naturally, his physical education had not been neglected. During his cadet years, he had developed into a good gymnast, a fine horseman, and an excellent swordsman who occasionally bested his instructors at the saber. This was the era of the student dueling society in Germany; dueling with sabers had long been a popular tradition. Strict rules enshrined in a written code specified where and how an affront to personal honor might be answered; participants wore appropriate padding; seconds supervised. Happy was the cadet who finished one of these encounters with a clean facial scar—the ultimate signifier of German military virtue. As far as we know, Paul von Lettow avoided dueling; his father, the aging general, a no-nonsense pragmatist, disapproved.

Paul, more his mother's child in many ways, still held his stern father in a reverence mixed with terror that approximated the average person's feelings toward a deity. The two of them—sometimes with Paul's younger siblings in tow, sometimes without—often went to swim in the bracingly cold Baltic at Brosen. One can imagine them there after a morning swim, father and son, clad in the heavy woolen bathing suits of the era. They sit side by side but not too close, on the rocky shingle beach on a cloudy day, each locked in his own thoughts, barely speaking a word.

Paul von Lettow-Vorbeck rose from this rocky beach—so to speak—alone. His career in the German Army, the career for which he'd been foreordained by the deeds of his ancestors going back 1,000 years and by an excellent military education, now began in earnest. He embraced it with the enthusiasm of the young Lee in Mexico, or Napoleon in the years after Brienne.

In *Mein Leben* von Lettow writes nostalgically of his decade as a junior officer in the Kaiser's Imperial Army: There were dawn inspections in the biting cold, regimental maneuvers, glimpses of the luminaries of the day— the Kaiser, Crown Prince Friedrich, the "Man of Gold" Field Marshal Count von Moltke, who was Germany's greatest military strategist, and others. There were drinking parties with fellow officers, card games till all hours, and splendid dances in Berlin—the young women shivering in their off-the-shoulder dresses, the new officers in bright, stiff uniforms—followed by the mad rush to catch the last train back to Spandau barracks for morning roll call.

The Berlin-Spandau trains ran until midnight, before the dances were over, and resumed again at five a.m., long after curfew. Unwilling to leave the dancing early, von Lettow and his companions would kill the small hours over coffee and endless cigarettes in the Kaffe Bauer, dress swords clanking on the tile floor, careful to conceal the ornamental topknots on the hilts, which to any passing superior officer would quickly identify their particular regiment. It was perhaps at the Bauer that von Lettow acquired the fierce cigarette habit he maintained throughout his life. Later, in Africa, cigarettes were his one essential luxury; during the course of a battle he could be seen chain-smoking furiously, pacing back and forth and issuing orders in a billowing cloud of nicotine.

His years of barracks duty over, the young von Lettow found a place in Berlin on the Great German General Staff—Count von Moltke's organizational achievement, equivalent to the Joint Chiefs in the U.S. modern armed forces. Before von Moltke, the various branches of the German military operated semiautonomously and in a disjointed fashion, with separate command structures, making cooperation complex and difficult.

Staff work can be awfully dull. Men of action are often at odds with its necessary emphasis on the smallest details of logistics, on paperwork and organizational structures. Many officers dread such a posting—the long hours of meticulous planning, the endless memo writing, the boring meetings—though a staff position can be an especially good springboard for fast promotion. But von Lettow was that rare sort of officer who, though decidedly a man of action and a highly capable field officer, also excelled at staff work. His strict, finicky upbringing had drummed attention to detail into his skull at an early age.

If von Lettow enjoyed intimate female companionship during his years of staff work in Berlin (as he did, undoubtedly; if not a womanizer, he definitely had an eye for female beauty), he does not say anything about it. His reticence in all matters sexual is old-fashioned and complete, befitting a gentleman of his day and utterly alien to the tell-all citizenry of our own. For him, there were probably a few of the kind of women who frequented the young officers of 1890—"Spanish" dancers after the mode of the notorious Lola Montez, heartless courtesans like Cora Pearl, and anonymous *Biergarten* girls. Von Lettow does complain, however, over the lack of "acceptable" young women, the kind one might take home to meet the parents in Pomerania.

"There were many young married couples," he wrote of the dances in Berlin of this era. "Almost no single girls for us young officers, and we had to dance with married women. . . ." All too often the available ones were undanceable: "I recall an older officer scolding a younger one because at a ball he failed to ask a young woman who was without a partner to dance. Offenses against chivalry were not tolerated."

When not dancing or on duty, the young officers of von Lettow's Berlin went out hunting in the countryside around the city. Hunting, more than just the preferred diversion for the aristocratic classes of the nineteenth century, had become, in a time of peace, a training ground for war. The famous World War One German ace Manfred von Richthofen—the legendary Red Baron—an avid hunter like many others, devotes a disproportionate amount of space to hunting in his brief memoir of aerial combat, *Der Rote Kampfflieger.*

Von Richthofen experienced the same ecstasies stalking the "aurochs" on the hunting preserves of the Prince of Pless as he did shooting down English pilots over the Western Front. Hunting gave him the "same fever that grips me when I sit in an aeroplane, see an Englishman, and must fly along for five minutes to come at him." He further distinguishes "hunters"—for whom killing is an art, one of the elemental aspects of being alive, like making love— from "shooters." In the shooter, the hunting passion is transformed by the machinery of war. He cited his brother, Lothar, as one of the latter:

"My brother makes a distinction between a hunter and a sportsman and a shooter. . . . When I downed an Englishman, my hunting passion was quelched. I seldom tried to shoot down two. . . . It was different with my brother."

This difference the Red Baron describes as a kind of bloody-mindedness, a ruthless willingness to kill in pursuit of victory and keep killing until victory is achieved. The same ruthless willingness to kill was shared by von Lettow, and—despite protestations to the contrary—by von Richthofen himself. Von Richthofen's memoir is about his transformation from hunter to shooter; von Lettow's is about the limits he will impose on himself for the sake of victory in German East Africa: In short, there are none. War is sport only to a point, perhaps only in its first, exciting hours. After that it quickly boils down to its most basic component: killing as many of the enemy as possible.

And yet von Lettow reserves some of the most lyrical passages in his own autobiography for the hunt. One has the feeling that he reserved for it the depths of sentiment other men experienced during love affairs. This passion, more than the dearth of "acceptable" women in Berlin society of the day, might explain von Lettow's persistent bachelorhood: For several years during this period he lived in a pleasantly squalid bachelor pad near the barracks at Spandau with another officer, his cousin Axel von Loeper—himself an avid hunter. Von Loeper kept a dog and a selection of well-oiled shotguns he and von Lettow took hunting in the Kaiser's reserve in the Spandau City Forest. During hunting season, they would leave their military duties behind at four in the afternoon, quickly change out of their uniforms into old clothes, and reach their shared snipe blind as evening fell:

"Many a snipe met its end at the stands, after showing off in the wonderful spring evening. . . . Of the dozen shots that would ring out, some of them were at moths, whose flight after dark, under the shining stars, was absurdly like that of a snipe."

Later, von Lettow and von Loeper and a few other dedicated hunters of the regiment pooled their resources to rent a private hunting ground bordering on Rhensberg. It was "a magnificent domain of lake and forests," von Lettow wrote. "Red deer and roebuck were plentiful, with numbers of small game. . . . I killed many a fine stag there, and one morning four fat deer. . . . The whole experience, the sunny August mornings on the Seradella was so magnificent that it has remained an especially blessed memory." His passion for hunting and the marksmanship skill honed by shooting snipe and elk and other wildlife in the deciduous forests of the German countryside would save von Lettow's life in tropical latitudes in thicker forests with bigger game and under dire circumstances. There would come a time, in the remote bush of German East Africa, when von Lettow and the hunters of his Schutztruppe would supplement dwindling rations with what they could bag in the bush, decidedly more impressive targets than the European snipe: On the march, his men preferred hippo lard, flavorful and full of protein. They spread it on bread like it was butter. Elephant fat, though also quite nutritious, was an acquired taste.

It is worth noting here that Adolf Hitler, a vegetarian, detested hunting, which he called "one of the last remnants of a dead feudal world."

Meanwhile, in the midst of all this hunting and dancing and staff work, von Lettow's military career moved forward with painful slowness. Advancement in the German Army, traditionally torpid (in the era following the Napoleonic Wars, one could remain a lieutenant for thirty years), heated up slightly after the unification of 1871. Field Marshal Count von Molke made more room for men of talent in the higher echelons of the army: like Napoleon, he believed in merit. Von Lettow soon developed into an excellent staff officer, reliable and detail-obsessed—but his father, the old general, wanted something better for his son, something more glorious, that would affix the family name forever in the annals of Germany's military heroes. He insisted his son stand for the examinations that would admit him to the Kriegsakademie—the war college of the German Army. This examination, one of the toughest of its kind, weeded out more than three-quarters of the applicants.

At first, von Lettow was ambivalent about his father's desires. But at last, he shrugged and gave in to paternal ambitions—somewhat after the manner of von Richthofen. ("I was not particularly eager to become a cadet," the Red Baron wrote in his memoir, "but my father wished it and I was not consulted.") After several attempts and several failures, von Lettow finally passed the examination and advanced to the next phase of his military education.

The war college delivered exactly the sort of training its name promised; it schooled the nascent commanders of the next generation in the art of war. Von Lettow studied there for three years, under such luminaries of the Imperial German Army as Field Marshal von Bülow (the ultimate soldier's soldier—so von Lettow says—and a hero to the young officers in his care). Of the war college, von Lettow notes, "There was certainly no so-called mechanical obedience," or learning by rote. And indeed, he emerged in March 1899 with a deeply personal understanding of the science of war. He was then assigned more or less at random to the bureau of the German War Department that dealt with the Kaiser's recently acquired overseas territories and also with England. This quirk of staffing would lead him on to his years of destiny in Africa.

In his new assignment, von Lettow met a variety of interesting and unconventional men whose knowledge of warfare extended far beyond what could be gleaned from leather-bound editions of von Clausewitz or leaden monographs written by the generation of 1870: There was Major von Estorff, who would help defeat the Herero guerrilla leader, Hendrik

Witbooi, in the deserts of German South West Africa; Heydebreck, who had been with the brash adventurer Zelewski in the struggle against the Wahehe in German East Africa; Captain Freiherr von Reitzenstein, the famous long-distance rider who had been a keen observer of the floundering British fight against the Boers in South Africa in 1881. And the great explorer Count von Goetzen, discoverer of Lake Kivu, who, like Stanley, had crossed the African continent on foot from east to west.

From von Reitzenstein, in particular, von Lettow absorbed a contempt for British military leadership. During the Boer War, von Reitzenstein observed, the British Army's cumbersome maneuvers cost them dearly in both men and supplies. Meanwhile, the "commandos" of the Boers—mobile corps of up to 10,000 mounted men—ranged freely over impossible terrain and across vast territories the size of Europe, seemed to be everywhere at once, and were impossible to defeat using conventional methods.

Also, as a part of his duties, von Lettow attended lectures given by members of the General Staff. The so-called Schlieffen Lessons, a famous series of talks given by Chief of Staff Alfred von Schlieffen (originator of the invasion plan that sent German armies careening across Belgium in 1914), were a great influence on von Lettow's developing military brain. And during this period, he worked ever more closely with Count von Goetzen— at one point they shared a desk—who would soon be appointed governor of German East Africa. From this shambling, indomitable ex-explorer, he absorbed fabulous tales of the rigors and excitements of colonial life and the sheer magnificence of landscape in Equatorial Africa—and something else: a determination to see it all for himself.

But as von Lettow approached thirty, in 1900, his life seemed unfulfilled. He had become a dedicated career officer, successful, respected, undervalued. Still unmarried, he was too devoted to his work for any serious romantic relationships. "Take-home work cost me many nights," he later admitted ruefully—though he still found large uninterrupted blocks of time for hunting.

His first solo apartment in Berlin gradually filled with the trophies and accoutrements of his favorite pastime in a pleasant jumble. Stags' heads, stuffed and mounted and impressively pointed, hung on the walls. Expensive English shotguns and the delicately engraved hunting rifles for which German gunsmiths were famous resided in a special dust-free cabinet. Ready-to-go rucksacks stuffed with old clothes and basic necessities lay propped near the door. And at one point, fourteen German shorthaired pointer puppies—the multitudinous offspring of his mated pair of hunting dogs—invaded the place. They slept here and there, messed the furniture, peed on the carpets. But they were so beautiful, von Lettow says, "my comrades gladly adopted all of them." From this comment, one can easily imagine the carefree disarray of an apparently confirmed bachelorhood: the hunting togs left in unwashed heaps, the half-drunk bottle of beer on the mantel, the ashtrays full of cigarettes from last night's card party with fellow officers.

As yet, Paul von Lettow-Vorbeck, born within the sound of heavy guns and trained for the rigors of war, had known only peace. Except for a few minor colonial conflicts, the Great Powers had been in a state of armed détente since 1870. Europe was now led by a generation of men who happily contemplated dying in their beds. Like Caesar—who, upon turning thirty, famously lamented before the statue of Alexander at Rhodes that he had done nothing with his life at an age when the great Macedonian had conquered the known world—von Lettow hungered for battle. He was a saber made to shine in war, its blade slowly beginning to rust from lack of use.

Chapter 6

AT WAR WITH THE BOXERS

Years later, in Africa, in the jungle, Paul von Lettow-Vorbeck remembered China. After the fall of Morogoro in August 1916, the commander of the Schutz-truppe paused in his carefully orchestrated fighting retreat from General Smuts's vastly superior forces to dine with a few German ladies at the mission station at Mgeta. The ladies brought out the last of their scanty luxuries for the occasion—canned fruit and fresh bread made with all the remaining flour, a garnished roast of unnamed bush meat—all washed down with a bottle of the ubiquitous "antimalarial" Italian red vermouth—and, best of all, two or three of the precious bottles of beer rescued from the German brewery in Dar es Salaam, destroyed by British naval bombardments before the capital fell into their hands.

The ladies set the table with a white cloth and laid out the surviving German silverware. The commander, in an expansive mood, answered their many questions about the war as honestly as possible. What could he say to them that might offer some hope?

True, the Kaiser's small force in East Africa could not prevail in open warfare against the several Allied armies engaged against them. Yes, the Schutztruppe fought on, but German territory dwindled, as did their fighting strength. This trend showed no signs of abating. But as long as the Imperial German flag still flew somewhere in the colony, von Lettow assured the ladies, German East Africa remained German and thus undefeated. Besides, his strategy had never been to win the war outright; from the beginning a traditional sort of victory had been clearly impossible. But to win the peace, this might be just within reach.

The ladies exchanged puzzled looks at von Lettow's explanation; the commander attempted to clarify: He aimed to keep up the fight in Africa until German arms triumphed on the battlefields of Europe—his goal being to divert many thousands of Allied soldiers and millions of pounds worth of war material from the main theaters to this hopeless little sideshow in German East Africa. If successful, this odd reverse strategy might, in the end, constitute victory: Soon, maybe not this fighting season or the next, but soon, with the war won by Germany in Europe, the Schutztruppe would emerge from the bush and march into Dar es Salaam again, its regimental band playing, to the cheering of the crowds. And the German colony would pick up where it had left off in August 1914.

But the ladies seemed baffled by all this talk of tactics and the necessary strategy of losing well—so von Lettow changed the subject. He paused, drank a little of the precious beer; the chattering night sounds of the jungle pressed around them. Then he began to talk, and talked for a long time about another conflict a world away and a lifetime past: the Boxer Rebellion in China in 1900. It had been his first overseas adventure and his first taste of battle. He had volunteered to serve as an adjutant with the German East Asian Expeditionary Force—the Kaiser's contribution to the Allied armies sent to rescue those few foreigners still left unmassacred in Peking in the months following the initial Boxer uprising.

Now the ladies listened, rapt at the commander's descriptions of the tattered, medieval splendor of the last days of the Chinese emperors and of the desperate contrasts of the great city aswarm with coolies and mandarins, concubines and eunuchs, princesses carried in sedan chairs and legless beggars crawling in the muck.

"He ate very little and only sipped his wine," one of the ladies wrote in her diary. "Halfway through the meal, a message came for him that an English division was driving towards us from the Uluguru Hills and we were in danger of being cut off. 'We must leave quickly, Colonel,' his staff officer said. He replied 'Not until we have finished our meal.'"

Unperturbed, he continued to talk about China—now turning to the famous Siege of the Foreign Legations by the Boxers and Imperial Chinese troops controlled by the fearsome Dowager Empress Tsz'e Hsi.

For roughly two months, from June 19 to August 14, 1900, the ministers of the Great Powers (England, France, Germany, the United States, Austria-Hungary, Russia, and Italy), along with their families and employees and servants and several thousand Chinese Christian converts, were trapped and besieged in the hastily fortified diplomatic quarter in Peking. This cataclysmic event, in the memorable phrase of one of the most eloquent historians of the conflict—Peter Fleming, brother of spy novelist Ian—"once formed a part of the iron rations of general knowledge which everyone carried in their head, one of those episodes of history like . . . the Boston Tea Party or the Black Hole of Calcutta, which we all remember to have occurred, their picturesque qualities acting as preservatives."

Alas, even "iron rations" will spoil after a century on the shelf. The biases of our own moment in time have covered everything past beneath a presentist pall. Now only the vague outline of deeds once deemed great can be descried beneath the thick gray cloth of historical revisionism—though, admittedly, the origins and causes of the Boxer Rebellion remain obscure, even to those who were there.

"Basically," von Lettow muses in his autobiography, "it was a Chinese national reaction against the foreigners who had gained more and more control of the Chinese customs and commerce. As often happens in such cases, the movement degenerated into robbery and terror."

By 1900, China, once one of the world's great empires, had sunk into decay. Great rotten chunks of territory had fallen off China's main body and fallen into the European maw; significant portions of her commercial and political life were now controlled by the European powers then basking in the bright sun of colonialism's high noon.

The Germans had seized Kiaochow and Tsingtao on the Shantung Peninsula as compensation for the murder of the two German priests previously mentioned. Tsingtao, said one observer, was "rapidly converted into a sort of Oriental Prussia, with verboten signs all over the place, engineers swarming and missionaries proselytizing. Within a few years, Tsingtao was . . . a Far Eastern Dusseldorf, the most orderly, the neatest, cleanest, and least Chinese city in China." (The German-style lager beer of the same name available at Chinese restaurants everywhere is perhaps the last cultural artifact remaining from the German presence in this region of China.)

Meanwhile, the Russians had extorted via the threat of military action a lease on Port Arthur and the port of Darien; the French, who had earlier bitten off Cochin China and the Mekong River Basin, had recently obtained Kwangchowan. The British, in addition to their lease on Hong Kong, now occupied We-hai and maintained influence over the Yangtze Valley; the Portuguese had long since seized Macao. Thus, thousands of square miles of Chinese coastline all along the South China Sea, with additional territory penetrating miles into the interior, now lay in the hands of foreign governments.

Indeed, no area of Chinese life existed beyond the sphere of European influence. European-built railroads had put thousands of Chinese boatmen and porters out of work; European-style bureaucracies had supplanted the time-honored, corrupt ways of the Chinese civil service; European mores and manners had scandalized the foot-bound ladies of the Chinese upper class. But most irritating to the existing order in China was the progress made by European missionaries in the mass conversion of the Chinese peasantry from their ancient and closely held superstitions to one or another form of Christian belief.

Though nominally Buddhist, the average Chinese person of 1900 still believed in a pantheon of gods and a host of spirits inhabiting all things, including inanimate objects. To an original monotheistic concept of a dualistic Supreme Deity—T'ien and Shang Ti, who were different aspects of the same divine person—had been added, according to the magisterial 1904 Eleventh Edition of the *Britannica*, "a worship of the sun, moon, and constellations, of the five planets and of such noticeable individual stars as Canopus, which was looked upon as the home of the God of Longevity. Mother Earth came in for her share of worship, indicated especially by the God of the Soil, and further distributed among rivers and hills. Wind, rain, cold, thunder, and lightning, as each became objects of desire or aversion, were invested with the attributes of deities. The various parts of the house—door, kitchen stove, courtyard, etc.—were also conceived of as sheltering some spirit whose influence might be benign or the reverse. The spirits of the land and of grain came to mean one's country, the commonwealth, the state; and the sacrifices to these spirits by the emperor formed a public announcement of his accession to the throne. Side by side with such sacrificial rites was the worship of ancestors, stretching so far back that its origin is not discernible."

In their most extreme manifestations the ancient gods of China, when offended, could only be appeased through human sacrifice: The Boxers themselves were to torture and sacrifice thousands of victims, mostly Chinese Christian converts, on barbaric altars in temples heaped with gore. An extreme and aggressive resentment of all foreigners and foreign influence—in effect a severe case of the traditional and time-honored Chinese xenophobia—swept across China in the decade leading up to 1900. A series of disasters, both natural and military, augmented this xenophobia and contributed to the cataclysmic explosion of Boxerism. Chinese armies, antiquated and gaudily dressed, many of their soldiers equipped only with pikes, swords, and primitive matchlock muskets, suffered a stinging defeat at the hands of an already modernized Japan, whose efficient khaki-wearing troops carried the latest European-style bolt-action rifles. The Treaty of Shimonoseki in 1895, obtained by the Japanese victory, ensured the independence of Korea and gained for Japan the Pescadore Islands and Formosa. Then two consecutive Chinese harvests failed, leading to famine and mass death from starvation; this was followed by a plague of locusts, itself followed by disastrous flooding in which thousands of villages washed away. The dirty brown waters of the Yangtze River, clogged with at least 100,000 putrefying bodies, led to an epidemic of typhus.

Thus, it seemed to the Chinese that the traditional gods of China were displeased—angered, no doubt, by the establishment of vigorous new foreign gods on their own soil and by un-Chinese innovations like the railroad and the steamship, and also by the reforms of the Manchu emperor Kwang-Su. This pallid monarch was just then attempting to wrestle China into the modern age through a series of imperial edicts written with the "vermillion pencil" of imperial power. The Japanese had modernized at an amazing pace following the opening of Japan by U.S. Commodore Matthew Perry and his armada of American warships in 1850—why not China? So a handful of brave and forward-looking Chinese reformers thought—and they had the ear of the emperor.

New imperial edicts overhauled the fossilized system of state examinations that had allowed the rise of fools and manipulators in the Imperial Service and created a modern state department out of the rubble. Other edicts encouraged the teaching of Western sciences in newly established Western-style universities. But from a Chinese perspective the most outrageous of the edicts did away with the obligatory wearing of the long pigtail—the "characteristic feature of national dress," once a badge of subjugation imposed upon all Chinese males by conquering Manchu emperors in the seventeenth century—a custom that, in a kind of turnabout, had been cherished for centuries. All bitterly resented the new law that now forced them to cut it off.

Had the reforms of Emperor Kwang-Su adhered, the subsequent history of China might have followed a different course and been, perhaps, significantly less sanguine. It was not to be. The naive Kwang-Su had failed to reckon with the powerful forces of reaction at court, in particular with the shadowy power wielded by his aunt, the Dowager Empress Tsz'e Hsi—one of the most tenacious dragon ladies of Chinese history.

The dowager empress acted quickly to preserve the traditional order. She had previously obtained the loyalty of the army, and during the night of September 20, 1898, at her behest, soldiers invaded the Forbidden City and secured the divine person of the emperor. Before they got to him, Kwang-Su was able to warn some of his friends in the Reformist Party—including the famous scholar Kang Yu Wei, known as the "Modern Sage"—who thus escaped a painful death at the empress's hands. The emperor himself was immediately forced to rescind all the reformist edicts that had sprung from the colorful lead of his vermillion pencil. The hapless Kwang-Su was then imprisoned with a few of his favorite concubines on an island in the middle of an artificial lake, called the Ocean Terrace. The dowager empress explained to alarmed representatives of the Great Powers that the emperor's health, worn down by weighty matters of state, had undergone a sudden decline. He was now compelled to seclude himself from the world to rest and recuperate for an unspecified period, she explained. Until the emperor's much-anticipated return, she would reluctantly act as regent and rule in his place.

Dowager Empress Tsz'e Hsi's rabid hatred of foreigners dated to her youth in the 1860s and the punitive destruction of the fabulous Summer Palace by British and French troops during the Second Opium War. Like the Boxers whose antiforeign rage she sought to channel, she wanted to turn back the clock 500 years and rid China of all foreign influence. Her official name, Tsz'e Hsi, which means "motherly and auspicious," usually modified on Chinese state documents by a string of superlatives including "Most Orthodox, Heaven-Blessed, Prosperous, All-Nourishing, Brightly Manifest, Calm, Sedate, Perfect, Long-Lived, Respectful, Devout, Worshipful, Illustrious, and Exalted" exudes more than a whiff of surreal absurdity. She was, in reality—with the exception, perhaps, of "Long-Lived"—none of these things. Rather, she was one of the most treacherous and power-hungry rulers China had seen in 1,000 years. She had reportedly murdered her sister, her nephews—one of them briefly emperor—and "encouraged her son, the young emperor, in debaucheries which hastened his death." Or, other sources say, this unfortunate ruler may have been murdered by Tsz'e Hsi's motherly gift of an embroidered facecloth infected with smallpox bacilli. Tsz'e Hsi was also thought to have taken a hand in the poisoning of her son's pregnant widow; all this dynastic nefariousness to smooth her own way to China's glittering Peacock Throne.

According to the learned sinologist—and noted fabulist—Edmund Backhouse, whose erotic adventures in China, both real and imagined, literally fill volumes, the dowager empress was a woman of unique sexual appetites. She possessed, he tells us, an "abnormally large clitoris which she enjoyed rubbing against her lovers' anuses." This fact he discovered for himself, he says, when singled out for an imperial sexual encounter: According to an account in his unpublished memoir, *Décadence Mandchoue*, preserved in the Bodleian Library at Oxford, he was taken to the dowager empress's bedchamber wearing only an embroidered silk teddy. Candles blazed from jade fixtures; mirrored walls reflected the sixty-something but remarkably preserved empress lying naked on her phoenix couch:

"My bed is cold," Backhouse has her saying. "Now exhibit to me your genitals, for I know I shall love them."

To the dowager empress and the Boxers, Europeans were "First Class Devils," their Chinese Christian converts "Second Class Devils," and any Chinese who worked for a foreigner "Third Class Devils." All these devils, the Boxers believed, could be driven from China by the use of martial arts, repetitive rituals, and magic charms, with the aid of military ghosts from China's glorious past. Along with their brother organization, the Big Sword Society, they believed that "a combination of deep-breathing exercises, magical formulae, and the swallowing of chains made their bodies invulnerable to bullets, as if they were protected by a golden bell."

The name Boxer is a European transliteration of the Chinese characters *I Ho Ch'uan*, meaning "Righteous Harmonious Fists." Though the virulently anti-Christian and nationalistic society had been around for centuries and probably inspired the expulsion of the Jesuits from China in 1749, their true origins remain obscure. Many similarly mystical martial-arts-based sects existed in China from the earliest days: the White Lotus, the Eight Diagram Sect, the Red Fists, and the Big Knives, among others. Of these, the Boxers—with members drawn from the disenfranchised peasant classes—were the most violent and certainly the most theatrical. They produced elaborate traveling shows, full of calisthenics, hypnotic chanting, banner waving, dancing, and gong music, similar in character to the popular Chinese operas of the day. And they printed up thousands of dramatic illustrated *pronunciamentos*, secretly circulated from hand to hand, in which they promised they would soon conjure an army of 8,000,000 ghost soldiers to massacre all the Foreign Devils of every classification on Chinese soil.

The typical Boxer fighter wore a dingy white tunic scrawled over with red Chinese characters and belted with a red sash, his head wrapped in a tattered red turban. In the villages and towns in the provinces of Shantung, Chihli, and Kiangnan through the last years leading up to rebellion, these fanatics proselytized and recruited followers through their magic shows, put on free of charge in the village square. One of the main Boxer tricks illustrated their supposed imperviousness to rifle fire. Of course, the shooter used a blank cartridge, but everyone present, even the Boxers themselves, willingly suspended disbelief.

As the new century dawned, the Boxers gathered thousands of recruits and enough confidence to commit outrages upon the innocent. First they visited their massacres and tortures on the Second Class Devils—the Chinese Christian converts—of whom hundreds were slaughtered, then gradually upon the missionaries themselves. On December 31, 1899, in Shantung Province, Boxer thugs murdered a British missionary, the Reverend S. M. Brooks. They chased him down as he was trying to escape to safety in Peking, chopped off his head, and threw it in a gully at the side of the road. Though the murderers were quickly apprehended and executed by the imperial governor, the Dowager Empress Tsz'e Hsi refused to condemn the Boxer movement as a whole. She declared on January 11 that the Boxers were a nonviolent religious sect, nothing more than "peaceful citizens who banded together and practiced the martial arts for their self-defense . . . a part of Chinese life."

With this edict, she set the imperial stamp of approval on the coming People's War against the Europeans. She hoped to use the Boxers as a proxy army to rid China of all foreigners and their adherents. Should the Boxers succeed in this aim, so much the better; should they fail, she would claim helplessness in the face of a movement over which she had no control. Accordingly, Boxer militiamen began harassing Europeans in the streets of Peking. It became unsafe for a foreigner to go about in the capital without an armed escort.

The European ministers protested this treatment fruitlessly during daily visits to the Tsung-li Yamen, the office of the Imperial Chinese Court set up to deal with foreign matters. A visit to this Kafkaesque governmental institution—kept deliberately drab and comfortless as an insult to the foreign dignitaries bound to convene for hours within its precincts—was little more than an exercise in futility. The European ministers would wait all day for an audience with the dowager empress's representatives, only to be told at dusk that the official in question had taken ill earlier and gone home. Would the foreign gentlemen kindly return in the morning?

Meanwhile, Sir Claude MacDonald, the British minister and senior European diplomat, foreseeing the coming siege, set about organizing the defense of the Legation Compound. With the blessing of Sir Claude, Frank Gamewell, an American Methodist missionary and engineer, organized work parties of Chinese Christians who had taken refuge in the compound. Gamewell and his coolies and every other able person of a dozen different nationalities united to make a fortress out of the warren of streets and official buildings that comprised the compound: Barricades were erected; trenches dug; loopholes cut into the sides of the residences; sandbags made from silk curtains, sheets, anything at hand. Provisions were stockpiled and committees formed to deal with the distribution of food and ammunition. If they could just hold out until a promised relief column of Allied troops reached them from the coast! This polyglot army of Russian, French, English, American, and

Japanese sailors and marines currently idled on a variety of naval vessels now anchored at the mouth of the Pei-ho River 100 miles distant.

Some of the ministers maintained that a reasonable and peaceful resolution to the crisis might yet be achieved. But the dowager empress had gone to a place beyond the appeal of reason. As for peace, she had never liked it much in the first place. She was, a snarky French diplomat had observed, the "only man in China," and she was determined to fight. Also, she half believed the Boxers' claim of magical invulnerability and, "little by little, became fascinated with the thought of adding the supernatural" to the arsenal of weapons with which she would defeat the foreign devils and drive them from her Celestial Kingdom.

Reportedly, she "listened intently to eyewitness accounts of how the Boxers practiced ritual exercises to induce their gods to possess them. Her passionate love of Chinese theater made her particularly susceptible to tales of how the Boxer devotee was seized with . . . spasms, catalepsy, or epilepsy, and often passed into something resembling a state of trance or hypnotism. They seemed to be literally mad men, daring everything and fearing nothing. When the trance period had been passed through successfully, the worshipper was held to be quite invulnerable."

On June 19, 1900, the vermillion pencil now wielded by the dowager empress composed another edict: All foreigners were to evacuate Peking within twenty-four hours; their safety could no longer be guaranteed by the imperial government. The European ministers debated the ramifications of this order all through that day and night. Some insisted all would be massacred once they set foot outside the Legation Compound; others that they should trust the Chinese, pack their families and a few things, and leave immediately, a baggage train of carts and wagons being requisitioned for this purpose. But Sir Claude MacDonald, citing the example of the Siege of Cawnpore during the Sepoy Rebellion in India forty-odd years before, warned against placing their fates in the hands of the Chinese. On that occasion, British personnel and their families, guaranteed safety by the treacherous Nana Sahib should they surrender the Cawnpore Fort, surrendered and were all slaughtered. The women and children not killed in the initial attack were later hacked to pieces, the resultant bits thrown down a well.

As the ministers debated, restless Boxer hordes now completely surrounding the Legations were joined by a multitude of "Kansu Braves," fierce Chinese-Muslim fighters commanded by the virulently antiforeign Muslim General Tung Fu-hsiang. Suddenly, the German minister, Baron von Kettler, a staunch European Imperialist whose brusque manner the Chinese found particularly obnoxious, and who held them in equal contempt, informed the assembled ministers he would personally make one last visit to the dowager empress's representatives at the Tsung-li Yamen. He would protest the evacuation order strenuously; as he was German, the Chinese would have no choice but to listen to him! The European ministers attempted to dissuade von Kettler from this foolish mission to no avail. The mandarins at the Tsung-li Yamen, they said, would refuse an audience, as always.

"Thereupon, von Kettler who is, or rather was, a very passionate and excitable man," wrote Sir Charles in a private dispatch to the British Foreign Office, "banged his fist on the table and said 'I will go and sit there if I have to sit all night!'"

In the company of his aide, a certain Herman Cordes, von Kettler ordered up two sedan chairs and Chinese porters to take them to the Tsung-li Yamen. These chairs, fitted with scarlet and green hoods and easily recognizable, were used only by traveling dignitaries and foreign ministers. Von Kettler, dressed in his best diplomatic duds, mounted his chair, nonchalantly smoking a cigar and carrying a thick book with which he planned to while away the hours he would be forced to wait in the Tsung-li Yamen's dismal precincts. According to one witness, he looked "as if he were going on a picnic."

This was the last time anyone in the Foreign Legations saw him alive. Halfway to the Yamen, the sedan chairs in which he and Herr Cordes rode were attacked by Imperial Chinese troops. Though shot through both thighs, Cordes miraculously managed to crawl to safety, surviving to report what he saw next:

"The Minister's chair was three paces in front of me," he testified. "I saw a banner soldier, in full uniform with a mandarin's hat and a button and blue feather, step forward, present his rifle within a yard of the chair's window, level it at the Minister's head, and fire. . . . I affirm the assassination of the German Minister was a deliberately planned, premeditated murder, done in obedience to the orders of Chinese government officials by an Imperial Bannerman."

The war with China had begun.

News of Baron von Kettler's murder reached the Kaiser in Germany via telegraph within a matter of hours. This was the last reliable report that would be had by an anxious European public from the Legations in Peking for many weeks. The Boxers, not entirely ignorant of European technology, cut the telegraph cables and Peking went silent.

As the Boxers went about their work of destruction, the joint British-Russian-American-Japanese-German relief expedition under British Admiral Seymour at last set out from the coast via railroad to Peking. But the Boxers had torn up the tracks and the expedition was forced to disembark halfway to the capital and turn back. Marching along the banks of the Pei-ho in steaming heat and through shoulder-high fields of millet, the countryside raised against them, the wells poisoned, they suffered heavy losses and were saved only by the timely intervention of a unit of Cossack cavalry. At last, they gained the safety of the foreign quarter of the walled coastal city of Tientsin—but there they would find no respite. They had arrived just in time to endure another siege.

A vast Chinese army quickly invested the native sectors of Tientsin and began battering the walls of the foreign quarter with artillery. This army, composed of trained imperial troops, was now backed by thousands of Boxers; the empress had clearly made common cause with the rabble. Seemingly, every Chinese male who yesterday had been a carter or a grocer's assistant or a dockworker had today joined the Boxer cause. And their numbers were now further augmented by a contingent of young Chinese women called the Red Lantern Girls, after the incendiary lamps they carried to help burn down missionary buildings. These female fighters, between the ages of twelve and eighteen, were regarded with superstitious awe. Supposedly, the Red Lantern Girls could "pull down high-storied houses with thin cotton strings, and could set fire to a house by simply moving a fan." They could also fly, and were seen by the credulous in the air above the spires of the burning Christian churches in Tientsin, circling like crows, untouched in broiling sheets of flame.

Europe waited with terrible apprehension for more news from China. Everyone feared the worst. How could a few thousand Europeans, even armed with the latest weapons and a steely Caucasian resolve, hold out against a nation of three hundred yellow million? At last, in July, the dreaded, expected news came: The *London Daily Mail* received a dispatch from their special correspondent in Shanghai detailing the massacre of all the foreigners in Peking: THE PEKING MASSACRE, the headline ran. *All White Men, Women, and Children Put to the Sword!* The *London Times* later confirmed this report, describing how "Europeans fought with calm courage to the end against overwhelming hordes of fanatical barbarians thirsting for their blood. . . . When the last cartridge had gone, their hour had come. Of the ladies, it is enough to say that in this awful hour, they showed themselves worthy of their husbands." Other major newspapers, including the *New York Times*, reported more horror stories: The heads of murdered U.S. Marine guards had been paraded around the streets on spears; the public executions of foreigners had gone on for ten solid days. Rather than fall into the hands of a merciless enemy, the women of the Legations had poisoned themselves the moment the Boxers breached the walls.

The Western world mourned.

Queen Victoria was "quite miserable, horror stricken" at the fate of her envoys and their families and at the violent deaths of all the Europeans. What could be done to make China pay for these crimes against humanity? A grand public memorial service for the victims of the Peking Massacre was scheduled for July 23, 1900, at St. Paul's Cathedral in London.

In Germany, the Kaiser fulminated, particularly enraged at the loss of Baron von Kettler, who had been a special favorite. He decided to send an army to avenge von Kettler's murder and the murder of his German subjects in China—an army that would, incidentally, expand his influence in the Far East. The Kaiser's plans coalesced into the German East Asian Expeditionary Corps, under the command of Field Marshal Count von Waldersee. It would be one of the major components of the cooperating foreign forces being organized to exterminate the Boxers. They would ferret them out and destroy them, dislodge the dowager empress and her murderous clique, and establish in its place a new order favorable to European interests.

Among the first volunteers eager for action was Leutnant Paul von Lettow-Vorbeck, just then in his second year as a logistics officer on the Great German

General Staff. Von Lettow got himself appointed adjutant under General von Schwarzhoff, a military pragmatist whom he greatly respected and who would soon be recognized as an outstanding officer of "towering confidence," and acknowledged as "the heart of East Asian operations."

The soldiers, sailors, and marines of the Kaiser's expeditionary force assembled at Bremerhaven on July 27, 1900. The great transport ships lay dockside, their pennants unfurled, the white, black, and red ensign of the Imperial Navy flying from the lanyards. Among these was the 13,000-ton *Batavia*, which would be von Lettow's vessel for the 5,000-mile journey to China. Still furious over von Kettler's murder, the Kaiser mounted the podium to address the departing troops. Against the wishes of his advisers, he began to speak off the cuff, departing from the prepared text given to the press, and made statements that would have unfortunate echoes in the years to come:

"You must know, my men," the Kaiser shouted into the rainy afternoon, "that you are about to meet a crafty, well-armed foe! Give them no quarter! Take no prisoners! Kill him when he falls into your hands! Even, as 1,000 years ago, the Huns under their king, Attila, made such a name for themselves as still resounds in terror . . . so may the name of Germany resound through Chinese history. . . . Never again will a Chinaman dare so much as look askance at a German. . . ." Etc.

This speech, extemporaneous, hurriedly given and barely understood by restless men awaiting embarkation, nevertheless became notorious. A lone journalist, who had not trotted off with the rest of his colleagues at the heels of German press officers for a prepared luncheon and free beer, hastily transcribed the Kaiser's words. He quickly relayed them to his newspaper via telegraph; from this source they were picked up by other newspapers, translated into many languages, and circled the globe. The pejorative "Hun" and its derivatives (Hunnish, Hunnishness) to describe Germans and their activities derived from the Kaiser's speech that day.

As it turned out, reports of the fall of the Legations in Peking and the massacre of all foreigners in the city had been greatly exaggerated. In fact, they were entirely false—the highly effective fabrications of the *Daily Mail*'s special correspondent in Shanghai, an American con man named Sutterlee. Actually, the Legations held out heroically against the Boxer siege, their supplies and ammunition dwindling, until the relief of Peking by a second and larger Allied army on August 14, 1900.

The heroism of the defenders of the Legations against the Chinese assault became proverbial, part of the "iron rations" invoked by Peter Fleming. But it was the unprecedented and efficient cooperation between European nations that saved the day—ironic, as little more than a decade later, these same nations would be busily engaged in a war of mutual extermination. Dramatic details of the siege, enough to fill many engaging volumes, were reported in a slew of memoirs published shortly after the events, and in several excellent, comprehensive accounts published over the years since. But in another sense, the journalistic con man Sutterlee had gotten it right when he described the remorselessness displayed by the Boxers in his fictitious massacre: During their brief, bloodthirsty reign of terror over the summer of 1900, the Boxers managed to slaughter all the Christian missionaries in the interior of the country and at least 30,000 Chinese Christian converts.

By September 1900, the defeated Boxers, dispersed to various provincial strongholds, contemplated the totality of their ruin. Many of them now believed the European soldier could "render himself invulnerable by smearing his face with menstrual blood." The reason Boxer assaults had failed, they asserted—especially the attack on the Pietang, Peking's Roman Catholic cathedral—was entirely magical in nature. Apparently, at the Pietang, "the defenders had draped the skins of women from the embrasures," thus ensuring through a special kind of dark, psychosexual magic that Boxer bullets would not hit their mark.

Also, the Boxers especially blamed the French Roman Catholic bishop Favier, whom they saw as an immensely powerful supernatural being, the "Chief Foreign Devil" in Peking. Bishop Favier had invoked powerful anti-Boxer foreign magic by nailing naked women and fetuses torn from the bellies of the pregnant to the facade of the Pietang—this the Boxers believed contrary to the evidence of their eyes. They also believed that the foreigners were in possession of a powerful magical weapon, the "Ten Thousand Woman Flag" woven entirely from female pubic hair, which in some unexplained fashion vitiated the magic of the Boxer gods. However, in these assertions, the Boxers were in error. No such bizarre enchantments had been needed to defeat them, and the Ten Thousand Woman Flag has never been found. Rather, European tenacity, superior firepower, and international cooperation had done the trick.

And also, as the 1904 *Britannica* explains: "It was to Jung Lo," who almost alone of the dowager empress's advisers had opposed the war, "that the legations owed their escape from extermination." Jung Lo, a general of artillery and a political moderate among radicals, had somehow failed, despite orders, to bring his most modern fieldpieces to bear against the Legation's walls. After the siege, brand-new Krupp guns bought by the Chinese government from Germany in 1899 were discovered in a nearby warehouse, still sealed in their packing cases. With these modern guns in play, European defenses wouldn't have withstood the battering of a single afternoon.

———————

By the time Leutnant von Lettow-Vorbeck and the German East Asian Expeditionary Force under Count von Waldersee got under way, the worst of the fighting in China was over.

The Chinese attack on the Legation Compound had been repulsed; the Allies had taken Tientsin and Peking with the forces available. The dowager empress, whose hatred of foreigners had been the immediate cause of the war, had fled to the northern hinterlands with her nephew the emperor—now, as a result of his incarceration on the Ocean Terrace, a childish semi-idiot. Before she left the palace, in a fit of pique, she ordered his favorite, the Pearl Concubine, thrown down a well by her eunuchs.

But the brutal work of pacification had just begun. The mopping up remained, the rooting out. Also, the epic looting of Peking, treasure-house of untold ages, by Allied troops was just gathering momentum. None of these developments were known to von Lettow aboard the *Batavia*. Preparing for war, he sought to keep his men fit, to maintain their morale. He drilled the rank and file daily on deck, organized target practice, fitness regimes. For his officers, he mandated French lessons—French being, literally, the lingua franca of the Peking Legations. And, via an Irish-born German officer, classes in English, the common language of joint military operations.

The *Batavia* passed through the Mediterranean—stopping at Gibraltar, where von Lettow watched brown-skinned urchins dive for coins tossed into the clear water—and traversed the Suez Canal. Plague raged at Port Said; the expeditionary force, many of whose members now suffered from chronic seasickness, was not allowed to disembark. In the Red Sea, beneath a blazing sun and in conditions of "insane heat," von Lettow made an important discovery about himself: He could take it. Indeed, his precocious personal stamina would be put to the test time and time again over the years ahead fighting in punishing tropical climates. The equatorial temperatures aboard the *Batavia* felled many aboard, sent many more to the hold unfit for duty with ice packs on their necks. Not von Lettow. The heat hardly bothered him at all—a resistance he attributed to his fit physical condition, honed over a youth and young manhood in Germany spent outdoors, hunting in all sorts of weather, from autumn's hoarfrost to the torpor of July.

At Singapore, eighteen days out of Port Said, the *Batavia* finally reached the Far East. This, more than the punishing weather, acted as a shock to von Lettow's system. He had never seen anything like the mass of humanity that shouldered its way through the narrow streets of the teeming port city: "Pigtailed, sweating Chinese trimming coal amidst unending clamor; refined Chinese merchants in silk costumes wearing European Bowler hats with the pigtails sticking out oddly from under them." But he was most alarmed by the multitude of rickshaws. These two-wheeled conveyances pulled by a man struck him as an insult to human dignity. He sat in them reluctantly, only because they were the sole vehicles capable of negotiating the overcrowded thoroughfares, and always overpaid his fare. But he could not reconcile himself to being "pulled around by a man as if he were an animal." In his deeply felt reaction to the sufferings of the rickshaw drivers, von Lettow articulates his belief in a basic, shared humanity, revealing an empathy for the struggles of fellow human beings of any race. This element of his character was to become as powerful a part of his contradictory psychology as its reverse—which is to say his ferocious dedication to war and the military life.

Also while in Singapore, von Lettow observed for the first time a foreign army going about its duties. A crack British regiment strutted around smartly kitted out in pressed khakis—these in contrast to the oddly drab and unseasonably warm "tropical" uniform of the German East Asian Expeditionary Force, which consisted of jackets and pants of an easily rumpled, thick mustard-colored corduroy. On their heads, as the single concession to the climate, they wore ridiculous-looking *Südwesterhuts*, which is to say wide-brimmed straw hats, folded up on one side.

Before they re-embarked for China, von Lettow and the GEAF received two pieces of welcome news. First that the Legations had been relieved and the besieged inhabitants saved from massacre. Second that Field Marshal von Waldersee had been appointed commander in chief over all Allied armies in China as a concession to the Kaiser for von Kettler's murder. Whether von Lettow was secretly chagrined at the cessation of major hostilities, he does not say. In any case, his duties as adjutant, heavily logistical, would most likely have precluded him from partaking in any protracted fighting.

After Singapore, the *Batavia* stopped in Shanghai, then proceeded to Tientsin, so recently embattled, now the disembarkation point for Allied troops. In Tientsin, von Lettow organized quarters for his superior, General Schwarzhoff, and staff at the Astor House Hotel. This venerable establishment still stands today, a rare survivor from China's colonial past, complete with wood-paneled lobby and brass spittoons, its creaky cage elevator lurching fitfully from floor to floor as it did more than 100 years ago.

From Tientsin, von Lettow arranged a caravan of packhorses and mules—the railroad not yet refurbished—to carry the staff to its final destination, Peking. The journey, which even then took only a few hours by train, took von Lettow's caravan over four days. Along the way, they passed through a hellish landscape: burned-out villages, unharvested crops rotting in the fields, the bloated corpses of dead Chinese in decomposing mounds. Packs of feral dogs roamed the countryside, fattened on human meat. Thick black clouds of flies swarmed everywhere. At last von Lettow and company caught sight of the ancient city in the distance. It was a sight he would never forget: Peking's massive medieval fortifications, its high walls so wide that "wagons could stand cross-ways upon them. The main streets led through tremendous gates, recently battered down by Allied cannon. Bargaining, haggling Chinese swarmed. . . . Sweltering heat and that special Chinese aroma of onions and garlic lay over everything." This memorable, all-penetrating odor, commented upon by nearly every European visitor to Peking in those days, encompassed more than just frying food and "night soil" (human feces)—but the trace of something mysterious, indefinable: The future polar explorer Sir Ernest Shackleton called it the "smell of the moth-eaten centuries."

The amount of plunder available for sale within Peking's walls astounded von Lettow. The ancient city had been gutted and turned inside out by Allied troops. The treasures of the ages—priceless jade objects and rare furs, fantastically detailed ivory carvings, gold and silver jewelry, diadems, porcelain—everything and anything, was being traded for the equivalent of a few dollars or a pack of smokes. Not just treasure, but a great nation's history lay in heaps on the street corners, stolen by common European soldiers armed with bolt-action rifles and bayonets. Nothing like this had been seen since the sack of Byzantium by Venetian doge Enrico Dandolo and the Crusaders in his pay in the dreadful Fourth Crusade of 1204: After thoroughly raping that legendary city, for a bit of fun, the Crusaders installed a prostitute on the sacred throne of the Byzantine Patriarchs in the Basilica of the Hagia Sophia.

Von Lettow immediately found himself fascinated by Chinese culture. Its immense age intrigued him; beneath everything, every gesture, lay centuries of complex civilization and a behavioral code that most Westerners—even old Chinese hands like Edmund Backhouse—might study for a lifetime and fail to grasp.

"There were still refined Chinese to be seen," von Lettow asserted. "They had just begun to emerge in public after the paroxysm of plunder and rapine that had engulfed the city after the Allied victory. But even the coolies showed China's ancient culture when they replied to greetings in an especially gracious manner." And one has the feeling that von Lettow felt a sort of kinship between himself and the mandarins he met—Junker codes of conduct being similarly complex.

At first, his logistical duties as adjutant to General von Schwarzhoff consumed all his time. When Supreme Commander von Waldersee arrived at the Taku anchorage, von Lettow was charged by his immediate superior with finding suitable quarters for the multitude of General Staff and with installing a functioning HQ for the German Army in the Winter Palace of the Chinese emperors. The famous Winter Palace, a labyrinthine complex of highly flammable wooden pagodas hundreds of years old, had been built around the large lotus pond bordering the Forbidden City. Much clearing of rubble and construction work was required before this district could be inhabited—so thoroughly ransacked had it been by Japanese and Cossack troops in the days immediately following the siege.

Meanwhile, the endlessly curious von Lettow set about learning as much as he could from his experiences in China. He cultivated the friendship of many Chinese people from all classes and walks of life. Often eschewing the officers' mess, he shopped in the cacophonous native markets and patronized native businesses, living—as the expression goes—"on the economy." He sought out members of the Chinese bourgeoisie and often dined in their homes in the interest of promoting cross-cultural understanding. Under their tutelage he improved his knowledge of conversational Chinese, becoming good enough to communicate regarding the basic necessities, but—so he says, regretfully—inadequate for any serious conversation. He often attended the Chinese opera and, despite his inability to understand the niceties of plot and dialogue, enjoyed the garish performances on the level of spectacle—finding particular amusement in the ultrastylized and unnatural falsetto employed by the actors to declaim their lines.

Reticent as always regarding sexual matters, von Lettow nevertheless lets drop a few tantalizing hints in his memoirs: Like all occupied cities, the Peking of 1900–01 was by necessity a whorehouse—which is to say, its body was for sale for a few coppers, desperately needed food, a jar of face powder, the small comforts of life. Von Lettow expressed contempt for the Allied ransacking of the city, and refused to participate in the auctions of looted objets d'art that now regularly occurred in the Legation Compound and at pop-up bazaars elsewhere. Women too were available for purchase. Taking a beautiful Chinese mistress was considered the best way to learn the language and the culture; women acquired for this purpose were called "sleeping dictionaries." Of course, von Lettow, then a vigorous young man barely thirty, was not immune to the charms of Chinese femininity. One evening at the opera, he tells us, "a silk-clad feminine leg pushed itself onto the chair next to me and its owner said 'Good evening, *Herr Leutnant.*'"

This woman, whose name he never reveals, spoke perfect German and had lived in Berlin where she had been a secretary at the Chinese embassy. She took it upon herself to translate the opera line by line close in his ear as it unfolded on the stage. It was a classic, she told him, from the period of the Ming Dynasty. Afterward, von Lettow allows, they went for a glass of champagne. He doesn't say what happened once the champagne had been consumed—and with that, lets the matter drop.

As a staff officer and adjutant to General von Schwarzhoff, von Lettow might easily have avoided action entirely. Many staff officers did. Why waste your time getting shot at if your services were urgently required at headquarters? But von Lettow had not volunteered for the expeditionary force to sit in an office overseeing logistics for the General Staff. He had come to China to fight and—as he saw it—to avenge the death of Baron von Kettler, whom he had known in Berlin. And though the battle for the Legations had been won and Peking taken, fanatical elements of the defeated Boxer armies had entrenched themselves in out-of-the-way strongholds in the far north. There they counted on the magical powers of the Boxer gods to keep all Foreign Devils at bay.

In January 1901, von Lettow joined a column of German troops ordered to reduce a Boxer fortress in the wild terrain northeast of Peking. Northern China is a region of climatic extremes, sweltering in the summer, freezing in the winter. Von Lettow, bundled in furs and heavily armed, made his way toward the enemy with the German column via forced marches in deep snow. Temperatures dropped to subzero. Icy winds blasted falling snow into a blizzard. The Boxers, secure behind the walls of their fortress and unused to making war in winter (spring and summer were the traditional fighting seasons in China), had not expected an attack. After a short, intense firefight, the German column took the Boxer position by storm.

Von Lettow says little about this encounter, only that it went well. He tells us nothing about how he felt, pulling the trigger of a rifle for the first time on living men who were in the process of shooting back; nothing about his "baptism of fire." The first experience of battle in a life henceforth marked by war passes nearly unremarked, and we can only guess at von Lettow's emotional state. Though, given his utterly cool demeanor during similar situations throughout his military life, our guess might at least be called educated: He probably smoked all through the encounter, as he did later in Africa, the rising clouds of cigarette smoke the only visible sign of his agitation. Then the bolt-action Mauser carefully aimed, the trigger squeezed, the first shot. What went through his mind as answering enemy fire splashed into the frozen ground all around him? Did he hear in the moment after the bullet's sharp report the shriek of a comrade wounded by his side? Or did he hear other voices, farther away? The voice of his father the general, and his grandfather the general, and his great-great-granduncle the general to whom Frederick II had given the Pour le Mérite—the voices of von Lettow fighting men out of the ancestral gloom of 1,000 years, out of the shadows of the Baltic forests. Fear is not an option, failure is not an option. Not for a Junker with a pedigree dating back to the wars of the Teutonic Knights.

Von Lettow emerged from this nameless action both bloodied and victorious. He participated in a few more such expeditions of pacification, one with a contingent of Austrian marines to the south of Peking. This time, the Boxers, again surprised in their hideout, didn't put up much of a fight. They surrendered and were immediately taken out and shot in accordance with martial law. Whether he found these summary executions distasteful, he doesn't say. Victory was the anticipated result, total eradication of the Boxers the definition of that victory.

Back in Peking, von Lettow's practical military education continued. He showed a great interest in the behavior of foreign armies, both in the field and at rest—which is to say, he focused equally on tactical capabilities and logistical skills. How quickly did that army maneuver—especially in difficult terrain; how efficiently did it acquire and distribute much-needed supplies? "An army fights on its stomach," as Napoleon famously observed. An army must be fed before it can march and fight. Had Bonnie Prince Charlie's Highlanders been well-fed the night before Culloden in 1746, the results of that disastrous battle might easily have been different; a Stuart might now occupy the British throne.

Another universal truth, militarily speaking, has it that an army destined for war in foreign lands must carry its own supplies—at least until local sources of food and fodder can be captured or organized. At Bremerhaven, the *Batavia*'s capacious hold had been loaded in a traditional and "excellent seamanlike manner," as von Lettow points out, "with the heavy cannon barrels in the lower holds and lighter provision packed over them. Under way, however, the sacks of peas, beans, and lentils took the rolling badly and burst, their contents pouring down over the cannon barrels." This amounted to a logistical disaster when the *Batavia* reached her destination after seven weeks at sea. Stevedores found everything compressed into a "tight cake in which the cannon barrels stuck like almonds."

Weeks later, this rat's nest of food, weaponry, and munitions had yet to be disentangled, leaving the German East Asian Expeditionary Force short of supplies and provisions. Von Lettow knew that in a more closely contested war this logistical mistake might have resulted in military defeat. Meanwhile, the British, with their considerable experience of smaller-scale colonial warfare, employed an easy solution to just such a predicament. They used less capacious transport ships with the arms and provisions supplied to each column stowed not in tightly packed layers but side by side with other necessary gear in such a way as to be immediately accessible upon disembarkation.

Von Lettow learned several other valuable military lessons observing foreign armies in action in China. Most important, perhaps, for his conduct of future wars, he found that British troops, otherwise excellent, were "abysmally led." Their officers could never seem to coordinate the movements of columns in the field, often missing rendezvous points critical to the outcome of battle:

"With the English, it was always delay, delay, and delay, and combined exercises didn't work so well," von Lettow notes acidly. "With us Germans, the precise coordination of large groups in modern warfare has always been a question of life and death."

In April 1901, von Lettow-Vorbeck's superior and mentor, General von Schwarzhoff, died in an accidental fire at the Winter Palace—though some credulous Chinese blamed this blaze on the secret work of Red Lantern Girls, floating invisibly in the sky. Von Lettow, saddened by the loss of a talented soldier who had become a personal friend, transferred to the command of General Lothar von Trotha.

By this time, von Lettow had soured on China. Or rather, he had learned everything he had come to learn and knew it was time to move on to other theaters of war and other experiences:

"The more I entered into Chinese life," he wrote, "the clearer it became to me that I was dealing with a culture and way of life that was fundamentally different from the European, and which would take me more than a few years to understand. It would take decades, perhaps even a lifetime, and I felt no inclination to do that."

Von Lettow's personal obsession, the course of study to which he had devoted his life's energies, was—as unheroic as this might sound—essentially logistical: He had become increasingly obsessed with the idea of perfecting the most efficient operational strategies for a modern army in the field. In this obsession, he believed, lay victory for future German armies. He now realized a return to the Great General Staff would better suit his chosen career path in the army. Though he had found China endlessly fascinating, though he respected its history and traditions and recognized a people whose "underlying strengths" had yet to be fully tapped, the demands of his military career made it pointless to remain any longer.

The *Batavia* sailed for Bremerhaven in November 1901, her departure coinciding with the general withdrawal of the foreign expeditionary forces from China. Aboard her went von Lettow, recently promoted captain. Typhus and dysentery haunted the long voyage home. At every port, the critically ill were off-loaded so they might either recover or expire in local hospitals. Many died at sea. Their bodies wrapped in shrouds, they slipped into the deep far from home, the military salute from the ship's guns timed to follow the rising and falling of the waves.

Chapter 7

HEREROLAND

Overseas colonial empires are acquired in any one of several ways, none of them entirely pleasant: some through outright conquest, like the French in Algeria, Morocco, and Indochina; others, like the British in India and elsewhere, through a slow, almost haphazard accretion—a combination of reluctantly applied military force and the economic blandishments available to history's first industrialized superpower. By the late nineteenth century, most of the world was divided in two parts—Europe and those other places directly or indirectly residing within the European sphere of influence. Only in Equatorial Africa were the borders of "Magna Europa" not yet firmly set.

In 1899, the English journalist and politician L. S. Amery traveled to Berlin to—as he put it—"sit at the feet of the great German classicist Theodor Mommsen," then a venerated historian and public intellectual in his late eighties. In Mommsen's "stately and magnificent presence," Amery, still fresh from his own historical studies at Oxford, hoped to "learn more of the government of Imperial Rome." Instead, he was treated to a vehement private lecture on the rightness of Germany's desire to found a new Fatherland in Equatorial Africa and "a diatribe on England's wickedness; how we had filched an empire while Germany was weakened by the Thirty Years' War and subsequently engrossed in the long and costly struggles between Prussia and Austria and against France. Now the time had come, Mommsen asserted with some violence, to change all that."

The amiable and reserved Amery confessed himself shocked by Mommsen's anti-British and rabidly procolonialist stance, but then pointed out that such crazy talk had been heard all over Germany in the generation since 1870—stridently articulated by the popular imperialist historian Treitschke among others. Its echoes had long since reached the Kaiser's one good ear—he was, as everyone knew, more or less deaf in the other.

During the fifteen years following Germany's unification in 1871, Chancellor Otto von Bismarck's good sense and proverbial iron will prevented Germany from joining the "Scramble for Africa" initiated by other European powers. The always prescient von Bismarck voiced what others blindly refused to admit: Colonies simply didn't pay. The costs of pacification and administration far outweighed any profits derived from the raw materials colonies supposedly possessed. The secret justification for colonialism lay in the hearts of the colonizers and was a moral—or aesthetic—rather than a financial imperative. And the Iron Chancellor, one of history's great practitioners of realpolitik, had little patience for aesthetic considerations:

"The advantages expected from colonies . . . rest for the most part on illusions," he said in 1868. Following the German victory at Sedan, he quickly quashed the impulse to take for the new German Empire France's colonies in North Africa as part of the latter's indemnities for starting the war.

"I want no colonies," he announced again in the Reichstag in 1872. "They are only good for providing offices. For us, colonial enterprises would be like the silks and sables of the Polish nobility, who otherwise have no shirts."

But realpolitik can be a difficult blade to wield properly. In 1884, the ever-sensible von Bismarck suddenly reversed his anticolonialist stance and "embarked on a career of colonial annexations right and left." This abrupt volte-face, prompted by what historian A. J. P. Taylor calls "considerations of European politics," and only tangentially by pressures from German commercial interests and procolonial societies, initially focused on one of Africa's last blank spaces: The "long stretch of inhospitable desert coast and the vast area of semi-arid and thinly peopled country between the Orange River (the British South African Cape Colony) and the recognized administrative limits of the Portuguese colony of Angola, nearly a thousand miles to the north."

During the preceding half century, intrepid German missionaries had made small penetrations into this region—soon to become German South

West Africa—setting up mission stations, pushing through a few roads, building one or two Christian schools, in the forlorn hope of bringing the blessings of Christianity to the heathen population of an arid, pagan land. Most, garnering few converts, died in the attempt, the victims of disease and tribal warfare, ultimately committing their German bones to the alien dust. A few enjoyed mild success—which is merely to say they did not fail outright.

What motivated such people? Certainly not financial gain or a desire for territorial conquest, but something stronger than these, yet utterly immaterial and stronger for its immateriality: An unshakable faith in their Christian God.

Before the arrival of the first missionaries in South West Africa, its history is steeped in neolithic obscurity. The area's original inhabitants, the Khoisan peoples (various tribes of hunter-gatherers including the Bushmen, whose stature rarely exceeded four feet) and the Hottentots, all spoke a venerable dialect of the Khoisan language that incorporated many unusual and melifluous "clicking" sounds. This language sounded so strange to the ears of the first European explorers, they wondered whether the strange little people who spoke it were people at all, or rather some unknown species of primate. Reinforcing this perception, the Hottentots in particular quickly demonstrated a near-animalistic savagery in warfare. They regularly perpetrated, wrote one missionary, "the most atrocious barbarities. . . . [Our] men were unmercifully shot down; the hands and feet of the women lopped off, the bowels of the children ripped out, etc., and all this to satisfy a savage thirst for blood."

But excepting the occasional burst of ultraviolence, most Hottentots lived in a condition of Stone Age torpor. They seemed immune to all change, a part of the ageless cycles of the natural world. Then, sometime in the mid-eighteenth century, wide swaths of Hottentot territory succumbed to the invasion of a tribe of Bantu cattle herders from the north—the Hereros. This warlike people first occupied the region's arable upper plateau, ideal for cattle grazing—a flat brown landscape resembling the Texas panhandle. Agricultural duties, which were minimal, they relegated to captured Hottentot slaves.

Over the remaining decades of the century, the Hereros slowly drove the Hottentots into the dry, rugged hills farther south and east. The newcomers, much taller and far more warlike than the indigenous Khoisan peoples, were possessed of the fierceness that comes from basing one's way of life on a single source: Everything they valued, all wealth and status and personal happiness, had to do with cattle. Regarding the care and protection of their herds, the Hereros showed themselves utterly merciless, and far more "savage" than the Hottentots had ever been. Because of their dominating ways and elegant bearing, the few Europeans who encountered Herero tribesmen in the early days regarded them as the region's "natural aristocrats."

"The Herero, generally speaking, are an exceedingly fine race of men." This according to the Swedish explorer Charles John Andersson in 1850. "Indeed, it is by no means unusual to meet with an individual six feet and some inches in height, and symmetrically proportioned. Their features are good and regular, and many might serve as perfect models of the human figure. Their air and carriage is very graceful and expressive." Though a closer association with them eventually modified his opinion: "Both sexes are exceedingly filthy in their habits. Dirt often accumulates to such a degree on their person as to make the color of their skin totally indistinguishable, while to complete the disguise, they smear themselves with a profusion of red ocher and grease. Hence, the exhalation hovering about them is disgusting in the extreme."

Of course in a land without water, the Hereros might be excused a reluctance to indulge in European-style bathing, but Andersson's next charge is somewhat more damaging: They were also, he says, infamous for their extreme cruelty, deceitfulness, and cunning—and had become a far more dangerous opponent than the comparatively innocuous, clicking Hottentots.

For the 100 years or so from their first appearance in South West Africa, the Hereros and Herero cattle lived in an uneasy truce with their Hottentot neighbors—though in matters regarding the theft of cattle, they became implacable and vicious enemies, as is witnessed by the vengeance taken on a hapless Hottentot cattle rustler, caught in the act:

"We came across a few Hottentots whom of course we killed," admitted a Herero warrior interviewed by German authorities around 1895. "I myself helped to kill one of them. First, we cut off his ears, saying to him, 'You will never hear Herero cattle lowing.' Then we cut off his nose, saying, 'Never again shall you smell Herero cattle.' And then we cut off his lips, saying, 'You shall never again taste Herero cattle.' And finally we cut his throat."

This was a justice of the most primitive kind, preserved from the original bloody assizes at the dawn of the world.

The Hereros themselves forgot why they had come into the country to begin with. They had no written history and few stories to explain themselves to themselves and like the Hottentots inhabited an eternally unfolding present. Around 1920, German ethnographer Heinrich Vedder interviewed a wizened elder in search of the lost Herero past. This dusty, antique gentleman provided a picture of Herero history that might have come from the days before Homo sapiens began their great migration out of Africa 50,000 years before:

"Have not the Hereros been cattle breeders ever since God created them? As cattle breeders, do we not always live in the self-same way? We trek with the herd wherever water and grazing can be found, and in the meantime, the cattle increase. Sometimes they are stolen by our enemies, sometimes no cattle thefts occur for years at a time. This is the life of a Herero; that was the life my father lived and my grandfather and great-grandfather. When we live exactly the same way, there is not much to be told. . . . This country has no owner, unless we are to regard the Bushmen who live in the veldt like wild animals as owners."

But the one constant in human life is change, no matter how glacial its pace. Around 1830, the *Difaquane*—or Time of Wandering—came to Hereroland and everything succumbed, metaphorically speaking, to the advancing ice. Briefly, the *Difaquane* encompassed a complicated series of wars of conquest set off by the ambitious, brutal Shaka Zulu—who may rightly be called the African Hitler—in far Natal, on the other side of the continent. Shaka's tactical innovations and ultradisciplined Zulu "impis" (celibate regiments of spearmen) swept all competing tribes from neighboring territories with maximum brutality and created a Greater Zululand—of which he declared himself emperor. Crops went unplanted; cattle died; famine and cannibalism followed in Shaka's wake; uncounted, unknowable millions died. The tribes of the far interior were eventually dislodged from their grazing lands by the Zulu-inspired holocaust; they in turn dislodged and slaughtered others. This domino effect eventually reached South West Africa, there manifesting as a Herero vs. Hottentot struggle over territory and grazing land. The goal—as in all wars of the *Difaquane*—became a complete annihilation of the enemy. *Totaler Krieg* long before the Nazis perfected the strategy.

The Herero-Hottentot Wars occurred in four increasingly brutal phases, each one roughly twelve years long: the First Herero-Hottentot War, 1830–42; the Second, 1846–58; the third, called the Herero War of Freedom, 1863–70, in which the Hereros temporarily gained the upper hand over their now-hereditary enemies; and the Fourth Herero-Hottentot War, 1880–92. The cumulative effect of almost sixty years of warfare was near-total devastation. South West Africa, already an arid wilderness, barely able to support its minimal population, had been reduced to an utter wasteland. The vicious, never-ending nature of the conflict at last gave the Germans the excuse they were looking for to establish their first colony in Africa: The Fourth Herero-Hottentot War bankrupted the handful of intrepid German traders who had managed to establish themselves in the territory by selling guns, alcohol, and other necessities to the antagonists. The Imperial German government moved in to restore order and make sure everyone got the guns and alcohol they needed.

"The classic nineteenth-century justification for imperial expansion was that only by the imposition of *force majeure* could peace be brought to the uncivilized world, and without peace civilization was impossible," asserts Jon Bridgman, one of the few modern historians of the Herero-Hottentot-German conflicts. Though he admits that in the case of South West Africa after the series of four brutal, disastrous Herero-Hottentot Wars, this argument had "a certain plausibility."

———

In 1883, a German entrepreneur named Adolf Lüderitz purchased the Atlantic harbor of Angra Pequena, later called Lüderitz Bay, from a Hottentot chief for 2,500 deutsche marks, 200 rifles, and a selection of toys that included—in an ironic bit of foreshadowing—a detachment of lead German soldiers. Cheaply bought perhaps, but considerably more expensive than Manhattan. From this tenuous foothold, the German presence in South West Africa exploded. As so often happened in the colonial era, traders and entrepreneurs acted as trailblazers, establishing trading posts and commercial towns that quickly proved impossible to defend from native elements who did not understand the concept of private property. These entrepreneurs, soon embattled, ended up calling upon the help of home governments who were then obliged to send out troops and establish a rudimentary colonial administration, which led to territorial status, metamorphosing at last into a full-fledged colony, dependent on the motherland for just about everything, but especially military protection.

Exactly this pattern was followed in South West Africa. In 1885, Bismarck sent Dr. Ernst Göring, father of future Nazi Reichsfeldmarschall, to replace Lüderitz, establish the new government, and make treaties with Hottentots and Hereros alike. But Göring, an arrogant and high-handed administrator, only managed to antagonize the region's native peoples. He also insisted that black Africans be kept out of the colony's Schutztruppe, just then forming—a dreadful mistake not repeated by German administrations later in East Africa. Nonetheless, by 1888 through the efforts of Lüderitz, Göring, and others, Germany's first African colony had taken shape. The new protectorate covered a vast area from Portuguese Angola to the Orange River, spanning the interior across the deserts to the central plateau, the prime grazing land of the Hereros. At 835,100 square miles, it exceeded the size of the German Empire in Europe by half.

But German South West Africa was trouble from the beginning. "Despite being suited, climatically, to white settlement," the colony proved— says the redoubtable Mary Townsend, the doyenne of colonial German historiography—"the most difficult and burdensome to pacify and to organize. The presence of extremely strong and independent tribes kept the territories in a turmoil of native uprisings, while the nature of the country required tremendous sums of capital to develop. Its inaccessible coasts demanded harbor construction; the high inland plateau, so admirably suited to stock raising, necessitated irrigation; its mineral wealth needed expensive

machinery to make available; and the vast stretches of the country, uncon-
nected by natural waterways, made the construction of roads and railroads
on a large scale inevitable."

Thus, with the acquisition of German South West Africa, exactly the
sort of economic and administrative burdens the far-seeing Bismarck had
sought to avoid landed squarely in his large German lap.

By 1904, after less than twenty years of German colonial rule, the Hereros
of German South West Africa, now a subject people, felt themselves on the
verge of extinction. Hereroland had been plunged into a sort of Teutonic
nightmare. The ever-industrious Germans began to build cities, pushed
through a railroad from the coast to the new capital at Windhoek, and were
determined to create in Africa another Germany, though with a distinctly
medieval flavor: The indigenous peoples would happily labor in a kind of
permanent serfdom, so the Germans intended.

Millions of acres of grazing land had been alienated from the Herero
tribes through debt and sharp business practices and given over to a new
class of German immigrant farmers who regarded GSWA's tribal peoples
as little better than "baboons"—a derogatory term then commonly used to
refer to Herero and Hottentot indiscriminately. More and more Germans
arrived each year, among them a number of "ne'er-do-wells," Townsend
observed, "not a few of them criminally inclined younger sons of aristocracy, packed off to Africa to prevent them from disgracing the family name
at home."

At this point in its development, the colony had attracted about 4,000
white men and only 700 white women. Life was tough and dirty; what right-
thinking German woman would want to leave the comfy and pleasantly moist
Fatherland to marry a lout in a primitive land that got no rain? Thus, German
men without wives, driven mad by sexual cravings, turned to the dreadful
expediency of *Verkafferung*, which is to say the stealing of Herero women
from native kraals, or *Schmutzwirtschaft*, which came to mean sexual assault
on any native woman who came to hand. That just such an incident was responsible for setting off the cataclysmic rebellion of the Hereros makes perfect
historical sense: Herodotus tells us history itself began in this way—with

Greeks stealing women from the Trojans, which in turn began a tit-for-tat series of similar female thefts, culminating in Paris's ravishing of the beautiful Helen, which ended, as everyone knows, in ten years of war and ten years of wandering and two great poems describing that war and its aftermath.

In January 1903, a sex-starved German trader named Dietrich, his horse having died, was walking from his homestead to the nearby town of Omaruru to buy another. Halfway to his destination, a wagon driven by the high-ranking son of a prominent Herero chief passed Dietrich on the road. In the wagon with the chief's son were his young wife and child. The chief's son graciously offered the horseless Dietrich a ride—a common courtesy in Hereroland. That night, they camped; Dietrich got very drunk. After everyone had fallen asleep, Dietrich, crazed with booze and lust, attempted to force himself upon the wife. She resisted; he shot her; she died. Later, Dietrich was arrested and brought to trial for the woman's murder. The unrepentant trader claimed the shooting had been accidental: He woke in the middle of the night, he said, choking with fear and thinking himself under attack by Herero renegades; he had fired his pistol blindly into the darkness, unfortunately hitting the woman and killing her.

The German court in Windhoek decided to believe Dietrich's unlikely version of events and acquitted him of murder. He had also probably been suffering from "tropical frenzy," they added, attempting to explain Dietrich's "night terrors." Tropical frenzy was a new, pseudoscientific disease invented by German settlers to explain their violent mistreatment of the Hereros, and lately lent some credence by the German medical establishment in the colony. In this unfortunate incident and the naked outrage inspired by a murderer's escape from justice resided the spark that lit the fuse of the rebellion.

According to Major Theodor Leutwein, GSWA's new colonial governor, this murder "aroused extraordinary interest in Hereroland, especially since the murdered woman had been the wife of the son of a chief, and the daughter of another. Everywhere the question was asked: Have white people the right to shoot native women?" Leutwein was an honorable and fair-minded administrator, with much experience in Africa. Cut from the same cloth as von Lettow-Vorbeck, he judged each man based on his merits and not on the color of his skin. His fair-mindedness had earned him the respect and trust

of the Hereros and the loathing of many new German colonists who regarded him as a "race traitor." Over obstreperous objections, Leutwein insisted on a second trial for Dietrich before the colony's supreme court. This
time, the trader was found guilty of manslaughter and sentenced to jail.

But the underlying issues of which Dietrich's act of *Lustmord* was a
symptom remained: "The Hereros from early years were a freedom-loving
people," Leutwein later wrote, "courageous and proud beyond measure. On
the one hand, there was the progressive extension of German rule over
them, and on the other their own sufferings increasing from year to year."

Six months after the murder, the Germans sent a mounted troop of colonial police under a Leutnant Jobst to the Bondelzwart Hottentots, who
lived in the far south of the colony near the Orange River. There Jobst was to
register all guns in possession of the Bondelzwarts; in the event of resistance,
he was to disarm them completely. Among the Bondelzwarts—as in certain
regions of the United States today—an intrusive central government bent on
the forced registration of all firearms was bound to inspire a fierce resistance: Warned before Jobst arrived, Bondelzwart warriors lay in wait for the
German troopers; an ambush ensued in which Jobst and four Germans were
killed. The Bondelzwarts, fearing retaliation, fled to the nearby Karras Hills,
where they joined forces with gangs of landless Hottentot banditti already
hiding there; these latter used the region's inaccessible ravines and rocky
outcroppings as a base for their criminal operations.

Governor Leutwein, alarmed and fearing a general uprising that could
involve both Hereros and Hottentots united against their German overlords, overreacted. He denuded Hereroland of all but a few German troops
and personally led the GSWA Schutztruppe south to pacify the Bondelzwarts, hoping an example made of one rebellious tribe might deter others
from similar rebellions. The distances involved—vast, empty spaces, waterless and treeless and without roads of any kind—nearly swallowed Leutwein's expedition. Bondelzwart territory lay at the heart of Hottentot
territory, more than 500 miles from Windhoek. This was a very long way
on horseback over rough terrain.

Meanwhile, the Hereros had been waiting for such an opportunity. It
was almost as if they had coordinated the ambush of Jobst's police troop
with the Bondelzwarts and anticipated German overreaction. Later, rumors

circulated to this effect: In fact, the Herero chief of chiefs, Samuel Maharero, a wily giant of a man who favored operatic uniforms and tasseled bicorn hats, had met with his subordinates in secret conclave in April and May 1903, in a place called Okahandja in Hereroland. There they debated an all-out war against the Germans. The right blow struck at the exact right moment, Chief Maharero believed, might drive the hated white man into the sea. As with all African wars since the *Difaquane*, total annihilation of the enemy would be sought.

The Germans, though armed with modern weaponry (Mauser 88; rifles; six Maxim machine guns; four or five quick-firing Krupp mountain guns), could barely muster 2,000 men for the defense of the colony. Of these, only 776 were actually trained German troops; the rest consisted of colonial militias composed of farmers and fresh immigrants.

Against this inadequate army, Samuel Maharero brought a nation under arms (women and children often fought alongside the men) and 8,000 battle-hardened warriors. With strategic sophistication honed by generations of internecine warfare and a native's understanding of his own terrain, Maharero and his chieftains fixed upon a three-pronged campaign: First, they would attack the thinly held German military outposts; second, they would destroy the railway from Windhoek to Swakopmund on the coast, Germany's only lifeline to the outside world; third, a comprehensive attack would be made on German farms and cattle ranches. All structures would be burned to the ground; the Hereros would reclaim the land and livestock that had until recently belonged to them. To his credit, Chief Samuel Maharero, a Christian convert who spoke and wrote German well, forbade killing German women and children—an order only fitfully obeyed by rampaging tribesmen.

On the morning of January 12, 1904, the Hereros launched their campaign. They ripped out railroad beds, cut telegraph lines, burned everything in sight. The uprising took many Germans by surprise, even those missionaries who lived and worked closely with the Hereros in the bush. German farmers and traders, whose sharp business practices had done much to inspire the rebellion in the first place, were hunted down and killed, some pulled from their beds and slaughtered in front of their horrified wives and children. The sudden intensity of the Herero onslaught later recalled to Leutwein, a student of history, the Sicilian Vespers—an infamous medieval incident in which the aggrieved inhabitants of Sicily rose at a signal and murdered every single Frenchman they could lay their hands on, the French Angevin dynasty being the despotic masters of southern Italy at the time.

"In a way which we held to be impossible, the Hereros concealed their intention from us completely," Leutwein later admitted. "I had intimate contact with them for over ten years and came to believe I understood them, but would never have thought they might be capable of mounting such a coordinated, energetic effort."

Fortunately for the German colonists, their military experts, always anticipating such an uprising, had over the course of the previous decade constructed several dozen solidly built blockhouses in Hereroland. These self-sustaining minifortresses boasted massive brick walls, barracks, storehouses, various outbuildings, and a watchtower offering a commanding view of the surrounding terrain. All straddled a water source and had been stocked with enough food and ammunition to last a year. Now the handful of German soldiers who had not followed Leutwein south withdrew behind the walls. They were soon joined by those settlers from outlying farms who had managed to escape Herero raiding parties. All of these blockhouses, in places with strange-sounding names—Omaruru, Otjimbingwe, Gobabis, Outjo—now found themselves "loosely besieged." That is, the Herero, possessing no knowledge of siege warfare, contented themselves with harassing the scrubby countryside, burning German buildings, killing stragglers, and—according to rumor—castrating any male children who fell into their hands.

For nearly two weeks, the Hereros rampaged unopposed. The Germans, huddling in uncertainty and dread behind the walls of their forts, prayed for relief from Leutwein's army, from Germany, even from the British and Boers across the Orange River. At any moment, they feared, the Hereros might attack in overwhelming numbers, breach the walls, and finish them off. But the Hereros, like many tribal peoples, lived hemmed in by superstitions whose roots lay in the unremembered past. They did not like to fight in built-up areas, around buildings, and on streets, deeming any warfare made in such places unmanly, believing it would sap their fighting spirit. To the Hereros, a true warrior fought on open veldts or in the hills. Only cowards and the ungodly hid behind walls and killed their enemy at a distance with machine guns and artillery shells. In these ancient prejudices lay their undoing.

During their January offensive, the Hereros, properly organized, might have taken the German forts and achieved total victory. But they hesitated, shadow-dancing around the forts and the towns, and the moment was lost. At last, news of the uprising reached Leutwein in the far south and German vengeance—like the Eye of Sauron in Tolkien's *The Lord of the Rings*— slowly turned its pitiless gaze upon Hereroland.

Governor Leutwein, pinned down in a small war with the Bondelzwarts and not yet fully aware of the extent of the uprising in the north, sent only the 4th FK (field company) under Captain Otto Franke—later the unhappy commander of German forces against the British in 1914—to relieve the embattled German garrisons. After two days of marching, Franke learned from scouts the true gravity of the situation. He called his troop together, gave an impressive speech—"I must demand the utmost from every man, whether troops or officers," etc.—and managed to galvanize them to an impressive achievement: Forty-eight hours later, via forced marches, the 4th made Windhoek. They had marched more than 200 miles in 100 hours—a startling achievement over difficult, rocky terrain.

Captain Franke's arrival before Windhoek relieved pressure on the capital. Herero marauders dispersed before his advance, moved out into open country, regrouped, and prepared to meet the Germans on ground of their own choosing. Franke gave chase and finally came up against a large force out in the scrubland near Omaruru. Some of the opposing men he recognized; he had been friendly with them during the course of his peacetime duties. Seeking to avoid an all-out battle, both because he was outnumbered and because he wished to avoid further casualties, Franke tried a stratagem that might have come from the playbook of Hernán Cortés during the conquest of Mexico in 1519: He donned his spotless white dress uniform, mounted a white horse, and rode out alone to meet the Hereros. He thought the sight of himself so splendidly attired and mounted might overawe the enemy, whom he regarded as little more than childish savages; thus rendered pliable, they might then be willing to negotiate a surrender.

Of course, the Hereros were not childish savages. They were instead fighting men seeking to rid their homeland of an invader they deemed tyrannical. Franke on his white charger elicited only a determined fusillade. He retreated, barely escaping with his life. But the boldness of his gesture impressed the troops under his command. Even exhausted as they were from days of forced marches, they could not be held back.

The ensuing battle caused heavy casualties on both sides, but in the end the Hereros quit the field, leaving the road to Omaruru open and earning for Franke a commendation from the Kaiser—the coveted Pour le Mérite—and his future sobriquet: Hero of Omaruru. Franke later wore his new metal proudly around the colony, von Lettow tells us, and did his best to justify the reputation for heroism—all before falling afoul of morphine addiction and becoming the unsteady blunderer of 1914.

Franke's victory at Omaruru in February 1904 marked the end of the first phase of the Herero Uprising. The United Herero Army—for such it had become, disparate tribal groups uniting to fight a common enemy—melted into the landscape. The bulk of them, at Samuel Maharero's orders, congregated in the foothills of the Waterberg Mountains. Holed up in this isolated redoubt they remained just beyond the reach of German forces; they made their plans, tended to their wounded. Herero women and children and livestock slowly joined the warriors, until nearly the entire nation had assembled in the vicinity.

Governor Leutwein, as has been mentioned, respected the Hereros. It may even be said that he loved them, as a stern parent loves his rebellious children. That the causes of the war lay with the Germans did not escape his discernment. The Hereros had been despoiled of land and cattle and liberty; their free-ranging Paleolithic lifestyle, now endangered, faced a doubtful future. Soon they would all be confined to reservations and forced to serve their new German masters forever. Leutwein knew the wrath of the German Empire was about to fall on them and hoped to soften the blow. He sent desperate messages to Chief Samuel Maharero in hopes of negotiating an end to the war. In this, Leutwein acted on his own, heedless of the prevailing mood in Germany, which called for a bloody revenge.

"The Germans are filled with fearful hate," wrote a missionary about this time. "I must really call it a blood thirst against the Hereros. One hears nothing but talk of 'cleaning up,' 'executing,' 'shooting down to the last man,' 'no pardon,' etc."

German desire for retribution—for German lives lost, German settlers tortured and murdered, German farms razed, German infrastructure destroyed—only worsened over March and April 1904. But during these dreadful months, field companies sent out to capture or destroy the Hereros in the bush met with defeat after defeat. The Hereros themselves, emboldened by their unexpected success against one of the world's great modern armies, only grew bolder. They came to believe that "the Germans were too cowardly to fight in the open," and despite equipment shortages, the war seemed to be going their way.

The reasons for the Herero victories, though baffling to the panjandrums of the Great General Staff in Berlin, did not escape the analysis of open-minded fighting men like Leutwein and von Lettow, the latter now closely watching events in South West Africa from his desk in Berlin: The Hereros fought with the country rather than against it; they generally eschewed pitched battles and were extremely mobile, drawing heavily laden, plodding German soldiers on long, exhausting marches through waterless bush tangled with thorn scrub where German firepower could not be used with effectiveness. They knew the country intimately; it was in their blood, and their "tactical and strategic ideas," as Leutwein put it, "were adjusted to the realities of the land."

The Germans suffered more than defeat during the early months of 1904; they suffered humiliation, their brilliant modern army unable to defeat a rabble of "half-naked savages." Cries in the Reichstag, and from the Kaiser himself, for total eradication of the Hereros grew strident. When a leading member of the Social Democratic Party pointed out that the Hereros were as human as any German and also possessed immortal souls, he was howled down by the entire conservative side of the legislature.

At last, Leutwein, despised by many in Germany as a weakling "lacking ruthlessness," was sacked in favor of the ferocious General Lothar von Trotha—the same capable and relentless officer under whom Paul von Lettow-Vorbeck had served in China in 1900–01. Von Trotha, known for his harsh dealings with East African tribes during German colonial efforts in that part of the continent a decade earlier, believed only the most draconian measures would defeat the Hereros.

"I know the tribes of Africa," he wrote. "They are all alike. They only respond to force. It was and is my policy to use force with terrorism and even brutality. I shall annihilate the revolting tribe with streams of blood. . . . Only after a complete undoing will something else emerge."

The beginning of the "complete undoing" of the Hereros—later generations with the benefit of hindsight would call it "the first genocide of the twentieth century"—was some months away when, on May 20, 1904, the steamer *Eleanor Woermann* of the German East Africa Line, sensibly packed for war in the tropics, made ready to cast off from the quay at Hamburg. The band played "*Muss i'denn zum Städtle hinaus*," that most sentimental of German melodies, as loved ones waved from dockside and wept and held up new babies for one last look at dear Papa, and orders were given to cast off. Then, with the kind of grave stateliness only available to the large ships of the past, the *Eleanor Woermann* slipped her mooring lines and made her way down the lower Elbe toward the open sea.

Aboard that day, in addition to Lieutenant General von Trotha, 72 officers, 496 soldiers, a doctor, sundry colonial officials, and 420 horses, was Captain Paul von Lettow-Vorbeck, who would act as adjutant for the entire GSWA Schutztruppe. Standing in the bow, von Lettow felt the ship, its engines shuddering, begin to "breathe" as brackish waters gave way to salt. The German General Staff had learned from its experiences in China four years earlier—informed, no doubt, by von Lettow's sound advice. Instead of a few massive superships stuffed to the scuppers with supplies, ammunition, and guns for the entire army, the *Eleanor Woermann* was the first of many smaller vessels sent out from Hamburg during May and June 1904. Each ship carried two companies of the 4th Regiment and all of the supplies and horses required to put those companies in the field within twenty-four hours of arrival on foreign shores. No more of the endless detangling, the "seed-cake studded with cannon barrels" that had hampered the German Army in China.

With the exception of a small epidemic of seasickness in the Bay of Biscayne, the voyage out to Africa passed uneventfully. They put in at Las Palmas and Monrovia for refueling and three weeks after leaving Hamburg made the arid coast of German South West Africa at Swakopmund. Von Lettow says little about his first impressions of the place—the endless lines of breakers, the low dunes, the smell of blood in the air, the atmosphere of incipient disaster. Though he does remark on its stark difference from his previous colonial posting:

"The theater of war in South West Africa was the exact opposite of China in every respect," he later wrote. "Water holes were rare with long dry stretches between them. There was scarcely a sign of agriculture and great difficulties with food supply. A ridiculously sparse and scattered population existed at the cultural level of pure nomads, but their warriors were as cunning as poachers. And they had firearms; some were of the most modern models." Von Lettow fails to add, however, that many of the latter were taken off the bodies of dead German soldiers.

Swakopmund was not a harbor in any sense of the word, rather a mere indentation in an otherwise undifferentiated coast. The British enclave at Walvis Bay, a small corner of the British Empire surrounded by German territory and the only true harbor within 1,000 miles, was not available to German military vessels. Lighters and other small craft soon appeared in the roads off Swakopmund. Bosun chairs swung General von Trotha, von Lettow, and the other staff officers onto the lighter *Harbicht*, and within a couple of hours all had taken their seats in one of the spartan passenger cars of the narrow-gauge German railroad—its terminus at distant Windhoek, several days and hundreds of miles away. At Karibib, a day's journey up the line, von Lettow met Captain Franke, already proudly wearing his Pour le Mérite, and records a favorable impression of this ill-fated man.

Von Lettow's ultimate destination, Okahandja, about halfway to the capital, a few weeks before little more than a railroad depot, had just assumed the bustle and importance of a major military outpost. Von Trotha intended to stage his assault on the Hereros, who had now completed their foolish relocation to the slopes of the Waterberg, about 100 miles due north. Also, over the previous months, the deposed governor, Major Leutwein, despite his reputation as a do-nothing pacifist, had carefully herded the last

Herero war bands toward this rugged region—a running battle in which his forces had incurred heavy losses.

For reasons that will never be known, Chief Samuel Maharero now decided to dig in and await the German offensive, abandoning the traditional Herero guerrilla tactics so recently successful against superior German forces. Clearly, he intended to risk all in a grand defensive battle—a fateful contest that might lead to total victory, or encirclement and doom. Maharero had been called by some in Germany the "Herero Napoleon," and perhaps had come to believe this flattering assessment. In any case, he had not reckoned with the range of German artillery and the destructive power of the Maxim gun.

Von Lettow quickly settled into the duties of regimental staff officer at Okahandja, duties that kept him at his desk until the small hours—though his conscientious work habits were derided by more easygoing, card-playing comrades, including his bunk mate, the fractious logistics officer Natchtigall. As ultimate authority shifted from Major Leutwein to General von Trotha, new officers continued to roll into the regiment. Field command passed quickly from Oberstleutnant de Beaulieu, a German of French descent, to the very Prussian colonel von Deimling, for whom von Lettow developed the greatest respect. For his part, von Deimling immediately recognized von Lettow's tireless efforts on behalf of the regiment—here was an ambitious, talented officer who had somehow yet to make his mark!—and bumped him up to the post of chief of military personnel.

In this capacity, von Lettow assumed responsibility for the rehabilitation of those officers among his peers who had disgraced themselves in Germany in the peacetime army. These unfortunates were guilty of what he euphemistically calls "matters of honor," which is to say, drunkenness, dueling, womanizing, brawling, gambling, insubordination. The officers seeking rehabilitation came to von Lettow for any assignment in the line of battle dangerous enough to redeem their lost reputations and fallen careers. This was a task von Lettow relished. He liked nothing better than to see a fellow officer picked up, dusted off, and set back on his feet, preferably while gunfire exploded all around his head. In this, both the fundamental decency of his character and his devotion to military values emerges.

"In the assessment of matters of honor," von Lettow noted in his autobiography, "I believe the chief approved my judgment without exception."

No amount of routine regimental duties, however, could obscure the main fact: Okahandja was an armed camp at the edge of a war zone. Beyond the next scrubby hill, German soldiers and Herero warriors fought bloody, inconclusive guerrilla skirmishes amid thickets of impenetrable thornbushes sharp as barbed wire. And as battle approached, conditions in the camp worsened. Soon enough, "Okahandja was full of sick and wounded," von Lettow observed. "With dysentery and typhus claiming more and more victims."

Together these two diseases, the scourge of all premodern armies, were responsible for more deaths than any actual fighting. The longer the army stayed at Okahandja, the more soldiers fell ill and died. But General von Trotha, one of the most thorough German officers of his era, was just then in the process of setting an elaborate trap in which to catch the Herero hordes. Methodically, slowly, he drew his forces tightly around the Waterberg. He intended to surround the mountain completely—and at last, with men and munitions in place, advance upon the Herero positions from all sides at once.

The Hereros had by now drifted en masse to the extensive bush country in the foothills just south of the Waterberg's main slope. "Thus offering," von Lettow remembered, "something rarely encountered in guerrilla warfare, a chance to defeat them in a single operation. But it had to be done rapidly—a maneuver that was extremely difficult."

Ironically, had the Hereros merely withdrawn from the vicinity and fled another 100 miles north, it is doubtful whether the German Army, utterly dependent as it was on the railhead at Okahandja, would have been able to pursue them effectively. For many more months or perhaps years—at least until another railroad might be built to reach them—the Hereros might have lingered there at the edge of the desert, just beyond the reach of German vengeance. But Samuel Maharero, as taken with dreams of glory as his European counterparts, had decided to fight. His warriors waited in caves and huts behind the wall of low hills as the 2nd Field Regiment slowly arrived at Swakopmund from Germany, loaded its heavy artillery onto trains and massive Boer wagons drawn by teams of twenty-four oxen, and slowly advanced toward the front lines.

Von Lettow took advantage of this lull to explore the comparatively lush country around Okahandja, home to "enormous quantities of guinea fowl." As always, he recommended his favorite sport to all soldiers who must fight unconventional wars in primitive parts of the world. In "a typical guerrilla war," he counseled, soldiers "needed considerable expertise as hunters, and must be able to keep their bearings in an unknown wilderness by using the sun to find the way."

In the anxiety-filled weeks before the big battle, to stave off precombat jitters, von Lettow accompanied various patrols of the 2nd into the deep bush. In late July, the officer commanding one of these forays, a Major von Glasenapp, took him to Owikokavero, the site of a deadly Herero ambush in the early days of the uprising in which scores of German troopers and several officers had been killed. There von Lettow found a grisly, yet somehow beautiful, reminder of this recent struggle: On the ground, near the tangled roots of a thornbush, lay "an elegant desiccated hand." Though whether it gestured the German Army onward to victory or another humiliating defeat he could not yet tell.

The Battle of the Waterberg occurred along the length of a brutally hot day—August 11, 1904. The various sections of General von Trotha's small army, outnumbered by the Hereros six to one, moved out from their entrenched position around the periphery of the mountain in the gray hours before dawn.

All available personnel, including staff and logistical officers—among them von Lettow—attached themselves to a field company to fight with the army. Okahandja was left deserted, except for the sick and wounded in the hospital tent and a few medical orderlies. Von Trotha had carefully divided his force into six parts that, at a signal, would advance toward the main Herero camps from all quarters of the compass. He intended to deal the Hereros a smashing blow from which they would never recover.

"General von Trotha was blamed," von Lettow later wrote, "by some people for his ruthlessness, but I believe that an insurrection on such a scale must be immediately stamped out, by every means available. . . . Of course once authority has been completely reestablished, everything has to be done to redress grievances and to placate the indigenous peoples."

In his first assertion (the small matter of winning the war you are currently fighting), von Lettow was in accordance with both his commanding officers and sound military theory. In the second, on questions of humane treatment of conquered peoples, he was not. He was also at odds with prevailing German attitudes—with the notable exception of the former territorial governor, Major Leutwein. Leutwein saw the indigenous people of Hereroland as its greatest natural resource, a human treasure to be nurtured—elevated from barbarism to modernity by the example of German civilization. For this progressive attitude, he was reviled, deposed, and demoted.

Indeed, the average German, reading only of Herero atrocities in the newspapers at home, prayed for revenge—though understandably, the Herero practice of cutting off the hands and feet, ears, nose, and lips of captured German soldiers made for brutal tabloid reading. Also, the age-old Herero custom of mutilating the genitalia of corpses on the battlefield, usually perpetrated by women traveling in the van of Herero war parties (like similar acts committed by the War Women of the Apache in our own Southwest), only served to further enrage the average German. In the end, these primitive terror tactics were self-defeating: German soldiers who found their dead comrades thus disfigured were not likely to show clemency to the perpetrators.

General von Trotha knew, however, that the death blow he hoped to deliver to the Hereros could not be achieved by his own small army alone. He had already surrounded them in the Waterberg; now he would attack and let their own hard country finish them off. He had allowed only one avenue of escape, the way to the Omaheke Desert. He expected the Hereros, meeting stiff resistance elsewhere, to withdraw into this waterless desolation. There they would die, destroyed by the inhospitable landscape.

Four of von Trotha's six field companies advanced without difficulty.

"The largest, Section Deimling, was to attack the Hereros from the west along the base of Mount Waterberg," wrote von Lettow. "The third battalion, commanded by Lieutenant Colonel von Müller of the first regiment, was ordered to attack from the south. . . . Major Estorff, commanding the first battalion of the first regiment, was to lead the attack from the east. To the north two smaller sections were stationed to block the passes through the Waterberg . . . to prevent any escape in that direction. Finally, the second battalion of the first regiment, commanded by von der Heyde, was to attack from the southeast."

All this looked beautiful on paper, neatly laid out on military maps with colorful stickpins, and was expected to unfold precisely as planned. But von Lettow, riding on the flank of Müller's forces, tells a different story: The fighting quickly became confused and disorganized, obscured by clouds of impenetrable dust and slowed by terrific heat. Herero warriors behind every tree, rock, and shrub kept up a continual barrage of rifle fire that took a fearsome toll on the advancing Germans. Armed with deadly war clubs called *kirris* and captured Mausers, the Hereros were excellent shots; their sharpshooting skills—as von Lettow guessed—had been honed by generations of subsistence hunting. The commander of the 11th Field Company was soon killed by a single shot, as were several other officers.

"You could see nothing in the bush," von Lettow wrote in his journal, a state of controlled panic shading his words. This was, after all, his first major battle. At one point, pinned down behind a Boer wagon in a supposed "safe area," von Lettow returned fire until his ammunition gave out. The enemy had only to advance to take him but, perhaps reluctant to leave the protection of their thornbush redoubts, did not advance. He was thus saved by a whim of fortune. Years later, he learned that a native scout serving with von Trotha's army had deserted to the enemy; this deserter gave up the German positions and nearly turned the course of the battle in the Hereros' favor.

"A soldier from the 11th Company came by and said, 'The Captain's dead, all the officers and most of the men are dead, and the rest can't hold out much longer,'" von Lettow remembered. "It was 9:37 a.m. I had made a mental note to write down the time immediately after the hour during bush fights like this one. Impressions are so strong, they can erase each other."

Scrambling around in the choking clouds of dust, he came upon the guns of the 5th Battery abandoned, their crews killed. He ensconced himself behind a termite hill and laid out covering fire as staff officers from HQ stepped up to man the guns, adding the battery's ear-shattering roar to the general concussion of German artillery booming across the valley.

At last, night fell and the firing quieted. No one in von Lettow's vicinity knew whether the battle had been lost or won. He set out after dark to gather intelligence and count the German dead and wounded. "Finally, I found three men of the 11th Company who said all the others were dead," he noted. Had a modern European army been defeated by primitive tribesmen armed with a few stolen weapons and, literally, sticks and stones? If so, the Battle of the Waterberg might add up to one of the worst European defeats of the colonial era.

"Thank God it wasn't as bad as all that," von Lettow soon realized, making his way through the German lines. Then he "stepped on something soft—the stomach of First Lieutenant von Kriegsheim." Von Kriegsheim was not dead or disemboweled, only reclining with a bottle of good champagne—abandoned by his colonel, who had been wounded in the fighting—after a hard day's work. The Germans had won, von Kriegsheim said. The Hereros, squeezed by von Trotha's enveloping maneuver and pummeled by the heavy artillery bombardment, had fled toward the Omaheke as planned. They had fallen into von Trotha's trap, abandoning their women, children, cattle, and possessions. German artillery had easily pulverized the massed Herero bands—roughly 50,000 crammed into a rectangle five miles long and ten wide. They'd had no choice but to abandon their positions.

"Whatever lay within reach of our guns had been destroyed," noted another officer. "Everywhere we saw signs of a wild, panicky flight. In the lean-tos cowered old men and women and children who had been left behind. The wounded, sick, and dying awaited their fates crouched in corners. Everywhere there were numerous cattle . . . and cattle were sacred to the Hereros—as evidence of the hysterical flight. Wagons filled with goods, furs, household items . . . had been left behind. Numerous blankets, jewelry, whole cases of feathers strewn about. The whole national wealth of the Hereros lay on those roads."

Meanwhile, von Lettow settled down with the lieutenant to do justice to the bottle of the colonel's champagne: "I must confess," he wrote, "that I have seldom had a drink that tasted as good as that one."

Though close by their jolly little celebration, gruesome deeds were unfolding. The von der Heyde Division, decimated by the Hereros in early fighting, alongside other hard-pressed German companies, now engaged in an orgy of vengeful killing. Von Trotha himself had specifically ordered Herero women and children spared—in a tacit acknowledgment of Samuel Maharero's similar order regarding German women and children. But the German soldiers, incensed by the Herero War Women's mutilation of their dead, would not be restrained. "Now a fearful punishment rained down upon the Herero," wrote one colonial official. "They will never recover from it."

"We hesitated to kill women and children, but the Germans spared no one," a native scout and eyewitness later testified. "They killed thousands and thousands. I saw this slaughter for day after day."

News of the wholesale slaughter of surviving Hereros filtered back to Germany, where Reichschancellor von Bülow—Bismarck's successor—outraged at the possible stain on the German escutcheon and worried about the reaction of other European governments, demanded an accounting from the army chief of staff, von Schlieffen. The latter explained that Herero women had gleefully participated in the torture of German prisoners and the mutilation of German dead, and were thus themselves legitimate military targets. He said nothing about the killing of children. In any case, the German public, cheered by a long-awaited victory in GSWA, failed to greet reports of massacres with the expected outrage.

The fighting there, von Schlieffen further explained, had turned into a "race war," and in that kind of conflict, men lost control of their reason. Overwhelmed by the rage to kill, they were "not responsible for their actions." It was another version, grandly put, of Dietrich's "tropical frenzy" that had touched off the conflict in the first place.

The smashing German victory in the Waterberg Mountains, the last major battle of the Herero-German War, did not end the conflict. Samuel Maharero and the rest of the Herero leadership, well provisioned and with a few thousand men, escaped into the Omaheke Desert and—it was rumored—had crossed into the British Kalahari, thus placing themselves beyond German jurisdiction. Still, skirmishing continued. The Germans fortified the perimeter of the desert, setting up heavily armed camps at Epikuro, Ras Fontein, Klein Okahandja, Okatabawaj, and Otjinene—the very names redolent of remote and barren vistas. A few of the Herero bands, driven mad by thirst and heat, tried to break through the German cordon but were thrust back. Their desperate excavations in the deep desert in search of water, later found by German patrols, often reached a depth of forty feet, to no avail—even the substratum was dry.

Samuel Maharero had gambled with the fate of his people at the Battle of Waterberg and lost. But could he have won? Could he have pushed the Germans out of South West Africa for good?

"Was Samuel's plan reasonable?" asks Bridgman in his concise account of the conflict, *The Revolt of the Hereros*. Though the Hereros did not possess much in the way of modern weaponry, they possessed superior numbers and up-to-the-minute intelligence from highly mobile scouts. And they wisely relied on the trackless thornbush and the waterless distances they knew intimately, to act as their chief ally. In the end, Bridgman concludes, the Battle of the Waterberg, hence the revolt itself, was, as Wellington said of Waterloo, "a close run thing." The Germans nearly lost on that day of confusion, dust, and heat. Only the accuracy and ferocity of their artillery saved them from disaster.

In October 1904, General von Trotha issued his infamous *Schrecklichkeit*, a general order directed at those Hereros who had managed to remain alive after the Battle of the Waterberg.

"Hereros are no longer German subjects," it read in part. "They have murdered, stolen, they have cut off the noses, ears, and other body parts of wounded soldiers. . . . Any Herero found within the German borders will be shot. I shall no longer receive any women or children; I will drive them back to their people or I will shoot them." Etc.

In other words, von Trotha had decided to eradicate the Hereros completely. Out of a total 80,000 Hereros before the war, about 60,000 had survived the debacle at Waterberg and been driven into the desert. A year later, when they were finally allowed to surrender themselves to German justice, only 20,000 remained alive: At last, the Kaiser, under pressure from von Bülow, ordered von Trotha to rescind his *Schrecklichkeit*. This order, von Bülow successfully argued, was unchristian, difficult to implement, and made no economic sense: Why strip the indigenous labor force from the colony and at the same time give Germany a black eye, morally speaking?

Many Germans at home now agreed with von Bülow. A defeated enemy is always easy to pity, and mercy can aggrandize the ego—though most were sincere in their desire to see a more lenient policy applied to native peoples. Major Leutwein was one of these. The Hereros had considered him as a sort of father figure and made a place for him at their campfires. Now they were gone, their campfires extinguished. One must imagine the man rattling around some gloomy Swabian *Schloss*, missing the open heaven of the Hereros and regretting his role in their extinction. One must also imagine Paul von Lettow-Vorbeck as another who preferred a more lenient policy—though, as a junior officer, he had as yet no role to play in policy-making. He eschewed more than a passing comment on the bitter end of the Herero War and the actions taken by von Trotha that have since been construed as genocidal. Given the respect for Africans von Lettow would soon demonstrate in the 1914–18 war in German East Africa, his views on the matter might be inferred.

But von Lettow's—and Germany's—attentions were soon diverted to another theater of war, in rougher terrain and against a tougher enemy, farther south.

Chapter 8

A RED SOUP WITH BLACK DUMPLINGS

In the spring of 1904, while the Germans were otherwise occupied with rebellious Hereros, Hendrik Witbooi, grand chief of the Witbooi Hottentots, came under the influence of a mysterious self-appointed Christian prophet named Sturmann. Of mixed Dutch and African blood, Sturmann had lately smuggled himself into German South West Africa from the British Cape Colony across the Orange River. He believed Jehovah had appointed him to preach a gospel of extirpation—that is, he sought to rouse native tribes in a jihad that would drive all white men from the continent forever. To this end, he preached massacre and fire. Africa by God's grace for the Africans! Such was the slogan of this ragged mystagogue, cut from the same cloth as other violent prophets through the ages, God's instruments all: Think of Savonarola in Florence, submitting Renaissance masterpieces to the bonfires; of John Brown's massacres in Bloody Kansas; of the Mahdi at Khartoum, directing his dervishes to cut down the brave but unfortunate British general Charles George Gordon.

Since, as Scripture has it, *God has chosen those the world deems absurd to shame the wise* (1 Cor. 1:27), Sturmann's apocalyptic preaching found ready purchase in the wise old brain of Hendrik Witbooi. Hendrik was eighty-three. He had carefully shepherded the Witbooi Hottentots through war and diplomacy for the past fifty years and had long been a German ally. During the brutal struggle between the Kaiser and the Hereros he had directed his people to remain neutral—acutely aware of both the fighting capabilities of modern European armies and the technology gap between industrialized European civilizations and tribal African cultures. When

Governor Leutwein repeatedly reminded Hendrik of his relative helplessness vis-à-vis the Kaiser, hoping to impress upon him the necessity of staying out of any Herero-German disagreement, the Hottentot chief replied testily: "I know very well that the German emperor is more powerful than I, but you don't need to keep telling me about it."

Leutwein was mollified, but shouldn't have been. In other words, the certainty of defeat, Hendrik believed, was no reason not to start a fight in the first place. For God directed the outcome of battles and would protect His people with military miracles.

Since early youth, Hendrik Witbooi's brain had been readying itself for the implantation of the kind of apocalyptic visions peddled by Sturmann: Hendrik—educated by Rhenish missionaries and a devout Christian of the Calvinist variety—forbade the consumption of alcohol among his subjects, vigorously enforced the sanctity of the Sabbath, and meted out the death penalty for fornication and adultery. His own daughter, pregnant from an extramarital affair, gave birth in secret and killed the baby rather than face her father's biblical wrath. Inevitably, Hendrik discovered his daughter's transgression and sentenced her to death; only the timely intervention of the German authorities, in the person of District Officer Captain von Bergensdorff, saved the girl's life. All ended well, with parent and offspring reconciled—a happy outcome reminiscent of the bit in Genesis between God and Abraham over the fate of Isaac, with von Bergensdorff playing the part of God.

Then, in August 1904, as the Hereros perished on the dry escarpments of the Waterberg and upon the Omaheke's burning wastes, Sturmann's ravings convinced Hendrik the time had come to act. "God the Father," Sturmann announced, eyes blazing with righteousness, "will free the earth." It is probable that Hendrik—part biblical patriarch, part Machiavelli—had been waiting for the Germans to destroy his hereditary enemies, the Hereros, before going to war. In any case Hendrik wrote an open letter to the chiefs of the other Herero tribes, explaining his decision to attack the victorious Germans in phrases redolent of Holy Writ:

"I have now stopped walking submissively," he wrote. "I have put on the white feather of war. . . . The time is over when I will walk behind [the Germans] . . . and the Savior himself will now act, and he will free us through his grace and compassion."

On October 3, 1904, while the German Army dug in at the edge of the Oma-heke, District Commissioner von Bergensdorff rode into Hendrik's main camp nearly 1,000 miles away at Marienthal in Namaland—the home turf of the Hottentots—to reason with his old friend. Word of Hendrik's bellicose letter had reached him; he also had it from informants that the Witbooi Hottentots were about to revolt. How could this be true? Time and again, the Witboois had made common cause with German forces to put down local squabbles; a state of peace had existed between Chief Hendrik Witbooi and Kaiser Wilhelm for twenty-five years. But Bergensdorff was shot out of the saddle by a Hottentot named Solomon Sahl moments after he entered their camp and hit the hard-packed, dry earth of Namaland dead.

Whether Hendrik Witbooi had ordered the death of his friend von Bergensdorff—who had made fair dealing with the Hottentots a point of honor—or whether his death was a bloody whim of Solomon Sahl's is beside the point: It was the first act of the Hottentots' general uprising. Over the next few days, rampaging Hottentot war parties killed every German soldier and civilian they could get their hands on, in a few bloody afternoons throw-ing off the yoke of European civilization they had worn for a generation.

This time, German settlers in Namaland, in a high state of anxiety since the Herero rebellion and thus on their guard, had managed to reach the security of local German blockhouses before the main attack, and the massacre failed in its primary objective. The German Army of the North under von Trotha, though still hunting down Herero stragglers, responded immediately. Colonel von Deimling headed south with six companies and two batteries of artillery. As the new year rolled around, about 5,000 German troopers were on the ground in Namaland, along with about 3,000 horses; everyone expected a speedy resolution to the crisis.

But the local terrain was even more waterless, more remote, and more hostile to German endeavors than Hereroland had been. And Herero terri-tory, bisected by the Swakopmund-Windhoek Railway, had been far more accessible to arms and supplies from Germany. A railroad spur to Namaland, proposed by von Trotha, had been nixed by the Reichstag—too expensive and too hard to build. Only a single road, the Baiweg Trail, linked Namaland to Lüderitz Bay, the nearest "coastal indentation" where supplies could be brought ashore via lighters. The Baiweg Trail hardly merited the name; more of a general direction than a trail, it crossed the fearsome Namib Desert, its path continually obscured by shifting sand and marked only by the half-buried carcasses of the horses and oxen that had died along the way. Clearly, a German Army operating in a region as remote as Namaland would experience critical shortages of vital supplies. Everything, including water and down to the last bullet, would have to be trekked across the desert from the sea—a journey that took at least twenty-five days.

The Hottentots, though perhaps not as overtly warlike as their enemies the Hereros, were nonetheless cleverer and famously skilled in bushcraft. They proved, over three years of fighting, nearly impossible to catch and kill. Like the Hereros before them, they counted on the remote and forbidding nature of their homeland as a natural ally against the Germans. But they had an even greater ally they hadn't counted on and didn't understand: the *Rickettsia* bacteria, the infectious agent responsible for typhus. *Rickettsia* belongs to the obligate intracellular parasitic type of bacteria, which is to say it cannot live for long outside a host cell and makes the jump from animal to animal and from animal to human and from human to human and back again with relative ease, transferred via the excrement of the common body louse. Discovery of this louse-poop vector was still some years away, though medical authorities knew outbreaks could be controlled by frequent bathing and changes of clothes—preventative measures not available to men fighting in hot, waterless climates. Thus, typhus swept through the German Army in Namaland like a scythe.

On the march with von Deimling's forces, von Lettow tells us, "water was so scarce that . . . there was not enough for washing. We had neither doctor nor thermometer. . . . I didn't know I had typhus." Patients crammed together in oxcarts heading for hospitals in Windhoek, he says, "died unnoticed." Meanwhile, Schain, the surgeon general of the German Army in GSWA, faced with an overwhelming number of new cases and helpless to control the spread of the disease, went mad and had to be transported back to Germany—leaving in his place a handful of undertrained company physicians. For von Lettow's company there was only a veterinarian named Moll. Moll, quickly infected, quickly died.

Typhus is characterized by a painful blotchy rash, high fevers, weakness, vomiting, and a certain fuzziness of thinking. A powerful immune system and an iron will to live were von Lettow's only weapons in the fight. He survived the worst of the disease, he says, *while in the saddle*, and given his resistance to other infectious parasites later in East Africa, this is not beyond the realm of the probable. Von Lettow's batman, a tough, hulking German peasant named Droste, came down with typhus and, reduced to skin and bones, wept with helplessness—though dehydrated as he was, only dust fell from his eyes. Von Lettow barely made it to Windhoek alive. He recuperated there for a while, thought himself cured, then suffered a relapse and became so weak he could barely raise a hand or hold a pencil. At last they evacuated him to Swakopmund, which, after a few months, sea air and ocean bathing, effected the cure at last.

When von Lettow returned to Namaland in late 1905, he found a countryside afire with war. A cumbersome, bumbling German Army had suffered many small defeats and a few middling catastrophes at the hands of a much smaller force of highly mobile Hottentots.

"Although the Hottentots were not as physically robust as the Hereros," they needed far less for survival," von Lettow observed. "They were entirely armed with modern weapons and were excellent shots. We faced an opponent who was hard to come to grips with, and who would slip through our fingers and disappear, sometimes to regroup in our rear without us being aware of it. Their leaders were very able tacticians. Anyone who had to deal with old Hendrik Witbooi had to be extremely alert."

Also, in von Lettow's absence, Hendrik had been joined by a half-Hottentot/half-Herero desperado named Morenga, who commanded a large band of skilled cattle thieves. Morenga quickly proved himself just as difficult to defeat as Hendrik Witbooi—he was known for his intelligence and was notably humane to a defeated enemy. He spoke five languages, had worked the copper mines of the Cape Colony, and—it was said—had lived briefly in Europe. He refused to kill women and children and even forbade looting. Forced to live off the land, taking the livestock and produce of native herdsmen, he presented them "with a precisely itemized requisition that guaranteed the recipient a period of immunity" from further such depredations. He possessed, so the Germans reluctantly admitted, *Grossmut,*

Umsicht, and *Tatkraft* (magnanimity, prudence, and energy), traits that in the end made him the most dangerous enemy of all.

Shortly after Morenga joined the fight, von Lettow, who had yearned for an independent field command, got it at last: von Deimling put him in charge of the 8th Company of the 2nd Field Regiment—80 riders, 160 horses, 4 ox wagons, 140 oxen, and 4 mules with carts and drivers—all tasked with the capture or killing of Morenga. Von Lettow then quickly assembled a staff of his own. They were capable officers and underofficers experienced in guerrilla warfare, "men who never missed a Hottentot track, could find their way on the land, knew the natives and their fighting methods, and were immediately aware when there was any danger of ambush." Among these were a former trick rider from an American circus, a young Boer intimately familiar with the hills and canyons of Namaland, who, with his blond hair and blue eyes, looked like a Teutonic knight in the saddle; and von Lettow's old batman, Droste, who had made a full recovery from the typhus that had killed so many of his comrades and had now become "a capable guerrilla fighter."

The 8th penetrated Morenga's territory at Ukama Station, not far from the Orange River, in February 1906. The sight of the river's brown-orange flow, colored with the red mud of the region, gave von Lettow's men pause. Most of them, except for von Lettow himself, fresh from the beach at Swakopmund, hadn't seen a body of water larger than a puddle in more than two years. But despite the best efforts of the men of the 8th and others, the wily Morenga proved elusive. Still free, he had destroyed a dozen isolated German encampments, emerging seemingly out of nowhere and disappearing again into the bush. He had pulled off one of his greatest victories in this manner at Hartebeestmund the previous October, overrunning the entrenched German lines and killing forty-three officers and men in a matter of minutes.

"The whole German position in the southern part of the colony was shaken by a few score men," as Bridgman puts it, "who were outnumbered at least twenty to one."

―――――――

In the spring of 1906, von Lettow and his new command finally tracked Morenga to Ondermaitje, a flyspeck of a place, not far from the water hole at Duurdrift. It was evening. The sun dropped behind the sandveldt and a bright moon rose. Von Lettow did not abandon the pursuit, but rode on and on, the trail lit by bright moonlight. Around midnight, they saw the glow of campfires on the horizon in the direction of Duurdrift. They approached this ephemeral light stealthily, crawling to the top of a hill overlooking the watering hole, and were grimly elated by what they saw below: Down there Morenga and his men carelessly relaxed around two or three campfires over the remains of their evening meal. Von Lettow ordered his troops to surround the position under cover of darkness. At first light, when the Hottentots made better targets, they would attack.

Dawn broke at last. Von Lettow's men took aim with their new bolt-action Mausers; at his signal they would open fire. Then, to his horror, he saw that one of his platoons had worked itself into an exposed position within the perimeter of Morenga's camp during the night. Morenga's men, just now aware of the Germans in their midst, were already scrambling for their weapons.

"My plan was ruined at the last minute," von Lettow later lamented. "Now there could be no hesitation. I fired the first shot, which, at 400 meters, hit near a large man, making a dust devil on the cliff face. Firing became general, Morenga's brother made a great leap and fell, shot in the head."

But the Germans had lost the critical element of surprise. Soon, von Lettow's company found themselves pinned down by the extremely accurate fire of Morenga's Hottentots. We all deem ourselves immortal in our secret hearts; no soldier—indeed, no human being, no matter how experienced—could be truly prepared for what happened next:

"Suddenly, a large bang went off in front of my face," von Lettow continued. "Everyone around me shouted, 'Explosive shell!' in astonishment. I felt a heavy blow to my left eye, which seemed to slosh in my head like a red soup with black dumplings."

Critically wounded, von Lettow attempted to fight on but could not. The horses drifted toward the watering hole, where some of them were taken off by Morenga's men. Fighting continued all day. When it grew dark, the Hottentots simply slipped off into the bush. It rained that night. Lightning rent the sky; each bolt felt like a saber slash against von Lettow's damaged eye. The right eye had meanwhile become dangerously infected; von Lettow feared he was going blind. In pain, in a state of tightly controlled panic, unable to see anything but shadows and led by Droste, his loyal batman, he made the dangerous seventy-kilometer journey to the dressing station at Ukama.

There, to his great good fortune, the military doctors on duty had both done early training in ophthalmologic surgery in Berlin. After several dangerous procedures during which a quantity of pus and "lenticular matter" was cleaned from his left eye, and after periods of enforced darkness with both eyes bandaged, von Lettow managed to retain full use of the right one. The left, though not glass as rumor later had it, was essentially dead. With his good eye closed, he could only make out the faintest gradations of light and dark.

After three more months of recuperation in Windhoek, several more surgeries, and several more weeks spent in total blindness, Paul von Lettow-Vorbeck was judged fit for evacuation back to Germany. The Hottentot War, now over for him, ground on in his absence. More German soldiers died along with uncounted numbers of Hottentots. Hendrik Witbooi himself was killed during a raid on a German supply train; Morenga escaped across the Orange River into British territory and was heard from no more. At last, on December 21, 1906, the surviving Hottentot chiefs and Colonel von Estorff, representing the Imperial German Government, signed a treaty of peace. The Hottentots, through clever fighting and sheer obstinacy, had managed to secure far better terms of surrender than the unfortunate Hereros. They were allowed to remain on their lands and in many cases retained their arms—as long as they accepted German suzerainty. They had been beaten but not defeated.

But a modern German Army, equipped with the latest armaments, had nearly been driven out of Africa by one tribe of "half-naked savages" at the Waterberg; and after years of bloody, inconclusive fighting, they had been forced to make peace with another. Lothar von Trotha, the man regarded in some quarters as a Hero of the Fatherland and in others as a butcher and an architect of genocide, returned to Germany under a cloud. The Kaiser, as if to defend the rightness of the struggle in South West Africa against its liberal detractors in the Reichstag, awarded him the Pour le Mérite.

Even in von Lettow's state of temporary blindness, the Herero and Hottentot Wars presented a series of lessons he could not fail to see. Lessons that would seep into the very marrow of his bones: Military bungling on a grand scale was only possible with grand armies, replete with layers of hierarchy and mired in red tape and politics. Traditional military strategies did not work in Africa, where distance, disease, inhospitable terrain, and the difficulty of obtaining supplies were as much an enemy as the enemy. Smaller, tighter forces worked much better in such an environment. And most important, by using mobile hit-and-run tactics, by fighting with the terrain and the weather and not against it, a small army, even a very small army, could harass, incapacitate, and perhaps eventually defeat an army many times its size.

In the end, von Lettow realized he owed a great debt to South West Africa and its inhabitants, a debt he never failed to acknowledge:

"It was from these brilliant and fantastic Hottentots that Lettow-Vorbeck learned the bushcraft that was to prove of such value to him in his war against the British in East Africa," wrote the great English popular historian Leonard Mosley. "When [Hottentot guerrilla leader] Samuel Izaak was captured and brought in for questioning, it was von Lettow who conducted the interrogations. . . . His questions were about how to live off a country which offers no apparent sustenance, how to run in conditions when most men have barely the strength to walk, how to condition the body to go without food or water, and most important of all, how to become so much a part, so absorbed into an unfriendly wilderness that survival is possible as the snakes and land crabs and lizards survive."

Chapter 9

PEACETIME ENNUI

In those fervent, uneasy years 1907–13, the world changed. Motorcars began making their appearance on the cobbled boulevards of Copenhagen and Berlin. In Vienna, Sigmund Freud was hard at work creating new myths to explain the inchoate desires of men and women. In Paris, Pablo Picasso had just discovered cubism and Proust was hard at work on *À la recherche du temps perdu*. In America, everyone started going to the movies.

The Great German General Staff in Berlin appointed Paul von Lettow-Vorbeck corps adjutant of the garrison at Kassel, where he had spent his formative years as a cadet. They made him a major and gave him a few medals for his service and combat wounds in Africa, but other than that, they didn't exactly know what to do with him. He had become, somehow, a figure out of time. With his refined sense of honor, his problematic sympathy for native peoples, and his family connections to the now unfashionable Otto von Bismarck—a cousin—von Lettow could be neither overtly praised nor entirely dismissed.

He did not seem to belong to the new age of the flying machine and the motorcar; he disdained the new Daimler-Benz issued to his commanding officer at Kassel. Instead—now financially comfortable on his major's salary—von Lettow slowly acquired a small stable of fine horses, including an expensive, spirited Hungarian stallion that gave him "considerable trouble" but that he loved dearly. He also conceived a passion for the bicycle—just then acquiring pneumatic tires—both as a means of exercise and as an easy way to see the countryside. He would often bike twenty-five kilometers to a rented wood, shotgun and bird bag strapped to his back, leaving Kassel in the early morning and returning, bird bag full, shells spent, just in time for afternoon inspection. Fully recovered from the wounds and privations of the war in South West Africa, he felt, he said, "young and fit"—though he was now in his late thirties, still a bachelor, and subject to the melancholy of men without women in their lives.

He continued to wait for an assignment that would be commensurate with his talents and suit a developing taste for distant lands and primitive peoples. In other words, von Lettow wanted another colonial war. Even as late as 1913, no one really thought that the nations of Europe, each armed to the teeth, would actually endanger a century of progress and go to war with one another. So a local war in one desert or jungle colony or another, against one or another restless, belligerent tribe, seemed the only chance for escape from the dull routine of peacetime duties.

To this end, von Lettow applied to the Kolonialamt (Colonial Office) for a Schutztruppe command anywhere in the Overseas German Empire, preferably with the garrison in Tsingtao, in China, for which he left himself well-prepared by his experiences during the Boxer Rebellion in 1900. Much to his surprise—and chagrin—his application was rejected, his status noted as "unfit." True, he had lost the use of an eye in the war against the Hottentots, but his strategic judgment and his aim with a rifle had never been sharper. Years later, this snubbing still smarted: "I don't suffer from delusions of grandeur," he wrote. "But I still think that judgment was a bit harsh."

Thus, two or three years back from Africa, Paul von Lettow-Vorbeck's military career had again begun to stagnate. As Ulysses S. Grant had waited in Galena for the Civil War to lift him from the mire of everyday life, so von Lettow waited at Kassel—but with no similar conflict in sight. Meanwhile, he played the role of a successful, cultured officer living a happy life. He regularly attended the opera, went to museums both in Germany and abroad—Guernico's *Repentant Magdalene* at the Capodimonte in Naples he visited "again and again, moved by how she looked with pain at the crown of thorns in her hand, her expression at the same time alive with resignation and comfort."

While not Berlin or Paris, Kassel could boast "a vivid cultural life," and "balls with 200 guests that were the social event of the province." Also, "large numbers of senior military staff officers and civil servants and their families made for an active social scene." And yet this period of von Lettow's life seems tinged with a sense of personal failure. Though introduced to many young ladies in society, like Frédéric in Flaubert's *Education Sentimentale*, he suffered the atrophy of his heart. Meanwhile, stories spread regarding von Lettow's refusal to accept an arranged marriage with the daughter of a senior officer on the Great General Staff.

"There was a rumor current at the time," writes Mosley, "that his failure to contract a suitable union had mitigated against his promotion in the army. He had rebuffed an approach from one of his influential superiors, it was said, to make a match with his daughter, and this had never been forgiven." Though Mosley asserts, "Lettow-Vorbeck assures me this was untrue," the latter does admit to a serious rift with his father—the formidable general, the hero of 1870—caused by a matter he does not specify but that most likely had to do with a woman. Whether this woman was the superior's rejected daughter or another the elder von Lettow deemed unsuitable is a matter for speculation.

"In my late thirties," von Lettow admits, "I was introduced to many a fine young woman. . . . Economic considerations were no longer a barrier, but unfortunately, for other reasons, I was in so serious a disagreement with my father that I could not introduce a young woman into my family."

The full story, the family scenes and private dramas, the gray German afternoons when all seemed lost, the hopeless love letters burned in the grate—these things are ashes now and will never be retrieved from the rubbish heap of the past.

———————

Alienated from his father and his family home, chafing under the round of petty, time-consuming duties at Kassel, the ever-ambitious von Lettow had perhaps reached the nadir of his fortunes. The lot of a warrior in a peacetime army is never an enviable one. Other veterans of the struggle in GSWA—surely some of the worst fighting seen by any army in the early part of the twentieth century—no doubt also suffered from the same ennui. Stung by the Kolonialamt's blunt rejection, von Lettow also suffered from rejections of a more personal nature: Another woman whom he does not name, with whom he had been in love since his days as a fresh-faced young lieutenant, had suddenly married another.

"I had deliberately distanced myself from her, so as to give her complete freedom to act," von Lettow offers cryptically. "Now my dreams were shattered." Another woman, pursued on the rebound from this devastating love, also rejected him, contributing to the sense of loss and personal confusion. Around this time, von Lettow found himself at a banquet at his old regiment in Berlin. Chance sat him next to Count Dohna, a fatherly older gentleman with an aristocrat's easy view of life. Von Lettow, perhaps missing his own father's advice, poured out his soul to Count Dohna—his professional disappointments, his romantic debacles. He felt, he said, "broken inside"—a startling admission from a military man who had faced the withering fire of the Hottentots in a place reminiscent of the surface of Mercury. Dohna listened patiently, over cigars and digestifs—one imagines a strong schnapps, distilled from pears, particular to the regiment—and at last offered some words of comfort: He assured von Lettow that all would be well, that the German Army could not long afford to neglect military talent such as his. And also, one day—hoariest of clichés—he was sure to find the right woman.

But von Lettow did not believe Dohna's well-intentioned predictions. "I didn't see it that way at all," is how he put it, grimly. Everything looked bleak, and no one could convince him otherwise. Soon, however, the old man's prescience became manifest:

Much to von Lettow's surprise, he was appointed commander of the 2nd Sea Battalion—which is to say Marine Commandant—at Willemshaven, on the North Sea. This promotion von Lettow ascribed to the intervention of a man he barely knew—General Count Huelsen, chief of the Kaiser's military cabinet. Known for his fair and disinterested judgments—like Count Dohna—General Count Huelsen was removed from the petty intrigues and factionalism of the Great General Staff by his personal closeness to the ruling monarch. For reasons that remain obscure, Huelsen had taken a liking to the energetic, frustrated von Lettow and had paid close attention to his military career: When they met for the first time at a breakfast party given for the visiting Kaiser at the home of Kassel's commanding general, von Lettow stepped up smartly, Prussian-style, to introduce himself. Count Huelsen, smiling, returned his stiff military greeting with informal geniality:

"You do not need to introduce yourself to me," he said. Adding mysteriously, "I know you very well."

Von Lettow shook Count Huelsen's hand warmly, surprised but moved. The rest of the party passed in a kind of pleasant daze: His untiring efforts on behalf of the German Army, his strict attention to military detail, his perfectly balanced sense of honor had not gone unnoticed by those in a position to dispense preferments. Perhaps he would not be stuck at Kassel forever. Among the virtues of an aristocratic system of government is the freedom to make judgments unfettered by political motivations, judgments that rely on intuition and an aesthetic understanding of life. Count Huelsen's personal judgment regarding von Lettow's character and abilities, whispered into the Kaiser's good ear, had led to—of all places—the Imperial Navy!

In late 1909, von Lettow found himself by the shores of the North Sea wearing an unfamiliar uniform, attached to an alien branch of the service with a new command and entirely new duties to learn. He knew almost nothing about the navy. There were boats, sailors; together, they often went out to sea for long periods. The navy lacked, he soon discovered, the formality and addiction to rules and precedence so familiar to him from his service in the army. The Sea Battalion was a place for iconoclasts and independent thinkers. Because of this freewheeling attitude, the Kaiser himself could often be found in Willemshaven dining at the mess, where "in the company of officers, he took no offense at a sharp comment, especially when the year's events were picked apart at a stag party."

Paul von Lettow-Vorbeck spent four years commanding the Sea Battalion—an experience that rounded out his military education. Indeed, he became, almost by accident, one of the most well-rounded officers in the entire German Army: By 1910, he had experienced colonial warfare in both Asia and Africa; in the first case mastering logistical operations, in the second grappling with the brutal expediencies of combat in bush and desert. Now he found himself frequently aboard the heavy cruiser *Roon*, observing fleet maneuvers in the North Sea and along the Scandinavian coasts—the sky alive with the northern lights, a world away from the dense heat of subtropical Africa. On land, he trained his marines in two relatively new disciplines—night fighting and the all-important use of the infamous Maxim machine gun, whose full potential in battle had not yet been realized. Two Maxims, its adherents insisted, properly sited and sufficiently supplied with ammunition, could pin down an entire regiment in the field—an assertion later confirmed in the trenches of the Western Front.

"Drills were . . . carried out thoroughly," von Lettow wrote with characteristic understatement. "A discipline grew that was based on the inner confidence of subordinates and on self-reliance. This was totally different from what those who do not understand call 'mechanical obedience.'"

And yet, despite his success at Willemshaven, von Lettow was not a navy man at heart. He longed for the exotic vistas and perils of an overseas command and again let it be known he was available for a posting to the Schutztruppe—still, preferably, Tsingtao, but anywhere within the borders of the empire would do nicely. When other, less experienced officers were promoted in his stead, von Lettow reacted with astonishment and dismay: "A prominent officer in the military cabinet"—perhaps Count Huelsen—"also expressed his astonishment to me when staff officers were repeatedly picked for Tsingtao with less seniority than I had . . . against customary procedure."

If von Lettow had a few supporters in high places, he clearly also had his detractors. He names only one of these, the Grand Duke von Oldenburg, with whom he'd had a serious disagreement on a matter of honor that might have caused "a breakdown in relations with the nobility that could have been disastrous" for his career, he says. Von Lettow was clearly an officer who inspired strong reaction, praised by some for his refined sense of honor and joie de vivre, criticized by others as a humorless martinet. Grand Duke von Oldenburg viewed him as a person who "doesn't allow himself to like anything." And to a few subordinates, "life in his immediate neighborhood was a trifle oppressive." No doubt there is some truth in this last assessment: Von Lettow famously demanded total dedication from the men in his command and was not chary dealing out punishment duty when his expectations went unmet.

"Certainly [von Lettow] knew how to get the most out of those who served under him," says Byron Farwell, one of the foremost historians of nineteenth- and early-twentieth-century British military. "He insisted on the best from his officers and men, white and black, but he recognized men's frailties, knew well that not all men can endure hardships with equal stoicism or face bullets with equal courage. Strict but fair, he inspired an exceptional loyalty."

In other words, von Lettow's best traits emerged under pressure, in battle, and on the march over punishing terrain, rations down, water scarce. But all this could only be guessed at by the German military authorities of the jittery, glossy Belle Epoque years leading up to the Universal Conflict. True, von Lettow's abilities as a staff officer were generally agreed to be excellent. But his command capabilities in the field—muted by typhus and wounds in GSWA—could only be inferred. Von Lettow's detractors wanted him reserved for logistical roles; his supporters believed he would make a fine field commander. Then, in August 1913, a telegram arrived at staff headquarters, Willemshaven, that neatly solved the dilemma:

HIS MAJESTY INTENDS TO APPOINT YOU COMMANDER OF THE SCHUTZ-TRUPPE FOR GERMAN EAST AFRICA. Paul von Lettow-Vorbeck's supporters—via what behind-the-scenes maneuvering we shall never know—had won the day. The command in GEA brought with it an automatic promotion to *Oberstleutnant*—lieutenant colonel.

The news came as a shock to von Lettow himself. Here was yet another of his reversals of fortune. He had given up on a promotion to the Schutztruppe, was essentially unprepared for it, and set about scrambling to prepare himself in a frantic burst of energy: He sold his stable of much-beloved horses—including the feisty Hungarian stallion he loved, the sale of which brought tears to his eyes. He read all available books and government documents dealing with the situation in German East Africa, studied and mastered Swahili in a Berlitz-type crash course, had several Schutztruppe uniforms made for himself by one of Kassel's finest military tailors:

The basic Schutztruppe officer's tropical field uniform, at once severe and dandified and cut out of German yellow-brown khaki, was topped by the inevitable gray *Südwester Hut*—this one made out of gray felt, with one side rakishly pinned to the crown by a small imperial cockade. Two more uniforms were de rigueur for the well-dressed commander in the colonies: tropical white for ceremonial and special occasions, and the pale gray dress *Tuchuniform* for winter home service, all outfitted with Swedish cuffs and gold Lintzen braiding. In von Lettow's case, each uniform was piped in white, the color associated with German East Africa. Piping colors indicated the colony of service: white for GEA, blue for GSWA, red for German Cameroon, green for Togo and New Guinea, yellow for China.

But just as von Lettow had gotten all his affairs in order, horses sold, uniforms made, personal possessions neatly packed, he learned that his command might not be the German East African Schutztruppe after all, but the smaller and less important Schutztruppe in German Cameroon. It seemed the pro– and con–von Lettow factions were not quite done with each other yet, this flip-flop the latest manifestation of the struggle. Von Lettow protested that he had already made arrangements for GEA. He had learned the language, studied the topography; German Cameroon was a very different kind of place altogether! The military cabinet would not countenance his complaint. He would hold himself open for both positions, they replied tersely; the final decision would come soon.

But von Lettow didn't hear anything for months. He waited, fretting. Would he be sent to East Africa or the Cameroons, or would they reverse their decision entirely and keep him at Willemshaven or send him to the North Pole? Who could say? Wallowing in this uncomfortable limbo, emotionally vulnerable, he met in Willemshaven a woman for whom he felt an irresistible attraction. Now, poised on the cusp of a completely new career in another wild corner of the world with all its attendant dangers, he had fallen—ridiculously for a man his age—in love. He was forty-four years old! Though the attraction was mutual, they both knew nothing would come of it. The woman, Margarethe Wallrath, was held captive by an unhappy marriage that had already produced three children, all still quite young. Lucky at cards—von Lettow turned the old saw around in his head—unlucky in love.

Then, after "weeks of suspense," as he put it, in early December 1913, von Lettow's final orders came: He was to proceed immediately to Dar es Salaam, German East Africa. There he would report to his superior, the governor of the colony, Dr. Heinrich Schnee, and take command of the colony's Schutztruppe.

Von Lettow received a dispensation from General von Glasenapp of the General Staff to spend Christmas with his mother and father in Berlin. Now that Paul's career seemed to be moving forward, his father's attitude had softened and they had reconciled. In the last days of the month, von Lettow took his leave and made his way—via the Riviera—to Marseilles, where he would board the SMS *Admiral* of the Deutsche Ost-Afrika Line. Just to test his new-found good fortune, he stopped at the famous casino in Monte Carlo. His luck held. He made a killing at the tables, playing roulette and chemin de fer.

Chapter 10

GERMAN EAST AFRICA

The vast wilderness that became German East Africa—its mountains, among them Kilimanjaro, the highest on the continent; its deep valleys; endless thorn scrub *pori*; lakes; jungles; rivers; tributaries, so many they could hardly be named or counted—was handed over by a "half-mad" German scholar, adventurer, and sadist named Dr. Karl Peters to an ambivalent Otto von Bismarck on February 5, 1885, in Berlin, late in the afternoon.

Peters, "certainly an odd fish to find creating a new German empire in the wild places of Africa," was the unruly, unscrupulous, but brilliant son of a Lutheran clergyman from Neuhaus an der Elbe—in the year of his birth, 1856, still the capital of the independent Kingdom of Hanover. A small, provincial sort of place, its people were nevertheless known for their independence and industriousness, and a certain marked eccentricity of character. Like many of the offspring of clergy, having been raised so close to God, Karl Peters's tastes ran in the opposite direction. About most of his activities in East Africa in later years there hangs more than a whiff of sulfur. The natives he encountered came to call him *Mkono Wa Damu* in Swahili, the "Man with Blood on his Hands." Bismarck, with Bismarckian bluntness, merely called him "the Stupid Guy" and loathed him.

But during Peters's early years of scholarly endeavor, he seemed neither obviously murderous nor particularly dumb. He studied history and philosophy under the colonialist Treitschke in Berlin; in 1879 he was awarded the gold medal—German scholarship's highest honor—for a dissertation on the political life of medieval Venice. Peters then published a "brilliant" and well-received philosophical treatise, *Willenswelt und Weltwille*—the first of several dense tomes whose obscure subject matters included ancient gold mining practices and the archaeology of prehistorical Africa.

He was redheaded and diminutive and possessed a fiery temper. Photographs show him, appropriately mustachioed, kitted out for safari in khakis and puttees. The barrel of his hunting rifle, butt to the ground, reaches to his armpit; he looks like an eight-year-old with a fake mustache playing a dangerous game of dress-up with his father's gun. His education and publications seemed to destine him for a post teaching at the university level, but the narrow parameters of college classrooms and faculty teas could not contain his outsize ego or sense of mission—nor could, indeed, the inward-looking Germany of his early manhood. In 1880, he left the country and lived in London with a maternal uncle, a distinguished musicologist named Karl Engel who frequented the highest levels of English society. There Peters became infected with the virus of colonialism. As a German—the citizen of a nation without colonies—he felt himself inferior to the Englishmen he met. The English, with their far-flung empire, played their games of lawn tennis, so to speak, on the world stage; instead of a shuttlecock made of paste and feathers, Egypt and the Sudan and the Transvaal got bandied back and forth over the political net.

"I got tired of being accounted among the pariahs," Peters wrote of the sense of inferiority he felt in England, "and wished to belong to the master race." This phrase—to echo so ominously in the next century when Peters, long disgraced, rehabilitated by Nazi ideologues, would become one of Hitler's personal heroes—meant only one thing to him: To become the equal of Great Britain, Germany must acquire colonies in Africa.

Mad schemes blossomed in Peters's head in the first years of the 1880s. They grew feverishly in a mulch of unbridled ambition and ego—but how could one man, a scholar without a school, a teacher with no students, a more or less spindly intellectual who had never gone farther from Berlin than London, hope to influence the course of events 5,000 miles away, in Africa? Of course, history shows us that the most outrageous schemes are not beyond the realm of possibility when pursued with single-minded zeal by one man with an idea whose time has come.

Peters returned to Germany from England and there convinced two of his old university chums, Carl Juhlke, a handsome blond Teuton, and the "dashing aristocrat" Graf Joachim von Pfeil, to form a colonialist society (the GDK—Company for German Colonialism), one of the many private, procolonialist organizations springing up in Germany at the time. Peters had tapped into a deep national longing at the high-water mark—the desire, sprung perhaps from the long winter nights of the North Sea, for "a place in the sun" for the German people. This place to be located somewhere in Equatorial Africa.

Together, Peters, Juhlke, and Pfeil recruited other procolonialists for their society, mostly from their own class of solidly educated German professionals (doctors, lawyers, journalists, etc.), and in a few years had collected the funds necessary for a private expedition to the "Swahili Coast"—that is, the 650-mile-long stretch of Central East Africa bordering the Indian Ocean, nominally under the control of the sultan of the island of Zanzibar. This vast region, supposedly reaching 1,000 miles into the unexplored interior, the sultan claimed as his personal domain—though in reality, he was a puppet of the British and barely in control of his own affairs. Meanwhile, the Swahili Coast itself had been dominated for centuries by a handful of ruthless half-Swahili, half-Arab sheiks who lived in heavily guarded fortified compounds and prospered off the slave trade.

Peters, Juhlke, and Graf von Pfeil, with barely enough resources in hand for a safari of five weeks' duration, sailed for Zanzibar in 1884, disguised as plain German workmen. Their secret plan, after the imperialist fashion of the day, was to secure "treaties" with the various local tribal chiefs, placing the chiefs' territories and people under the protection of the Imperial German Government. Peters's treaties, purely private in nature and with no official sanction, would then be handed to Bismarck as a fait accompli—an instant empire for Germany in Africa. Meanwhile, Bismarck himself, who seemed to know everything happening in Germany—indeed, the world—at any given time, got wind of Peters's scheme. When the three adventurers arrived in Zanzibar, they found a cablegram waiting for them from the Reichschancellor stating that the German government in no way supported any treaties they might make. They could not act in the name of the Fatherland, nor unfurl the Imperial flag in any official capacity on African soil.

Karl Peters read this cablegram with dismay—and immediately discarded it. He and his companions had come to Equatorial Africa to found a German colonial empire, and this was what they would do! For the next five weeks, they tramped through jungle and swamp, accompanied by a couple of dozen native porters paid to carry their gear—and occasionally themselves—on crude litters made from canvas and wooden poles. They visited one native chief after another in quick succession, unfurled the forbidden black, white, and red Imperial flag, read an unintelligible proclamation, produced trade beads, American cotton cloth (called *merikani* by the natives), and the various glittery gewgaws that so impressed tribal chiefs of the era, and then—crucially—got each chief very drunk on rum and schnapps.

At this point, with the chief good and soused, they promised the protection of the Kaiser in distant Germany and the blessings of German civilization and brought out a document printed all over with dense gothic script, to which they persuaded the hapless, drunken potentate to affix his personal mark. In this way, they delivered both chief and tribe into German hands. Signature procured, Peters and company quickly packed everything up and tramped on to the next tribal chief, where the performance was repeated, again and again over the next three months. Using these gaudy medicine show tactics, Karl Peters acquired, on paper at least, a vast, secret empire in East Africa for Germany.

This putative new empire encompassed a landscape of such variety and lushness as to represent within its borders everything characteristic of the continent itself: Its great lakes (Victoria Nyanza, Tanganyika, Nyasa) were broader or longer than anything found in Europe, its rivers more numerous, its rift valleys deeper and—having seen the evolution of the human species in eons past—arguably more fecund. The highest African peak, Kilimanjaro, has already been mentioned, but the no less impressive ranges of the Uluguru, Pare, and Nguru suggested the Swiss Alps in summertime—their slopes temperate and well suited for cultivation. Meanwhile, on the plains that spread below, all sorts of game of the type that had been extinguished elsewhere for thousands of years roamed free: elephant, rhino, gazelle, giraffe. In the tangled river deltas the hippopotamus and the crocodile proliferated.

Peters's new German colony offered a glimpse of the world as it had been at the dawn: The native population, about 7,000,000 divided into more than 100 tribes—some warlike and cannibalistic, others peaceful and nearly vegetarian—lived in and around the animals, as much a part of the landscape and the natural world as the animals themselves. And like the animals, subject to the whims of nature and weather and the hunt—in this case the vicious parties of Arab-Swahili slave traders who maintained fortified trading posts on the coast and nominal allegiance to the sultan of Zanzibar. A few of these trading posts, grown into small, easily defended port towns—Tanga, Banga-moyo, Dar es Salaam, Kilwa—had been fought over by Portuguese and Arabs in centuries past, often changing hands many times.

Endless monsoons lashed the country twice a year. The southeast mon-soons began in March or April and lasted three months. Parts of the inte-rior were swept with inundating rains later in the winter months; other parts—the *pori* or *bundu*—in the northwestern quadrant just beyond Kili-manjaro received little precipitation. Covered with dry thorny scrub, the *pori* boasted few watering holes and was susceptible to abrupt changes of weather and plagued by clouds of thick red, choking dust and intense heat.

Despite this natural profusion, the territory that would become German East Africa was, to the materialistic Peters, "perhaps not a colony of the first class. It is not a British India, nor may it be compared with the rich islands of the Malay Archipelago, or the West Indies. But it offers splendid open-ings in several directions, and if properly managed it may be developed into a wide and very important field for German enterprise, and take its great share in the commerce and prosperity of the world."

None of Peters's caveats regarding the East African colony were apparent when he returned to Germany and secured his fateful interview with Bis-marck in February of 1885. His arduous journey through the thickets and swamps of the Swahili Coast had indeed nearly killed him and his friend Juhlke. Both in the end had become so delirious with fever that they had to be carried by the last few porters who had not deserted. At last, they made the coast at Bangamoyo, where an order of German Catholic monks had recently established a mission church, complete with an oversize crucifix and stained glass windows carefully shipped from Bavaria. Peters crawled out of his makeshift palanquin and stumbled into the church. After the rigors and privation of his foot safari, the unexpected sight of sun stream-ing through the stained glass and the sound of a pipe organ playing Cath-olic hymns stunned him into near hysterics:

"I cannot describe the impression it made on me," an emotional Peters told Bismarck. "I am not ashamed to say that I broke down in uncontrollable sobbing."

Bismarck, though moved by Peters's tale, still insisted that Germany had no need for a colony in East Africa that—he correctly predicted—would someday require German garrisons to subdue and prove an immense drain on the national treasury. "As for my part," he famously maintained, "I am not a colonial animal."

But the unashamedly manipulative Peters would not be discouraged by Bismarck's opposition: "It was an astonishing sensation," Peters later said, "to feel those great penetrating eyes of the Iron Chancellor turned on me. His gaze seemed to plumb the depths of my soul and read my innermost thoughts."

This critical scrutiny, however, did not deter Peters from his next gambit: Since the German Reich wasn't interested in establishing a protectorate in East Africa based on his hard-won treaties, he said, then surely Leopold II, king of the Belgians, would not disdain the offer. After all, the aggressively forward-looking King Leopold had already acquired territory in West Africa and the Congo many times the size of his small nation and would welcome the chance for a continent-spanning Belgian colony, stretching from the mangrove-clogged mouth of the Congo River to the green-blue waters of the Indian Ocean.

The great Bismarck fumed. How dare this upstart blackmail the German Reich! "I am opposed to colonies," he reiterated. "To the kind of colonies where officials must be placed and garrisons established!" But Bismarck, the deal-maker, the master of realpolitik, had been outdealt by an upstart *herr doktor* from the middle classes whose head brimmed with impossible schemes. A man who—Bismarck was forced to admit—rode the tide of German public opinion in a way he himself did not.

A few days later, on February 17, 1885, Bismarck signed a charter in the name of the Kaiser that founded a company for the commercial development of East Africa—now yoked willy-nilly to the rising German star. Backed by a squadron of German warships that appeared a month later in the Zanzibar Lagoon opposite the sultan's palace, the charter elucidated the new order of things. Henceforth, East Africa was part of the German Reich.

———————

But the course of empire never does run smoothly.

One of Germany's more laudable intentions in the region was the suppression of the Arab-Swahili-run slave trade—established there since time
immemorial and decried by the English explorer/saint Dr. Livingston as he
drew his last breath by the banks of the Molilamo in 1873: "All I can add in
my solitude," reads the last pitiful entry in the bloodstained diary found
among Livingston's possessions after his death, "is may heaven's rich blessing come down on every one . . . who will help to heal this open sore [of
slavery]." Unfortunately getting rid of the peculiar institution in East Africa
would prove extremely difficult: Slave raiding and selling was the chief industry of the Swahili Coast; more, it was a way of life for both Africans and
Arabs.

The Arab-Swahili slave traders naturally objected to the new foreigners
whose design it was to abolish their main commercial enterprise. Resistance to the Germans occurred not long after they established their first
permanent trading post at Dar es Salaam and began carving up the surrounding bush for plantations of sisal and cotton. In September 1888, an
Arab firebrand named Abushiri raised an army of 20,000 men—a volatile
mixture of Arab clansmen, Swahili Muslim slave raiders, and armed
slaves—all united against the prospect of German rule. This first revolt in
a German colony established a pattern that would become familiar over the
next twenty-odd years: Germans, seeking to impose dominion over native
Africans, were hunted down and killed, their plantations burned. Survivors
of the initial attack retreated to their strong places—in this case the towns
of Bangamoyo and Dar es Salaam—which had been fortified with trenches
and barbed wire, to wait out a long siege, eventually relieved by an infusion
of fresh troops from Germany.

When news of Abushiri's revolt reached Bismarck, the Iron Chancellor
contemplated abandoning the new enterprise in East Africa—still not an
official colony—to its fate. He hadn't wanted a German presence there in
the first place; that damned upstart Peters had twisted his arm. This revolt
was as good an excuse as any to rescind the charter. But the German public
would not contemplate such an outcome. Now German prestige was at

stake; Germans had been savagely killed by fuzzy-headed natives, and the national honor demanded swift vengeance.

In January 1889, Bismarck secured a grant of 2,000,000 marks from the Reichstag for a punitive expedition against Abushiri and his Arab-Swahili minions and appointed Hermann von Wissmann, a talented German colonial soldier, to lead the expedition. Bismarck sent von Wissmann off to fight on the equator with a single instruction: *"Siegen Sie!"* ("Go and conquer!")— and left the details of how he would do it entirely up to von Wissmann himself. The latter gathered a small staff of talented young officers in Germany. The army they would command was recruited on African soil and at first comprised mostly Sudanese soldiers demobbed from the Anglo-Egyptian Army and rounded out with a number of battle-hardened Zulus who had recently fought the British in South Africa's Zulu Wars.

From the beginning, von Wissmann, known for fairness to both black and white soldiers, inspired a fierce devotion. His command—called the Wissmanntruppe—became the basic model for the Schutztruppe of later days and established the tradition of a native rank and file led by a German officer, perfected by von Lettow in 1914–18. Though a fatherly presence to his men—the very figure of the commander—von Wissmann could be brutal to the enemy. He quickly retook the port towns of Tanga and Pagani, relieved the sieges of Bangamoyo and Dar es Salaam, and inflicted thousands of casualties on Abushiri's undisciplined army. The achievement of total victory occupied von Wissmann's considerable energies for a little over six months. Abushiri himself was captured and executed in December 1889.

Unlike many other German colonials, von Wissmann did not relish killing. Peters, by contrast, confessed to a kind of pleasurable "intoxication" experienced when killing Africans. Once order had been reestablished in the colony, von Wissmann issued a general amnesty to any native who had served under Abushiri—he had come to win, he said, not to punish. This gesture might have initiated an era of peaceful development in German East Africa. Instead it presaged more than a decade of colonial conflicts—small, bloody wars in which massacres of German colonists by members of one disgruntled tribe or another in response to real or perceived German brutalities led to increasingly brutal German reprisals.

At least, with Abushiri's defeat, the Germans could point to the extinguishment of the Arab-Swahili slave trade as a genuine achievement. Sadly in its place a kind of native serfdom emerged, with the Germans playing the role of feudal overlords—a role they had already assumed in German South West Africa. Thus began the era of East African *"kiboko rule"*—the *kiboko* being a dreadful whip made of tough hippo hide that, wielded properly, could cut the flesh of a man's back to the spine with a single stroke. "It was not as much an instrument of punishment or discipline, but of terrorism," wrote Leonard Mosley, "used everywhere to turn the natives into cringing animals, ready to do everything their masters demanded. . . . In some areas in the south, once a month was designated kiboko day . . . when men were chosen at random to be whipped simply as an example to others."

The Germans, a new and supposedly civilized presence on the African continent, quickly became as cruel as the Arab slavers they had superseded. Germans had not emigrated in sufficient numbers from the Fatherland to manage the new, impressively large plantations of sisal, cotton, coffee, and other cash crops von Wissmann's victory had enabled them to develop. Many were forced to rely on Arab or Swahili overseers called *akidas* to handle their farms. These "Arab or Muslim educated natives ruled like profligate monarchs, took bribes, bullied, oppressed, wenched, secure in the knowledge that the German authorities . . . would back them because they had no other choice."

During this period, as a reward for Peters's role in creating the colony, the Kolonialamt installed him as Reichskommissar of the Kilimanjaro region with his HQ at Neu Moshi. Peters lived there, within view of the snowy peak of the great mountain, like a despot out of Herodotus, like Cyrus or Xerxes the Great. He maintained a private army and an impressive harem of native girls confiscated from local villages. He tortured and burned at the first signs of resistance; he hanged men on a whim and seemed to enjoy the act of murder. When he discovered his favorite concubine, a young woman named Jagoda, in bed with Mabruk, his Swahili manservant, he tried them for treason and hanged them both. Not satisfied with this quasi-legal act of vengeance, he also burned their home villages to the ground. This incident provoked a rebellion led by the Chaga Tribe—Jagoda's people—which was brutally suppressed at great cost to the colonial government.

Details of Peters's corruption and sadistic behavior at last reached the
Reichstag in the early 1890s. He was recalled and forced to work a desk job
at the Colonial Office while his record in Africa underwent several investi-
gations. His revealed penchant for flogging and hanging Africans, the ex-
altation he experienced while watching them die reeked of a murderous
pathology and proved too much, even for a nation that was supposed to
thrive on "blood and iron." The German press took to calling him
Hängepeter (Hangin' Peters) and he was denounced by liberal legislators on
the floor of the Reichstag. Chief among his detractors was Baron von Eltz
of the Catholic Center Party and August Bebel of the Socialists:

"What have you achieved by perpetual fighting, by acts of violence and
repression?" Baron von Eltz thundered. "You have cut the knot with the
sword and have transformed this most beautiful country into a battlefield!"

In 1897, the Reichstag dismissed Peters from the colonial service without pension. He retired, disgraced, to private life, never understanding the
enormity of his crimes or expressing remorse for the deaths—the number
must have been in the thousands—of Africans in his care. Unfortunately,
Germans with the conscience of Baron von Eltz and August Bebel—and
even von Wissmann—were rare, both in the colonial service and in the
class of emigrants now coming to East Africa.

A growing catalogue of cruelties—beginning with rampant overuse of
the *kiboko*—perpetrated by German planters and their *akidas*, a punitive
"hut tax," and the loss of arable land for sustaining essential native crops
like millet led directly to another series of violent uprisings in the period
1890–1905. The last and bloodiest of them all was the bizarre Maji-Maji
Rebellion of 1905–07, which neatly coincided with the Herero-Hottentot
Wars on the other side of the continent. That these altogether separate rebellions may have been coordinated, in an unusual, perhaps unique example of intertribal cooperation during the colonial period, is not beyond
conjecture: "Moreover . . . the Herero in rebellion in German South-west
Africa sent word to the east coast natives to follow their example, an instance of the growing solidarity of the black races of Africa." So postulates
the writers of the Eleventh Edition of the *Britannica*, though this assertion
is not corroborated by any other contemporary sources.

———————

While the Maji-Maji Rebellion had its roots in the moment Karl Peters first set foot in Africa, it began in earnest in mid-July 1905, when a Matumbi tribal spirit medium named Kinjikitile Ngwale became possessed by a snake spirit that called itself Hongo. Together Ngwale and Hongo became a third entity, Bokero, and in this guise began calling—once again—for the massacre of all Germans in Africa.

Ngwale/Hongo/Bokero were not entirely without resources in their struggle against the Germans and their Mausers and Maxim guns. Working together, they developed a "war medicine" called *maji-maji*, which would magically turn German bullets into water—*maji* being the Swahili word for water. *Maji-maji* war medicine was composed of water, castor oil, and millet seeds, decanted into small bottles, and worn around the neck. This potent elixir, first presented to warriors of the Matumbi Tribe, infused them with sufficient gumption to attack the Germans armed only with spears, poisonous arrows, and the occasional stolen rifle, which they didn't know how to shoot properly. These "soldiers of Hongo" came to include warriors from several different tribes, including the Muslim Ngoni people. All gleefully set about the task of killing Germans, first falling upon a party of German missionaries, including the Roman Catholic bishop of Dar es Salaam, who was speared to death on his way to Mass one Sunday.

As they had done in GSWA, the Germans retreated to their fortified blockhouses, here called *bomas*. The Maji-Maji rebels overwhelmed and destroyed the German garrison at Hakara on August 16, as a prelude to an attack on the major German outpost at Mahenge. Here the commandant, Lieutenant von Hassel, backed by sixty *askaris* and a few hundred loyal tribesmen and armed with two Maxim guns, fought off an attack of more than 3,000 spirit warriors protected—somewhat inadequately—by their *maji-maji* bottles from the Maxims' deadly spray of 600 rounds per minute. Most of the spirit warriors were killed at a distance of 1,000 yards; a few managed to reach the shadow of the battlements before falling. The rest, upon witnessing the fate of their comrades, disappeared into the bush, their faith in the *maji-maji* shaken forever. But soon after this debacle, the Ngoni Tribe brought 5,000 more warriors to join the struggle against the Germans. This Ngoni army was surprised in its encampment near Mahenge by a small contingent of German troops who had now gone on the offensive. The Ngoni, caught in the cross fire of the Maxims, broke and ran, discarding their magical bottles of *maji-maji*. Pitiful cries of "The *maji* is a lie!" echoed in the bush as bullets bit at their heels.

The governor of German East Africa, the competent, aggressive Count Gustav von Goetzen (later von Lettow's desk mate at general staff HQ, Berlin), would not let the matter rest there. The Maji-Maji rebels were not completely defeated. They had merely melted into the landscape and continued to raid and burn German farms, paying particular attention to German-planted cotton fields, which had displaced their native millet. Thus, the Maji-Maji Rebellion metastasized into a vicious guerrilla war that consumed the southern half of the colony. If not ended quickly, von Goetzen feared, it might undermine the authority of every German colonial administrator in Africa. He called for reinforcements from the Fatherland. One thousand regular troops arrived, supplemented by a contingent of saronged native warriors from the new German colony of New Guinea.

With this heterogeneous army, von Goetzen embarked upon his own *Totaler Krieg*, destroying villages and burning native crops all over the south. As a result of his scorched-earth strategy and the anticipated starving time that followed, more than 120,000 men, women, and children died in the southern half of the colony in 1906–07. Famine and fire at last quelled the Maji-Maji Rebellion. By its end, so many dead and rotting corpses lay scattered about the landscape unburied that local lions, particularly in the Songea Region, developed a taste for human flesh that, it is said, has not left them to this day.

As the stench of destruction and rotting flesh drifted in clouds over the German South West and East African colonies, a cool reforming wind blew it northward, until it settled like a fog in the chartered streets and electrified avenues of the German capital. By August 1906, the average German citizen, now well-informed by a robust, inquiring press, was horrified to learn of the bloody excesses committed by their soldiery in Africa in the name of peace. A kind of national revulsion spread rapidly, inspiring the forces of reform with a new zeal: at last the Catholic Center and Social Democratic parties gained the upper hand in the Reichstag.

Savagery in the suppression of savagery led only to more of the same and served to perpetuate the struggle, the Catholic/Socialist coalition argued. More, it was simply bad for commerce and thus offended plain old German common sense. General von Goetzen's scorched-earth policy in East Africa, von Trotha's *Schrecklichkeit* order in South West Africa, and other similar chastisements amounted to the same thing: a counterproductive and wholesale extermination of the native peoples of Africa. The peace that was now descending on the colonies, wrought by German arms, was the rancid peace of the ossuary; indeed, vast stretches of GEA had now been rendered into fields of bones.

"We solved the native problem," wrote one German commentator, "by smashing tribal life and creating a scarcity of labor."

The German elections of fall 1906 swept the conservative parties out of power. This was the only election of the colonial era in any European country in which colonial issues played the deciding role in the outcome. Under the newly elected progressive regime, German colonial policy swiftly changed its basic character from cruel and exploitative to something resembling caretaking and compassionate. Amazingly, the Germans became, almost overnight, the most progressive and forward-looking European colonial regime on the African continent. Now began a brief golden age of German rule in East Africa. A new Colonial Office was created with a sympathetic technocrat, Dr. Bernhard Dernburg, at its helm. Dernburg was a large, genial man, fond of cigars and good food; his father was a liberal German-Jewish publishing magnate and his mother was the daughter of a Lutheran minister. Perhaps because of his "mixed" background he felt a particular sensitivity to the sufferings of the Africans in his care. He was also a hard-nosed businessman and knew that a population ruled by the whip would not work as efficiently as a society of free men who might profit by their own labor. The goal of any colony, in his view, was to generate revenue for the colonial power, but only if that revenue did not destroy the colony from whence it was derived and a goodly portion returned to its source in the form of improvements to infrastructure and education. As Bismarck had predicted, Germany's colonies hadn't generated anything other than corpses and debt. Dr. Dernburg made it his goal to change all that. To everyone's surprise, he largely succeeded:

He "accomplished in five years what previous German administrations had failed to do in two decades," says African historian Charles Miller. "During his incumbency, incompetents and sadists were summarily removed from office. Not a few had to stand trial for acts of cruelty or malfeasance."

Eventually, Dernburg was driven from office by his political enemies, but his handpicked successors at the helm of the Colonial Office, often personal acquaintances or friends, continued his forward-looking policies. Albrecht von Rechenberg, the next governor of GEA, outraged the colony's German planters when he declared that "the most important factor in our colonies . . . is the African native." He authored regulations curtailing use of the dreadful *kiboko*, except for egregious offenses and only with a doctor present. He outlawed forced labor—slavery by another name—on German plantations, wrote new land laws preventing German colonists from appropriating native farms. Meanwhile, the Africans themselves, supported in their efforts to grow cash crops with hybrid seeds and modern farming technologies, were given access to new markets for their produce.

Amazingly, the colony prospered. It became, in a remarkably short period, the prime example of what an enlightened colonial policy could produce—which is to say, more nearly self-sufficient than any other colony in Africa. Some began to call German East the "gem of the Swahili Coast." Dr. Wilhelm Solf, Rechenberg's successor, flatly stated that "the natives have a right to demand that they be regarded by the more highly developed races as an end and not a means." Under his regime, railroads intended to open the hitherto remote interior to commerce were built using paid African laborers. The Northern Railroad, completed in 1911, linked the port city of Tanga to Neu Moshi in the shadow of Kilimanjaro. The Central Railroad, an even more ambitious undertaking, would connect Dar es Salaam with the distant shores of Lake Tanganyika via 700 miles of track laid through an impossible terrain of jungle and *pori*. It neared completion in the fall of 1913. This achievement and other advances would be celebrated at a grand international Colonial Exhibition in Dar es Salaam scheduled for the following year.

But perhaps the most overtly progressive of the German colonial administrators was the new governor, Dr. Heinrich Schnee. Appointed to the office in 1912, Schnee—who somewhat resembled the comedian Charlie Chaplin—was slim, jittery, punctilious, socially awkward—and dedicated to the cause of African welfare that would be, he said, the "dominant feature of my administration."

But, weirdly, his greatest fear went hand in hand with this dedication and became a kind of obsession: He sought to avoid, at all costs, a reprise of the bloody rebellions, massacres, and native uprisings of the early years of the colony. To this end, he studied the archives of the Maji-Maji Rebellion feverishly, familiarizing himself with its daily atrocities, and grew ever more certain that such an uprising would occur again. Thus, he partially defeated his most noble aims and lived with a constant paranoid delusion that he might be murdered in his bed at any moment by blood-crazed natives. Personally, he never liked or trusted Africans; but as so many academics and theorists before and since, he liked the *idea* of Africans. To put it simply, happy Africans made for a happy and prosperous colony, and this, ultimately, Schnee believed, would both keep him safe at night and benefit the German Fatherland.

Schnee, a successful son of the educated professional class, was the perfect exemplar of the "new man" in Germany. He had followed in his father's footsteps—the latter had been a district attorney in Neuhaldensleben, Saxony—and studied law at Heidelberg. But against his father's wishes, Schnee cast his eye toward a career in the Kolonialamt. There, by dint of hard work and the crucial ability to ingratiate himself with his superiors, he worked his way up through the power structure. He achieved deputy governorships in New Guinea 1900–04—where he put an end to the consumption of human flesh by cannibal tribesmen—and German Samoa 1904–09, where he met his forward-thinking English wife, Ada. But it was Schnee's appointment to the governorship of German East Africa, the pinnacle of his diplomatic career, that marked him out as an instrument of the liberal elements in the Reichstag.

Upon arrival in the colony, Schnee immediately set about implementing the most progressive agenda of any colonial administration in Africa: He believed strongly in native education and built more than 1,000 free elementary, secondary, and vocational schools for Africans, all well funded and supplied with a first-rate curriculum and staff. These schools filled quickly, boasting a capacity enrollment of more than 60,000 after just one year. They were still functioning in the 1930s when an American observer commented, "In regards to schools, the Germans have accomplished marvels. Some time must elapse before education attains the standards it had reached under their rule."

In other areas, Schnee proved himself an exemplary governor. He improved roads, built native hospitals, and funded scientific research centers. Chief among the latter was the biological research center at Amani in the Usambara Mountains, dedicated to the development of equatorial agriculture and the study of tropical diseases. Its most famous researcher, the bacteriologist Dr. Paul Erhlich, invented the "magic bullet" serum, which became the first effective treatment for syphilis.

By late 1913, as Dar es Salaam prepared itself for the Colonial Exhibition, German struggles in East Africa appeared at an end. Charles Miller puts it this way: "On the basis of its achievements in medicine and agriculture alone, the German presence in East Africa seemed more than justified." It was as if the German people had sought to atone for the dark atrocities of the kiboko era. Dar es Salaam itself had become a showpiece with new dock facilities, botanical gardens, and an excellent state-of-the-art brewery producing a light, tasty pilsner, suitable for life in the tropics. Graceful houses built in a sort of hybrid Arabo-Germanic style lined the broad boulevards. Compared to this colonial splendor, Nairobi, the capital of British East Africa just to the north, appeared little more than a "shantytown."

But German East Africa possessed another asset, also unmatched on the continent: its Schutztruppe, the colony's defensive force, officered by Germans and composed of native recruits and—most important—native NCOs. Honed by decades of bush warfare, educated in the hard school of the Abushiri Rebellion, the Wahehe Revolt, the Chaga Insurrection, and the Maji-Maji Rebellion, trained in guerrilla fighting by great military minds like von Wissmann and von Goetzen, GEA's Schutztruppe was probably one of the most professional, disciplined, and effective small armies anywhere in the world. It had become the perfect implement, awaiting only the hand of a soldier of genius to wield it properly.

This soldier stepped aboard the SS Admiral of the Deutsche-Ost-Afrika Line in Marseilles in December 1913, bound for Mombasa on the Swahili Coast.

Chapter 11

A ROMANTIC INTERLUDE

The SS *Admiral* followed a southeasterly course through the Mediterranean, touching at Naples, where, in the last days of December 1913, it took on more passengers from the northern lands—Germans, Swedes, and Danes—before continuing on its way toward Port Said on the North African coast.

The Mediterranean can be rough that time of year, the "wine-dark sea" turning a kind of ominous blue-black under oppressive clouds, and the *Admiral* tossed in the waves. Many of the new passengers stayed in their cabins during the stormy crossing to Africa: among them, Prince Wilhelm of Sweden with his royal entourage, off to British East Africa to hunt lions; a German doctor of tropical medicine making his twenty-third visit to the Dark Continent in search of the cure for sleeping sickness; a couple of English officers posted to Nairobi and the KAR (King's African Rifles), British East Africa's version of the Schutztruppe. And a frail, pretty young Danish woman, traveling to Africa for the first time to make a marriage of convenience with a man she didn't love.

The woman's name was Karen Dinesen, called Tanne by her friends; her fiancé was the profligate, charming Baron Bror von Blixen, big game hunter and international playboy—before such a term was widely used to describe his antics. Marriage to Bror would confer many privileges in status-conscious British East Africa, just then being settled by an energetic crop of the second sons of European aristocracy who had decided to seek their fortunes below the equator. It also came with property—a struggling coffee farm in the Ngong Hills above Nairobi—and an impressive title, Baroness, and soon, a membership in Nairobi's exclusive Muthaiga Club.

But Tanne could not reconcile herself to her fate. To her, marriage to the charming, worldly Bror came as a diminishment, poor compensation for the loss of her true love, Bror's twin brother, Hans, who had married another. Regretting to the point of despair her decision to marry—or because of seasickness, or the rough crossing, or all three—Tanne had stayed in her cabin until the *Admiral* reached Port Said, at the mouth of the Suez Canal. Here, pale and tearstained, she emerged at last, thrilled despite everything by her first footsteps on African soil and by the vivid life of the teeming port city:

"Beggars displayed their sores; the blades of the sword swallowers flashed in the burning sun; the smells of dung and mint mixed with the dust," wrote her biographer, Judith Thurman. And this from Tanne in a letter to her mother: "Everything was for sale: silks and scimitars, opium, whisky and small children."

Port Said in those days was a kind of border town, like Tijuana before the Mexican drug cartels rendered it too dangerous for a visit—salacious, exotic, rough-and-tumble, without being necessarily deadly. The English novelist Evelyn Waugh describes a visit a few years after the war: There were streets composed entirely of brothels catering to all tastes and budgets; one of these cut through a city block, with an entrance on two different streets, one more upscale than the other. Depending on which side you entered, prices varied from reasonable to extravagant—but it was exactly the same establishment with the same whores on offer.

Whether Tanne visited Port Said's more raffish neighborhoods as a wide-eyed Danish tourist is not known, though certainly, given the writer she became—one of the twentieth century's greatest storytellers with a vast knowledge of mores and men—a passing visit might be inferred. It is also not known at what point in the voyage she caught the eye of a distinguished military gentleman also traveling aboard the *Admiral* to Africa—Paul von Lettow-Vorbeck. One can imagine the recently lovelorn, newly promoted *Oberstleutnant* watching from the ship's upper railings as the delicate Tanne picked her way down the gangplank in the company of an older lady, a German woman named Martha who had become her shipboard chaperon.

A contemporary photograph shows Tanne as an insouciant gamine in a white dress, her hair stylishly done, boyish and coquettish in equal measure, the obligatory parasol just out of frame. No doubt she disappeared into the crowd of hawkers, sellers of lemon water, and rug merchants as von Lettow watched, slightly alarmed on her behalf. Perhaps he followed her and offered his services, being a man and a soldier with much previous experience of Africa. In any case, she soon became his companion at dinner. Typically reticent, he says only that they "became friends over the course of the voyage," and that "she was an intelligent, highly educated young woman who later shot a number of lions."

This terse description catches Tanne precisely—half ingenue, half Amazon. About him, she wrote many things, all of them redolent of a young woman's infatuation, carried on into later life. To her he was a figure of legend, a myth: "He belonged to the olden days," she wrote in *Daguerreotypes*, a book of autobiographical essays published decades later. "I have never met another German who has given me so strong an impression of what Imperial Germany was and stood for." To her mother at the time, she wrote simply: "He has become such a good friend to me."

As it turned out, they had both drunk from the same deep, inexhaustible well of European culture—imbibing Goethe, Dante, Voltaire, Byron, Rembrandt, Schiller, Schopenhauer, Stendhal, Beethoven, Wagner, Mahler, and all the rest. They shared the same references, loved the same literature and art, and quickly discovered a shared history: Their ancestors had fought against one another in at least three European wars.

Tanne's adored father, Wilhelm Dinesen—brilliant, extravagant, a wanderer, and ultimately a suicide—had served as a young officer in the Dano-Prussian War of 1864. A daguerreotype exists in which he poses in his elegantly braided, elaborately collared officer's coat, the red and gold kepi fixed to his head at a jaunty angle, a purposeful, holstered parrot-head Colt darkening the opéra comique atmosphere of his pretty uniform. Denmark suffered a humiliating defeat in this small, forgotten war. In the Prussian Army's first demonstration to the world of its dreadful efficiency, they abruptly seized the provinces of Schleswig and Holstein from the Danes as they would seize Alsace and Lorraine from the French two years later. Seeking revenge for Denmark's losses, Wilhelm offered his services against

Prussia to Napoleon III in 1870. As captain in command of a company of *Tirailleurs*, he again suffered a military defeat, equally humiliating, in the process coming up against men like von Lettow's father, the implacable, efficient Prussian general.

At last disgusted by war and its killing fields, Wilhelm Dinesen fled to America, where he lived alone in a log cabin in the deep woods outside Oshkosh, Wisconsin. There he became a friend of the Chippewa and the Fox and Sauk Indians. He came to admire their grave dignity and "natural arrogance," their unquestioning submission to elemental things, to land-scape and weather and the vagaries of fate. Years later back in Denmark, disillusioned and stricken with syphilis, he hanged himself from the rafters of his apartment not far from the national legislature. He had become a politician; disillusioned with politics, he married and fathered five children—his favorite, Tanne, was ten when he killed himself—but he had never been able to settle down. A congenital restlessness led him inexorably to his death as it has led to the premature deaths of many other similar types: from Clive of India to Lord Byron and General Eaton, hero of the Barbary Wars, to Jim Morrison of the Doors.

Tanne idolized her father, whose untamed life and wild stories had both frightened and entranced her. Perhaps von Lettow reminded her of the man she had lost. She confided in him recklessly on the long nights of their passage to the Swahili Coast. They were never apart. Before the era of air travel, long ocean voyages often engendered a temporary, intense intimacy be-tween strangers. The "shipboard romance" was a common hazard: living in close proximity, suspended between one life and the next, men and women fell prey to desires easily resisted on dry land.

"There was dancing in the salon," notes Judith Thurman, "and games of bridge." New Year's Eve 1914 found von Lettow fetching Tanne's cham-pagne. They shared a toast, one must imagine, with arms intertwined, drinking to the new year, which would bring such horrors to the world and such changes for both of them.

As the *Admiral* slid down the fetid sluice of the Suez Canal, crossing the old caravan routes to Syria, they gazed from the railing at the ancient land passing slowly below the iron walls of the ship. They watched the *fellaheen* plowing their dry bits of field—brown and naked in the sun, slaves to the waterwheel and to the pack animal, their lives much the same as the lives of distant ancestors in the times of the pharaohs. The chalet of the old Khedive rose at the mouth of Lake Timsah, an architectural folly echoing the ruins of the Serapeum of the Ptolemies, nearby. The *Admiral* glided out onto the still waters of the Great Bitter Lake and into the bottleneck of the Lesser, and at last made Port Ibrahim and the Red Sea churning ahead and the rugged coast of the Arabian Peninsula. Meanwhile, bright equatorial constellations filled the night sky with an unfamiliar glitter.

"We sat out on deck during the starry, clear tropical evenings and chatted together," Tanne later wrote. "During one's life one does not meet many so-called great men. Those whom I have known personally have been reserved people. I thought of another great personality or hero from Africa whom I had the good fortune to know, the philosopher of religion and physician, missionary, and interpreter of Bach, Albert Schweitzer. . . . [Von Lettow and Schweitzer] have in common in their deportment an unusual modesty and thoughtfulness toward their fellow human beings, and one can scarcely imagine either of them raising his voice. People have had to listen to them, and have listened whenever they have spoken."

The hero worship felt by the inexperienced young woman for the worldly, battle-scarred officer more than twenty years her senior is described by Thurman as "a chaste flirtation." But Thurman wrote at a distance of several decades and did not know Tanne or von Lettow personally. Ulf Aschan, Bror von Blixen's godson, believed that Tanne's relationship with von Lettow had quickly metamorphosed from friendship into something else. "It has been hinted that they were lovers," Aschan coyly asserts in the memoir he wrote about his godfather, *The Man Whom Women Loved.* Whether hinted or not, the evidence, seen today, seems heaviest on the affirmative side of the scale:

When the SS *Admiral* reached its destination on January 13, 1914, Tanne and von Lettow "stood close together . . . in the narrow, fiery street in Mombasa which looks out over the blue Indian Ocean." This is her description of their emotional parting. *"Wir kommen nicht wieder so jung zusammen,"* von Lettow murmured to her. ("We will not meet again so young.") But they did make plans to meet again soon, in six months' time, and to go on a safari together. The war and all its unfortunate consequences intervened. "No, God knows we did not go on that safari," Tanne lamented, "and much water has gone over the dam and much blood into the earth since then, and those times have not returned."

On that last day in Mombasa, blind to a probable future that would find them on opposing sides of a bitter conflict, Tanne agreed to source ten good breeding mares for the cavalry arm of the Schutztruppe. Decent horses were rare in most of German East Africa, afflicted by the tse-tse fly, which can kill a healthy horse in a matter of days, and she was well-known as an excellent judge of horseflesh. This arrangement, on the eve of all-out war between Germany and England, made her, effectively, a German agent. As if to seal his devil's bargain, von Lettow gave her an autographed photograph of himself wearing the uniform of commandant of the 2nd Sea Battalion, mounted on his beloved Hungarian stallion. To this, he added an erotic verse, written on an engraved card and surreptitiously handed to Farah, the Somali manservant sent to escort Tanne to her waiting fiancé. The verse was to be given to Tanne, von Lettow specified, only on the day of her wedding to Bror:

Das Paradies der Erde / liegt auf dem Rücken das Pferde / in der Gesundheit des Leibes / und am Busen des Weibes! (Earthly paradise is found on the backs of horses / in the pleasures of the body / and in the bosoms of women!)

Of Tanne's intended, Baron Bror von Blixen, there was initially no sign. This was a foretaste of the many days during their marriage when he would be absent, in the arms of one of his numerous mistresses. But rumor spread with lightning speed in the closed world of the white colonials of British East Africa. It is not impossible that news of Tanne's interlude with the impressive Oberstleutnant Paul von Lettow-Vorbeck had already reached her fiancé, himself fresh from dalliances elsewhere. Rumor to this effect certainly made the rounds of the British residents of Nairobi. Shortly after Tanne arrived in that polyglot city, the whole place was already abuzz with the news that she had consummated an affair with the new German commander.

"It was a wonder that she was not arrested," Ulf Aschan wrote, concerning a period later in the war, when British authorities, driven to hysteria by defeat after defeat at von Lettow's hands, began a witch-hunt for supposed German spies. Somehow Tanne escaped incarceration, though "her friendship for von Lettow was well known." And, he says, Tanne's commission to buy horses for the enemy and the "general agreement that she and von Lettow had been lovers" was widely discussed.

Nor was British Nairobi's suspicion of the Danish Karen von Blixen and of British East Africa's sizable Danish community helped by the enlistment of many Danes from South Jutland in the Kaiser's navy. Scores of these seaborne Scandinavians, sailing aboard German blockade runners, would eventually jump ship and serve with von Lettow's forces in GEA. As a Dane living in British territory, Tanne felt caught between the warring parties. She held herself to a kind of haughty neutrality until her husband's eager involvement in the British war effort compelled her to support his actions against Germany in the field. Eventually, she organized several ox wagon safaris to deliver supplies across the Masai Reserve. For months on end, she was the only white woman encamped in this dangerous territory—an experience memorably described in *Out of Africa*, her most famous book, written under the pseudonym of Isak Dinesen.

But Tanne's true sympathies were for neither army. Rather she felt a helpless compassion for the native African porters of the Carrier Corps of both sides. In the absence of pack animals, the Carrier Corps porters followed the soldiers, bearing all supplies, armaments, and munitions on their backs or on their heads—usually divided into sixty-five-pound loads. Over the course of the war, the mortality rate of the unarmed and vulnerable Carrier Corps porters, never officially tabulated, was certainly far higher than that among the combatants themselves.

"For me, the war in Africa was a great tragedy because the black people in the carrier corps suffered so much in it," Tanne wrote in *Daguerreotypes*. But the next sentence perhaps reveals her heart's true allegiance: "It was nevertheless entertaining to hear about the contest between the united English and South African troops and von Lettow's few men," she admits. "It generated sparks. When the Armistice came, his enemies mourned his disappearance from their lives; there was 'nothing left remarkable beneath the visiting moon.' . . . During the war, I heard him mentioned every day by the English officers who were fighting against him. They spoke of him with great respect, not only as a skillful commander and a brave soldier, but as a chivalrous enemy. . . . The English developed a sort of love for him, a pure infatuation such as the hunter feels towards a particularly fine piece of game."

One must suppose that the love and infatuation of which she speaks was not shared by the English alone and in some way reflects her own experience. On all her safaris ferrying munitions and supplies to British troops across the Masai Reserve, Tanne carried the equestrian photograph of von Lettow as a sort of magic talisman against capture. If taken prisoner by the Germans, she would show them the photograph and hope for lenient treatment. On the obverse she had written, from memory and in garbled German, the erotic verse von Lettow had passed to her servant in Mombasa in January 1914.

"She took that picture along," von Lettow confirmed years later, "when she drove transport for the English in the war—so that in case she fell into German hands, she would be able to offer proof that she was a friend of mine." Von Lettow admitted that he was "bothered a little" by this subterfuge. It was as if whatever affections they had shared in their romantic interlude aboard the SS *Admiral* from Naples to Mombasa had been harnessed to the war effort, their brief idyll tainted by the bitter tang of gunpowder and blood. Another casualty of the vast conflagration that would soon consume so many lives.

Chapter 12

OPENING MOVES

Dar es Salaam—its name means Haven of Peace—glittered in the sun in the last days of July 1914. The weather remained pleasant. A balmy low eighties during the day, sixties at night, its palm-lined streets swept by refreshing breezes from the Indian Ocean beyond the magnificent new floating dock in the harbor. Lace curtains fluttered in the open windows of the graceful, galleried homes. Adorned with tropical gingerbread and wide verandas, they presented clean white exteriors—like freshly starched shirtfronts—to the strolling crowds of visitors from Germany and elsewhere who had come to attend the Colonial Exhibition slated to open officially on August 13.

Hotels had run out of rooms. German planters from the interior, newly arrived by goods train, complained about the prices—Dar was getting as expensive as Berlin! Nonetheless, the restaurants and *Biergartens*, proudly serving pilsner from the new brewery, were full. The hour of dusk echoed with music from military bands; later, at the Dar es Salaam Club, the orchestra played new tangos from Buenos Aires via Paris and young officers and their ladies danced a little too closely. In the gentleman's club rooms, overhead fans stirred the air, thick with cigar smoke and loud with the self-important thrum of male conversation—the topics generally limited to war (was it coming?) and, as always, business.

The excuse for the coming celebration of German achievement in Africa was the completion of the Central Railway, linking Dar es Salaam with Kigoma on the shores of Lake Tanganyika, nearly 800 miles away. Its narrow-gauge tracks passed through thick jungle, deep swamps, arid *pori*, and the towns of Morogoro, Kikombo, Dodoma, Kilimatinde, and Tabora on their way to the great lake. Now, with the railway, the rich red soil of the western districts would be open to greater cultivation. This meant more acreage devoted to sisal, a species of agave cactus that produced the fibrous stuff used for rugs and matting and rope the world over; more coffee on the foothills of Kilimanjaro; more cotton planted in the bottomlands, by the many rivers. The green hills cried out for the foundation of new cities and towns. At last the German people would have their "place in the sun."

The future of the colony, seen from any veranda in Dar es Salaam, looked bright. Everyone agreed German East had become, in an astonishingly short period of time, the showplace colony in Africa. Perhaps all the blood spilled during the brutal early years of German colonization had not been for nothing. Perhaps history had a purpose: to bring greater prosperity and the blessings of European civilization to more and more people of all races. Certainly, the new liberal regime in the Colonial Office in Berlin, helmed by the benign Dr. Solf and his man on the ground in GEA, Governor Heinrich Schnee, believed so—and passionately:

"Colonialism means missionizing," Governor Schnee had said in a recent speech given at Government House, the new, opulent quasi-oriental palace built to house the German executive at the heart of the city. "The task of the colonizers is wide and diversified: The natives are ignorant, they must be instructed. They are indolent, they must be taught to work. They are unclean, they must be taught cleanliness. They are ill with all manners of distempers, they must be healed. They are savage, cruel, and superstitious, they must become peaceful and enlightened." And, echoing his mentor, Dr. Solf, "They also have a right to demand that they should be regarded as an end and not a means."

Paternalistic and ethnocentric to modern sensibilities, perhaps—but shockingly radical stuff to the assembled colonials and planters who were Schnee's audience. Many among the planter class already reviled him as "a weakling and a pacifist," who had curtailed the use of their beloved *kiboko*—though most were not displeased by his next proposal: In the event of a European war, Schnee asserted, he would pursue a policy of total neutrality for the colony. He had arrived at this decision out of a near certainty that the economic and social progress made by Germany in East Africa would be derailed by the carnage of war—and also out of his secret terror of the Africans he ruled. To Schnee, war meant social upheaval; social upheaval meant the possibility of another bloody native uprising.

"All responsible individuals must realize that the provocation of wars in Africa in which black men would be forced to fight against white men would deal a deadly blow to the prestige of whites among blacks, just when they are beginning to look up to us," he continued. "The extension of European conflicts to African peoples is contrary to that spirit of humanity which should inform modern colonization."

This statement elicited a smattering of applause. While the planters didn't care much about the welfare of black Africans, they knew a war in Africa pitting England and her allies against Germany meant an interruption of commerce and possible financial ruin for many who had so recently achieved prosperity. With the exception of a few rabid patriots and military men like the new Schutztruppe commander, there existed at the moment no real warlike spirit in German East Africa. German colonists, who now numbered around 6,000, had become too fat and happy in this difficult but rich land to want war.

"There is no stomach for fighting" among the German colonists, observed Norman King, Britain's consul in Dar es Salaam, in a coded cable to his superiors in London. "So long as the white population . . . can be guaranteed reasonable security from native unrest or bombardment from our ships, they will exert their influence against the minority elements who wish to provoke hostilities."

Schnee's antiwar leanings—craven as they might have seemed to a few—also fell in line with international agreements going back nearly thirty years. The Congo Act, instigated by Bismarck and signed by the great European powers in 1885, had created a free trade zone in East and Central Africa, which is to say, German East Africa, the German Cameroons, Uganda, Nyasaland, and parts of French Equatorial Africa, Rhodesia, and the Belgian Congo bordering on German territory. More to the point, it also pledged the signatories to bring about the neutralization of their colonies in the event of a European war. Belligerent parties "would be required to refrain from carrying out hostilities in the neutralized territories and from using them as a basis for warlike operations," the treaty stipulated.

By invoking the neutrality clause of the Congo Act, Schnee hoped he could keep his colony out of the coming war. He would declare the colony's ports—including the capital, Dar es Salaam, and Tanga, its second largest city—"open," that is, free of war matériel and garrisoned troops and offering no support to warships or military transports. In any case, Schnee viewed a possible war with England as already lost; German East Africa, surrounded on all sides by enemies, was also beset from the sea: England's Royal Navy—the most powerful in the world—could easily blockade the entire Swahili Coast and stop the flow of supplies and war matériel from the Fatherland. In the event of war the colony would be effectively cut off from any outside help.

This left GEA's woefully undermanned Schutztruppe as the only force available for her defense. As of January 1914 it consisted of 216 German officers and 2,450 black *askaris*. This small army would be called upon to defend a territory larger than Germany and France combined, and with antiquated weaponry: Most of the Schutztruppe *Feldkompanies* had been issued outdated surplus Jagerbuch Model 71 rifles, the same single-shot black-powder weapon adopted by the Imperial German Army a generation before, right after the Franco-Prussian War. Though the Schutztruppe also maintained sixty-seven modern Maxim guns and a couple of useful if aging fieldpieces of middling caliber, the ubiquitous Model 71 represented a tactical disadvantage in the field—specifically, they were best used at night. When fired during daylight battles, they emitted billowing clouds of distinctive black smoke, a dead giveaway of *askari* positions for enemy artillery spotters.

But none of this mattered to Schnee. As far as he was concerned, the war would not be fought: "All that is necessary, gentlemen," he concluded his speech, "is to make sure that in no way, except in our thoughts and sympathies, shall we in this colony do anything that might be considered aiding the Fatherland militarily. It will be a difficult time for us—we all know where our hearts lie. But for the ultimate good of Germany and the furtherance of our aim to keep the flag of the Fatherland flying in these savage territories, it will be our duty in the colony to refrain from any belligerent activity."

Schnee's policy of noninvolvement seemed prudent to the planters and businessmen present that day. If any one of them felt misgivings or pangs of conscience over the probable surrender of Germany's premier colony without a fight, they kept it to themselves. But just then, visible from the ornate windows of Government House, moored to the floating dock down in the busy port, rose a sight that appeared to negate Governor Schnee's pacifistic declarations: The 3,400-ton Imperial battle cruiser SMS *Königsberg*, the "most formidable seagoing engine of destruction in the Western Indian Ocean."

The natives of German East Africa had stood in awe of SMS *Königsberg* as she made her maiden voyage down the Swahili Coast in June. They gaped from docks and the decks of dhows as she steamed into port. Allowed aboard as tourists, they admired her guns and gleaming brightwork, her massive engines. Her tall smokestacks functioned as a simple yardstick by which they measured a vessel's destructive power: the more smokestacks, the meaner the ship. *Königsberg's* triple funnels led to her admiring Swahili sobriquet, *Manowari na Bomba Tatu*—Man of War with Three Smokestacks.

Sent supposedly to grace Dar es Salaam's Colonial Exhibition, *Königsberg's* true mission was far more bellicose: Her orders specified that, upon outbreak of hostilities, she would become a commerce raider. She would seek out and destroy British shipping in the Indian Ocean and beyond. At 375 feet long, she showed the elegant lines of an oceangoing yacht and had been chosen as escort to the Kaiser's royal flotilla on his official visit to England back in 1906. But her fearsome armaments were more suited to a naval battle than a pleasure cruise: Ten long-barreled 10.5cm naval guns bristled from her deck; twin torpedo tubes protruded from the bowline. Her crew, equally warlike, consisted of 322 seasoned, handpicked officers and sailors led by a savvy, aggressive captain in the person of the indestructible Maximilian Loof.

Though a native of landlocked, mountainous Alsace, Loof had conceived an early and irrational love of all things having to do with the sea. He had enrolled in the German Imperial Naval Academy at Kiel in 1892, served aboard a variety of ships, both sail and steam, and participated in the German East Asia Expeditionary Force during the Boxer Rebellion, where he had come into contact with von Lettow. Physically dissimilar from the tall Prussian *Oberstleutnant* (Loof was short, genial, inclined to pudginess, eschewed cigarettes for an impressive pipe like a proper sailor), he nonetheless resembled von Lettow in more important ways: They were both pugnacious, industrious, obstinate; both utterly dedicated to the Kaiser; both natural leaders—which perhaps accounts for the persistent friction between them— and both ultimately jealous of each other's military fame.

But without one or the other, as we shall see, the war in German East Africa could not have been fought.

———————

Among the crowds of visitors aboard *Königsberg* when she reached Dar es Salaam on July 13, 1914, was the shambling, apparently innocuous British consul, Norman King. A favorite at the Dar es Salaam Club, always an amiable fourth in a game of bridge, pink gin in hand, he ambled about the town taking care of the few official matters involving British citizens in the German colony in an apparently lackadaisical fashion. That day, strolling about *Königsberg's* wide, glossy deck, he buttonholed the sailors on duty, asking many seemingly innocent questions in an unnervingly fluent German: How many guns did the ship have? How much ammunition did she carry? And what, exactly, was her top-end speed?

To Captain Loof, receiving Dar es Salaam's elite on the bridge in his best dress uniform, King asked, in a tone of studied unconcern, a few questions about *Königsberg's* role in the event of war: not a war with England, of course—everyone knew that Germany and England would never go to war, wasn't England's King George first cousin to the Kaiser? No, he meant a war with Imperial Russia. Would Captain Loof take *Königsberg* through the Suez Canal and into the Black Sea? Or would he perhaps steam around the Indian subcontinent and through the Malay Archipelago and engage Russia's Far East Fleet in the Pacific Ocean?

Korvettenkapitän Loof politely refused to answer. Questions regarding military matters must be addressed to the Admiralty in Berlin. Privately he fumed, outraged at King's "unbelievable impudence," and gave strict orders to his officers and crew not to speak to the man to whom he referred as England's "spy consul" in Dar es Salaam. Loof, an acute judge of character, was right about the consul: King was a caricature of a certain English type, but not the type (amateurish, aristocratic, bumbling, an avid golfer) he wished everyone to believe. His apparent harmlessness masked a vivid intelligence. He was indeed a spy consul, a figure straight out of one of the new popular thrillers by John Buchan or Erskine Childers. And he ran an elaborate network of agents both in Dar es Salaam and Zanzibar, a short twenty-five-mile hop across the channel, roughly the distance from Calais to Dover. On regular visits via Arab dhow to that island of spices and slaves, King maintained regular contact with the Foreign Office in London, sending and receiving coded messages over the undersea cable that connected Zanzibar to India, and India—over thousands of miles of telegraph wires—to England at the far end of the world.

As the hot summer days of 1914 faded one into the other, the prospect of a major war in Europe became distressingly probable—now fueled by the assassination of Archduke Ferdinand of Austria and his wife, the Archduchess Sophie, by the Serbian terrorist Gavrilo Princip in Sarajevo on June 28. War was coming, everyone agreed. A few questions remained: Where? When? Who would fire the first shot? In the last week of July, Consul King, determined that the first shot would not come from one of SMS *Königsberg's* 10.5cm guns, sent an urgent wireless message to Rear Admiral Herbert King-Hall, commander of the Royal Navy's African Cape Squadron—consisting of the admiral's flagship, HMS *Hyacinth*, and two heavy cruisers, HMS *Astrea* and *Pegasus*. King-Hall had just anchored for maintenance in the port of St. Louis on the tiny island of Mauritius, a British possession in the Indian Ocean 530 nautical miles off the coast of Madagascar.

But the admiral was instructed to abandon any current plans and immediately proceed to Dar es Salaam with his squadron. Once there, he would patrol the harbor mouth and monitor *Königsberg's* movements. If she left the harbor, he would follow closely; when war came, he would engage in battle. Though *Königsberg* could outgun any of King-Hall's vessels one-on-one, the German cruiser would not be able to stand up against the guns of an entire squadron. Pummeled by all three British warships, *Königsberg* would be destroyed.

Admiral King-Hall and his squadron weighed anchor on July 25 and made haste toward Dar es Salaam. On July 27, they were forced to stop for coal at Diego Suarez on the northern end of Madagascar. Here they lost precious time loading "patent black Natal"—coal of an inferior grade (Korvettenkapitän Loof called the stuff "poison")—not the sought-after high-grade coal from Welsh mines, ideal for peak efficiency in the highly stressed engines of a warship. This Natal coal also caused a debilitating condition known as "furring," wherein the insides of a ship's boilers became caked with an oily residue and thus far less efficient. Furring necessitated a periodic dismantling of the boilers and a vigorous scrubbing out—just the operation Admiral King-Hall had been about to commence on Mauritius before Consul King's summons.

In Diego Suarez, the British squadron faltered, unavoidably detained. Officers and men loaded the Natal coal at a heroic rate around the clock; everyone knew they might be unable to reach Dar es Salaam in time to blockade *Königsberg* in the harbor. Then, for the British, another stroke of bad luck: Lookouts aboard the Deutsche Ost-Afrika liner *Tabora* spotted King-Hall's battleships at Diego Suarez and wired a warning ahead to Loof. The wily Loof had already prepared his ship and crew for a quick escape. On the afternoon of July 31, *Königsberg* slipped out of the harbor and headed south along the coast without a moment to spare: Bearing down on him were the Cape Squadron's warships, Admiral King-Hall's *Hyacinth* in the lead. They had arrived just ninety minutes too late to frustrate *Königsberg*'s escape. Though expected momentarily, hostilities in Europe had not yet been declared and King-Hall could not order his gunners to fire on the German ship. Instead he deployed his squadron in a screening formation behind *Königsberg*, cruising along at twelve knots per hour, just within bombardment range of 3,000 yards. When news of war came, they would open up with their guns and send *Königsberg* to the bottom.

Königsberg, though capable of twenty-four knots per hour, could not outdistance the three pursuing ships without guile or an act of God. Both were on hand for the fortunate Loof: He had ordered his chief engineer to build up a ferocious head of steam in the ship's boilers—a motive force able to slingshot the vessel forward at top speed. Meanwhile, he damped down the smoke that might signal his plans to the British cruisers. But this level of steam pressure could not be maintained for long without release into either *Königsberg*'s engines or the atmosphere; to keep it pent up for long might lead to a disastrous explosion. Tense hours passed. Aboard *Königsberg*, Loof's engineers nervously watched the needles on the boilers' pressure gauges edging toward the red. To an observer ashore, it must have seemed the four massive battleships, their white hulls now painted gray for wartime service, were making a stately parade down the Swahili Coast. How long could this splendid martial processional last? Until one or the other ran out of coal? Until *Königsberg*'s boiler blew and she sank to the bottom in pieces?

Then, at the last possible moment, the Divinity intervened in the shape of a blinding tropical squall descending out of the southwest. All four ships disappeared into a turmoil of lashing seas and driving rain, visibility reduced to a distance no farther than the next wave. Loof acted seconds after losing sight of his pursuers: The command "Full speed ahead!" released nearly 1,400 horsepower from *Königsberg*'s dangerously overheated boilers to her twin screws. A sharp turn of 180 degrees took her out of formation and toward the unseen horizon over the deeper waters of the Indian Ocean.

The tropical squall blew itself out after no more than ten minutes. But now night was falling. Last light revealed an empty sea-lane beyond *Hyacinth*'s bow; the *Königsberg* was nowhere to be seen. One can only imagine Admiral King-Hall's dismay as he surveyed the watery vacancy at the other end of his binoculars. *Königsberg*'s disappearing act called into question his seamanship, his grasp of naval tactics. He had clearly been bested by a superior strategist—the pudgy little German captain from Alsace, a hilly, provincial place hundreds of miles from any ocean.

As far as anyone knew, war had still not yet been declared. King-Hall and His Majesty's forces in Africa maintained an advantage in this regard. The British had cut the international cable from Zanzibar to Dar es Salaam; British signal jammers were hard at work intercepting and scrambling radio transmissions sent from Berlin to German forces in Africa, via the tall, ultrapowerful Telefunken radio tower in Windhoek, GSWA. Dar es Salaam's own radio tower, situated on a promontory overlooking the port, a smaller version of this behemoth, would be the primary target for naval bombardment upon commencement of hostilities.

Meanwhile, the atmosphere above Africa crackled with static and secret codes, barely audible to *Königsberg*'s radio operator, Oskar Neimyer, his ears pressed hard to the Bakelite disks of his headset. *Königsberg* had escaped—but for how long? Like her sister ships currently prowling South Asian waters—the soon-to-be-infamous SMS *Emden* and Count Luckner's unique sail-powered *Seeadler* among them—she awaited word from Berlin to begin her career as a commerce raider. Which is to say, a lethal weapon aimed at the heart of British shipping.

This was Admiral King-Hall's worst fear. He had let a panther loose upon the seas. The admiral slept uneasily in his bunk aboard the *Hyacinth* that night. He tossed and turned, now in the grips of an obsession: At all costs, *Königsberg* must be found and sunk!

————————

Several months before SMS *Königsberg*'s lucky escape, deep in the interior of German East Africa, Oberstleutnant Paul von Lettow-Vorbeck, the colony's new Schutztruppe commandant, fell into a hole and got "water on the knee."

He had been making an extensive, thorough, and—for him—most entertaining tour of the colony. He had familiarized himself with all active-duty Schutztruppe detachments; with every available rifle, Maxim gun, fieldpiece, munition, and map. He had ordered supply dumps hidden in out-of-the-way spots all over the colony, just in case; had gotten to know the *askaris* who made up the army he would command and the officers and underofficers who would command them. He had visited white plantations and African tribal villages, sipped Moselle with the planters and guzzled palm wine with the chiefs and had improved his Swahili to near fluency.

Between January and July 1914, he traveled more than 1,000 miles around GEA, often on foot and alone, sometimes on bicycle, its pneumatic tires overinflated to deal more readily with the roots and bumps of jungle tracks. On his way to one Schutztruppe encampment near Neu Moshi, ambling along, chewing on a stalk of sugarcane, he met a young officer who had gone AWOL—that is, run off to town for a couple of beers without permission—and was now returning to base drunk and cocky. Von Lettow was not in uniform; the young officer took him for a local planter and began voicing his doubts about the new commander, due any day for an inspection visit. Rumor had it that the commander—a certain von Lettow—a real

Prussian bastard, had a stick up his ass for military discipline. Von Lettow listened affably, munching away on his sugarcane, not saying much.

When the pair reached the guard post at the base, the sentry on duty immediately recognized the *Oberstleutnant* whom he had seen in Dar es Salaam, and he drew himself up and saluted smartly. In that moment the AWOL officer, instantly sober, realized to his horror the seriousness of his indiscretion. Trembling, he stood to attention, expecting the worst. But von Lettow only smiled. "What passed between us on the road was a conversation between two comrades," he said. "That bastard the commander doesn't need to know about it."

And with that, the matter was closed.

When von Lettow had completed his military inspections, he moved on to a similar scrutiny of the colony's transportation infrastructure: He walked the long tracks through the bush, floated down the navigable rivers, traveled the two major railways end to end. He slept in freight cars and on the ground—sometimes accompanied by a few staff officers, among whom were his adjutants Major Kepler and Leutnant Göring (son of the Göring who had been, briefly, military governor of German South West Africa and brother to the future *Reichsmarschall*). Mostly, however, von Lettow went on his way unencumbered by either luggage or companions.

"I fully enjoyed the magic of the tropics," he later wrote, nostalgically, "disappearing into uninterrupted bush far from any civilization. And the magnificent game. And nights spent under gleaming star-filled heavens, listening to the terrible roaring of the lions in the distance."

But he was truly entranced by the Africans he encountered in this journey of discovery: "I realized that the natives were, for the most part, very intelligent people. Although they were a few millennia behind Europeans in terms of culture, they had nonetheless developed remarkable things by themselves. They had a greatly affectionate family life, unity in tribal society—often under the guidance of very capable village elders and chieftains—and remarkable handicrafts: I once watched a blacksmith in the forest bellow-up a charcoal fire to make sickles and swords. Awed, I realized this is what it must have been like during that obscure period of German history when Mime forged Siegfried's sword, Balmung."

Then, perhaps hunting buffalo—unsuccessfully, von Lettow says—or running from a comically got-up war party of ostrich-feather-bedecked cannibals in the deep bush—he fell into that hole. "Water on the knee," a swelling produced by a torn meniscus or ACL, in those days before laparoscopic surgery was cured only by staying off it for several weeks. And so he went for recuperation to the plantation of his old friend from cadet school days, Tom von Prince. Von Prince farmed a huge, fertile spread in the Usambara Highlands; he grew sisal and coffee and kept an excellent stock of Rhine wines on hand for guests. The two old friends sat on the veranda of Tom's comfortable, German-style house—von Lettow's leg propped on a pillow—drinking bottle after bottle and reminiscing.

"A handsome, bearded adventurer," von Prince had thus far lived a life even more eventful than von Lettow's and possessed an unusual biography for a German colonist: Born a British subject, he had remained one even as he fought for Germany's interests in Africa, helping to forge the colony in its early, brutal days. Since then, he had become more German than the Germans themselves, a patriot fanatically devoted to the Kaiser, eager to fight Great Britain and her armies in East Africa. His father, a Scot, had been superintendent of the British Colonial Police Force on Mauritius, his mother the daughter of a German missionary. Orphaned young, both Tom and his sister had been sent off to England and educated at English schools. Thus, despite his later allegiances, von Prince's early heroes were the great figures of British military history: Admiral Nelson, Wellington, and, most of all, General Charles George Gordon—then called Chinese Gordon for his role in the Taiping Rebellion, and later Gordon of Khartoum—whom he had met on Mauritius as a child.

The circuitous path upon which von Prince eventually reached Africa reads like something out of one of the romantic adventures by H. Rider Haggard, author of *King Solomon's Mines*. Sponsored by his German mother's family, von Prince attended the German military academy at Kassel but, as we have seen, quickly got himself expelled for various insubordinations. Chief among these was the passionate, forbidden courtship of Magdalene von Massow, the fourteen-year-old daughter of a retired general. For those who left Kassel without a degree, enlistment as a ranker in the German Army was mandated by law; von Prince evaded this obligatory service by rediscovering his British citizenship at the last minute—and thus traded tedious garrison duty in provincial Germany for the prospect of African adventure: In the late 1880s, he sailed for Zanzibar, consumed by half-formed dreams of riches and glory. There he hoped to make his fortune as a diamond prospector or an elephant hunter or something of that sort.

On his way from Zanzibar to the mainland, von Prince's dhow struck a reef; he swam ashore, wandered the bush a bit, and finally joined up with von Wissmann's seminal Wissmanntruppe, just then fighting Abushiri and his mob of Arab-Swahili slavers. Quickly talking himself into a position of authority, von Prince became an officer in command of a company of *askaris*, freshly recruited from the Anglo-Egyptian Army of the Sudan. Also serving with von Wissmann at the time was a rash soldier of fortune named Zelewski. Like recognized like; von Prince became Zelewski's great friend. Unfortunately, Zelewski became the East African Custer: The slaughter of his command during the Wahehe Rebellion of 1890—led by Mkwawa, a "wily, ruthless, and magnificent sultan"—might be called an East African Custer's Last Stand. A lone Sudanese trooper escaped the general massacre to report Zelewski's picturesquely defiant last moments: A spear through his throat, Zelewski nonetheless continued firing his revolvers into the dark, screaming mass of Mkwawa's advancing hordes. At last, bullets spent, he was overwhelmed and dismembered.

Vowing to avenge the death of his friend, von Prince became consumed by an appalling bloodlust. The *askaris* he commanded in his long rampage against the Wahehe came to call him *Bwana Sakharani*, "The Man Who Is Drunk with Fighting." They regarded him as a terror, a man possessed by demons; a born warrior who would not shrink from battle no matter the odds against him. Von Prince fought the Wahehe in East Africa for more than a decade, always greatly outnumbered, almost always victorious, armed with sheer guts and the Maxim gun—particularly effective against primitive tribes whose single and unchanging battle strategy relied on a wild assault with overwhelming numbers. With the Maxim gun, the charging tribesmen could be mowed down before they got close enough to throw their spears:

"Whatever happens, we have got / the Maxim gun and they have not," as Hilaire Belloc's cynical ditty puts it.

Gradually, von Prince wore down Wahehe resistance. At last, with a company of *askaris* at his back, he stormed the Wahehe Citadel at Iringa,

atop the Uzungara Escarpment, 7,000 feet above sea level. Rather than sub-
mit to capture, Sultan Mkwawa murdered all his wives and was about to
commit suicide when the opportunity for escape presented itself. But von
Prince, hell-bent on destroying the destroyer of Zelewski once and for all,
tracked Mkwawa relentlessly through the bush for more than a year and in
1898 finally had him cornered. This time, the "Magnificent Sultan," realizing he could not escape, put a pistol to his head, and blew out his brains.
The Wahehe had thought Mkwawa immortal, a supernatural being protected from bullets by an alliance of evil spirits and a magic horn that grew
out of the center of his forehead. His death ended this supposition, but the
mythical horn actually existed: When von Prince cut off Mkwawa's head,
the horn was found to be a poorly healed bullet wound, oddly mounded
with scar tissue. Eventually, his much-shot-up skull, defleshed and bleached
and complete with gaping hole and cartilage horn, was put on display in an
anthropological museum in Germany. After the war the skull was to be
repatriated by special stipulation of the Versailles treaty, but could not be
found: the magical skull of Mkwawa had vanished mysteriously, perhaps
fallen into the chasm between one historical epochand the next.

Tom von Prince, more savage than the savages he fought, was also a sentimentalist. In the midst of his brutal, personal struggle with Mkwawa, he
took a hiatus from the fighting, returned to Germany, and again paid court
to Magdalene von Massow, his sweetheart from cadet school days. Now a
ripe young woman of twenty-six, she had waited twelve years for his return.
Von Prince had just been officially awarded the honorific "von" by the Kaiser for his mad exploits against the Wahehe and was, briefly, a national
hero. To old General von Massow, he seemed like a different man, his
youthful wildness tamed by manners, his unsuitability as a son-in-law di-
luted by the honors that had been heaped upon him. The general now con-
sented to the union he had formerly proscribed; von Prince and Magdalene
were married and immediately departed for German East Africa.

There the war against the Wahehe continued. Toward the end of this brutal struggle, the von Princes kept a hostage in their East African home—a
polite, likable Wahehe chieftain named Mpangire of whom they both became

very fond. Unfortunately, Mpangire was brother to the unruly Mkwawa. Despite a pledge to remain neutral, Mpangire was found to be in secret communication with rebel forces. Mpangire and his lieutenants, immediately court-martialed for treachery, faced a firing squad; Tom overruled Magdalene's appeals for clemency and the courtly Mpangire fell, riddled with bullets.

"I wept bitterly . . . and even now I am in mourning for the black gentleman," she wrote in a letter home. "Tom is also quite upset."

Not long after this execution, the brutal, aggressive *Bwana Sakharani*, momentarily sated by blood, put up his guns, became Tom von Prince again, and settled down to the private life of a planter on his farm at Usambara. There, for some years, he enjoyed a placid domestic existence with his beloved Magdalene. To the Africans who labored on his farm, he showed himself a stern taskmaster who did not refrain from putting his hand to the *kiboko*—even after its use had been forbidden by the new, enlightened colonial regime in Dar es Salaam. By 1913, von Prince's active career in the colony's wars would seem an artifact of his receding youth. But now, as he tarried over wine on the veranda of his house with his old school chum, von Lettow, and talk turned from battles past to the possibility of war with England, it became obvious that the cast-aside persona of the bloody-handed warrior had easily reasserted itself:

Von Prince confessed to the *Oberstleutnant* that he had already organized the local German planters—among whom were many military veterans—into Schutzenkompanies, mounted corps of sharpshooters, each armed with his own expensive hunting rifle. Under the guise of a hunting club, the planters got together regularly for rifle drills and maneuvers. These Schutzenkompanies, von Lettow saw immediately, had "real military value." And it was perhaps to von Prince on one of these boozy evenings that he first discussed his grand strategy for the wartime defense of the colony.

What was their "duty as East African colonials in a war with England?" von Lettow asked. And answered: "We must divert as much enemy fighting strength as possible away from the decisive battles in Europe to our secondary theater of war. The survival and future of our Fatherland is at stake and we cannot just stand by and watch. On the contrary, we must act! Germany has about 8,000,000 people suitable for military service in its protectorates, both African and white. These cannot be allowed to remain idle during a struggle for the very existence of the Fatherland. We cannot move this population to Europe as England rules the seas, but we can force the enemy to employ troops in East Africa that will otherwise go to Europe.

"We must attack the enemy aggressively in British East Africa, concentrating our troops on some critical objective they will be forced to defend. I believe this objective to be the British Uganda Railway, BEA's lifeline, which runs parallel to our northern border. A defense all along its great length would require masses of troops; even so, it could never be adequately protected. Thus, in the event of war, I envision moving most of our units to the Usambara-Kilimanjaro District."

In May 1914, von Lettow further articulated this strategy in a carefully worded memorandum to Governor Schnee in Dar es Salaam.

"The war here is likely to be nothing more than an incident," he concluded. "But our small war and the big war outside can have their mutual influence on each other. We have it in our power to hinder the enemy by sheltering our navy during its campaign against their transport, and by keeping as many of their troops pinned down in Africa as possible. The Schutztruppe under my command is ready to do anything in its power to help win the war."

It remains the privilege of governors to ignore written entreaties from their subordinates, particularly when these entreaties contain absolute truths of the most vital importance—though, in this case, Schnee deigned to favor his military commander with a tepid, dismissive response: "So far as I can see," he wrote, "there have been no developments here which could be considered to have changed the situation in any way."

But as the summer wore on and the assassination of the archduke made war inevitable, the situation changed with startling alacrity: To address evolving circumstances, von Lettow hopped a goods train from the deep bush to the capital for a secret meeting with Governor Schnee.

When von Lettow arrived in Dar es Salaam on the morning of August 3, he found a city in panic. The Colonial Exhibition had been canceled, the undersea cable to Zanzibar cut. Since before *Königsberg*'s escape on July 31, there had been no news from Europe or anywhere else. Clamorous crowds of tourists, businessmen, and others mobbed the docks, desperate to catch a ship to British-controlled Zanzibar. Many paid exorbitant rates for a bit of deck space on Arab dhows, crouching atop their luggage, cheek-by-jowl with penned-up goats and baskets of salted fish. Indian merchants, being citizens of the British Commonwealth and fearful they would be interned in POW camps, were among the most frantic to get away. While they waited for their passage, they still managed to occupy themselves selling the flags of neutral countries (the U.S., Sweden, Switzerland) to nervous dhow captains, the latter anxious not to be fired upon by warships of either side—though arguably, a Swiss-flagged dhow was a floating absurdity that might merit a shell or two.

Von Lettow, still in jungle khakis, stood off to one side, observing this spectacle, greatly amused. His native adjutant, who'd been bludgeoned all his life with the certitude that any white person was superior to any black, looked on the frightened evacuees with a kind of wonder: "I never thought, *Herr Oberstleutnant,*" he said, "that I would see white men behaving this way. Our women could show them how to act."

Later that afternoon as the tropical sun dipped over the vast interior of the continent, von Lettow mounted his bicycle and rode slowly over to Government House for his meeting with Schnee. He pedaled through deserted streets, the shutters of the pretty tropical houses closed against all possible invaders. Von Lettow found the governor in his office in a state of nervous agitation. The silence imposed on the colony by the cutting of the Zanzibar cable, and the lack of any news regarding impending war with England, had driven him to distraction. He immediately handed his military commander a Reuters dispatch that had been smuggled aboard one of the dhows from Zanzibar: France and Russia had declared war on Germany. No news yet from England, but it was only a matter of days or hours.

The following exchange between governor and soldier was jotted down by Leonard Mosley during interviews with von Lettow himself, and further reconstructed from the latter's notes and diaries. No doubt it represents, roughly, the substance of Schnee and von Lettow's actual conversation that night, though it reads like a one-act play written for two characters of completely different sensibilities, both nonetheless equally poised on the cusp of war. (The stage directions are the author's.)

The Scene: Governor Schnee's office, Government House, Dar es Salaam, August 3, 1914. Shelves of thick, leather-bound official reports contrast oddly with the zebra-skin rug and the horns of an eland mounted on the wall. The red, white, and black Imperial German flag hangs limp in a brass stand. Beyond the open Moorish-style windows, palm trees stand dark against a scarlet dusk blooming over the Indian Ocean. A large painting of the Kaiser looks down sternly on all.

Opposing each other across a wide desk strewn with papers, Oberstleutnant Paul von Lettow-Vorbeck, commander of German East Africa's Schutztruppe, and Heinrich Schnee, governor of the colony. The latter is a thin, nervous man wearing a formal suit and pince-nez spectacles. There is something about him of a country schoolteacher, dangerously out of his depth. He presents a study in contrast with the upright soldier confronting him on the other side of the desk: Oberstleutnant Paul von Lettow-Vorbeck is tall, muscular, and balding and seems to exude authority. He wears nondescript military khakis without insignia of rank, though he is obviously a man used to command. One of his eyes, perhaps made of glass, is fixed and staring. He is affable, controlled, aristocratic— but intense, and perhaps dangerous when crossed. At the moment, he is carefully reading the Reuters dispatch he has just been handed.

VON LETTOW: *(Handing the dispatch back to the governor.)* Good. I shall send word to my troops to stand by for orders.

SCHNEE: *(Coldly.)* What orders?

VON LETTOW: It's obvious what we must do. There is only one way we can help the Fatherland win this war, and that is by pinning down British soldiers here in Africa. We can do that best by attacking them where they are most vulnerable.

SCHNEE: *(Astonished.)* You actually want to *attack* the British?

VON LETTOW: Of course, Excellency. And the obvious place to do it is in the north, in the vicinity of Kilimanjaro, where we share a frontier with British East. Just on the other side is the Uganda Railway. If we cut it, Britain's supply line from Mombasa on the coast to Nairobi and the interior will also be cut. Britain cannot afford to let that happen. She will react.

SCHNEE: *(Angrily.)* You need to understand this situation clearly, *Oberstleutnant*—I want no confusion in the coming days. I did not call you here tonight to hear what plans *you* have formulated or what orders *you* wish to give your troops. I called *you* here to receive *my* orders.

VON LETTOW: *(Calmly.)* I do not think it is within your powers to give me orders, Excellency. I am responsible to the supreme commander of colonial troops at the Kolonialamt in Berlin; he is responsible to the High Command of the Army.

SCHNEE: Berlin is dead to us, Colonel! We are completely cut off. This is likely to be the case for some time. I remind you as governor of this colony, I am commander in chief of the Schutztruppe and *you* are under *my* orders. I have already worked out with my advisers what *you* will do. I have already made plans for the welfare and security of Dar es Salaam and the other ports. By midday tomorrow I order you and all your troops to leave Dar es Salaam. I repeat the word again—*order.*

VON LETTOW: *(Angry, but tightly controlled.)* How can the evacuation of my troops possibly help the security of this city or the welfare of its citizens? What are your intentions?

SCHNEE: I am under no obligation to discuss my plans with you. You have your orders! I warn you that I intend to see that they are obeyed, even if that means relieving you of your command and putting you under arrest. Am I clear?

VON LETTOW: I would like to ask again, Excellency—what are your intentions? What will you do about Dar es Salaam and the other ports?

SCHNEE: *(Nearly hysterical.)* You have your orders! Do you obey them or not?

VON LETTOW: *(Pausing thoughtfully.)* If I am to remove my troops from the city, I ask one thing: permission to remove them not only from Dar es Salaam, but from all the other coastal garrisons. I will reassemble them at Neu Moshi in the Kilimanjaro District.

SCHNEE: *(Hotly.)* Permission refused, absolutely! Neu Moshi is too close to the British frontier. . . . *(Calming himself with effort.)* Given the delicacy of our situation, the presence of troops on the border might be construed as a provocation— exactly the kind of provocation I wish to avoid. You will take your troops from Dar es Salaam inland but keep them well away from the frontier. Understood?

VON LETTOW: *(With difficulty.)* Understood. *(He salutes and marches stiffly toward the door.)*

SCHNEE: Come back, Colonel. We will have a bit of schnapps before you go. Please understand that I am doing this because I am thinking of the welfare of the colony.

VON LETTOW: And I am thinking of the welfare of the Fatherland, Excellency.

Whether von Lettow shared that glass of schnapps with the governor is not recorded. It is certain, however, that for the moment, von Lettow had no choice but to obey the man who, pending further instructions from Berlin, remained his superior.

In the morning, a seething but outwardly emotionless von Lettow assembled Dar es Salaam's Schutztruppe garrison in Barracks Square. As an African band played *"Deutschland Über Alles,"* Schutztruppe underofficers hauled down the Imperial German flag in a stiffly ceremonial fashion—all under orders to avoid the appearance of panic. The rumor that the Schutztruppe was making an ignominious retreat in the face of danger and abandoning the city to its fate had to be squelched—as far as this was possible—by the soldierly behavior of the *askaris* on parade. A crowd of silent, solemn-faced white colonists assembled to watch this spectacle; one can only imagine their thoughts: Would they be shut up in concentration camps as the British had done to the Boers during the Boer War? The even ranks of smartly kitted out black soldiers marched once around the square and headed down the street out of the city, band still playing, standards waving. Von Lettow, properly mounted, erect as a Prussian officer should be, rode at their head. For their part, the African spectators present in the crowd tittered nervously—these matters of concern to white men seemed alien, far removed from their daily struggles. Had they realized that suddenly the concerns of white men were the concerns of everybody on the planet, they would have lost sleep that night.

Von Lettow marched the Schutztruppe most of the day, stopping at dusk outside the village of Pugu, twenty miles away. He had sent an advance column to commandeer the local telegraph post and had already prepared the ground for an encampment. He would go no farther than Pugu for the time being; close enough to Dar es Salaam and the Central Railway—which had a small station at Pugu—to mobilize his troops quickly if they were needed. That night, many messages snapped out over the wire from Pugu to Schutztruppe detachments near and far: They were to make haste to Pugu to join the main force and there make themselves ready for war with the British Empire.

A shadowy figure lurked behind Governor Schnee's decision to evacuate Dar es Salaam—none other than the shambling, apparently innocuous British consul, Norman King. Korvettenkapitan Max Loof had been right about forbidding his sailors to make conversation with the man: King was a true gamesman, a clever strategist wearing the bells and whistles of a motley fool. But the governor, at heart distrustful of military men, and desperate to keep his colony neutral, would not heed Loof's warnings or countenance von Lettow's daring and grandiose plans for an offensive strategy against the British. Instead he entered into long talks with Consul King in secret and at night at Government House—and between them, they hatched a scheme to keep German East Africa out of the war.

In his fixation on neutrality, Schnee now had most of the wealthy men in the colony on his side: businessmen who traded with the British in BEA across the border, planters who farmed thousands of acres with native labor that would certainly be tapped for service in the Carrier Corps. The colony's rich faced "bankruptcy at least and massacre at most if German East Africa should be subject to the turmoils of war" and, like the multinational corporations of our own time, gave their most passionate allegiances to the bottom line, and not to their nation of origin. In any case, hadn't Bismarck himself written them off years ago, in the 1880s, at the dawn of Germany's colonial enterprise? "I am not anxious to know," the great man had said, "how Germans who have shaken the dust of the Fatherland off their feet are getting on."

All of the above, and a fierce desire to preserve his social achievements in Africa—and thus his own legacy—had already driven Schnee into the arms of the enemy. In all likelihood, given the relative antiquity of the Congo Act, neither Germany nor England would abide by its pacifist clauses. But King had assured Schnee in mid-July that a private deal might be arranged between the two of them. If Governor Schnee could guarantee the closure of GEA's ports to all military shipping (especially the main ports of Dar es Salaam and Tanga) and destroy the radio towers in these places and order the Schutztruppe to restrict itself to minor police actions within the borders of the colony, then it might ride out the war unmolested. Schnee, overjoyed at the possibility of keeping GEA safe, nevertheless asked for a guarantee from the consul. A handshake between two gentlemen was one thing, but would it bind the nations they represented?

King sailed for Zanzibar on a dhow on July 24, 1914, ostensibly to secure his government's acquiescence to this arrangement. The same opportunity was not available to Schnee—no way to communicate with Berlin through a cut cable—but his actions would speak for themselves. King stayed away for two days, locked in the cable room at the British legation in Zanzibar. Schnee waited, fretting and biting his nails. At last, on July 26, King sailed back to report that His Majesty's government had agreed—in principle—to German East Africa's neutrality—though, tellingly, he had no written document or official communiqué to prove this fact. For the time being, neutrality in East Africa would have to remain a gentleman's agreement, a matter of personal guarantees between Schnee and himself.

At this point, the desperate Schnee was prepared to believe anything. But, according to Mosley, "it seems doubtful whether the British government ever gave such a pledge. King seems to have been bluffing. . . . Schnee was not to know that." The gullible governor nonetheless took Consul Ving's word at face value and at a dramatic meeting with his advisers on July 27 announced that German East Africa's neutrality had been secured, and that the work of civilizing the savages could continue unhindered by a European war played out in Africa. Von Lettow, still off on his inspection of the interior, knew nothing of these developments. He would not be informed until the fateful meeting at Government House on August 3. But later, he criticized the obvious strategic failings of any such agreement, which to his mind played squarely into the hands of the enemies of the Fatherland:

"In the event of neutrality we, who did not command the sea, would have to remain inactive, with a force which, though initially small, had behind it a loyal population . . . suitable for military service. The English, on the other hand, would have no need to employ a single man in Africa on our account. After providing a limited force for internal security in British East, they would be able to take away their very last fit *askari* for employment in other, more important theaters. Therefore it would be an advantage for England if any agreement existed which condemned us to neutrality."

With these thoughts in mind, and bitter over what he considered Schnee's cowardice in the face of a potentially aggressive enemy, von Lettow obeyed Schnee's orders but would withdraw no further than Pugu, there to await the outcome of events. He did not have to wait long: At six fifteen a.m. on August 5, 1914, Dar es Salaam's radio tower received a curt, almost anticlimactic message through the world static from the Telefunken tower in Windhoek: *England declared war on Germany August 4.* No more, no less. A short, simple sentence to mark the beginning of one of the greatest cataclysms the world has ever known.

In response to this intelligence, Schnee ascended into a fever pitch of hysteria. Acting as if his personal agreement with Norman King held the weight of international treaty, he launched on his scheme to castrate the offensive capabilities of German East Africa's ports and armed forces. In his first official wartime proclamation he announced that he would "preserve order and safeguard the interests of the colony," by sinking Dar es Salaam's pride and joy, its new floating dock, in the main shipping channel, thus putting the harbor out of commission for the duration. This he accomplished, though not before the supply ship *Somali*, loaded to the gunwales with top-quality coal, squeaked out of the harbor on her way to a prearranged secret rendezvous with the *Königsberg*, set to begin her career as a commerce raider. Having, he thought, disposed of the Schutztruppe and their unruly commander, Schnee then ordered the colony's constabulary to "withdraw immediately in the event of contact with enemy forces." Though, in the meantime, they must still do their best to keep the "natives peaceful."

Schnee then committed his greatest outrage to German pride by blowing up Dar es Salaam's radio tower, the city's last link with the outside world. In this act of self-sabotage, he was inspired by HMS *Astrea*, which had returned from her fruitless search for *Königsberg* to threaten Dar es Salaam. She began to shell Dar's radio tower on its promontory above the town; one of the shells landed close enough to Government House to startle the skittish Schnee into precipitous action. He immediately ordered the radio tower destroyed by his own demolition men—thus fighting the British war against himself and apparently winning.

Radio tower gone, harbor incapacitated, Schnee raised a huge white flag over Government House and began packing. He appointed the city's police chief, the unfortunately named Geheimrat Methner, as the primary authority and government spokesman in Dar es Salaam, with the understanding that "at all costs, the bombardment of the city should be avoided." Then, with his wife, Ada, and much luggage, Schnee departed on an express train to Morogoro, 100 miles up the Central Railway, far beyond the reach of British shells. Dar es Salaam was now open for British occupation—although Sykes, captain of *Astrea*, had no such orders from his own government. His only instruction, he explained to Dar's harbormaster, had been to blow up the radio tower, which, thoughtfully, the Germans had already done for him.

Meanwhile, von Lettow, waiting with the Schutztruppe in Pugu, though aware that England and Germany were now at war, had no knowledge of unfolding events in the capital. He was not, however, idle. He spent his time drawing up plans for an aggressive hit-and-run campaign against the British Uganda Railway and telegraphed his bellicose friend Tom von Prince to stand ready with his Schutzenkompanies for the signal to move.

On the afternoon of August 6, Governor Schnee's train stopped briefly at Pugu. The governor met with von Lettow to insist once again that the Schutztruppe refrain from any actions that might antagonize the British. Hoping to avoid widening the breach between himself and his military commander, or perhaps because he now lacked the nerve for such a confrontation, he deliberately failed to inform von Lettow that a white flag of surrender flew over Government House and that the capital had been evacuated. These omissions illustrate the assessment of his character later set down by the controversial diarist Colonel Richard Meinertzhagen, a British Intelligence officer stationed in Nairobi, during the war: Schnee, Meinertzhagen wrote, was a typical example of a second-rate civil servant, and "definitely no gentleman"—despite the latter's pretensions to the contrary with Norman King.

As Governor Schnee hurried back toward his train, von Lettow, striding along at his side, asked in an offhand manner if he might move his small force to oppose a landing of British troops rumored—falsely, as it turned out—imminent at the flyspeck settlement of Konduchai, a little farther up the coast. Schnee, perhaps because he hadn't heard the question clearly, or hadn't thought through the implications of von Lettow's request, agreed. Then he hopped back on his train and chuffed away into the green dusk.

While moving his men toward Konduchai the next day, von Lettow intercepted two messengers from the abandoned capital, both bearing dispatches for the governor:

Apparently, Methner, the police chief left in charge of Dar es Salaam, in accordance with Schnee's wishes, had concluded a humiliating agreement with Captain Sykes of HMS *Astrea* now blockading the harbor and interdicting all shipping. Sykes promised not to initiate a bombardment with *Astrea*'s naval guns so long as the city remained neutral and all war matériel was either surrendered or destroyed. Sykes also insisted upon the signature of the officers and crews of several German merchant ships—now trapped helplessly in the harbor—on a broadly worded neutrality document. In the document they recognized Dar es Salaam as an "open city" and pledged to sit out the rest of the war as noncombatants.

Von Lettow read this document with a growing sense of outrage. He claimed later that he had only glanced at it in a vague way, assuming that since the governor had failed to mention anything about the complete surrender of the capital, an overreaching police chief had concluded a separate peace with the British. Of course, this statement cannot be taken at face value. It is doubtful that an officer as famously nitpicky and thorough as von Lettow would have failed to examine a document of this significance closely. His next actions underscore the point: He halted his march toward Konduchai, turned his forces around, and headed straight back to Dar es Salaam. He sent the same two messengers ahead to notify civil authorities that he was assuming command of the city and its defenses.

"All negotiations with the enemy must be conducted through me alone," he told them. Then he tapped into the nearest telegraph line and sent a message to Tom von Prince, waiting in Usambara at the head of several hundred armed men:

> WE HAVE INFORMATION THAT THE BRITISH ARE SENDING HEAVY REINFORCEMENTS OF INDIAN TROOPS TO MOMBASA FOR SERVICE INLAND. THE DESTRUCTION OF THE UGANDA RAILWAY AND TELEGRAPH LINES ALONG IT SHOULD BEGIN AT ONCE. YOU HAVE MY PERMISSION TO MOVE. DESTROY STATIONS AND RAILWAY LINES, CUT TELEGRAPH WIRE . . . FAST WORK AND SURPRISE ATTACKS WILL HAVE THE BEST RESULT. TAKE THE INITIATIVE. WIPE OUT THE BRITISH ON THE FRONTIER.

For Oberstleutnant Paul von Lettow-Vorbeck, the Kaiser's war in Africa had begun.

Chapter 13

THE WAR AT SEA

Far out to sea, the SMS *Königsberg* rode the swells off the southeast curve of Cape Agulhas, within raiding distance of the rich shipping lanes between the Cape Colony and the British Empire in India. On August 4, 1914, she encountered heavy seas. Twenty-foot waves crashed over her bow as she plunged into the deep shadows of the troughs. Korvettenkapitan Loof ordered lifelines rigged along the deck for her crew manning battle stations even in the teeth of the gale.

But despite the roar of the wind and the crash of wild water and the clatter of gear breaking loose belowdecks, all was silence in the radio cabinet amidships. Radio officer Neimyer sat quietly with his ears pressed to his headset, oblivious to the noise of the storm, listening for the coded signal that would unleash *Königsberg*'s destructive power on enemy shipping. There had been nothing for days, not a dot or a dash through the world static. Meanwhile, *Königsberg*'s precious coal supply was running perilously low; soon she would have to put in somewhere or run out of fuel. Neimyer listened all through August 4 as the storm raged, barely pausing to take a little food and relieve himself. Use of the wireless in these early days required special skills; a good wireless man needed a finely tuned sense of hearing and a deft touch on the big, clumsy dials.

On August 5, the storm cleared but undersea currents continued to roil the surface of the ocean and heavy waves still broke across *Königsberg*'s plunging bow. Sailors stood precarious watch, their binoculars trained on the horizon, searching for anything—a British cruiser, twin plumes from the stacks of a French merchantman—but the *Königsberg* might as well have been the only vessel left afloat on the Indian Ocean. And in Officer Neimyer's radio cabinet, only silence. At last, that evening, following a deep red sunset, the waves calmed, the moon rose in a clear sky, and Neimyer picked up the signal from Windhoek at last—not a word exactly but a sequence of five letters endlessly repeated that nevertheless spoke volumes: EGIMA EGIMA EGIMA EGIMA EGIMA. The significance of this code was well known to Officer Neimyer and within moments to Korvettenkapitan Loof and within the hour to all the sailors and marines aboard the *Königsberg*: EGIMA meant war between Germany and the rest of the world.

Korvettenkapitan Loof immediately sent out another coded radio message to all German vessels in the vicinity: Proceed to Dar es Salaam (he was as yet unaware of the sinking of the floating dock in the main shipping channel or the "open" nature of the city) or nearest neutral port and there await opportunity to join the war effort. One of *Königsberg's* crew, Gunnery Mate Richard Wenig, went topside after hearing the news, half expecting nature herself to have acknowledged this epoch-shifting moment in human affairs, half expecting to find the word WAR! written in the stars like a headline. Instead all was exactly as it had been before reception of the EGIMA code:

"Strange how the moon shines on," he writes in his slim volume of reminiscences of the African war, *In Monsun und Pori*, "how the sea roars, the rigging wails—nothing has changed! How is that possible?" Then he answers himself with another rhetorical question and much Teutonic fatality: "What does the quarrel of atoms mean to the universe?"

———————

The next morning dawned fair and calm, sun shining on a flat sea, conditions perfect for naval combat. And all of a sudden, the shipping lanes seemed crowded with enemy steam. Before eight a.m. *Königsberg's* lookout spotted a plume of smoke in the distance; she closed to bombardment range, only to find the German Lloyd liner *Zieten*, making for Dar es Salaam as instructed, with a company of 100 marines heading back from China for home leave in Germany. To a man, the marines had volunteered to serve with von Lettow's East African Schutztruppe, which meant—though they did not know it at the time—no more home leave for five long years.

As *Königsberg* closed with *Zieten*, another column of smoke appeared on the horizon. This proved to be the German freighter *Hansa*, also hastening to comply with Loof's radioed directive of the previous evening. Loof sent both *Zieten* and *Hansa* on their ways with a "Godspeed," and a moment later a third vessel was sighted by *Königsberg*'s busy lookouts. This vessel, a freighter, refused to identify herself. Instead she executed an abrupt evasive maneuver and hurried off south. *Königsberg* gave chase—each nautical mile eating up more of her precious coal supply—at last came within range, and fired a warning shot. The unarmed freighter stopped all engines but raised her colors defiantly: the Imperial German flag. She was the *Goldenfels* out of Hamburg; she had taken the pursuing *Königsberg* for a cruiser of the British Cape Squadron. Loof, dismayed over the waste of coal, merely waved the vessel on her way.

The day waned. The long green afternoon of the tropics dropped slowly over the sea. At about four p.m., yet another vessel swam across the ken of the lookout's binoculars—surely this time! But it was a Japanese passenger ship of the Nippon Line, the *Yusen Kaisha*, on which, ironically, Loof himself had once sailed to the Far East. Japan's secret treaty with the British Empire was not yet known by Loof or any other German nationals in African waters; whether it was known to *Yusen Kaisha*'s captain is a matter for conjecture. In any case, the *Königsberg* drew alongside, a cordial greeting passed from one captain to another, and *Yusen Kaisha* passed on—perhaps to take up a role as troop transport in the Anglo-Japanese assault on Tsingtao or one of the German possessions in the South Pacific.

Dusk fell at last, vivid as always, followed quickly by a dense tropical dark. *Königsberg*'s lookouts scanned the shipping lanes with night glasses. At about eight p.m. one of them spotted a dim silhouette against the greater ocean blackness. After a day of frustration, Korvettenkapitan Loof greeted this sighting with low expectations, but this time his hunt for enemy shipping had found a proper quarry. *Königsberg*'s slim, Germanic lines and atypical silhouette eluded identification in the darkness; the unidentified vessel hove to, and prepared to receive a representative of her country's navy. In this, her captain was mistaken and caught by the enemy unawares: She was the *City of Winchester*, a brand-new British freighter built at a cost of 400,000 pounds sterling—millions in contemporary money—loaded down with a valuable cargo of precious tea for the home market worth millions more.

Königsberg's capture of *City of Winchester*, the first Allied ship to be taken on the high seas in the World War, caused two distinctly different kinds of panic, one financial, the other naval: First, the "bottom dropped out of the London tea market when news of her capture reached England," leading to shortages of the nation's favorite beverage until late in the war. Second, the "brass hats" at the Admiralty back in London—including First Sea Lord Winston Churchill—went into a tizzy, with *Königsberg* looming large in their nautical nightmares. Soon, she was seen everywhere and credited with dozens of merchantmen captured and sunk off the Arabian coast. Another highly fanciful report—that she had shelled the railway lines leading from French Somalia to the Abyssinian Highlands—was also widely believed.

In truth, *Königsberg* now lacked sufficient coal for anything but the shortest cruise. Her bunkers had not been filled to capacity when she sailed out of Dar es Salaam on July 31 and she had burned days' worth of coal in her race to evade Admiral King-Hall's Cape Squadron. In the days following the capture of *City of Winchester*, Loof and his men replenished *Königsberg*'s bunkers from the former's supply, but it was coal of the worst sort—super-low-grade Bombay, even more poisonous for her boilers than the dreaded patent black Natal. When the last of the poor-quality coal had been off-loaded and *City of Winchester*'s crew transferred as prisoners to the *Zieten* idling nearby on Loof's orders, he sent two torpedoes into the British freighter's hull below the waterline and she sank to the bottom with her tea untouched in the hold. The Germans were coffee drinkers. *City of Winchester*'s crew must have wept as the water closed above her shiny, still-new hull, their ship transformed into a giant tea bag in an instant.

For the next couple of weeks, *Königsberg* patrolled the Indian Ocean fruitlessly, meeting only a cruiser of the Royal Navy's East India Squadron in what might have been the first naval battle of the war. But with night falling and the seas running at half-gale, Loof chose to run. He didn't have the coal to spare. The British ship fired a few unanswered salvos and *Königsberg* wagged her stern and disappeared into the darkness. As it turned out, Loof's presence in the Indian Ocean had caused both the British and French Navy to interdict all unprotected merchantmen from the area. First Sea

Lord Churchill ordered that "no convoys of transports are to go across the Indian Ocean or Red Sea unless escorted by at least two war vessels, one of which must be stronger than the *Königsberg*."

Loof quickly realized that he must take his ship into ever-more-distant waters to find the prey he sought. *Königsberg*'s cruising radius, with bunkers loaded to full capacity and boilers unfurred, should run to 5,000 nautical miles. But after one month of cruising and despite a partial refill from the *Somali* in a midocean rendezvous arranged by wireless code, *Königsberg*'s operative radius had been reduced to a few hundred miles—no farther than Madagascar. While several French Messageries Maritimes liners had sought refuge in the Portuguese port of Diego Suarez, heavy coastal defenses prevented Loof from pursuing them there. He needed another prize like the *City of Winchester*, preferably loaded up with better-grade coal. *Königsberg*'s dwindling coal supply also meant a reduced water ration for her crew: On warships of the era, drinking water not hauled aboard in barrels could only be obtained via a process of charcoal distillation that required coal. Dwindling water supplies meant that now Loof allowed his men only one pint a day.

Like all great sailors who must expect to encounter shipwreck and all sorts of privations in a life spent at sea, Loof knew how to make do with resources at hand. Deprived of a friendly shipyard where he might put in for fresh water, refueling, and defurring, he decided to make one for himself. He needed only a sheltered anchorage, close to shore but hidden from the scrutiny of passing ships, to which *Königsberg* might repair unmolested. He cast an eye across his charts of the Swahili Coast and fixed upon the tangled labyrinthine delta of the Rufiji River, a wilderness of mango swamps, shoals, jungle, crocodiles, and snakes opposite Mafia Island about 150 miles southwest of Dar es Salaam.

The Rufiji was one of German East Africa's mightiest rivers. Its channels and tributaries, though mostly uncharted, were known for their surprising depths—deep enough, Loof hoped, to allow passage of a battleship. Before piloting *Königsberg* to this jungle lair, he sent out a fake wireless message using a naval code known to have been cracked by the British. The false message called for all German raiders in African waters—Loof knew there were none but *Königsberg*—to rendezvous at a fixed location in the open sea below the southwesternmost point of the Arabian Peninsula. From there they would form a squadron to attack British troop convoys heading from the Indian subcontinent to the European theater.

British Naval Intelligence picked up this coded message and was deceived. The startling news, passed on to the Admiralty, immediately caused a panic; First Sea Lord Churchill ordered all available warships to intercept and destroy the fictitious German squadron. Anticipating a major naval battle and the certainty of British victory, the sea lords sat back, rubbing their hands with glee. Loof waited calmly for the seas to clear of Royal Navy warships—now a regular presence in the blue-green waters off GEA—then, after a few days, scurried off to hide in the Rufiji Delta. In the second week of September 1914, with lighters going ahead to sound the channel, *Königsberg* inched up creeper-clogged tributaries and found a convenient spot ten miles upstream from the river's mouth, near the little-known hamlet of Salale. But she wasn't there for long. Just as Loof was about to dismantle *Königsberg*'s boilers, he learned via a network of spies and secret German wireless stations that one of Admiral King-Hall's ships, HMS *Pegasus*, had put into Zanzibar for defurring.

Loof owed this critical bit of intelligence to the indefatigable von Lettow: During the new *Oberstleutnant*'s 1,000-mile peregrination around GEA in the months before the war, he had overseen the recruitment of a network of German agents who were then installed in British territory: "He had agents in Mombasa and several other towns," one of his biographers affirms, "and a remarkably effective espionage service in Zanzibar."

One of these agents, a respected German doctor with a practice divided between Zanzibar and Dar es Salaam, sailed back and forth across the channel on Arab dhows at least once a week. In his black bag, alongside various pills and sulfur treatments for his patients, he carried a coded report on British activities on the island—to be delivered to German authorities. It was from him that news of *Pegasus*'s distressed condition reached Loof: She lay there in the rank, oil-stained waters of a Zanzibar harbor manned by a skeleton crew, with two of her boilers reamed out—splayed and helpless, so to speak, as a patient etherized upon a table. Loof did not hesitate. The Rufiji Delta lay about 100 nautical miles from Zanzibar, a journey that, even in her furry condition, the *Königsberg* might easily accomplish. Squadrons of British warships currently searched the heavy seas off Aden, so there was nothing to fear from that quarter. *Königsberg* could make the Zanzibar run, destroy *Pegasus*, and return to her safe anchorage in the jungle undetected.

On September 19, under cover of darkness and led through the labyrinth by her lighters, *Königsberg* slid down the Rufiji, powered over the bar, and eased into the Indian Ocean. On the morning of September 20, a dense mist covered the ocean just beyond the harbor mouth at Zanzibar. Just before first light, Commander Charlewood of HMS *Helmuth*, one of the British vessels patrolling the shipping channels, caught sight of a large ship steaming toward him out of the mist. The *Helmuth* was an armed tug, formerly German, now British, commandeered on the first day of the war. From behind the instrument binnacle on its bridge, Commander Charlewood watched as the approaching ship gradually solidified, its identity painfully clear all at once:

"To my horror," he later wrote, "I saw she had three funnels and I knew she must be *Königsberg*. At that instant, German colors broke from her foremast head and the peak of her gaff and a blank shot warned us not to pursue our enquiries further." Charlewood watched helplessly as *Königsberg* steamed to within bombardment range of the incapacitated *Pegasus* and let loose with her 10.5cm naval guns. "After two or three salvos, every shell was finding its mark. *Pegasus* put up a heroic fight. . . . Her shells were falling short and there could only be one end to the duel."

Helmuth, now situated between *Königsberg* and *Pegasus*, could not maneuver out of the way fast enough for the German gunners. They sent a small-caliber shot over her bow a little too far; a second shot fell short. The third would blast *Helmuth* out of the water. Charlewood ordered his crew to abandon ship, and everyone—except for the Indian engineer—jumped over the side without life preservers. As predicted, the third shot found *Helmuth*'s main boiler, which exploded, killing the hydrophobic engineer. Meanwhile, *Königsberg*'s big guns kept blasting away at *Pegasus*, now silent and on fire, her hull full of holes. One last explosion ripped her open belowdecks and she was finished, with eighty sailors killed or wounded.

Work of destruction done, *Königsberg* came about and made ready to head back to sea, but not before slowing long enough to throw Commander Charlewood a life preserver: "I was astonished to hear a voice call out in

English 'Are you all right?' My response was not compatible with that of an officer or a gentleman," he admitted. "I declined to make use of the life buoy, fearing that a line might be attached to it and I should be hauled aboard and made prisoner."

At this, the *Königsberg* shook her hip at Charlewood's ungraciousness and left the swearing Englishman treading water. In a few minutes, she had disappeared from view and within twenty-four hours was safely ensconced again in her hiding hole up the Rufiji. To the British, soon scouring the sea-lanes of the Indian Ocean for any sight of the German menace, it must have seemed as if she had sailed off the ends of the earth.

SMS *Königsberg* and Captain Loof had scored another first: the first sinking of a British warship in the World War. To the sea lords at the Admiralty back in London, it was as if she had sailed up the Thames itself and bombarded Whitehall. In the ten-minute engagement between *Königsberg* and *Pegasus*, "Britain's only naval protection in East African waters had been wiped out." Worse, "British naval prestige had suffered a heavy blow, and the *Königsberg* was still at large and obviously off on a career as a sea raider. It was vital that she be sought out and sunk as rapidly as possible."

To this end, First Sea Lord Churchill ordered the creation of a new squadron of English warships whose sole purpose was to find and destroy *Königsberg*. These consisted of the heavy cruiser HMS *Chatham*, then patrolling the Red Sea, and the light cruisers HMS *Dartmouth* and HMS *Weymouth*, with Captain Drury-Lowe of *Chatham* in overall command.

This "Destroy *Königsberg* Squadron" assembled at Zanzibar on the last day of September and immediately began scouring the Indian Ocean for any sign of the German raider. Drury-Lowe's *Chatham* alone outgunned *Königsberg* and could possibly outpace her; *Dartmouth* and *Weymouth* were nearly as deadly. Drury-Lowe had strict but somewhat contradictory orders from the sea lords as to the scope of his mission: Nothing, not the incidental destruction of any other German ship, nor any sort of offensive blow against the Germans in East Africa, should be contemplated if it might conceivably take his attention off finding *Königsberg*. But, should Drury-Lowe's squadron encounter German vessels in the shipping lanes, "on no account is time to be wasted by taking or sending any captured ships into port." Reading between the lines, this order automatically doomed any German vessel encountered during the hunt for *Königsberg*; it would be sent to the bottom immediately, pirate-style. No mention was made about what to do with survivors.

The Destroy *Königsberg* Squadron combed the sea-lanes of the Indian Ocean for over a month with no sight of the quarry. She had become a ghost, a legend, as unreal to sailors aboard *Chatham* as the Flying Dutchman. But, unbeknownst to Drury-Lowe, his squadron's intelligence officers were already in possession of two important clues—gathered early in the search for the German cruiser—which, had they been properly considered, would have led quickly to *Königsberg*'s jungle hideout. Unfortunately, like most vital intelligence, the clues were not properly considered. Ignored, they had the ultimately tragic effect of touching off a general war in German East Africa, still slumbering under its makeshift neutrality.

The first of these clues, a chart depicting the Rufiji Delta in great detail, had been taken from the captain's cabin of a captured German merchant ship, the *Präsident*. A further perusal of the captain's log showed that the *Präsident* had just made a journey up the Rujifi with a hold full of food and coal and returned empty. Inexplicably, these discoveries did not lead to any further investigation. The second clue involved the capture of a German reserve officer in a hut on tiny Komo Island opposite the mouth of the Rufiji. Interrogated, the German officer told the squadron's naval intelligence officers that he had been sent from Dar es Salaam to man a signal post. This was true, but also mostly a lie. To whom was he signaling and what? A diary found in his possession mentioned the *Königsberg* and a town called Salale. British charts showed no such place— significantly, the German chart taken from the *Präsident* was not consulted. Was "Salale" code for another place? Did it have any meaning at all?

While the naval intelligence officers debated these matters with all the urgency of monkeys grooming lice from each other's fur, an obscure informant apparently working for the British brought a report to Zanzibar: The *Königsberg* had been seen in the harbor at Dar es Salaam loading coal and stores. The informant's story, believed without question, was relayed to Drury-Lowe aboard *Chatham*. Though in possession of reports—unread, one must assume—describing the sinking of the floating dock in the main channel and the destruction of Dar es Salaam's harbor facilities, Drury-

Lowe proceeded thence immediately, anchoring in the roads two miles off the Makatumbe Light on October 21.

Dar es Salaam was still an open city, officially stripped of all military personnel under Governor Schnee's orders, and nominally under control of the police chief, Methner, as the only remaining civil authority. It must be said that in the first months of the war, the city's German population approved of this arrangement. Still on the side of Schnee and neutrality, they remained unconvinced that Europe's colonies in Africa would be drawn into the war in a major way—this, despite von Lettow's adamant insistence that a war between the Fatherland and Great Britain was a war between Germans and Englishmen everywhere, even in Africa. Von Lettow had attempted in vain to arouse the colonists' German patriotism. But believing themselves safe in their remote backwater, they preferred not to fight. In fact, he had argued the case for war so stridently in the Dar es Salaam Club and elsewhere in the months leading up to the war that many of his fellow Germans had mocked him behind his back. Governor Schnee's aides had quickly dubbed their new military commander "the Mad Mullah"—a nickname that would stick for years, and one that von Lettow would adopt with his usual self-deprecating humor.

But to engage in warfare properly, an army must have the support of the civilian population for which it fights. As of October 1914, such support existed only in small pockets in GEA. Von Lettow was determined to shake the colonists out of this dangerous complacency one way or another. And so in all likelihood, he devised the "obscure informant" stratagem and concocted the false report concerning the whereabouts of the *Königsberg*. He knew the British, desperate to destroy the German cruiser, would fall for any ripe piece of misinformation—a rumor that *Königsberg* had returned to Dar es Salaam would bring on Drury-Lowe, guns blazing. And a full-scale British bombardment of the city might be just the thing to neutralize Governor Schnee's neutralization policy and drive the colony to von Lettow's side.

For some reason, when *Chatham* dropped anchor off the German East African capital on October 21, the giant white flag that had been flying from the pinnacle of the lighthouse since August 5 had disappeared. One might suspect von Lettow's hand in this, though he fails to mention the matter in his war diary or his volumes on the campaign. An overeager Drury-Lowe, scanning the harbor through his spyglass, thought he could see *Königsberg*'s masts poking up in the harbor on the far side of the intervening mangrove swamps that acted as a natural breakwater—six miles away. *Chatham*'s lookout, hoping to please his captain, confirmed that the masts most probably belonged to *Königsberg*.

Now Drury-Lowe went through the motions of observing the "open-city" agreement made weeks earlier when Schnee had voluntarily blown up Dar es Salaam's radio tower: He sent up a signal flag demanding the immediate presence of an official from the city aboard *Chatham*. When the official appeared, Drury-Lowe would expect an explanation for *Königsberg*'s obvious presence in the harbor. But Drury-Lowe allowed less than a half hour for a response—not enough time for the Germans to send a boat loaded down with the correct officials six miles across open ocean. After twenty minutes had elapsed with no Germans in sight, he began to fire his big naval guns at the city. The bombardment lasted for an hour. When the billowing funnels of smoke cleared, much damage had been done to both government buildings and private homes and to the German freighters *Feldmarschall* and *Konig*, trapped in the harbor by the sunken floating dock, with some of their sailors still living aboard. Suddenly it appeared that Dar es Salaam had surrendered—though it had never been at war—unconditionally: Myriad white flags—which is to say bedsheets, freshly ironed shirts, ladies' undergarments, pillowcases, tablecloths, anything white—flew from every balcony and open window in the city.

Soon, the requested boat made its way out of the harbor and headed toward *Chatham*. When the officials came aboard, it was discovered that not one of them could speak English. Incredibly, no one aboard *Chatham* could speak German—even the intelligence officers. Through the use of sign language and a bit of French, the officials managed to make it known that *Königsberg* was not in the harbor; that indeed, the harbor was itself kaput to vessels of any size and also neutral and defenseless. Consul Norman King (now at large), whose flawless German had only improved with the outbreak of war, was sent for from Zanzibar and arrived the next morning. In the afternoon, he accompanied British officers into the harbor. There they ascertained that the sunken floating dock was indeed still sunk, and that *Königsberg* could not have entered the harbor.

King and the officers returned to *Chatham*, and the battleship steamed off to resume the search for *Königsberg*—without a word of apology from Drury-Lowe to the civilian authorities for having shelled a neutral port. As far as he was concerned, Drury-Lowe sniffed, when *Königsberg* sank *Pegasus* at Zanzibar, all pretenses of neutrality had been cast to the winds. In response to the bombardment of his defenseless capital, Governor Schnee eventually sent a sternly worded letter of protest to Consul King. In the letter, he did not renounce his policy of neutrality following the egregious bombardment of his capital; rather, he confirmed it:

"I again draw your attention to the fact that Dar es Salaam and Tanga are defenseless harbors and that their inhabitants have undertaken no warlike acts. . . ." Etc.

But the time for diplomacy had passed, blown away by *Chatham*'s six-inch naval guns. The bombardment of Dar es Salaam, its destroyed buildings and casualties, convinced the inhabitants of Germany's premier colony that neutrality would not keep them safe. In other words, the war that had already come to von Lettow had now come to German East Africa. His ploy had worked. Now the tide of public opinion shifted from Schnee's evanescent neutrality to the inevitability of war, and the *Oberstleutnant* became "confident that [he] need no longer worry about the governor's orders"— though this confidence was, as yet, a bit premature.

In the days following the bombardment, many men, hitherto apathetic, flocked to the colors, signing on with von Lettow's Schutztruppe for the duration. Among them, sixty-five-year-old Kurt Whale, a retired general, formerly of the Army of Saxony, who would become one of von Lettow's indispensable commanders in the war and the oldest combatant fighting on either side. Whale had arrived in Dar es Salaam as a tourist back in July, intending to visit his planter son and take in the Colonial Exhibition; the outbreak of war had stranded him in the colony with no choice but to join the fight.

The shift of the balance of power in German East Africa from Schnee to von Lettow had occurred at a critical moment: Goaded by the sinking of *Pegasus*, the British had decided to subdue the colony once and for all. Expeditionary Force B had just sailed from Bombay with more than 8,000 British and Indian troops aboard twenty-one rickety transports, escorted by two aged battleships, HMS *Goliath* and HMS *Fox*—their destination some unknown, vulnerable hamlet along the Swahili Coast of German East Africa.

Chapter 14

TANGA

Major General Arthur Aitken lounged in a deck chair reading a novel aboard the P&O luxury liner SS *Karmala*—requisitioned as a transport for officers and staff—anchored in the roads off Tanga on the morning of November 2, 1914. It is not recorded what novel occupied the general's attention, whether *War and Peace*, *Little Women*, or something by Trollope. But Norman King, former British consul in Dar es Salaam, now Major King, newly appointed intelligence officer attached to the British-Indian Expeditionary Force B, thought the activity frivolous at best, at worse, dangerous: Force B was about to embark upon the largest invasion of East Africa by British troops since the expedition against the despotic Abyssinian emperor Theodore III in 1868—and General Aitken didn't seem especially interested.

Force B had been at sea for nearly three weeks. Not a single vessel in the motley flotilla could make more than seven knots per hour. Conditions belowdecks recalled those aboard the slavers of the Middle Passage. The 8,000 Indian troops crammed in the holds of the wallowing ships had barely been allowed topside for fresh air. Most "staggered, slipped, crawled, and lay prone in shifting pools of their own vomit." And though the flotilla had paused for an afternoon at Mombasa, General Aitken had gruffly brushed aside suggestions that his confined troops might benefit from a period of training ashore—during which they might recuperate, drill together, and cohere as an army. Instead, he insisted, Force B would head straight for the port of Tanga, German East Africa. They could rest and recuperate after they had seized the town from the enemy.

Sadly, Expeditionary Force B wasn't much of an army to begin with. More a military hodgepodge of leftover soldiers and peasant draftees scrounged from all over the subcontinent, the best and most experienced Indian troops having been sent off to fight in Europe. Now, with the invasion of Tanga imminent—and General Aitken's intelligence staff completely in the dark as to whether they would face resistance from German forces holding the town—the general lay in his deck chair reading his novel, unconcerned. Officers of his command swirled around him, anxious over the embarkation of 8,000 troops on a hostile shore and the battle sure to come. Worried, they trained their field glasses on the mysterious mangrove tangle of Africa a mile off the port bow.

At last, Aitken put the book aside and gestured for Norman King to approach. King knew Tanga almost as well as he knew Dar es Salaam, having designed the town's nine-hole golf course—golf course design being one of his favorite hobbies—for German planter friends before the war. The newly minted IO stepped up, major's pips on the collar of his uniform glittering in the tropical sun. Expecting to be peppered with questions regarding terrain and military strategy (Would they face a determined resistance or none at all?), he was surprised to find these and similarly pressing matters decidedly *not* on the general's mind. Baffled, King answered Aitken's many questions regarding plans for British administration of the colony *after* they had seized it from the Germans. Which the general regarded as a fait accompli.

Major King, who described this episode in his diaries, answered the general's questions as politely as possible, but with growing alarm. How could any military commander show himself so utterly disinterested in the logistics of an invasion about to take place? Certainly, it seemed to King, the Germans wouldn't give up the town without a fight. But General Aitken dismissed King before the latter had a chance to voice any concerns, and went back to reading his book.

King would remember this episode for many years to come. It had not boded well for the Indian troops still crammed head-to-toe in the stinking, sweltering holds, waiting to face their doom.

Tanga, German East Africa's second-largest city in 1914, with a population of 24,000 native Africans, 700 Indians, Goanese, and Arabs, and 600 Germans to rule them all, sat about 100 miles north of the equator. The climate, as might be expected in such latitudes, was either sweltering or damp, or both, depending on the time of year. The tropical sun, always overhead, blazed down on its palm-lined waterfront and on the lush copra plantations and coconut groves and rubber trees that spread out from the outskirts for several miles.

Tanga's first-class port facilities, greatly improved by the Germans in recent years, extended for two miles along the shore at the southern end of a wide natural harbor. The gingerbread-white tropical houses of the European Quarter lay along a neat grid of streets leading to a pleasant square dominated by the town's largest structure, the Kaiserhof Hotel. Behind the port rose the peninsular headland of Ras Kasone, atop which stood two houses, one red, one white, used by German plantation overseers. Below Ras Kasone to the south lay a skirt of mangrove-clogged beaches that gave way to tough scrub punctuated by baobab trees and impenetrable fields of maize and sawgrass.

The beach upon which Aitken had chosen to land Force B, though shielded from the town by the bulk of Ras Kasone, was a small wilderness of mangrove swamp terminating at a fifty-foot cliff—unsuitable for a landing of any kind. Over the cliff, a mess of impassible vegetation cut across with a few narrow service roads led to the railroad tracks at the edge of town.

"It is bad country for fighting," wrote Expeditionary Force B intelligence officer Captain Richard Meinertzhagen in his detailed but often untrustworthy and certainly illegal diaries. (Intelligence officers, for obvious reasons, were not supposed to keep unofficial written records.) And though there are many unbelievable assertions and outright fabrications in Meinertzhagen's text—which stretches for many, many volumes and covers most of the twentieth century—this is not one of them. Meinertzhagen was there. "Very thick bush and palm," he continued, "with jumpy troops, I fear the worst." That the Indian troops of Force B were "jumpy" is one of Meinertzhagen's rare understatements. He goes on to describe them as "second rate," "disgraceful," "unreliable under fire," "showing no military spirit or grit, the worst in India whose senior officers are nearer to fossils than active energetic leaders of men."

For his part, General Aitken chose to believe his pan-Indian army would crush any resistance mounted by black Africans led by Germans: "The Indian Army," he huffed, according to Meinertzhagen, "will make short work of alot of niggers."

Expeditionary Force B was composed of two brigades—the 27th and the Imperial Service Brigade—consisting of roughly ten regiments apiece. The latter commanded by Brigadier General Richard Wapshare (Wappy, Meinertzhagen derisively called this cautious, blustering officer), the former by Brigadier General "Fighting" Mickey Tighe, hard-drinking and reckless and always spoiling for a fight. Various other detachments, including a unit of mountain artillery, a Carrier Corps, and other camp followers, brought total British strength to just under 9,000. Among the flotsam and jetsam were at least two reliable units—the Loyal North Lancs, raised from white European residents of India, and the famous Gurkha mercenaries of the Kashmir Rifles. These tough fighters from the arid hills of Nepal, famous for their deadly curved knives called kukris, still serve with Indian and British armies to this day.

But taken as a whole, Force B, "a grab-bag lot, hastily thrown together," was one of the least-prepared armies in British colonial history. Two of the regiments—the 98th Indian Infantry and the 63rd Palamcottah Light Infantry—hadn't been under fire since the 1880s. Another regiment, the 13th Rajputs, upon whom would fall the bulk of the fighting, was "hopeless"—another one of Meinertzhagen's assessments. He knew this regiment well, having trained with it two years earlier in Delhi: "They were considered inefficient," he wrote, "and had been reported as unfit for active service."

Both Wapshare and Tighe were strangers to their commands. Barely a week had separated assembly at Bombay and embarkation for Africa, and neither general had visited the stinking holds to which the Indians had been consigned for the voyage. Major General Aitken simply couldn't be bothered. He was a soft, portly man, the son of a Protestant minister from New Brunswick, Canada. His brother, the famous press mogul Lord Beaverbrook, friend of Winston Churchill's and well-connected in Parliament, was to become the model for Lord Copper, relentless editor of the *Daily Beast* in Evelyn Waugh's darkly comic novel of journalistic shenanigans, *Scoop.*

Aitken had served with the British Army in India for the previous thirty-five years, his record blameless but entirely undistinguished. Promotions had come to him over the backs of other, more talented officers, perhaps because of his powerfully connected brother. As commander of the Expeditionary Force, Aitken had nobody's confidence. According to a junior officer—as so often happens in the world—Aitken had been made commander *because of,* not despite, his incompetence: He had been "kicked upstairs," as Meinertzhagen put it, "because he was not wanted as District Commissioner in India."

Ashore at Mombasa on October 31, while the Indian troops sweated and puked in their airless hulks, Major General Aitken and staff discussed plans for the imminent conquest of GEA with Sir Charles Belfield, governor of the British colony, and General John Stewart. Stewart, another Indian Army general, had landed back in September with a force of 3,000 subcontinentals designated Expeditionary Force C. He planned to attack a Schutztruppe field company under Major Kraut—one of the ablest of von Lettow's subordinate officers—who had fortified the crater of an extinct volcano at Longido between Lake Natron and the northeastern slope of Kilimanjaro.

The assembled "red tabs" discussed matters for the better part of the afternoon. Expeditionary Force B's original target had been Dar es Salaam, but this was now changed by Aitken, who insisted on Tanga for strategic reasons: The Northern-Usambara Railway with its terminus at Tanga originated 120 miles upcountry at the German stronghold of Neu Moshi. Aitken felt that an occupation of the town would give them control of the railway. This would in turn, as they advanced up the line, give them control of the interior as far as Kilimanjaro, a region just then hotly contested by the British African troops of the King's African Rifles (KAR) and von Prince's elite, if amateur, Schutzenkompanies.

General Stewart would at the same time transport Expeditionary Force

C from Mombasa, via the British Uganda Railway, and retake Taveta—just over the border from German East Africa—dislodging von Prince and his men, who had occupied the town a few weeks before. (Von Prince's capture of this small railway depot in August 1914 marked the first seizure of British territory by German forces during the World War.) Following this action, Stewart's Force C and Aitken's Force B would converge and drive remaining German troops toward Dar es Salaam and the Indian Ocean. The capital would then be assaulted and quickly taken, ending the war before Christmas. The whole thing would be, Aitken asserted, "a cakewalk."

Other officers present voiced serious objections to Aitken's plan, pointing out the extreme difficulties of terrain—arid thornbushes, feverous swamps, mountain ranges—that lay between the British and their objectives. Not to mention the known professionalism of the German-trained African *askaris*. These objections Aitken brushed aside. He also curtly rebuffed an offer of help from Colonel Graham of the 3rd KAR battalion—seasoned native bush fighters to a man.

Among those horrified by Aitken's dismissive attitude, according to Meinertzhagen, was Meinertzhagen himself. To his infamous diaries is owed much of what is written about the Battle of Tanga and its aftermath—despite their multitudinous inconsistencies: For starters, they probably weren't diaries in the traditional sense, but memoirs composed from scraps of notes and with hindsight long after the events they describe. Unfortunately, Meinertzhagen, a fascinating Baron Munchausen–like character and quite possibly insane, remains one of the most articulate and entertaining eyewitnesses regarding the historical events in which he participated.

He "was a very efficient officer with lots of brains, no scruples, and quite unreliable," wrote a junior officer on his staff later in Nairobi. "I admired his knowledge, ability, and skills as an I.O. officer. . . . I wouldn't trust him a yard or believe a word he said unless I knew that it suited him to tell the truth in this instance."

———

Despite his German-sounding last name, Richard Meinertzhagen was the very type of the polymath English eccentric. An accomplished ornithologist, taxidermist, indefatigable diarist, skilled cartographer, brave soldier, self-promoter, and also—it appears—a "colossal fraud," he came complete with a barely suppressed murderous streak. All in all he calls to mind a Moriarty-like supervillain out of something by Arthur Conan Doyle.

The Meinertzhagens, a German merchant banking clan once on par with the Rothschilds, emigrated from Bremen in the early years of the nineteenth century and established a branch of their bank in London. Richard's father married into the hyper-talented Potter family; Richard's mother, Georgiana Potter, was one of nine beautiful and accomplished sisters—nieces of the author Beatrix Potter of *Peter Rabbit* fame. One of her sisters, also named Beatrix, an early feminist and ardent Fabian socialist, founded the London School of Economics along with a few others. The sixth of ten children, Richard was often placed in the charge of this aunt. He hated her and disliked many of the famous people, including Charles Darwin—upon whose lap he once perched uneasily—who frequented the Potter sisters' glittering intellectual circle.

Perhaps as a reaction to this liberal progressive background, Richard Meinertzhagen early on declared himself for king and empire. Even as a child, he hungered for the dusty, exotic regions of the world; Africa in particular occupied an especially vivid corner of his imagination. He read every book he could on the subject, questioned explorers returning from the "Dark Continent," and once, without his parents' knowledge, invited Henry M. Stanley—rescuer of Livingstone—to tea. After a brief, obligatory career in the family bank, Meinertzhagen joined the army in 1899 and served in India and Madagascar, and for two years with the KAR in British East Africa, 1902–06. But wherever he went, he inspired controversy.

During his first African posting, Meinertzhagen was accused of assassinating a Nandi Tribe holy man called the Laibon. The Nandis, warlike and primitive, wandered the savannahs of British East Africa hunting and scrounging for grubs and groundnuts. They ambled about the vast landscape mostly naked except for coils of copper wire scavenged from British telegraph lines, which they routinely cut and deconstructed to turn into jewelry. For this and other vandalisms, the Nandis were constantly at odds with their British overlords. When Meinertzhagen's KAR detachment turned a Maxim gun on the Laibon and his crew at a prearranged peace talk—it remains unclear whether the Laibon fired first or whether Meinertzhagen or someone else pulled the trigger in this action, dubbed the "Ket Parak Massacre"—the Nandis ceased troubling British authorities. Morality aside, the Laibon's extrajudicial killing probably spared the tribe from the devastating consequences of an all-out war against them.

After directing the British Intelligence Service against von Lettow from Nairobi, 1915–16, Meinertzhagen went on to serve in Mesopotamia, where he was credited—or rather credited himself and was believed—with having invented the famous "Haversack Ruse" now a staple of military spycraft. The Haversack Ruse is a stratagem in which a knapsack or briefcase loaded with misleading "secret" military information is "lost" in a spot where it will be found by the enemy. This ploy was used to great effect several times, most notably in the Second World War: False documents misidentifying the location of the D-day Invasion were placed on the body of a dead British pilot dumped off the coast of Spain. Spanish authorities found the body, discovered the documents, and promptly handed them over to their friends, the Nazis, who fell for the ploy, strengthening their defenses along the wrong stretch of the coast against an expected invasion that never materialized. That time, the Haversack Ruse probably saved tens of thousands of Allied lives.

Meinertzhagen's postwar career bounced wildly from achievement to scandal and back again. He soon emerged as the last of the great amateur British naturalists, famous for his beautifully preserved bird specimens and deep understanding of migratory patterns. Then in 1924, he killed his second wife, herself a noted ornithologist, in a suspicious hunting accident. Her death might have been genuinely accidental or something more sinister: perhaps a William Tell–style display of marksmanship gone awry, or even a kind of duel precipitated by her discovery of the various frauds her husband had perpetrated upon the ornithological community. Or he might have murdered her outright to pursue an affair with his teenage cousins, one of whom became his life companion. The truth will never be known.

In later years, Meinertzhagen became one of the earliest and most ardent non-Jewish supporters of Zionism and is counted among the Righteous, along with Oskar Schindler and other notable non-Jews who supported the Jewish cause. A square in Jerusalem still bears his name. A famously vivid raconteur, he was a sought-after guest on country house weekends, and for decades hosted the most popular party at the Ascot Races, held on a converted London bus in the racecourse parking lot.

Meinertzhagen's diaries, published in abbreviated form in the late 1950s and early 1960s, now held at the Bodleian Library at Oxford, run to eighty souvenir-stuffed, handwritten, and typed volumes. They were long considered the standard go-to eyewitness text for any historian interested in British Imperialism's latter days: Meinertzhagen seems to have been everywhere and met everyone of importance, from Winston Churchill—with whom he had attended Harrow—to Adolf Hitler. At a 1938 meeting with Hitler in Berlin, Meinertzhagen claimed he had a gun in his pocket and might have assassinated the Führer just in time to stop the Second World War. Improbable perhaps, but not impossible; while the claim he countered Hitler's standard greeting "heil, Hitler!" (not something Hitler ever said—why would he "heil" himself?) with "Heil, Meinertzhagen!" sounds like something out of a Monty Python sketch.

Richard Meinertzhagen died at age ninety in 1967. In his final days, eccentricities forgiven, he had become a national monument. Men of his type, everyone agreed, would never again strut across the stage of history. In the years following his death, a number of uncritical biographies appeared, and a film was made about the Mesopotamia Campaign in which he was portrayed by British actor Anthony Andrews. The reputation of the Meinertzhagen diaries grew. These labyrinthine volumes came to be considered an absolutely indispensable source, the starting point for anyone writing about World War One in Africa and the Near East, or on just about anything else that happened in the British Empire from 1900 to the Partition of India.

But a few years ago, the Great Man's reputation began to unravel. An earnest 2005 *New Yorker* article accused him of being a fraud. His famous diaries when closely examined by historians were found to be full of inaccuracies and outright lies; of puffery and tall tales. Meinertzhagen's most determined detractors came from an unlikely source—the world of ornithology. Upon close examination, it turned out that many of the excellent bird specimens he had supposedly shot in Africa and elsewhere, stuffed, and donated to various museums, had been stolen from other museums and relabeled as his own. Or stolen, relabeled, and donated back to the very museums he had stolen them from in the first place! Worse, the migratory patterns these specimens supposedly illustrated were shown to be false. Ornithologists, a tight-knit, unforgiving, and meticulous flock, never forgave him.

"Great villains can make fascinating characters," wrote Brian Garfield in his 2007 exhaustive Meinertzhagen takedown, *The Meinertzhagen Mystery.* Meinertzhagen "was not a conventional villain. . . . His complexities were Shakespearean."

Meinertzhagen's diaries are both far less and far more than what they purport to be. Taken together they make up a kind of epic roman-fleuve, an exercise in experimental autobiographical fiction, like something by David Foster Wallace run amok. They are a baroque monument to Meinertzhagen's maniacal self-regard and, fraudulent or not, something of a literary work of art. In them, Meinertzhagen portrays himself as the indispensible man— always prescient about the turn of events, always warning the perpetrators of disaster about the disasters they are about to perpetrate, always at the center of every episode of historical importance in his general vicinity and the hero of many improbably heroic escapades: His accounts of the rescue of a series of young women—from death in speeding trains, or fates worse than death in the brothels of Port Said—read like bodice-ripping Victorian melodrama.

Since Garfield's 2007 book it has been fashionable to debunk everything Meinertzhagen wrote as fraudulent. But his depiction of events leading up to the Battle of Tanga, the battle and its aftermath, and other campaigns in British East Africa during the war are finely observed and ultimately believable—as is his assessment of the blundering British commanders involved. Whether originating at the time or in hindsight, many of his assessments have the ring of truth.

"As Aitken saw it," Meinertzhagen wrote of Tanga, "the enemy would crumble and run before the first British fusillade, and the natives would welcome Force B as their long-awaited liberators from the brutal German yoke." From such certitude, he added, military disasters are made. Other officers besides Meinertzhagen criticized the Force B invasion plan at the October 31 meeting in Mombasa, but Aitken rejected them all. And that afternoon, following a little light refreshment, the general and his staff returned to their comfortable berths aboard the SS *Karmala.* With the ragged flotilla of Force B lurching along behind, she puffed out to sea again and turned south toward Tanga.

In *Meine Erinnerungen aus Ostafrika* (*East African Campaigns*), Paul von Lettow-Vorbeck's volume of military reminiscences, he says he never had any doubt the British would open the land war in East Africa with an attempt to take Tanga. He had been warned of this probability by his extensive network of spies and by intercepted British documents that "spoke of an impending attack by an Indian expeditionary force about 10,000 strong."

Accordingly, von Lettow made a special trip to Tanga in the last week of October, during which he "drove all over the country in a car . . . and discussed matters on the spot" with the ranking Schutztruppe officer posted there, Captain Otto Adler, and District Commissioner Dr. Auracher, Governor Schnee's representative in the town. The latter had already received instructions from Schnee not to defend Tanga in case of British attack and that the colony must remain neutral, even if that neutrality involved handing itself over to the enemy. But the time for neutrality had passed, von Lettow explained patiently to the recalcitrant district commissioner; the war had begun in earnest. In response, Auracher handed von Lettow a recent telegraph from the governor: "Tanga is an open city," the telegraph announced. "A bombardment must be avoided at all costs."

Schnee hadn't yet learned the lesson taught by HMS *Astrea* to Dar es Salaam a few weeks earlier. Again, Leonard Mosley records the following brief exchange between von Lettow and Auracher—another one-act playlet—as reconstructed from the former's notes. (Once again, stage directions are the author's.)

The Scene: An open car, bumping along a narrow track between groves of dense green rubber trees. In the distance, the glitter of the Indian Ocean. Oberstleutnant Paul von Lettow-Vorbeck and District Commissioner Dr. Auracher in the back. Driving, Captain Adler of the Schutztruppe.

VON LETTOW: (*Reading the governor's telegram, then tersely.*) Ignore it!

AURACHER: (*Firm.*) Impossible, *Herr Oberstleutnant*. I am a member of the administration of this colony. I must obey our governor.

VON LETTOW: *(Pausing, then thoughtfully.)* But you're not *only* a
civil servant. You are also a reserve officer in the German
Army. Correct?

AURACHER: I held the rank of *Leutnant* in the army, it's true.
But it's been some years. . . .

VON LETTOW: Then as you know, in time of war, you may be recalled to duty, in which case your responsibility to the army
supersedes your duties to the civil government. So, be informed that you are as of this moment recalled to duty. I am
your superior officer and now I order you to prepare for the
defense of Tanga. Under no circumstances will you hand
this city over to the enemy. If you do so, you will be arrested
and court-martialed. Is that clear?

AURACHER: Yes, *Herr Oberstleutnant. (Hesitating.)* But—you
will absolve me of all responsibility with the governor?

VON LETTOW: You are hereby absolved.

Whether Auracher contacted Governor Schnee following this exchange
is unclear. But Schnee, still idling with his British-born wife, Ada, at Morogoro, GEA's summer capital, was somehow apprised of von Lettow's
determination to defend Tanga. He immediately fired off another irate telegram ordering von Lettow to abandon the place: "Tanga's town and harbor
not defensible," he concluded.

Here the Schutztruppe commander was faced with a quandary. His par-
tisans among the German colonists were not yet sufficiently fervent to allow
him to defy a direct order from the governor and expect public support while
doing so. In his next exchange with Governor Schnee, he indulged in a rare
equivocation: Might it be possible to bivouac a *Feldkompanie* of Schutztruppe
in the vicinity of Tanga temporarily, von Lettow inquired, politely, consider-
ing the town's healthful climate and proximity to cooling ocean breezes?

Schnee, believing he had at last put a collar around the neck of his troublesome military commander, agreed to this request, with two caveats: The
commander himself must rejoin his troops in the north without delay, and
the Schutztruppe must evacuate Tanga immediately in the event of a British
invasion.

Von Lettow promised to abide by these strictures with fingers firmly crossed behind his back. Before leaving for Neu Moshi, he confirmed District Commissioner Auracher's authority over the city. But as a newly drafted Schutztruppe reserve *Leutnant*, Auracher would be taking his orders from the ranking officer on the spot, Captain Adler, who himself followed the orders of the military commander, von Lettow. And von Lettow had neglected to pass on Governor Schnee's second telegram insisting Tanga not be defended to Captain Adler. The rebellious *Oberstleutnant* had always believed in the military necessity of allowing junior officers to act independently in times of crisis—and here was such a time. He departed for Neu Moshi knowing exactly what Captain Adler would do if attacked, because they had planned the defense of Tanga together.

As von Lettow rode the narrow-gauge train north on October 27, through the beautiful green landscape, he expected to be recalled at any moment by the booming sound of British guns.

———————

Just before first light on the morning of November 2, 1914, the motley flotilla carrying the 8,500 officers and men of Force B lay anchored in the roads about twelve miles off Tanga, not quite visible beyond the rim of the darkened horizon to the east. At Aitken's instructions, Commander Caulfield in HMS *Fox* steamed toward the harbor and cut engines within sight of the town. It was a few minutes before six a.m. Caulfield ran up a flag demanding the presence of a German official aboard *Fox*, as Drury-Lowe had done at Dar es Salaam weeks earlier. But Caulfield, an overscrupulous officer, did not begin an immediate bombardment as Drury-Lowe had done. Instead he waited for the Germans to appear.

Meinertzhagen describes Caulfield as "nervous yet pompous and shifty-eyed. . . . It struck me that he was definitely afraid and was always referring to the safety of his blasted ship." And he adds that, of course, he "was not much impressed by him." Major General Aitken, however, stood in awe of Commander Caulfield, as he did of the Royal Navy as a whole. "He appeared to be overawed by the Navy, and though Commander Caulfield was much his junior in rank, he always seemed to defer to him in argument," Meinertzhagen concluded. This attitude of subservience, unpleasant in an acquaintance, exudes the fragrance of disaster when present in the character of the commander of an expeditionary force.

Soon, District Commissioner Auracher made his way out to *Fox* in a small boat and came aboard, dressed in the dusty white linen suit of a minor colonial official. Outwardly, he was Governor Schnee's representative; inwardly, he was von Lettow's creature. Commander Caulfield received him imperiously. A lack of foreign language skills made the interview difficult: Caulfield could not speak any German—typically, neither could anyone else aboard—and Auracher's English was limited to what he'd learned in school. But *Fox*'s commander managed to make himself understood: Surrender of Tanga and its port facilities would occur in two hours, at 0800. Failure to surrender would result in an immediate bombardment of the town. Auracher equivocated, making the most of the language difficulties, buying time. As a junior official, he said, he did not have the authority to surrender Tanga himself, but must have the permission of his superiors. Therefore, Caulfield must refrain from the threatened bombardment until word could be had from Governor Schnee. Also, he emphasized, military forces were not present in the town, which was neutral—technically true as Adler's Schutztruppe *Feldkompanie* was bivouacked a mile or two beyond the city limits in a grove of coconut palms.

In the end, Caulfield agreed to allow Auracher time to contact the governor, but not much time. Should HMS *Fox* not receive word by 0930 sharp, the bombardment of Tanga would begin. Auracher returned to shore, immediately ordered a complete evacuation of all civilians, and telegraphed von Lettow in Neu Moshi: ENEMY HAS DEMANDED SURRENDER OF TANGA. REFUSED. EXPECTING BOMBARDMENT. He then concluded all pending business as district commissioner, signed letters needing signatures, and wrote a few others. The last of these was addressed to Governor Schnee and contained his resignation from the Civil Service. He then went home, took off his District Commissioner's togs, put on the gray *Tuchuniform* of a *Leutnant* in the Imperial German Army hanging mothballed in his closet, and rode his bicycle out to the 7th FK to offer his services to Captain Adler.

Aboard *Fox*, Caulfield watched, dismayed, as the white flag flying above the Tanga District Administrative Offices came down to be replaced by the Imperial German colors. This meant war. But nine thirty came and went and Caulfield did not commence his threatened bombardment. The British had planned to use Tanga's government buildings as their own administrative center for the invasion of GEA, and its pleasant colonial homes as quarters for their officers. Half a dozen well-placed rounds from *Fox*'s massive naval guns could reduce all that to rubble—and nobody wanted to occupy a pile of rubble for the predicted month or so it would take to secure the colony for the British Empire. Instead Caulfield weighed anchor and steamed back to rejoin General Aitken and the Force B flotilla just over the edge of the horizon.

Another meeting of officers was again called aboard SS *Karmala*. Now that there would certainly be a fight, Caulfield proposed dividing the invasion force to attack both Dar es Salaam and Tanga simultaneously—a plan that many regarded as strategically sound. But, unexpectedly, for once Aitken disagreed with his naval commander. They would deal with Tanga first, he insisted, landing the 13th Rajputs at dusk, under the command of Brigadier General Tighe. In the crepuscular light, Aitken reasoned, Tighe's dusky Rajputs would make less visible targets for any German sharpshooters that might be lurking on the headland above.

Ironically, the possibility of having to fight a divided invasion force greatly worried von Lettow, waiting with the bulk of his Schutztruppe up in Neu Moshi. He simply didn't have the troops necessary to protect both cities. He too decided to focus on Tanga—where he would dig in and concentrate his forces. He later admitted this decision was a "colossal gamble." According to Edward Paice, "had Aitken opted to split his force, as Caulfield had suggested, von Lettow-Vorbeck's name would have been soon forgotten." Here, aptly illustrated, was the gambler von Lettow, the man who had broken the bank at Monte Carlo on his way out to Africa in 1913. One is reminded of the single indispensable quality Napoleon looked for in his commanders—that they be lucky.

Caulfield sulked over Aitken's uncharacteristic decision not to heed his advice. When other officers including Meinertzhagen proposed the landing be made directly on Tanga's tidy stone jetties, Aitken refused. This time he deferred to Caulfield, who refused to lend the support of *Fox*'s guns unless the harbor were first dragged for naval mines. Though the presence of mines seemed unlikely—HMS *Pegasus* had visited the harbor at least twice between August 5 and her watery death at the hands of *Königsberg* at Zanzibar—to placate his top naval officer, Aitken ordered this task accomplished. British tugs soon began to drag the harbor. Among their number was the resurrected HMS *Helmuth*, somehow still serviceable, even after its direct hit from *Königsberg*, and still under the command of Lieutenant Charlewood, eventually fished out of the drink at Zanzibar. He dragged up and down all night and brought up nothing more threatening than sunken logs, all the while exposed to sporadic machine-gun fire from the darkened town.

Meanwhile, Aitken fixed on the mangrove-clogged beach below Ras Kasone for the first landing of the Rajputs. He no doubt saw himself enjoying a good night's rest in one of the two houses—whether red or white didn't matter—occupying the heights. But getting the Rajputs into the lighters took all day and far into the night of November 2. First, machine guns were laboriously fixed to the bows, then the seasick, poorly conditioned Indian troops lowered into them. For weeks, these men had been improperly fed; many, used to specific diets according to Hindu religious dictates, had had their colons tortured by army food. A number of them, softened by weeks of inactivity belowdecks, could barely walk; their leg muscles had atrophied. They were seen lumbering and wobbling about by German observers on the cliffs, who didn't know what to make of the display. Were the English soldiers all drunk?

At last, by nine p.m., the lighters, fully loaded, assembled in the shadow of the *Karmala*, a dense black cast by the tropical moon on a blacker sea. The troops huddled in the little boats, digestive tracts in an uproar, unsteady and afraid, their officers trying to steel them for the coming night landing—among the first of Aitken's many mistakes: Night landings are prone to confusion; troops imagine terrors they cannot see, death itself lurks out there in the darkness. Morale suffers. From General Aitken himself had come the simple battle orders: "The town of Tanga is to be seized tonight." They would land on the beach directly below the red house off the southern point of Ras Kasone. From there they would climb the low cliff, advance into the plantation of rubber trees and copra palms, and seize Tanga from the Germans, all before sunrise on November 3rd.

Tugs towed the first lighters toward the beach at four thirty in the afternoon. They quickly ran aground on an uncharted reef and lay there exposed to German Maxim fire for hours as other lighters crashed into each other behind them. A well-placed shell from *Fox* silenced the German machine gun post and the shooting dwindled to the occasional potshot. Still, the stuck lighters, loaded down with soldiers, could not be lifted off the reef. At last, the Rajputs, weighed down with packs and gear and carrying their Lee-Enfield rifles over their heads, jumped overboard and struggled forward in chest-high water, stumbling over the submerged mass of mangrove roots and scrambling up to the beach at last after dark. They lay there on the sand without the strength to continue, unsettled by the unfamiliar night sounds of Africa all around them, determined not to move another inch until first light. Hardly the beachhead of a conquering army. By ten p.m., barely two companies of Rajputs and a few scouts had managed to assemble there.

Off-loading continued. By midnight, the first wave of Expeditionary Force B to invade German East Africa had at last packed themselves onto the narrow mangrove beach, but so tightly they could barely move. Fortunately for them, the Schutztruppe's artillery—three ancient but effective brass field guns of 1870 vintage—waited with their crews miles away in Neu Moshi. A few rounds from one of these brass cannons would have wreaked havoc with the troops just now disembarking, in this case the 13th Rajputs and the 61st Pioneers. As yet, the British had landed no guns and none of the sappers who looked after the Expeditionary Force's explosives and grenades.

As three a.m. rolled around, sufficient numbers of both regiments had gathered on the beach to be considered operational strength by Brigadier Tighe, who had himself landed not long before. He now walked among them, reaching much the same conclusion as Meinertzhagen: These men were not ready to fight. But General Aitken's order left no room for equivocation: Tanga by sunrise! Tighe ordered the advance and the Rajputs, led by their British officers, clambered up the low cliff and stumbled over the dark, uneven ground, ignorant of where or when they would come into contact with the enemy.

The few scouts come ashore earlier hadn't done a very good job. Nearly blind in the darkness, they had felt their way forward through the dense bush, unable to locate the enemy and unwilling to explore very far inland.

The Schutztruppe's 17th FK under Captain Adler, now joined by Reserve Lieutenant Auracher and a company of native police, had meanwhile dug themselves into a fortified position between the jetties of the port and the curve of the tracks of the Northern-Usambara Railway, about 200 yards east of the terminus. Adler and his men hunkered down in their trenches, invisible, waiting. As dawn broke over the Indian Ocean, the leading Rajputs, commanded by Lieutenant Colonel J. A. Stewart, advanced to within range of the German trench. Adler and his *askaris*, outnumbered at this point by at least four to one, would soon shorten the odds.

In battle, numbers don't matter as much as resolve. The British Indian troops of the 13th Rajputs were fighting on alien soil on behalf of a cause they neither understood nor loved. German officers and the black *askaris* they commanded faced an invading army bent on conquest. The motivations of the *askaris* in this conflict bear some examination: Why risk personal destruction on behalf of a colonial regime that had, not twenty years before, ruled the land with an iron hand grasping the *kiboko*? The answer lies, perhaps, in the enlightened policy of the last few administrations in Dar es Salaam—which is to say in the 65,000 black African students now enrolled in German schools and the new understanding at the Kolonialamt in Berlin that colonialism's ultimate responsibility in Africa had to do with the welfare of its native peoples. Black East Africans had just begun to *feel* German. Why trade the devil you know for one waving the Union Jack? But there existed another factor, less quantifiable: The morning of November 3, 1914, was, quite simply, a good time for a fight.

Adler held his fire until Stewart and his men approached to a point where the *askaris*—already good shots—could not miss. As the Rajputs reached a ditch 200 yards from the railroad tracks, Adler gave the order. Suddenly the predawn gloom resounded with the murderous clatter of machine-gun fire; the humid air thickened with the billowing black-powder smoke from the *askaris'* old Model 71s. African porters carrying the Rajputs' gear marching in the van of the army immediately dropped their burdens and disappeared into the bush. The Rajputs attempted to return fire, but the men, disorganized and demoralized by their night landing and all that had gone before, couldn't manage much of a fusillade in return, and failed to advance under heavy German fire. A few dug in where they were;

others, according to Meinertzhagen, simply threw down their rifles and lay down, faces pressed to the ground, overwhelmed by mortal terror.

Presently, the sun rose over a distressing scene. The Indian troops in front refused to continue; the second half battalion of Rajputs came up unsteadily, followed by the 61st Pioneers. The Pioneers were not considered a fighting detachment—their role in the military pecking order being mainly logistical. Inclusion of the Pioneers in the battle plan indicated that Major General Aitken hadn't expected any resistance from the few Ger- mans left in Tanga. The Pioneers were the first to break. Faced with accurate Schutztruppe machine-gun fire, they turned without hesitation and ran pell-mell through the bush for the embarkation point on the beach at Ras Kasone. Exposing themselves boldly to the German fusillade, their British officers tried to rally the men and were cut down where they stood. Then the Rajputs themselves wavered and buckled. Terror is contagious. Though a few Rajputs held their ground, most joined the general rout, fleeing in the footsteps of the Pioneers. HMS *Fox*'s big guns added to the general chaos; lobbing a few shells at supposed German positions, they managed only to hit the fleeing Rajputs.

Now Adler aimed two machine guns at the right wing of the Rajputs under Captain Seymour. Seymour fell to this fire, as did his commanding officer, Colonel Doddington, and two other staff officers who had foolishly mounted a knoll to ascertain German positions. At last, with his battalion in total confusion, Brigadier Tighe ordered a retreat. Panicked and hyster- ical Indian troops, barely under the control of their officers, converged wailing on the beach, many bleeding from fresh wounds. Meinertzhagen, roaming the battlefield in his capacity as intelligence officer, was disgusted by what he saw—Indian troops, as he put it, "running like rabbits and jib- bering like monkeys."

Had the Germans pressed the attack, Meinertzhagen realized, the whole of Expeditionary Force B might have been captured or driven into the sea to drown. No amount of heroic example set by the British officers now availed—anyway, there weren't that many left standing: Officer after officer had been shot down by the Germans. But Captain Adler couldn't press his attack; the Schutztruppe simply did not yet have the troops to do the job. In the aftermath of the first day's engagement, Brigadier Tighe estimated

German strength at no less than 2,500 men. In truth, there were fewer than 250.

"The bubble of the Indian Army has now burst," wrote Meinertzhagen. "Our men behaved disgracefully, showing no military spirit or grit. . . . I doubt if even half the Indian Army are really reliable against modern fire. . . . To show in what state the Rajputs are, a sepoy discharged his rifle in error. This was the signal for immediate panic, the Rajputs and Pioneers rising up and rushing back to the shore, and were with difficulty persuaded to return to their bivouacs. These are jolly fellows to go fighting Germans with."

Meanwhile, von Lettow had not been idle. He had ordered a general advance down the line upon hearing news of the British landing, and the first Schutztruppe reinforcements now arrived in Tanga via the Usambara Railway. The small cars of the railway rattled in, packed to the gills with *askaris*, their German officers, gear, machine guns, and porters, all ably managed by Schutztruppe Railway commissaries Krober and Kuhlwein. The *askaris* disembarked in good spirits—as von Lettow had observed, any railway journey was always a treat for his African troops, to whom rail travel remained a novelty. Gear and weapons got unloaded; then the train turned around and rattled back to Neu Moshi for the next load. The railway, in addition to being a smaller-gauge line, possessed only eight engines. These ran ceaselessly for nearly forty-eight hours, their sleepless engineers surviving on adrenaline and coffee. By the morning of November 4, they had managed to move an entire army and all its ordnance right up to the front lines—conveniently located just a few hundred yards from Tanga's railway terminus.

Though the first day's action had been disastrous for the British, with more than 300 killed and many more wounded, Aitken was not prepared to give up. The Loyal North Lancs and the dauntless Gurkhas of the Kashmir Rifles had managed to set up a security perimeter on the evening of November 3, fortifying the Ras Kasone Peninsula and commandeering both the red and white houses as operational headquarters. Expeditionary Force B would make a big push with all personnel in the morning. Even at full strength the Schutztruppe would be outnumbered by British troops by more than eight to one, an overwhelming advantage backed by the naval guns of HMS *Fox* in the harbor.

Meinertzhagen spent that night on the lawn of the white house, on a mattress made up from "the underclothing of the lady of the house, nice soft bits of lingerie, and for my blankets, a Union Jack and three German flags. My pillow is palm leaves stuffed into the corsets of a stout lady whose name I do not know." But as Meinertzhagen slept on his lingerie bed, Oberstleutnant von Lettow-Vorbeck arrived from Neu Moshi in the darkness, among the last of his forces to invest Tanga.

Captain Adler had withdrawn the 17th FK to their encampment in the coconut grove on the outskirts, reasoning that one field company of *askaris* and a few German officers couldn't conceivably hold the town against the expected onslaught—this, despite his vastly successful action of earlier that day. Surely, the British would return in full force and this time better organized and, with the support of *Fox*'s guns, crush any resistance.

"Where are the British now?" von Lettow asked. "Have they occupied the town?" None of his subordinate officers seemed to know the answers to these questions. Quietly furious at this startling lack of intelligence—though equally pleased over his troops' performance in the first phase of the battle (their fighting spirit, he said, had shown itself to be "magnificent")—von Lettow now decided to do some reconnoitering on his own. He applied blackened cork to his face and along with two volunteers—Captain von Hammerstein and Schutztruppe Dr. Vogel—proceeded into Tanga on bicycle. They found the streets completely deserted, haunted by moonlight. The white villas of the European quarter and the galleries of the Kaiserhof Hotel glowed otherworldly in the bright tropical night.

Von Lettow looked around wide-eyed, astonished by this oasis of peace—could it be that German East Africa was actually at war? But soon the distant murmur of activity from the harbor drew his attention. He and his companions abandoned their bicycles and, creeping in and out of shadows, gained the waterfront. There, on the far side, less than a mile away, a British warship disgorged more men and war matériel under bright, smoking theatrical lights. Von Lettow now came to the conclusion that the previous day's action had been a feint on the part of the enemy, designed to test the strength and determination of German resistance. As he watched the activity below, doubt crept into his mind: Perhaps it might be best to heed Schnee's telegraphed orders. Another, even more sternly worded missive from the governor now lay folded in his breast pocket: *You are forbidden to subject Tanga and the defenseless citizens of the town to the vigors of war. Should the enemy land in force, there will be no resistance. Tanga must be saved from bombardment.*

"We estimated six thousand had landed already with more coming," von Lettow remembered later. "We Germans had scarcely 800 men available. The rest were still in transit. Should I commit my small force to battle against a greatly superior army entirely armed with modern weapons and supported by the guns of its warships? Most of our people were still armed with the old black-powder M71 rifles, some marked with an 'X' as unserviceable, and we didn't have a single piece of artillery."

Von Lettow considered his options—none of them good—as he and his companions crept back to their bicycles. But the decision had already been made: Calling to mind the clumsy maneuvering of British forces in China in 1900, and their disastrous record in the Boer War, he believed they could be defeated, even with such inferior numbers. The British would be fighting in "very close and completely unknown country . . . where the slightest disorder was bound to have far-reaching consequences," he wrote. While the Schutztruppe's officers were "well acquainted with the country around Tanga and the *askaris* were completely at home in the bush. Thus they had a reasonable prospect of taking advantage of the enemy's weak points by skillful and rapid maneuvers."

Then, just as von Lettow and his companions reached the center of Tanga, chance nearly put an end to his plans: An outlying Indian sentry challenged the reconnaissance party from a darkened doorway, demanding in Hindi the password of the day. Taken by surprise, von Lettow responded with "Stambuli!" the German countersign. All hung in the balance; one shot from the sentry or a simple loud exclamation might bring an entire company of Indian soldiers down upon them. Who would command the Schutztruppe with the commander a prisoner of the enemy? But after a moment's hesitation the sentry simply turned and ran off. The Germans, relieved, hurried to their bikes and rode back out to the coconut grove to prepare for battle.

As the morning of November 4 dawned, the sound of sporadic firing could be heard from German and English patrols in the vicinity of Ras Kasone. This was nothing, just the result of nervous trigger fingers; battle lay some hours off. Much time was needed to move the assembled Schutztruppe companies into their defensive positions around Tanga. This required skill and more than a dash of military prescience: Von Lettow guessed the British would concentrate their attack on the German left flank, between the railway workshops and the sea. He positioned detachments of the 16th and 17th FK along this line, establishing his HQ behind them with the reserves—consisting of Tom von Prince's bellicose, patriotic all-German Schutzenkompanies. Meanwhile, he added the 6th FK to the defensive perimeter along a half-mile front at the eastern edge of town. It was a long and vulnerable line but, in part, solidly backed against a thirty-foot-high railway cutting.

"From a tactical standpoint, the defense of Tanga was very well planned," allowed the British-leaning Charles Miller in his analysis of the battle. "Even so, von Lettow would be opposing an invading force of eight thousand with less than a thousand men." And though the resourceful *Oberstleutnant* had carefully laid his plans, taking a stand here would be the greatest gamble of his military career: A loss would certainly lead to court-martial proceedings. In defending Tanga he would be disobeying direct orders from the governor of the colony; only a smashing victory would save him from this fate. Of course, von Lettow's decision went beyond personal considerations: With the town's extensive modern port facilities under British control, they might easily land more troops and drive up the line to Kilimanjaro as, unbeknownst to him, Aitken had already planned. The fall of the colony wouldn't be long after that. "There was nothing for it," von Lettow concluded. "To gain all, we must risk all."

The tropical sun beat down on the Schutztruppe all in place by nine a.m. Snipers poised in the branches of baobab trees were grateful for the shadows of the leaves. Everyone was cautioned to spare the water in their canteens; it must last all day. Meanwhile, some of the *askaris* knocked coconuts out of the trees, cut them open with bayonets, and showed their German officers how to drink the water inside. A few bottles of Moselle were filched from the wine cave at the Kaiserhoff and passed around. The African NCOs, who—as von Lettow readily admitted—were the backbone of the army, ginned up a fighting fervor among the men: *"Tutaharibiwa waingereza!"* (The English will be destroyed!) and *"Wahindi ni wadudu!"* (The Indians are insects!) they chanted, soon echoed as call-and-response up and down the line. Calling someone an insect in a land infested by many annoying varieties of bug was considered a mortal insult.

The hot hours of the morning slowly passed without even a whiff of battle. The forward-posted snipers took a few potshots at the enemy, but no general engagement had yet materialized. As it turned out, Aitken had checked the advance of his army to make sure everyone in Force B, officers, men, and orderlies, ate a good breakfast. For many, it would turn out to be their last. This caesura, though intended to bolster British fighting spirit, had the opposite effect. Indian troops grew more and more restless as the day drew on. Increasingly afflicted by the heat, they soon drank up the contents of their canteens. The Germans, given time to settle in and improve their entrenchments—and fed on freshly made sausages distributed by the Schutztruppe butcher, Grabow—only grew more determined. Checking and rechecking their sights, the snipers waited in the trees.

At last, just before three p.m., an *askari* runner found von Lettow at operational HQ, fiendishly smoking his cigarettes. *"Adui tayari,"* the *askari* reported calmly. (The enemy is ready.) "Those two short words," von Lettow later wrote, "I shall never forget."

The British-Indian regiments began to advance in staggered ranks from the direction of Ras Kasone toward the German lines along the railroad cutting and farther east. Their attack formation might have been something out of the Crimean War, a frontal assault on entrenched positions, not so different from the Charge of the Light Brigade into Russian guns at Balaclava or the Highland Brigade's advance on entrenched positions at the Battle of the Alma in 1854. In the day of bayonets and muscle, such an attack might very well have prevailed. But in this new World War, the Maxim gun ruled and even ranks of men were easily mowed down with a few short bursts. Meinertzhagen found the British formation an absurd anachronism, which reminded him of "days long past."

Even the British government's *Official History* describes Aitken's battle plan uncharitably, "founded on an infantry drill and tactics not yet modified by fresh war experience." Translation from official British underspeak: a disaster brought on by the sclerotic military brain of a general who'd never fought a real battle. Worse, Aitken refused to allow for the customary "softening up" of the enemy via bombardment from the *Fox's* potent naval guns. He also refused to allow his sole artillery unit, the highly regarded 28th Mountain Battery, to land their guns and join the fight. In his desire to preserve the infrastructure of the town, Aitken allied himself unwittingly with Governor Schnee. And thus "unsoftened," the Germans awaited first contact in their neatly made trenches and brush redoubts.

Advancing British troops inched over the uneven terrain dense with growth between the rubber trees. The heat grew ever more intense; the parched regiments, some soldiers nearly delirious with thirst, began to break out of formation. Many lost contact with their officers, became entangled in the shrubbery, and crashed into each other: "In the dense, steamy rubber plantation it was hard to keep touch," wrote a battalion historian. "Consequently, the advance was slow; the whole force broke into open order or small columns, thus adding to the difficulty of control."

The weather shifted abruptly as it will in the tropics and rain suddenly came down in sheets. But the rain didn't cool; rather it engendered a steamy, moist heat unlike anything most of the advancing units had experienced, even in India. Now both brigades—Wapshare's as yet untested Imperial Service Brigade and Tighe's 27th Bangalore, still shaken by the rout of the previous evening—advanced together. Wapshare's ISB included the 63rd Palamcottah Light Infantry—said to have suffered more than most on the difficult voyage—and the 101st Grenadiers, both backed by the resolute Loyal North Lancs. They crossed through a field of maize on the German right—the damp stalks, taller than a man, rustling wetly as they passed through—harried by accurate German sniper fire from the baobab trees. Many fell with a cry and a crash in the corn and never rose again.

At last, they emerged onto a dirt road—leading on their right to the

German hospital and the sea, on their left through fields and into thick bush—running parallel to the Schutztruppe's entrenched positions, visible in the near distance. They crossed the road, the sun again blazing overhead. Three hundred yards of open ground lay before them; beyond that, the enemy. As the vanguard of Wapshare's ISB advanced across this open ground and into the sun, the Germans opened fire all at once, up and down the line. First came the chatter of the Schutztruppe's carefully positioned machine guns; a moment later, the *askaris'* booming M71 rifles, each soldier taking careful aim, each shot releasing hellish-looking clouds of billowing black smoke.

The effect of this sudden and relentless fusillade was instantaneous. The 63rd Palamcottah holding the center of the British advance faltered and, as the *Official History* puts it, "began to disintegrate." Those who didn't fall in the first thirty seconds threw down their rifles and began to run back toward the rubber trees, heedless of their British officers who desperately tried to stem the hysterical retreat. Meinertzhagen, on his obsessively precise maps of the action that day, renders the fleeing Madrassi troops as a series of tiny dots with arrows pointing toward the Indian Ocean, implying they would have swum home had it been within their powers to do so. His laconic notation records the time of this flight as "ten minutes after action commenced."

Panic is contagious. The 13th Rajputs and the 61st Pioneers following in the second wave now joined the general rout. Astonished, Meinertzhagen says he watched from nearby: "I could not believe my eyes," he wrote. "It was demoralizing. We collected most of them, made them lie down and keep quiet . . . but they were all gibbering and were not in it for any price. Individuals were shooting off their rifles in any direction and many of the men were firing at our advancing troops. . . . Nothing short of violence will stop this sort of thing. I had to use my boots and pistol to stop it."

Even so, the 101st Indian Grenadiers and the Loyal North Lancs continued to advance bravely in the face of the German fire, though unsupported by the regiments behind them. By this time, von Lettow had abandoned his headquarters—leaving Tom von Prince and his Schutzenkompanies to defend Tanga—and roamed up and down the line encouraging the troops and exposing himself to enemy fire, smoke from his cigarettes nearly as dense

as the clouds issuing from the *askaris'* antiquated rifles. Reaching the western end of the German positions, opposite the now-blood-soaked field of
maize, he saw to his astonishment that Aitken's battle plan indeed belonged
to another century: A straightforward frontal assault without any supporting flanking movement.

"Here, the counter-stroke would prove annihilating," he later wrote. He
gave the command to fire with devastating results. "No witness will forget
the moment when the machine guns of the 13th FK opened up a continuous
fire. . . . The enemy fled in wild disorder. Our machine guns converging on
them from front and flank mowed down whole companies to the last man."
The 101st Grenadiers had struggled out of the maize and were now within
striking distance of the German entrenchments, but moments later, "the
battalion had ceased to exist."

All the dots on Meinertzhagen's battle map at four thirty p.m.—that is,
the Indian troops of the 101st Grenadiers, the 63rd Palamcottahs, the 98th
Indian Infantry, and the 3rd Gwalior Rifles—now in full flight toward the
beachhead at Ras Kasone, were visited by another terror that soon became
legendary: African honeybees, far more venomous than their European
cousins, descended upon them in dense, stinging clouds. The beekeepers of
Tanga cultivated these unusually aggressive bees for the copious amounts
of honey they produced, but wisely kept them far off the ground in nests
made from wooden kegs suspended via ropes and pulleys in the very highest branches of the trees. Now thousands of pissed-off bees descended from
these aeries like a tiny air force, stinging and tormenting the fleeing Indians.
One sergeant later had 300 stingers removed from his head; an officer of the
Loyal North Lancs, knocked out by a German bullet to the face, was stung
back to consciousness by the bees and joined the rout, thus saving himself
from an *askari* counterattack.

For years afterward it was supposed that the stinging bees of Tanga had
been a German secret weapon, their wooden keg hives dropped on fleeing
British troops like barrel bombs—and in fact, the use of weaponized bees
in war was not unheard-of: Richard the Lionheart had catapulted angry
hives over the battlements of Acre during the siege of that city in 1191. But
von Lettow eventually put the lie to this colorful rumor. The bees, disturbed
by the commotion of battle, had attacked both British and German troops

alike, he admitted. They had even incapacitated four German machine gun companies fighting with the 13th FK.

The bloody afternoon waned. The smell of corpses already bloating in the heat hung over the battlefield. The British left had suffered a complete rout. But on the right, close to the harbor, a different battle began to unfold: The Gurkhas of the 2nd Kashmir Rifles, along with the 2nd Company of Rajputs and the hard-fighting Loyal North Lancs, fought their way across the railway cutting and into the town. The Gurkhas invaded the Kaiserhof Hotel, tore down the German flag suspended from the second-floor gallery, and installed the Union Jack in its place.

Askari machine-gun fire from emplacements installed on rooftops opened up on the invading Indians; Schutzenkompanie rifles protruding from every window joined the din. A classic street fight ensued. Gurkhas and Loyal North Lancs fought from doorways and behind trees. Determined to avenge the humiliation experienced by the Rajputs on the previous day's action, they refused to give ground. For the course of one hour, the battle seemed to sway toward the British. Aitken, at last persuaded by his subordinates, ordered *Fox* to bombard the town—too late. Battle lines in Tanga were now hopelessly intertwined. British and German troops fought at close quarters, often hand-to-hand in the center of town, and naval shells are no respecters of national identity. Most of them landed among British troops. One blew a hole in the roof of the German hospital where Schutztruppe doctors tended to the wounded of both sides.

Still, the British pressed forward and Tanga might yet have been taken. At a pivotal moment, more than a dozen *askaris* under the command of Captain von Hammerstein panicked and abandoned their position under heavy enemy fire. Von Hammerstein, the previous night's burned cork still darkening his pale German complexion, jumped out of the entrenchment to rally his men. Swearing, he hurled an empty beer bottle after them—a lucky hit—it bounced off an *askari*'s head. This soldier reeled around, rubbing his bruised scalp. Something about von Hammerstein done up in blackface like a vaudeville performer, shouting curses and throwing beer bottles as gunfire exploded all around him, struck the *askari* as very funny. He roared with laughter. This sound brought the other *askaris* back to the line just as von Prince rushed up with his German riflemen to stiffen their resistance.

The dangerous moment passed; the sun began to drop in the west, over the ocean. The unsupported Lancs retreated, moving backward in the gloom, firing as they went. Soon, Tanga was left to von Prince's men and von Hammerstein's *askaris*. The British assault on the town had failed. A vacillating Aitken at last ordered a general retreat to the British positions hastily established not far from the original beachhead on the Ras Kasone Peninsula. Von Lettow's Schutztruppe had won the day—but at a cost. His great friend Tom von Prince, the fearless *Bwana Sakharani*, one of the founders of the colony, had fallen, shot in the head in the very last moments of the street fight for Tanga. His was an absence von Lettow would feel keenly throughout the length of the war in Africa.

As night fell darkly around them, the Germans consolidated their hold on the town and most of the surrounding countryside. Triumphant *askaris* brought in many Indian prisoners. Many more wounded were delivered to the overburdened German hospital. Except for the bit at the top of Ras Kasone and the white house where Aitken now met with his subordinates, all else remained in German hands. The mood at the British powwow was at once contentious and subdued. Everyone present knew the battle had been lost; most refused to admit it. Meinertzhagen claims he agitated for a night attack beneath the risen moon; the Lancs eager to get back into Tanga were also eager to attack. Officers and generals debated heatedly. Some shouted; others sulked.

There then occurred one of those strange accidents that might have put Tanga squarely in British hands within the hour: An *askari* bugler blew a call from somewhere within the town. Aitken, alarmed, thought it was the signal for a German counterattack on the British lines at Ras Kasone; meanwhile, the Germans occupying Tanga heard it as the signal for retreat. According to Meinertzhagen, who had lived in a German garrison town for six months before the war, the bugler had indeed blown the retreat—a nearly fatal mistake: Schutztruppe *askaris* quickly abandoned their positions and withdrew to their camp at the coconut grove. Meinertzhagen urged Aitken to reinvest the town. Unbeknownst to both of them, it now lay abandoned in the moonlight, its streets empty, its trenches unmanned. The British might have waltzed in and taken the town without a shot. They did not.

"I begged him to allow us to collect what we could and go forward," Meinertzhagen wrote. "But . . . he was tired and seemed disgusted with the whole business. His one ambition seemed to be to get away."

But perhaps Aitken knew that his demoralized and poorly trained Indian troops were not up to the task and would have been unable to deal with the inevitable German counterattack. Now the disconsolate major general ordered Expeditionary Force B to re-embark. They were leaving German East Africa to the Germans. The invasion had been a total failure.

At dawn, von Lettow moved his Schutztruppe back into Tanga and reoccupied their positions of the previous day. They fortified the entrenchments and waited for the next British attack. But the attack did not come. Puzzled, von Lettow again approached the harbor on his bicycle—and could hardly believe what he saw: British troops clustered disconsolate on the waterfront and on the shore, waiting for lighters to take them back to the transports. Had the Schutztruppe any fieldpieces—the three 1870 vintage brass cannons still hadn't materialized—von Lettow might have inflicted huge casualties. The day was overcast and heavy with rain. It rained off and on as the British scrambled into the lighters, abandoning munitions and guns and other supplies on the beaches. At last, von Lettow organized burial parties to clear the battlefield of the now-putrefying dead; those few wounded who had lain exposed all night still alive were taken to the hospital, though most of these did not survive.

He now realized—though he still couldn't quite believe it—that the battle had been a great victory for the Kaiser, perhaps one of the greatest the war would see. The Schutztruppe, outnumbered eight to one and armed with inadequate and outdated weapons, had won the day. Incredibly, they had inflicted more casualties on the invading British force than there were soldiers in the entire Schutztruppe.

At five p.m., Major General Aitken sent Meinertzhagen ashore under a white flag to negotiate a cease-fire. He found von Lettow in an expansive mood: The German commander offered to repatriate all Force B captured and wounded, provided they gave their parole not to fight against Germany in Africa for the duration. This was a magnanimous gesture, more reminiscent of the courtly eighteenth-century wars of Frederick the Great fought by his ancestors than the current, bitter world conflict.

More British officers came ashore to help organize transport for the wounded, including Lieutenant Charlewood of the *Helmuth*, who was treated to a civilized dinner in the German officers' mess at the Kaiserhoff Hotel: "Several German officers came up and one of them addressed me in English," Charlewood recalled. "He astonished us by inviting us to supper. . . . Of all supper parties in my experience, this was the strangest. The food, which comprised soup, fish, and steak, all out of tins, was well cooked and the conversation astonishingly bright. The Germans said they thought the war would be soon over because they expected the French to give in, and then, of course, it would be useless for Britain to continue the struggle."

Charlewood declined to comment.

Other British officers then came ashore under a flag of truce—including the quartermaster general, a man named Dobbs, who began toting up all the supplies Aitken had ordered abandoned on the beaches. These included "twelve machine guns, field telephone equipment, hundreds of rifles, 600,000 rounds of ammunition, and coats and blankets enough to last them for the rest of the war." Another group of officers, taking advantage of the cease-fire, but with no official permission, came ashore in a lighter to enjoy a swim at the beach. Captain von Hammerstein, who had by now washed his face, expressed his amazement at this behavior to Meinertzhagen:

"You English are really quite incomprehensible and appear to regard war as a sport," he protested. "If they do not go back at once, I shall have to order my men to fire on them."

With some difficulty, Meinertzhagen persuaded the swimming officers to return to their ship.

On the night of November 6, the Force B flotilla sailed for Mombasa. In addition to the weapons and supplies, they left behind 800 dead and 500 more too wounded to transport, and hundreds of MIA. Von Lettow had lost fifteen European officers and fifty-four *askaris*—though among the former, he considered Tom von Prince irreplaceable.

Unbeknownst to Major General Aitken at the time—he had already, perhaps, returned to his novel reading—Expeditionary Force C under Brigadier General Stewart had also been defeated by Major Kraut at Longido and driven back across the border into British East Africa. With this loss, the first phase of the British invasion of German East Africa must be counted a debacle on all fronts. The Battle of Tanga, later described officially as "one of the most notable failures in British military history," was one for the record books: "A setback on a small scale perhaps," later commented the director of military operations at the War Office in London, "but as decided a one as we met with during the war."

As for Oberstleutnant von Lettow, the successful defense of Tanga both secured his authority and cemented his military reputation. Though the German public did not learn of von Lettow's victory until January, the colony now rallied behind him with unalloyed enthusiasm. Schnee and his dreams of neutrality would no longer stand in the way of a proper military response to British aggression. Von Lettow knew the war ahead would be long and bitter, and that the British would return with overwhelming numbers in the end—but at Tanga he had gained something invaluable: "The morale of the force and its confidence in its leaders had enormously increased," he wrote. "And at one blow I was delivered from a great part of the difficulties which so greatly impeded the conduct of operations." More particularly, "The continuous fire . . . had lost its terrors for our brave blacks."

He buried Tom von Prince and the other European dead beneath a spreading buyu tree and raised a memorial tablet inscribed only with their names. Then he allowed himself a small moment of triumph, and celebrated with beer and cigarettes amid the hearty congratulations of his men.

Chapter 15

WAR ON THE RUFIJI

Fairy lights, bonfires, strange flags, and domestic linens (bedsheets, shirts) fluttering pale against the dark bush followed HMS *Chatham*'s progress for miles down the Swahili Coast. Drury-Lowe, *Chatham*'s grimly determined captain, was reminded of a *feu de joie* (a parade-ground display of military pyrotechnics) as he watched this mysterious display from the bridge of his ship. Though to him, its meaning held no mystery: German spotters, hiding in the bush, were using an arcane signaling system to relay the relative position of *Chatham* and her sister ships in the Destroy *Königsberg* Squadron to wireless stations inland and thence to Loof aboard *Königsberg*. The squadron now included HMS *Dartmouth* and *Weymouth*—the first detached from a vital role as a troop-ship escort, the second seconded from the British Mediterranean Fleet—as well as a small flotilla of colliers and fast steam cutters designed to navigate shallow estuaries.

Drury-Lowe was sure *Königsberg* lurked in a secluded inlet somewhere nearby, between Dar es Salaam and the border of Portuguese East Africa. He knew the German cruiser's relatively shallow draft allowed her passage up rivers and tidal backwaters where the heavier British battleships could not follow. This slice of the Swahili Coast was *Chatham*'s beat. *Dartmouth* and *Weymouth* now patrolled the 1,000-mile-long run of the Mozambique Channel. Between the three of them, surely, *Königsberg* could not escape detection. The "*feu de joie*," however, indicated to Drury-Lowe that now *Königsberg* wasn't far off. All signs seemed to point to a hiding place between

Lindi, German East Africa's southernmost port, and Mafia Island, opposite the mouths of the Rufiji River.

The Rufiji Delta—a swampy green hell of intense heat, crocodiles, mosquitoes, more mosquitoes, tiny fanged monkeys, snakes, and other unpleasant creatures—was thought to be more or less unnavigable to a battleship of *Königsberg*'s size—but maybe not. The British Admiralty didn't know the Rufiji well. It had just been charted by the German survey ship *Möwe*, in the months before the outbreak of war. The new German charts—making use of *Möwe*'s data—taken off the *Präsident* had finally been examined by *Chatham*'s naval intelligence officers and compared with the diary of the captured German spotter: The *Präsident* had apparently been loading lighters with coal and supplies and sending them to a place called Salale, five miles up the Rufiji. Accurately described as a "forbidding cesspool," the Rufiji Delta divided itself into four main channels—Kikunja, Simba-Uranga, Sumninga, and Kiomali—all interconnected by a labyrinth of creeks and rivulets and debouching into the sea opposite Mafia Island, itself separated from the mainland by a skirt of smaller islands, uncharted coral reefs, and shoals. The perfect hideout for a shallow-draft battleship seeking to avoid detection.

But Drury-Lowe had to be sure before he summoned the rest of his squadron from patrol farther south. Meanwhile, dozens of false *Königsberg* sightings kept pouring in, some of them planted by von Lettow's agents in Zanzibar: She had been seen skulking about the distant Comoros; she had fired rockets off Dar es Salaam, making bright, provocative splashes in the night sky; she had filled her bunkers at dusk in Jeddah on the Yemeni coast and the next day basked in the sunlight a few miles out from Porto Amelia, Portuguese East Africa. Her searchlights, like the eyes of a giant sea monster, had been spotted hunting for prey off Mombasa after midnight. Drury-Lowe, a hardheaded and thoughtful officer, chose to disbelieve these fantastical rumors.

He followed his *feu de joie* display to the Rufiji and anchored *Chatham* five miles offshore in the lee of Mafia Island, held by a small garrison of German troops. Drury-Lowe anticipated British occupation of this island soon—it would make a nice land base for naval operations—but not yet. Now he launched his steam cutters through the reefy shallows to a wide beach at the mouth of the Simba-Uranga. From here a landing party cut through the thick bush until they came to a fishermen's village. There, the men convinced the village *jumbee*, or headman, and his associates at gunpoint to accompany them back to *Chatham*.

However coerced, once aboard, the Africans were treated royally, wellfed on navy beans and salt pork and gotten drunk on navy grog. At last, the ship's intelligence officers settled in for the interrogation, conducted in pidgin Swahili and sign language—but it didn't take long. The *jumbee* and his men, living in the almost total isolation of the Rufiji, couldn't see much difference between Germans and Englishmen and readily answered all questions put to them: Yes, the *"manowari na bomba tatu"* was now up the Rufiji, at a place called Salale, along with a smaller ship—the collier *Somali*, as it turned out—and several small tenders. For Drury-Lowe, this news was both good and bad: He had probably found the *Königsberg*. But Salale could not be reached by *Chatham*—not only because the river wouldn't permit the passage of so large a ship, but also because the Germans had fortified every approach with machine gun posts, rifle pits, and gun emplacements for *Königsberg*'s secondary 47mm artillery. All of this, hung with field telephone wires, was joined by a system of trenches manned by "Delta Force," a small, determined army of marines and sailors off the battle cruiser, and a contingent of Schutztruppe officers and underofficers. Any British incursion up the Simba-Uranga would run into a bitter storm of expertly coordinated fire.

The *jumbee* and his men were thanked for the information they provided and sent back to their village. But their testimony was still not the definitive proof Drury-Lowe had hoped for. After all, a native drunk on navy grog was apt to say anything. *Chatham* lingered uncertainly in the lee of Mafia Island for a few more days while Drury-Lowe considered his options. At last, taking advantage of the monthly high tide, he ran his ship as close as he dared to the mangrove-fringed shore to give his lookouts a better view of the delta, though *Chatham* couldn't come any closer than two miles before scraping bottom. A lookout then climbed her highest mast with powerful binoculars. He saw nothing for long minutes, then noticed something odd: One of the tallest trees in the jungle seemed to be moving. After intense scrutiny, the lookout was able to descry *Königsberg*'s masts about five miles away, artfully camouflaged with jungle greenery.

At last, the German cruiser had been caught, trapped like a rat in a cesspool. Drury-Lowe, it is to be imagined, cut a small jig on the bridge when apprised of the news. He now hoped to sink the trapped *Königsberg* with shells from his six-inch naval guns—revenge for the incapacitated *Pegasus* sunk at Zanzibar. His elation, however, soon darkened: *Königsberg* lay at least 14,800 yards away, up a sinuous and winding creek, protected by a dense tangle of wilderness and the entrenched Maxims of Delta Force. *Chatham*'s big guns could only reach a target at 14,500 yards, 300 yards short; still, Drury-Lowe decided to try. He ordered all ship's ballast shifted in the hold—an operation that took half a day—until *Chatham* listed at five degrees. This, he reasoned, might give her guns a higher trajectory and thus a longer range. With the lookout in the masthead acting as an artillery spotter, *Chatham* let go with her first salvo—a huge boom, the ensuing concussion, the ship rocking back dangerously—to no avail. *Chatham*'s shells fell short, doing rather more damage to British objectives than to the Germans, destroying a few trees and the element of surprise.

Another salvo. The explosion echoed through the jungle; palm trees, flung in the air by the blast, crashed down as if cut by a giant scythe; chunks of wood the size of men shattered over the creeks and byways of the delta. Loof and his crew, though comfortably beyond the reach of *Chatham*'s shells, now knew they had been found by the enemy. It was November 4, 1914. That very day 100 miles or so to the north, unbeknownst to both Drury-Lowe and Loof, von Lettow was winning his lopsided victory at Tanga.

For Captain Loof, discovery by the British couldn't have come at a worse time. The *Königsberg*, it will be recalled, had been forced into the torpid maw of the Rufiji by her dangerously furred boilers and a critical lack of coal. This necessary refuge had been chosen in lieu of a shipyard in which they might refuel and make repairs—the nearest, Dar es Salaam, rendered inaccessible by blockading British warships and the sunken floating dock. In the weeks leading up to her discovery, *Königsberg*'s bunkers had been filled by the *Somali* and other vessels bringing supplies over the bar and by teams of porters converging on her hiding place from points inland. But the furry boilers remained a problem. They were so badly coked up from the use of inferior Natal coal as to be completely useless. Only disassembly, repair, and refitment could render them—and the *Königsberg*—serviceable again.

Loof had pondered *Königsberg*'s predicament throughout the long, humid jungle nights. The stagnant air around the stranded ship pressed close, thick with the sounds of a million insects, as the British gradually closed in. Loof knew about *Chatham*'s approach, kept well-informed by his spotters and their system of bedsheet codes. He knew *Königsberg* would be found sooner or later and bottled up in her dank, malarial hideout. His goal was to join the Kreuzerkrieg—Germany's overarching naval strategy—which directed squadrons of fast, heavily armed cruisers like *Königsberg* in predatory hit-and-run attacks on Allied shipping all over the world. Loof wanted to get in on this action. To him, and to every other German military strategist, the struggle in East Africa seemed a minor distraction. (In late 1914 perhaps only von Lettow understood the African war's potential as a significant drain on Allied men and resources.)

But to join the greater war, Loof needed to repair his ailing boilers, an operation beyond the capacity of Salale's simple jungle workshops. For a few weeks, as Loof's men attempted the repairs, and swabbed the decks and reswabbed them and polished everything that needed polishing and did it all over again, it seemed *Königsberg* might rot in her fetid anchorage. Malaria, a far deadlier enemy than the British, had already attacked the crew, with over fifty cases. Accidents also took their toll: One sailor, suspended over the side to paint the hull, was attacked by a crocodile. Leg bitten off at the knee, he soon died from the unanticipated amputation. How long could *Königsberg* linger in this green hell? Her crew, though kept active by Loof's regime of spit-and-polish maintenance, soon began to feel the effects of sagging morale and monotonous diet. Hunting parties were organized for diversion and fresh meat. Loof himself brought down a hippopotamus—prized for the pleasant taste of its lard—with the new 9mm rifle he'd had specially made in Germany for African big game hunting. To his chagrin, he discovered the hippo, a nursing mother, had left a calf behind. He had the tiny hippo brought aboard *Königsberg*, and though the men made a pet of it and fed it as best they could on beer and canned milk, the sad little creature soon died.

At last, one of Loof's subordinates, Lieutenant Commander Werner Schönfeld, proposed a solution to *Königsberg*'s predicament. If the ship couldn't come to the shipyard in Dar es Salaam, perhaps her boilers might be dismantled and brought overland to the capital. There, they could be repaired carefully before being hauled back again and reinstalled. The sheer labor required by such an operation at first seemed insurmountable. Dar es Salaam lay more than 100 miles away, through trackless forest and swamp and over numerous rivers uncrossed by any bridge.

But Schönfeld had managed plantations in the Rufiji District before the war, knew its terrain, and still had many friends among local German planters. He now applied to these for the labor and timber to build two giant sledges that were then hauled by 1,000 Africans to Salale. Here the *Königsberg*'s damaged boilers, having been disassembled into their component parts (giant steel plates each weighing several tons), were lifted from the hold by brute force and lowered onto the sledges. Then the African laborers hauled the sledges off into the jungle in the general direction of Dar es Salaam. Was it thus, Korvettenkapitän Loof wondered, watching his ship's precious viscera disappear into the greenery, that slaves had hauled the building blocks of the pyramids across the Egyptian desert 4,000 years ago? For nearly an hour afterward, the rhythmic, throaty chanting of the Africans—*"Harambee!"* (Heave!) *"Harambee!"*—could be heard echoing through the still, hot afternoon.

The laborers, forced to hack a new road through the jungle, had a hell of a time going: Tow ropes often snapped with a sound alarmingly like a rifle shot; at this, everyone hit the ground with shouts of alarm. The sledges sank with wearying regularity into the soft muck of the delta; saplings had to be felled to pry them loose again. On downward slopes they often went awry, crashing uncontrollably into the underbrush. Primitive bridges thrown over the many streams between Salale and Dar es Salaam nearly collapsed as the sledges groaned over them. Though the going got a little easier when the laborers left the jungle behind, the dry landscape wasn't much easier on them, with potable water difficult to find and the sun burning overhead. Even here the sledges moved along at an insect's crawl.

At last, after three weeks of Herculean toil, the boilers bumped the final few feet into the Dar es Salaam shipyards, beneath the scrutiny of amazed crowds of bystanders. Work began immediately, and proceeded day and night for several days. The laborers, barely recuperated from their efforts on the outward journey, too soon picked up the ropes again for the journey back. This, over a track already hacked out of the bush, took half as much time—all in vain. The sledges bearing *Königsberg*'s private parts arrived at Salale just two days too late: *Chatham*'s lookout spotted *Königsberg*'s camouflaged masts the day after her boilers had been reinstalled. Tested, they were found to be running like new, but Loof's hopes for a quick escape down the Simba-Uranga channel, over the bar, and thence back to Germany to join the commerce raiders of the Kreuzerkreig fell to pieces in the moments after *Chatham* fired her first salvo.

Now *Königsberg* would have to fight her way out, 10.5cm heavy guns blasting all the way. But, even in top shape and with every shell hitting its mark, she would have a poor chance against the combined firepower of *Chatham*, *Dartmouth*, and *Weymouth*, the latter two warships summoned from points south to join the death watch on the Rufiji. In fact, *Chatham*'s salvo had sounded the beginning of the longest naval battle in military history, between Drury-Lowe's Destroy *Königsberg* Squadron—later commandeered by Admiral King-Hall—and *Königsberg* and Delta Force, with Loof in command. Eight and a half months would pass between first and last shots fired—255 days filled with schemes and counterschemes, countless minor skirmishes, and the use of an amazing new technology: the airplane.

Captain Drury-Lowe, frustrated by *Chatham*'s inability to engage the enemy, wired GHQ in Nairobi for backup. The navy alone couldn't capture or sink *Königsberg*, he argued, and proposed a joint army-navy sea-land operation: Troops would be put ashore on the delta while fast steam cutters would forge up the channels; between them, they would destroy *Königsberg* in her secret lair—though now even her camouflaged masts had disappeared from view. She had no doubt burrowed even farther up the inaccessible reaches of the Rufiji.

Brigadier General Wapshare quickly vetoed this plan. Following the disaster at Tanga, Wapshare had been put in charge of the land war in East Africa. Major General Aitken, rightfully deemed the architect of Britain's humiliating loss, had been sacked by an irate Lord Kitchener, England's chief warlord. Only Aitken's brother's influence spared the erstwhile major general—reduced in rank to colonel and placed on half pay—the disgrace of a court-martial. Tanga now colored every aspect of British military strategy. Wapshare wasn't about to sanction any operation using the raw, poorly trained Indian troops at his disposal. He had learned at Tanga, to his sorrow, that von Lettow's Schutztruppe had become one of the most disciplined and expertly led armies in Africa.

"I am decidedly of the opinion that the project of cutting out the *Königsberg* from the sea is impracticable from a military point of view," Wapshare wrote to Drury-Lowe. "The ship is twelve to fifteen miles up the river, the delta is most intricate with many islands and swamps and with roads known only to the enemy. There is sea-water right up to her—drinking water is only obtainable from wells, situation unknown, which could be easily damaged. . . . The climate is very bad. The foreshore is strongly held with many Maxims. . . . Whilst owing to the reefs, the warships cannot materially support a landing; and surprise is impossible. The water approaches may be mined and the whole area is covered by *Königsberg*'s guns. The operation would probably last a considerable time, and the Germans can be heavily reinforced from the Central Railway in four or five days. . . . I consider that were this proposal to cut out the *Königsberg* attempted, it would probably end in failure, if not worse."

In other words, Drury-Lowe could expect no help from the army in his personal vendetta against *Königsberg*. This vendetta, shared by Admiral King-Hall—who had let *Königsberg* escape from Dar es Salaam in the first place back in July—had also been taken up by the brass at the Admiralty back in London. First Sea Lord Winston Churchill, particularly obsessed, now deemed her destruction "a matter of the highest importance." Churchill decided that if they could not yet devise a way to kill *Königsberg* with a British battleship, they still might "block her in" completely. To this end, an ancient merchantman, the *Newbridge*, was found in the harbor at Zanzibar, loaded down with rocks and dynamite, and towed 150 nautical miles to the Rufiji. There she would be sunk in the Simba-Uranga Channel, down which—Drury-Lowe had rightly guessed—lay *Königsberg*'s most likely route to freedom on the high seas. This operation, so dangerous as to be nearly suicidal, would be attempted in the face of withering cross fire from Delta Force, occupying both banks of the channel. But when Drury-Lowe called for volunteers, *Chatham*'s entire crew offered to make the sacrifice. From among these brave men, Drury-Lowe chose fourteen, whom, he admitted, he "hardly ever expected to see again."

These volunteers manned *Newbridge*, her wheelhouse now shielded in inch-thick steel plate. Just before dawn on November 10, 1914, followed at a distance by the armed tug, *Duplex*, and several small, fast steam cutters, she nosed her way up the mouth of the Simba-Uranga. Of course, the sailors and marines of Delta Force were not caught napping: They opened up from the shore with a pitiless barrage of Maxim fire, supported by *Königsberg*'s small artillery, well concealed in the bush. Waterspouts caused by the expenditure of all this ordnance nearly hid *Newbridge* from view as her temporary captain, Commander Raymond Fitzmaurice, maneuvered to an anchorage astride the main channel. He calmly ordered "Stop engines" and dropped anchor as if *Newbridge* were coming home to a cozy berth in some placid English port. But his next order—"Abandon ship!"—sent *Newbridge*'s skeleton crew scrambling for the *Duplex* hove-to alongside. The *Duplex* withdrew, zigzagging across open water beneath a storm of steel from the German guns—but not before Fitzmaurice had a chance to remote-detonate the charges in *Newbridge*'s hold. The merchantman shook with a muffled explosion, burped up a giant bubble of oily water, and sank nicely in the middle of the channel.

Newbridge's heroic crew made it back aboard *Chatham* with two killed by German shrapnel and nine badly cut up. Drury-Lowe, who had been expecting a far higher body count, pronounced the operation a complete success. He radioed the outcome back to the Admiralty in London, who then issued an overly optimistic communiqué describing the action, extolling the sacrifice of the sailors off *Chatham*, and stating with certainty that *Königsberg* "was now imprisoned and unable to do more damage." They were wrong. The operation had been a failure. The Simba-Uranga Channel was wider and deeper than supposed and *Newbridge*'s corpse had failed to block the main channel at all. At high tide, *Königsberg* would still be able to slip out of the river and head out to sea. But, distracted by events

General von Lettow-Vorbeck, in retirement after the war.

Von Lettow-Vorbeck (*second from right*) relaxes with friends at Neu Moshi in 1914.

All photos courtesy of the author unless otherwise indicated.

Major Kraut, von Lettow-Vorbeck's second-in-command.

Richard Meinertzhagen, British officer, polymath, and colossal fraud.
Courtesy of Dr. Theresa Clay

The wreck of SMS *Königsberg.*
Courtesy of Bundesarchiv Koblenz

Transporting one of the *Königsberg*'s guns up-country.

A German machine-gun nest.

Askari warriors in camouflage.

Major Kraut leads a troop column.

The Nigerian Brigade on the Rufiji River in December 1916.

Askaris marching across Portuguese East Africa.
Courtesy of Bundesarchiv Koblenz

German supplies had to be carried across the *pori*.

Another lookout post, this one on the slopes of Mount Kilimanjaro.

Native beehives at Tanga. The aggressive African bees within
played an important part in defeating the British attack.

The Germans kept pet pelicans at Bukoba.
They refused to leave and were blown up with the fort.

Although slightly smaller than the super Zeppelin *L59*,
this view of *L53* gives a good look at the rear section of a German airship.
Courtesy of Luftschiffbau Zeppelin

elsewhere, Drury-Lowe and his masters in London discounted this possibility. News of German Admiral von Spee's victory over the British fleet at Coronel off the coast of Chile on All Souls' Day had just reached the Admiralty and once again *Dartmouth* and *Weymouth*, detached from the Destroy *Königsberg* Squadron, steamed south to join Admiral King-Hall's Cape Squadron, now momentarily expecting an attack from von Spee. Von Spee's East Asia Squadron of five battle cruisers and three supply ships had been spotted heading around the Horn, their goal, reportedly, to engage King-Hall's ships and bombard Cape Town. But King-Hall waited for an attack that never came. Not long after Coronel, von Spee was surprised in the middle of an attack on the Falklands Naval Station by eight heavy British battle cruisers under Vice Admiral Sir Frederick Sturdee. A vicious naval battle ensued on December 8, 1914. Outgunned and outmaneuvered, von Spee's entire squadron went down, including his flagship, SMS *Scharnhorst*, lost with all hands. The admiral's two sons, serving aboard sister ships, also perished, alongside 1,871 German sailors.

With this extinguishment of the German naval threat on the high seas, Admiral King-Hall once again turned his attention back to *Königsberg*. After the *Newbridge* incident, Drury-Lowe seemed to be sitting on his thumbs. For all he knew, the Rufiji's other major channels might be navigable by *Königsberg*; the German battle cruiser could still break out of her hiding place and must be destroyed once and for all. To this end, King-Hall conferred with Drury-Lowe and came up with a solution, daring in its novelty: If they could not reach *Königsberg* by land or by sea, perhaps they could reach her by air. Bombs dropped from an airplane might actually sink the German beast; they just needed to find her first. Thus was born Equatorial Africa's first Naval Air Service, though it lacked, as yet, the one essential component for such a service—an airplane. In fact, as far as anyone knew, none existed in all of Africa.

Admiral King-Hall, something of a homunculus at just over five feet tall and the self-described "ugliest man in the British Navy," was also one of its most determined. He began his search in the Cape Colony and soon found an aviator, complete with his own machine: an adventurous, affable barnstorming aviator named Herbert Dennis Cutler, who happened to be in possession of the Royal Flying Club's 189th-issued pilot's license and an airplane. King-Hall tracked down Cutler in Durban. The aviator earned a meager living making exhibition flights with his single-engine, American-made Curtis "flying boat" hydroplane—probably the primitive Model D, little more than a motorized kite with fabric-covered wings stiffened by wire struts. The pilot sat in a wicker seat fixed at the edge of the bottom wing with his feet practically dangling in the water and directly in front of the single rear engine, which "pushed" the plane through the air. Pontoons, substituted for wheels, transformed this entirely unsuitable aircraft into a "seaplane."

King-Hall bought Cutler's Curtis and offered him a commission in the Royal Navy Reserve. Cutler, tired of living on peanuts and tips, readily agreed. They loaded the Curtis aboard the *Kinfauns Castle*, a supply ship quickly refitted as a hydroplane tender, and headed north to the Rufiji Delta to join the war effort. No one at the time realized they were making military history: Never before had an aircraft been used in such an action against a naval vessel.

Cutler went up on his first mission a couple of weeks before Christmas 1914—though the homemade gelatin bombs he had brought along proved too heavy for the flight and had to be discarded. His main orders were to find *Königsberg* and return unscathed, but even minus the excess weight of the bombs, the underpowered Curtis could barely climb above the trees. Suddenly, her radiator sprang a leak and after flailing about in a cloud bank for a while, Cutler put down near a small islet, fortunately beyond the reach of German guns. A rescue party in steam launches found him there, calmly getting in a swim. He appeared undisturbed by his near brush with death. Drury-Lowe commented that Cutler, though "an entire novice at observation work," was nevertheless "a good pilot and absolutely without fear."

But Cutler's Curtis, with its radiator busted and unfixable, was now out of commission—rendering, for the moment, Africa's first Naval Air Service a failure. Then a sailor named Gallehawk remembered having seen a Ford truck on the streets of Mombasa. The Curtis hydroplane and the Ford truck shared certain mechanical components (Henry Ford and aviation pioneer David Curtis had been acquaintances), and the sailor speculated that the radiators might be a match. HMS *Fox*, recovering from her ignominious role in the non-bombardment of Tanga and idling in the harbor at Mombasa, received orders via wireless to locate the truck and requisition the radiator. Captain Caulfield dispatched a shore party; truck quickly found, radiator removed, and brought aboard *Fox*, she steamed south to join the Destroy *Königsberg* Squadron. The Ford radiator, though not an exact fit, was easily adapted. Cutler went aloft again in the Curtis—nicknamed "Cuckoo" by the sailors aboard King-Hall's flagship, *Hyacinth*, now leading the action on the Rufiji.

Cutler made three more flights in his winged death trap—later described by aviation historian H. A. Jones as one of the most "striking incidents in the history of naval aircraft in the war; there are few which, for quiet gallantry, can beat this story of an underpowered flying boat, patched and repatched . . . operating in monsoon weather from the beach of a tropical island over jungle swamp." On his third attempt, Cutler flew straight up the delta and, banking, spied *Königsberg* basking in a remote bend of the Simba-Uranga, her deck awnings up to shield her busy crew from the deleterious effects of the tropical sun. He turned back to the British flotilla, now assembled off Mafia Island opposite the mouths of the Rufiji. But something happened—a strut snapped or he ran out of gas, or the radiator crapped out again—and Cutler, dropping out of the sky, hit the choppy water at a sharp angle. The Curtis broke up on impact. Cutler himself, using up another one of his nine lives, swam to safety and clambered, grinning, aboard *Hyacinth*.

King-Hall, pleased at the success of Cutler's flight—they had located *Königsberg* at last!—would not be dismayed by the loss of "Cuckoo." Another Curtis hydroplane—this one, most likely the more powerful Model F—turned up in Durban, apparently a hotbed of early African aviation. This second Curtis was supposedly capable of taking two people aloft, a pilot and an observer—though once again, Cutler found added weight diminished the Curtis's performance to the point where it couldn't rise above the tree line. He made several more flights in this contraption, often under fire from Loof's Delta Force. Each time, he observed the *Königsberg* moving farther upstream. On his last flight, the Curtis's overheated, overtaxed engine quit—the hydroplane, designed for the clear lakes of Upstate New York, suffered under tropical conditions. Cutler plummeted toward the jungle, crash-landing in the mouth of the Kikunja Channel. The ubiquitous

Lieutenant Charlewood of the much-shot-up tug *Helmuth* ran his resurrected vessel up the channel beneath a shower of German lead to Cutler's rescue. He managed to get a tow rope on the Curtis, still afloat, and pulled it to safety, but Cutler was not aboard.

The entire squadron mourned Cutler's loss. Speculation had it that the intrepid aviator had fallen from the plane in its spiral toward the Kikunja Channel, or had been eaten by crocodiles, or had been shot out of the cockpit by the sharpshooters of Delta Force. In fact, Cutler had wrestled his Curtis to a relatively gentle landing, swum ashore, and been captured by the Germans. He suffered through the next three years in a German POW camp in the bush. For years, nothing concrete was known about his fate; according to historian Byron Farwell: "his subsequent history, like his prior history, is unknown. He was one of those people who sometimes appear from no one knows where, play their bit part in momentous events, and then return to obscurity."

Not quite. Cutler was a Londoner who had served in the balloon corps in England before the war. Freed in 1917 along with other POWs the Germans could no longer manage to feed, he returned to England and finished the war as a flight instructor. Although not much is known of his private life, he settled in his native London, surviving both the blitz and the birth of rock 'n' roll. He surrendered the last of his lives in 1963; whether he recalled the green hell of the Rufiji and the precarious hours spent aloft searching for *Königsberg* in his final moments is known only to God. His last Curtis, the tattered, exhausted wreck hauled by the *Helmuth* from the murky waters of the Kikunja Channel, could still be seen, until quite recently, in an aviation museum in Durban.

To Admiral King-Hall, Cutler had served his purpose. Cutler's observations had shown that *Königsberg* now lay at the confluence of the Simba-Uranga and Kikunja channels, down either of which she might decide to make her escape. Such an attempt, urged upon Loof by von Lettow, was, however, refused by the latter. Why the doughty sea captain would not make the attempt has long baffled historians of the war, as it did von Lettow himself:

"She had aboard her pilots expert in the ways of the Simba-Uranga, who would have guided Korvettenkapitan Loof past the sunken *Newbridge*," von Lettow later commented. "It is also true that she was short of coal, but she could have replenished her bunkers from the coal brought in by the *Rubens*."

The *Rubens* was a German blockade runner—officially designated *Sperrbrecher A* (Blockade Runner A) but disguised as the Danish merchantman SS *Krönborg*—that had recently made a heroic 1,400-mile journey from Germany, around the Hebrides to the Swahili Coast through radio silence and bad weather all the way. At the last minute, *Rubens* had been caught and sunk by Admiral King-Hall and HMS *Hyacinth* in the shallow waters of Suva Bay, GEA. Thinking *Rubens* finished, Admiral King-Hall steamed away—in what turned out to be one of the greatest mistakes of the war: *Rubens's* crew, mostly Danes from South Jutland, swam ashore with no casualties and would serve for the duration with the Schutztruppe. Meanwhile, salvage operations began almost immediately. Hundreds of rifles, hundreds of thousands of rounds of ammunition, machine guns, and tons of top-quality coal were brought up by divers in an operation that became the "talk of the coast"—all accomplished right under the noses of the British Royal Navy. Nis Kock, author of *Blockade and Jungle*, one of the best memoirs of the East African campaign, was a sailor aboard the *Rubens*.

Now von Lettow offered to bring *Rubens's* salvaged coal to *Königsberg* using a train of native porters, but Loof again demurred. It is about this time that the strong-willed Loof and the stronger-willed von Lettow came to dislike each other. The *Oberstleutnant* suspected Loof's military judgment if not his personal courage. Also, Loof was a good friend and supporter of Governor Heinrich Schnee's, which automatically opposed him to von Lettow. This association colored Loof's view of the military commander, whom he deemed a glory hound. But Loof knew—as von Lettow did not—the near impossibility of maneuvering *Königsberg* down the delta without being found out and destroyed by the blockading British squadron. Such a run would depend on the exact right moment—at dark of moon, at the highest of spring high tides, between the hours of midnight and three a.m.—and also on the British seriously neglecting their duties. Loof, a canny calculator of odds, knew that such a moment—barring impossibly miraculous circumstances—would never come.

Still, von Lettow griped: "It is a waste of manpower and seapower that the last of the German cruisers should allow herself to be immured in the cemetery at Rufiji," he wrote, "when she should be fighting for the Fatherland on the high seas."

For now Loof was content to wait. And in his waiting the stubborn sea captain employed a strategy very much like von Lettow's own: As long as *Königsberg* remained up the Rufiji, the British Navy would be obliged to position several battleships on the Delta Station to prevent her escape. Battleships that might serve the British war effort more profitably elsewhere.

Meanwhile, Admiral King-Hall, harried by hectoring, bellicose cables from First Sea Lord Churchill, grew only more determined to smoke *Königsberg* out of her lair. Cutler's excursions in his Curtis hydroplanes had convinced the gnomish admiral of the value of airpower in a naval operation. Perhaps the right sort of airplane, something more airworthy than Cutler's motorized kites, could move beyond simple reconnaissance to a more offensive role. A more powerful machine might carry bombs of sufficient size that, dropped on *Königsberg*, might actually sink her into the muck of the delta. He appealed to the Admiralty for the machines and men to fly and maintain them, and was promised an "air wing" of the newly formed Royal Navy Air Service. They were on their way.

And so the last days of 1914 dragged slowly out. Christmas—by which both sides had predicted the war would be over—dawned on the steamy delta of the Rufiji. Aboard *Königsberg*, the sailors made the best of the holiday, though many, bitten by malarial mosquitoes, rolled sweating with fever in their narrow bunks. Quinine supplies, so necessary for the survival of white men in the tropics, were running perilously low. The destruction of Admiral von Spee's East Asia Squadron meant that no succor would be had from that quarter. On Christmas Day, those men off the *Königsberg* not seconded to Delta Force played soccer ashore on a makeshift field cut out of a jungle clearing. Later they knocked back extra rations of schnapps. In the officers' mess, after dinner, a few bottles of champagne were opened to toast the Kaiser's health.

The British aboard the various ships of the Destroy *Königsberg* Squadron no doubt dreamed of plum pudding and snowy Christmases at home. A waggish radio operator sent a Christmas poem to his German counterpart, Radio Officer Neimyer, in the all-clear:

"Kony, we wish you the best of good cheer / But blame you for stopping our Christmas beer."

One of the British ships' carpenters emphasized the veiled threat implied by these lines with a macabre gesture: He carved a number of tiny coffins; rolled up in each, slips of paper on which were written darker provocations in something resembling dried blood: "Try our Christmas pudding," read one of them. "Large size six inch, small size four point seven"—referring to the caliber of the British naval guns. It's unlikely that any of these reached *Königsberg*, concealed in her backwater, though one or two of them were probably retrieved by the vigilant sailors of Delta Force. One can imagine them floating by a carefully camouflaged Maxim emplacement: a bobbing flotilla of rat-sized coffins, each containing its tiny bomb of sarcasm.

On New Year's Day 1915, *Weymouth* returned from patrol duty elsewhere, relieved Drury-Lowe's *Chatham*, and sent another radio message to *Königsberg*:

"We wish you a happy new year and hope to be seeing you soon."

Radio Operator Neimyer, with Loof's permission, broke radio silence with the luxury of a response:

"Thank you for the message. If you want to see us, we're always home."

Oberstleutnant von Lettow-Vorbeck, now directing operations against the British Uganda Railway from his HQ in Neu Moshi, had spent Christmas on an increasingly rare bit of sport—a hunting expedition with officers of his staff. Rations low, they ate everything they shot: "For variety of game, the country provided more than one would be likely to find anywhere in Europe," he wrote. "Hare, various dwarf antelopes, guinea-fowl, several relatives of the partridge, duck, bush-buck, water-buck, lynx, several kinds of wild boar, small kudu, jackal, and many other kinds of game abounded.

Once, I remember, to my astonishment, a lion silently appeared fifteen paces in front of me. Unfortunately, before I could bring up my rifle he had silently disappeared."

This stealthy, vanishing lion seemed a sign from von Lettow's personal deity, the God of Battles. And perhaps—as he later put it—a harbinger of "decisive events" to come.

Chapter 16

THE SIEGE OF JASIN

The machinery of war is never silent. It clanks along at a steady pace, grinding lives into powder and destroying towns and cities, even in periods when, officially, nothing much happens: Patrols are sent out; the enemy briefly engaged. One or two troopers fall to sniper fire, their bones left to the loamy jungle soil. The small action in which they died doesn't merit more than a line in dispatches, of consequence only to the families of the men who never return.

In the context of the entire war on the East African Front, 1915 was just such a time of inaction for the British. They called it the "Black Year," and experienced a period of lethargy and plummeting morale. But for the energetic von Lettow and his Schutztruppe, 1915 offered a vital and necessary respite, a time for marshaling the resources of the colony and harnessing all to the war effort—though, as shall be seen, it was a respite punctuated by the occasional sharp action, and one hard-fought, costly battle that changed the nature of the conflict.

In the first months of the year, von Lettow reorganized the Schutztruppe into three separate armies: Major Georg Kraut, one of the *Oberstleutnant*'s most talented commanders, would look after the northern part of GEA, including the Kilimanjaro Front, adjacent to the strategic British Uganda Railway. A southwestern front bordering lakes Tanganyika and Nyasa would fall to the elegant Count Falkenstein. Kurt Whale, the retired major general who had come to visit his planter son for the canceled 1914 Colonial Exhibition—now an indispensible addition to von Lettow's small army—would handle the west. Von Lettow also requisitioned a full company of sailors off *Königsberg*, over Captain Loof's objections. These, issued rifles and drilled in dry-land soldiering (target practice, bushcraft, Swahili lessons), would eventually become some of the most effective weapons in the Schutztruppe's human arsenal.

But most significantly, the basic character of the Schutztruppe changed in a manner that reverberates today, more than a century later. Simply put, in early 1915, von Lettow created "modern history's first integrated army." This new, race-blind fighting force grew out of the military necessities of the day. Von Lettow, its architect and commander, was motivated by practical military considerations and a willingness to sacrifice all race prejudice to the possibility of victory for the Kaiser. Like Napoleon Bonaparte— whose forces included black generals, notably the father of French writer Alexandre Dumas—von Lettow believed in merit, regardless of skin color or social background.

Accordingly, the forward-thinking *Oberstleutnant* spread the Schutztruppe's best fighters over every company, on all fronts. Many of his carefully trained *askaris* were transferred to the formerly all-white ranks of the Schutzenkompanies. German enlisted men took their place in the Feldkompanies, sometimes serving under African NCOs. More Africans were recruited and trained, bumping field company strength from around 160 to 200 men. All of this naturally created a more efficient fighting structure. More, it boosted morale and engendered a vivid fighting spirit in all von Lettow's men, both black and white. Now all fought in the same army, toward the same goal; there was not one army for Africans and one for whites. All side by side served the Kaiser.

One incident must suffice as emblematic of the spiritual transformation wrought upon the Schutztruppe by von Lettow's reforms: Leutnant Ruckteschell (the Schutztruppe's resident artist and one of von Lettow's favorite subordinates), hit in the face by a ricocheting British bullet during a skirmish on the Kilimanjaro Front, received immediate attention from the *askari* fighting beside him. As Ruckteschell stumbled back, blood pouring down his face, the *askari* dropped his rifle, quickly removed the precious sock he had worn without changing for two weeks, and used it to stanch Ruckteschell's wound—which, though bloody, proved minor. The *Leut-*

nant's surprise at this tender solicitude elicited a broad grin from the *askari*. "*Ni desturi ya mivita*," the latter offered. "*Hufanya kwa rafiki tu*." (This is a custom of war. You only do it for your friends.) Though whether Ruckteschell's surprise was elicited by the unexpected gesture of friendship or the ripe pungency of the sock remains open to question.

Von Lettow now turned his attention to various logistical matters plaguing the army and the colony as a whole. The British blockade of German East Africa—challenged briefly by *Königsberg* before she hightailed it up the Rufiji—was nearly a complete success. Shortages of basic necessities made themselves painfully felt everywhere. The colonists soon lacked adequate supplies of soap, toothpaste, candles, fuel, beer, booze, rubber, cloth, chocolate, castor oil, and, most important, quinine, without which life in the tropics became impossible for Europeans. One or two blockade runners reached the Swahili Coast after many handships—notably the *Krönborg-Rubens* and the *Marie von Stettin*—but these were heroic exceptions. The aim of any blockade—complete starvation of the enemy—seemed within reach of the British Royal Navy for the first few months of 1915.

Then, with the begrudging help of Governor Schnee, still stewing away at Morogoro, von Lettow organized the colony to produce some of the most needed items. German East Africa, rich in natural resources, mostly lacked the necessary infrastructure—factories, refineries, laboratories, warehouses—to turn these resources into commercial goods. But presently, the colonists took it upon themselves to manufacture a variety of products for both civilians and Schutztruppe—now reaching its peak popularity as patriotic enthusiasm, fueled by the victory at Tanga, swept the colony.

Planters' wives revived the neglected art of spinning using native cotton; African women, given scratch-built looms, wove bolts of cloth. Between them, they more than made up for the lack of imported fabric. Leather torn from the backs of native buffalo herds and tanned using chemicals extracted from the colony's plentiful mangrove trees got cobbled into the boots so critical for the Schutztruppe—soon to march unimaginable distances over rough landscapes, much of which could not be traversed barefoot. Candles materialized from tallow; rubber from tapped trees: carefully dripped along rope, the raw, milky stuff was then hand-kneaded into tires for GEA's few automobiles, including von Lettow's staff car. A kind of primitive, homemade gasoline called trebol powered these vehicles—it was a by-product of distillates of copra, which also yielded benzene and paraffin. Soap came from a combination of animal fat and coconut oil. Planters and small businessmen eventually produced 10,000 pounds of chocolate and cocoa and 3,000 bottles of castor oil. Meanwhile, new factories sprang up in Dar es Salaam to make nails and other metal goods, including some ammunition. Rope woven from pineapple fiber proved both durable and less susceptible to rot than hempen rope from Germany; cigars and cigarettes rolled from native-grown tobacco made their way into every soldier's kit. At Morogoro and elsewhere, home brewers distilled schnapps and moonshine. The latter, at 98 proof and optimistically labeled "whiskey," was issued to the troops as part of their basic rations.

All this ingenuity, however, would be rendered useless without quinine. Before the war, the colony had gotten its supply from distributors in the Dutch East Indies, now cut off by the blockade. Dwindling supplies meant European populations of the colony would have no defense against their greatest enemy—not the British or rebellious natives but the malaria-bearing anopheles mosquito. At von Lettow's urging, the famous biological research center at Amani turned its chemists to developing a quinine substitute in their laboratories. The chemists researched furiously, tried formulations of this and that, and at last came up with an effective type of liquid quinine distilled from cinchona bark. Called "von Lettow schnapps" by his men, this foul-tasting, much-reviled elixir nevertheless met most of the army's needs for the next year or so.

Gearing up for what he knew would be a long war, von Lettow signed on 8,000 additional carriers from the native population. These human pack animals, utterly necessary in a country without roads, where the healthiest horse or mule quickly succumbed to the depredations of the tse-tse fly, became the Schutztruppe's transport corps. Goods and ammunition, divided into the traditional sixty-five-pound loads, would be carried on the heads of native bearers over rough jungle tracks for hundreds, eventually thousands, of miles.

Von Lettow also initiated a recruitment drive for fighting men in outlying regions, sending platoons of crisply uniformed *askaris* goose-stepping into remote towns to the music of German military bands. There, for the benefit of village gawpers, they waved flags, offered marksmanship demonstrations, executed double-time drills, talked up the thrills of army life. These displays proved wonderfully effective, inspiring many restless young African men to join the colors. A similar drive, aimed at those German planters who had not yet stepped forward to defend the Fatherland, raised several more Schutzenkompanies. These, stationed at Lindi, Bismarckburg, Mwanza, Langenberg, and elsewhere, acted as a sort of home guard for those regions of the interior farthest from the British border, though—as always—they could be sent wherever needed at short notice.

All this effort on von Lettow's part had a salutary effect on the Schutztruppe. By year's end the army would reach its maximum strength at more than 10,000 officers and men.

Meanwhile, among the British, now under Wapshare's command, the rule of three also prevailed: Wapshare divided British forces in the colony into an asymmetrical trio of military zones—with General Stewart, erstwhile commander of Expeditionary Force C, trounced by Kraut at Longido, taking command of the capital. The all-important British Uganda Railway was given to Brigadier General Wilfrid Malleson, a recently promoted ordnance officer; the coastal areas from Mombasa to the German border entrusted to "Fighting" Mickey Tighe.

Of course, the ever-acerbic Meinertzhagen had something cutting to say about each of these soldiers: Wapshare, he observed in his diaries, was a "kindly old gentleman, nervous, physically unfit and devoid of military knowledge." And so terrified of von Lettow that each time he heard the *Oberstleutnant*'s name mentioned in the mess, he went into "shivering fits of apprehension." Stewart, though "a great gentleman," capable of "great charm," was to Meinertzhagen, nevertheless, "a hopelessly rotten soldier." But his most critical assessment, reserved for Brigadier Malleson, comes across as pure vitriol. A contemporary photograph shows Malleson as a handsome, smartly dressed officer, his polished puttees gleaming, insouciant cigarette dangling from his mouth, but Meinertzhagen saw only darkness: He was "a bad man, clever as a monkey, but hopelessly unreliable. He comes from a class which would wreck the Empire to advance itself."

Only for Tighe does Meinertzhagen show any sympathy. The aging brigadier general drank to the point where it affected his health and judgment, Meinertzhagen says, but he was a real scrapper, a fighter through and through—exactly what a military man should be, what he calls a "thruster." This he illustrates with a description of a night action along the Uganda Railway: A troop train attacked by German saboteurs derailed in the middle of the vast, vacant *pori*. Utter blackness reigned beyond the windows— suddenly lit with the staccato crackling of German Maxim fire. Tighe and Meinertzhagen, traveling in the same compartment, were "violently thrown together," as "bullets splattered through the carriage." Meinertzhagen, his rifle close at hand, leaped out "into the night, firing at enemy flashes." Tighe, however, traveled without a sidearm. Instead he followed, brandishing "a thick stick, vowing vengeance on any German he met," and swearing like a trooper.

The Germans vanished into the darkness, but Tighe had proven himself in Meinertzhagen's eyes. Here was a man who would go straight at anything, sufficiently armed or not.

———————

In the last days of 1914, Tighe, under orders from Wapshare, had advanced against a Schutztruppe column that had crossed the border a month before. This column's audacious seizure of a few villages in the Umba Valley region of British East Africa had alarmed colonial officials in Mombasa and bothered the indigenous Wadigo—one of the many hundreds of tribes inhabiting the colony.

The Wadigo lived on a fertile plain sandwiched between the littoral and the bush, punctuated with ebony trees and those peculiar, surreal baobabs, so characteristic of Africa, whose fat trunks concealed whole ecosystems of insects. Perhaps remembering the slaughter of their cousins during the Maji-Maji Rebellion a decade earlier, the Wadigo hated all Germans; now they called upon the British government to expel them from Wadigoland.

Tighe answered with 1,800 rifles. His force consisted of the Gurkhas; a remnant of the 101st Grenadiers, decimated at Tanga; and the black African troops of the 3rd KAR. Supported by the Royal Navy, Tighe pushed the

German columns back across the border and, exceeding his orders, advanced into German territory to take the plantation town of Jasin. This small victory proved surprisingly controversial in Nairobi. His reliance on the 3rd KAR, who had done the bulk of the fighting, was deemed unseemly by many whites. Von Lettow's similar use of his brilliant *askari* fighters had already been harshly criticized by newspaper editorialists in the British colony: To the *Nairobi Leader*, an "unstated rule" of European wars in Africa had it that "natives are not brought into the row." To them it violated that most wonderful of all oxymorons, "a civilized war."

Now Tighe had followed von Lettow's suit. The newspaper hacks spouted off against him, but the inhabitants of Mombasa—just a little way up the coast from Wadigoland—enjoyed a more restful Christmas because of Tighe's action. Colorful Japanese lanterns were sent floating above Mombasa Harbor to celebrate the holiday, as Tighe fortified Jasin in expectation of a German counterattack. He had established the bulk of his army in a malarial camp in the Umba Valley nearby, leaving Colonel Raghbir Singh at Jasin commanding the 101st Grenadiers and the Gurkhas. Jasin itself was little more than a plantation/industrial complex with outbuildings and a sisal factory, watched over by a crude but immensely strong stone fort or *boma*, built during the harsh, early days of Karl Peters's *kiboko* rule. A trolley line led to the more substantial settlement of Totohowu six miles to the south. Sisal plants, their spearlike leaves razor-sharp, and dense groves of coconut palms covered the vicinity of Jasin, its cultivated fields crossed by a few deep streams. This area of the coast, known for its pestilential heat and thick clouds of malaria-bearing mosquitoes and tse-tse flies, made punishing terrain for bush fighting.

Von Lettow waited until the second week of the new year before commencing retaliatory operations. Jasin, as German territory, deserved to be "defended with the last drop of blood and breath to help what is German to remain German, so that the confidence the Kaiser has put in his people here will not be misplaced," as one overly earnest German trooper put it in a letter home.

The *Bwana Obersti*—as the *askaris* called von Lettow—began his campaign carefully, by reconnoitering the area around the plantation with one Schutztruppe company on January 12—though they were quickly sent packing by a superior British force. Von Lettow's second reconnaissance probe in the vicinity of Jasin on January 16 was again quickly repulsed by Tighe's men, though it can be said they were driven off just as much by oppressive heat and vicious bugs as by British bullets. By this time, von Lettow had learned what he needed to know about the British defense of the area. He fixed on the morning of January 18 for his big push to retake the settlement.

Just before dawn, on the 18th, von Lettow moved quietly up the trolley line from Totohowu with nine companies of the Schutztruppe, including 244 German officers and men, 1,350 *askaris*, and an unreliable contingent of 400 Arab levies from Dar es Salaam. He intended to seize the fort quickly and move against British forces at Umba Camp, thus forestalling Tighe, whom von Lettow believed was about to launch another attack on Tanga, this time overland, from the north. Von Lettow did not know that Lord Kitchener, enraged by the incompetence displayed by the British Army at Tanga, had suspended major offensive operations in theater until further notice. Kitchener was sending his brother, Colonel H. E. C. Kitchener, down to assess the military situation in East Africa and make a report. Tighe, by seizing Jasin, had violated Kitchener's orders—though it could be argued that, as some of the plantation straddled the German-British boundary line, the action had been defensive in nature, taken only to secure the border from further German incursions into British territory.

The British, holed up in Jasin Fort, consisted of 138 rifles of the 101st Grenadiers, half a corps of Gurkhas, and a detachment of KAR machine gunners. Another company of Gurkhas had fortified a factory building adjacent. The rest of Tighe's army idled at the ready at Umba Camp. Within a few hours' march, they could be called up by distress rockets to support any action at Jasin.

Arriving on the outskirts of the sisal fields at dawn, von Lettow ordered the Arab Corps to lead the assault on the fort. But these men, until recently small-time merchants from the Arab quarter of Dar es Salaam, now contemplated a mutiny. Von Lettow, famous for his laissez-faire attitude with regard to local customs and sexual mores, had indeed learned "to take the African as he found him." The *askaris* had long been allowed to bring their wives and concubines along on campaigns. These hardy black women, often with children in tow, nursed the wounded, tended the campfires of the army, and satisfied the sexual needs of their men. The widows of *askaris* killed in battle would be sent back to their native villages with a ration of food and a death benefit, courtesy of the Kaiser. The Arabs, however, bound by the strictures of Islam, would not associate with women in public. Instead they traveled with a contingent of pretty young men who performed the same function as the *askari* camp followers. Von Lettow, ever the broad-minded interpreter of the world and its diversity, shrugged at this peccadillo:

"With these simple people," he wrote, "whose predilection for their ancient traditions and customs is further confirmed by Islam, and who are besides very proud and vain, it is particularly difficult to interfere with such Dusturis (customs)."

But for the advance to Jasin, von Lettow refused to allow camp followers of either sex to follow the army. The terrain around the plantations was too difficult, the heat too intense, the mosquitoes too virile, the outcome too uncertain. The *askaris* accepted their commander's decision without complaint; the Arabs objected vociferously. They would go nowhere without their boys, they insisted, and on the eve of battle demanded their discharge. Von Lettow, of course, refused—a decision that almost immediately led to disaster: As the Schutztruppe attained their positions outside Jasin Fort, in the moment before the signal to attack, the entire Arab Corps suddenly fired into the sky above the coconut palms, as if to warn the fort's occupants of the coming battle. Then they threw their rifles down and ran helter-skelter for the rear. The war was over for them in more ways than one: The outraged *askaris* of Captain Ernst Otto's 9th FK, coming up behind to support their attack on the fort, put an end to the mutiny by shooting them down to the last man.

The defenders of Jasin Fort—thanks to the Arabs, now aware of the presence of the German Army—immediately commenced a withering fusillade from behind the battlements. They raked the sisal fields with precisely aimed volleys and deadly accurate Maxim fire. The front rank of *askaris* advancing through the gloom, instantly cut down, fell into the sharp fronds of the sisal plants, soon slippery with blood. Then the sun rose on the day of battle and along with it, the most tremendous heat von Lettow and his men had yet experienced. "Thirst and exhaustion became so great," von Lettow wrote with typical understatement, "that several gentlemen usually on the best of terms with each other had a serious difference of opinion over a coconut."

The heat only increased as the day wore on. It became so hot in the dry, sandy creek beds where the *askaris* entrenched themselves that the bottoms of their feet burned through the soles of their boots; so hot that despite the withering fire from the fort, troopers couldn't run, could barely manage to walk for cover.

Von Lettow had planned a variation of the "Horns of the Buffalo" tactic, invented by Shaka Zulu for his dreadful *impis* of celibate warriors in the early nineteenth century. Von Lettow had used a similar formation at Tanga. Simple and deadly, it resembled the head of a buffalo attacking: The center of the line (the head) attacked straight on, while either flank (the horns) moved to encircle the enemy. The Arab Corps, supported by 9th FK, was denominated "head," Major Kepler with 11th FK and 4th FK "right horn," and Captain Adler, 15th FK and 17th FK "left horn." The Totohowu trolley line would act as a sort of digestive system, allowing von Lettow to move the wounded back down the line and his reserves (1st FK, 6th FK, and 13th FK) under Captain Schultz and the two brass C73 field guns under Captain Albrecht Hering up to the front as needed. But the revolt of the Arab Corps and their subsequent battlefield execution at the hands of 9th FK dropped a large coconut smack in the middle of von Lettow's careful strategies: Envisioned as an elegant encirclement, the attack on Jasin devolved into a bitter, multiracial brawl:

Later in the morning, black *askaris* led by German officers fought for the first time against the black troopers of the KAR hurried to the front by their British officers from Umba Camp. This, while the Schutztruppe tangled with the Indian Gurkhas in the fort and factory outbuildings, and all fought the deadly heat and mosquitoes. The action, noted one participant, was "as wild as any that had been fought thus far in the campaign." Otto's "head" assault on the fort, pursued in the absence of the Arab Corps, foundered in the sisal fields halfway to its goal. Though the fort's Maxim broke down early in the fight, methodical volleys from the battlements, directed by the determined Colonel Singh, continued relentlessly, proving as effective against the *askaris* as any machine-gun fire. Singh outranked the British officers commanding the 101st Grenadiers at his side—Captains Hanson and Turner. This was not the first or last time during the course of the war in Africa when a person of color would lead white men in battle.

Von Lettow, alarmed at the developing stalemate, ordered reinforcements up the trolley line. One of these, 13th FK, considered an elite unit, met with more of Colonel Singh's carefully aimed volley fire. Within minutes 13th FK lost all three senior officers—Spalding, Langen, and Oppen—exquisitely trained and irreplaceable from von Lettow's perspective. Meanwhile, Major Kepler, coming along with the "left horn" of the assault, had been cut down an hour into the fight. The day wore on. The heat, which could not possibly grow more intense, grew more intense. Some men were struck down by it; they dropped their rifles and pitched forward into the sisal, just as if they'd been shot.

Inside the fort, without shade or cover, the Gurkhas and the Grenadiers also suffered. The barrels of their rifles, burning hot from repeated firing, glowed in the sun. Water rations ran low, ammunition dwindled, but still the fort would not be taken. At last, the *askaris* of the horns, dodging between the clumps of sisal, worked themselves around the flanks of the fort and entrenched facing a small stream—the Sigi—separating Jasin from the road to Umba Camp. They put up machine gun posts and dug rifle pits and waited for the enemy to come down the road. The fort was now completely cut off from reinforcements; in any case, Tighe, summoned by distress rockets fired off in the early hours of the morning by Colonel Singh, had yet to materialize. Still in the process of assembling his main columns at a leisurely pace, Tighe hadn't yet left the camp. Should he at last advance to the Sigi, he would find the way across barred by von Lettow's well-positioned *askaris*.

Meanwhile, three small detachments of the KAR had already been sent ahead to assess the situation and relieve the fort if possible. These, soon caught in cross fire from *askari* Maxims, failed to ford the Sigi. Among their number, Color Sergeant Juma Gubanda of 3rd KAR earned the DCM (Distinguished Conduct Medal), one of the first medals of the war issued to a black soldier, for his action on the Sigi. He stripped down and swam back and forth across the river several times to report on German troop movements as the water whipped to a froth by bullets all around him. For a while, in the early afternoon, the KAR and *askari* facing each other across the stream traded insults and bursts of machine-gun fire. They seemed evenly matched.

Von Lettow, anxious to keep the British from crossing here, took personal command, directing fire and heartening the men with his calm composure, as usual half-obscured in billowing clouds of cigarette smoke. Later, in another example of Lettovian understatement, he wrote that the KAR fire directed at him at Jasin did "no serious harm, although one bullet through my hat and another through my arm showed that it was well meant." Translation: KAR fire, accurate indeed, nearly cost him his life. Had the bullet through his hat found its mark an inch or two lower, the Schutztruppe would have lost its commandant in only the second action of the war. Also, von Lettow's much-cherished orderly, *Ombasha* (Lance Corporal) Ragabu, seeking to emulate the exploits of KAR Color Sergeant Gubanda, died while crossing the Sigi, cut in half by bullets.

Von Lettow himself, though wounded, his arm bleeding, refused to retire. He seemed more concerned about the damage to his floppy felt field hat than the bullet through his arm. Quickly patched up by medical orderlies, he continued to smoke and supervise the *askari* defense.

At last, 3rd KAR made three successive wild charges, bayonets fixed, across a shallow part of the stream, but could not break through to their comrades in Jasin Fort. With these, they ruined themselves and were forced to retire. The Sigi front now secure, von Lettow turned his attention back to the fort. He ordered the fieldpieces up the trolley line from Totohowu and used them against the walls—to no avail. The ancient guns made only a few tiny fractures in the thick, permanent stone.

At the same time, 1,000 yards away, Adler and 15th FK had at last surrounded the Gurkhas defending the sisal factory. His *askaris* pounded away with rifle and machine-gun fire at the crumbling mud-and-plaster walls. The Gurkhas' ammunition gave out around noon. Subadar Mardan Ali, the highest-ranking Gurkha left alive in the factory, briefly contemplated the hopelessness of the situation. Surrender seemed their only option, but Gurkhas do not surrender. Instead he ordered his men to fix bayonets—though some preferred to draw their kukris—and ordered a reverse charge at the German lines. This unexpected assault broke through amid scenes of carnage; three-quarters of his men reached the relative safety of Jasin Fort.

The Germans now poured lead into the fort from all sides. The Gurkhas of the Kashmir Rifles and troopers of the 101st Grenadiers returned fire as best they could, often with deadly accuracy, but supplies of ammunition had almost run out—whereas von Lettow had but to order more of the stuff up the trolley line from Totohowu. The fighting intensified. More German officers and more *askaris* fell, but a worse blow was yet to come. At three in the afternoon, von Lettow's friend and confidant Captain von Hammerstein stopped a bullet from the fort with his stomach, the same von Hammerstein who at Tanga had thrown his empty beer bottle at a fleeing *askari* and arguably, with this exasperated gesture, turned the tide of battle:

"Suddenly, Captain von Hammerstein, who was walking beside me, collapsed," von Lettow later wrote. "Deeply as this affected me, I had to leave my badly wounded comrade in the hands of the doctor." Again, had the bullet aimed at von Hammerstein hit a few inches to the left, it could have deprived the Schutztruppe of its commander. But the *Oberstleutnant* had a battle to win and reluctantly stepped away from his dying friend. Gutshot is the worst way to go; the unfortunate von Hammerstein died in agony along with many other wounded in a makeshift hospital at Totohowu a few days later.

Not long after von Hammerstein's fatal injury, a trio of bedraggled, battle-worn officers approached von Lettow and begged him to withdraw. The battle had become a punishing stalemate, too costly in men and material. Mightn't it be best to regroup, try the attack again fresh in the cool of the morning? Even von Lettow admitted the heat had become "insupportable," but he refused their suggestion without hesitation. He would not surrender the initiative won by so many German dead, he said. In any case, he felt the battle turning, albeit slowly, in his direction, the stalemate loosening:

"The thought of the unpleasant situation of the enemy," he wrote, "shut up in his works without water and having to carry on all the occupations of daily existence in a confined space in a burning sun and under hostile fire, made it appear that if we only held on with determination, we might yet achieve success."

The battle continued all afternoon and into the night. *Askaris*, as von Lettow had frequently observed, were not at their best after dark. Prey to all sorts of primitive superstitions, they could easily imagine the night shadows peopled with risen enemy dead. Wild rumors now circulated among the besieging troops hunkered down in the darkness. The fort, the men whispered, was not occupied by Indian troops at all, but by a specially trained corps of South African Boer sharpshooters, legendary for their marksmanship and their ferocity. Some claimed they could hear them talking in Afrikaans in the rare lulls between firing.

The action finally slowed around 3 a.m. and picked up again at dawn. The rising sun would bring another fierce, hot day of fighting, and more casualties. In first light, the toy trolley cars heaved down the tracks to Totohowu, straining under the weight of German wounded. The fusillade from the fort suddenly reached a crescendo. Then the gates flung open and the survivors of the garrison attempted a sortie but were driven back by German machine guns. The gates slammed shut again, the firing picked up for a few minutes, then abruptly stopped.

In the next moments, in the unnatural silence, the Schutztruppe held its collective breath as the tattered Union Jack fluttered down from its flagpole above the fort and a white flag rose in its place. Jasin had surrendered. A throaty cheer went up from the Germans. Moments later, the gates opened again, this time slowly, and 300 Indian troops and a few exhausted British officers emerged in a ragged line, empty Lee-Enfield rifles held over their heads. These now-useless weapons they discarded in a heap. They had run out of ammunition; not a single bullet remained. They had also run out of water during the night and were now half-dead with thirst. Colonel Singh, killed the previous day, had left Captains Hanson and Turner of the 101st Grenadiers in command. These young officers presented their sidearms to von Lettow, in formal acknowledgment of the surrender.

Fortunately for them, moments before, an *askari* runner had handed von Lettow a telegram shuttled up from Totohowu. News of his victory at Tanga had at last reached Germany. In the telegram, the Kaiser offered his personal congratulations and a medal von Lettow would have to collect after the war. With this happy news folded neatly in his pocket, the *Bwana Obersti* assembled the captured Indian troops and praised them for their stubborn defense of the fort and for their bravery. He accepted Hanson's and Turner's sidearms as a token of surrender, at once returned them, and released the officers on parole on the condition they gave their word to take no further part in the African war. Later that night, the victorious von Lettow threw a dinner party in Totohowu with Hanson and Turner as the guests of honor. It was no doubt a disorienting experience for these officers who had so recently been fighting for their lives against the man now pouring champagne. Such were the military courtesies of a bygone era.

Despite his bandaged arm, von Lettow, buoyed up by the hard-won fight and the Kaiser's medal, laughed and joked and ate and drank with gusto. Jasin had been a victory—not only against the tough Gurkhas but against Brigadier General Tighe, who an hour after the fort's surrender had at last appeared on the other side of the Sigi with more than 1,000 men. Too late! Met with determined fire from the German garrison now safely ensconced within the fort's thick walls, he withdrew. Later, Tighe defended his slow response to Colonel Singh's distress rockets of the morning: Given the rations in the fort, he had assumed the defenders could hold out for at least a week, he said. Also, he had been waiting for HMS *Weymouth* to position herself where she might provide support with her naval guns. But he had not counted on von Lettow. If some at British HQ in Nairobi still considered Tanga a fluke, they now knew otherwise.

Von Lettow "had again reminded the British in a manner that hurt, that his was a force to be reckoned with, and that no piecemeal effort would quell him," wrote Meinertzhagen.

But when the dust of battle settled a few days later, and the Schutztruppe began to count their dead and wounded and all the ammunition and ordnance expended at Jasin, von Lettow's jubilant mood darkened. Yes, he had kicked the British out of German territory, but he had also learned a salutary lesson doing so. The victory at Jasin could only be called pyrrhic. They had won, but like the victory of Pyrrhus of Epirus over the Romans under M. Valerius Laevinus at Heraclea in AD 271, the cost of winning had been far too high, and in the end might bear a greater resemblance to defeat.

The Schutztruppe had expended 200,000 rounds of ammunition out of a current stock of 600,000 rounds. German casualties added up to over 300—admittedly, against 1,000 on the British side. Worst of all, among the fallen were his senior staff officer, Major Kepler, and six other German officers (which is to say one-sixth of his entire officer corps), including his great friend Captain von Hammerstein and eighteen German NCOs. All expertly trained and irreplaceable. The chastened *Oberstleutnant* now realized, sourly, that "such heavy losses as we had suffered could only be borne in exceptional cases. With the means at my disposal, I could at the moment fight no more than three actions of this nature. The need to strike blows only occasionally . . . was evidently imperative."

The conventional war ended at Jasin. The guerrilla war for German East Africa had begun.

Chapter 17

THE WAR AGAINST THE RAILROAD

The British Uganda Railway ran nearly 700 miles from the Indian Ocean port of Mombasa to its terminus at Kisumu on the eastern shore of Lake Victoria—for none of this length, actually in Uganda. Its 200,000 steel ties, 1.2 million sleepers, and umpteen million stakes and metric tons of gravel were all laid in British East Africa.

At Kisumu, lake steamers would relay the weary but exhilarated passengers to Uganda on the far shore. Between ocean and lake, the railway passed over a variegated and difficult terrain, both lush and arid by turns. It crossed scrubland, impenetrable thornbush thickets, and waterless desert; traversed mountains and swamp and forested plateau; cut through valleys—including the Great Rift—all gradually uphill to the Mau Summit, where the railway builders had faced sleet and snow and massive slides of freezing mud. Then it ran steeply downhill to the green shores of the lake.

What's left of the railway today—highways have now replaced portions of its length—remains an engineering marvel of the kind no longer possible in an age when physical reality has shrunk to the size of iPhone screens. Now neither the will nor the wallet exists for such an undertaking—but what lacks most of all is hubris, the imperial variety: Only an empire could attempt such an undertaking and succeed.

The massive construction project occupied the better part of five years, beginning in 1896. Nearly 30,000 coolies imported from India signed on as labor; 2,500 of these died alongside the tracks from accident and disease and murder and tribal warfare. But at least 28 laborers—and perhaps more than 100 natives from local villages—were killed by a pair of freakishly large man-eating lions. This occurred between March and December of 1898 at a Tsavo River crossing where the men were attempting to build a bridge. The word *tsavo*, as it turns out, means "slaughter" in the local Kikamba language. And though the place was pleasant enough, the river here shaded by overhanging trees, the water fast and cool, it had a bad reputation. Evil spirits supposedly lurked nearby; they were known to snatch workers from camp after dark. Certainly, many disappeared, never to be seen again.

But evil spirits, at least of the traditional sort, had nothing to do with the disappearances: It was all about the lions. Dubbed the "man-eaters of Tsavo," these particular lions, two aggressive, maneless males, had developed an insatiable hunger for human flesh. They stalked the workers' encampments relentlessly, always at night; fire did not deter them, nor did coolies beating on pots and pans. Leaping over protective thorn scrub palisades called "zaribas," the lions dragged screaming coolies off to be eaten in the darkness. Once, they pulled a white overseer from a railway car and ravaged him as his friends watched, horrified. The landscape beyond the immediate construction sites was scattered with bits of half-eaten human meat, gnawed-on bones, and larger pieces—rib cages stuck with tattered bits of fabric, feet still in shoes, heads. Dozens of coolies deserted in the face of this horror. The ones who remained threatened mutiny unless something was done to stop the killings.

At last, the railway commission sent an engineer who was also a renowned lion hunter, the dauntless John Henry Patterson. Patterson stalked the man-eating lions for weeks at Tsavo with a four-bore shotgun and a .303 Enfield rifle. He built hunting blinds in the trees, sprinkled hunks of dead antelope beneath his perch, and waited through many cold nights, weapons at the ready. Finally, the beasts took the bait and attacked. He shot each one of them, in turn. The last one took seven bullets and kept coming on, still trying to reach him when it died. Both lions measured over nine feet from tail to nose; eight men were required to haul each carcass back to camp. The lions' skeletons and skins, later donated to the Chicago Field Museum, may still be seen there today.

Patterson himself became a hero to the Indians he saved from being eaten—and something of an international celebrity: Newspapers cited him as a sterling example of English manhood; his name was mentioned favorably in Parliament. The surviving coolies at Tsavo gave him a silver bowl engraved with an affectionate inscription. A poet among them wrote an epic poem in Hindi, half as long as the *Iliad*, celebrating his deed.

Later, in the 1914–18 war, in Mesopotamia, Patterson commanded the Jewish Legion—the first all-Jewish fighting force to take the field in more than 2,000 years. Though not a Jew, Patterson, like Meinertzhagen, was an ardent early Zionist and is revered today in Israel as the "godfather of the Israeli army." He received the DSO and other commendations during his long military career, but the silver bowl from the coolies at Tsavo remained, he said, his single greatest honor.

Triumphing over lions and landscapes and mutinous workers, the British Uganda Railway at last reached the shores of the lake in 1901. Winston Churchill, a passenger on one of the first trains to Kisumu, extolled the achievement of the builders. "The British art of 'muddling through,'" he remarked on that occasion, "is here seen in one of its finest expositions. Through everything—through the forests, through the ravines, through prides of man-eating lions, through famine, through war, through five years of excoriating political debate, muddled and marched the railway."

Mombasa built the railway and the railway built Nairobi. The latter relied on the railway for everything. The goods it could not make and every nicety from England came up the tracks from the coast; the railway was also BEA's lifeline to the lake country and the deep interior. But to von Lettow, this pride of British Imperialism resembled a long, exposed jugular vein that might be severed with fatal consequences anywhere along its 700-mile length.

In February 1915, in preparation for an all-out guerrilla war against the railway, von Lettow divided his already small, mobile, racially mixed field companies into smaller patrols of twelve to thirty men, with the latter bearing one or two machine guns. These were in turn divided into detachments of eight to ten. The *Oberstleutnant* had learned the hard lessons of bush warfare from the Hottentots in South West Africa in 1906. The *pori* through which ran most of his guerrilla front could not support detachments of more than a few men at once. As in South West Africa, the distance between water holes stretched interminably. The intense heat, thick dust, and sharp thorns tortured men and boots. And, given the climate, the Schutztruppe could keep few horses and mules. Those that managed to survive the tse-tse fly von Lettow distributed between two elite mounted guerrilla companies.

He began his first major guerrilla campaign in March—one of his early targets, the bridge at Tsavo: A Schutztruppe demolition team took mere minutes to destroy what had taken the British several months, many lives, and the assassination of two horrible lions to achieve. The *Oberstleutnant's* strategic goal had not changed. Despite successes at Tanga and Jasin, the limited nature of German resources still meant he could not win the war outright. But he could prolong it and force the British to expend blood and treasure that would otherwise go to the Western Front. Though he fought in Africa, his eyes were always on the battlefields of Europe where—he had just learned to his sorrow—his younger brother had died fighting the French on the Marne.

After Tsavo and a few other strikes in the vicinity, Schutztruppe guerrilla efforts narrowed to the 100-mile stretch within a three-day march of the thickly wooded Kilimanjaro foothills where they maintained a series of base camps. This was warfare Robin Hood–style: German guerrilla bands rolled down from their hidden Kilimanjaro lairs north through the desert and east through the thornbush—arduous foot safaris whose end result was destruction. "If enough concentrated damage could be done," historian Charles Miller commented, "the British in all likelihood would bring in more and more troops—not just to protect their main artery of communications, but, if possible, to drive the Germans well behind their border and keep them there."

It is worth remembering that British strategy at this period had been limited by Kitchener to purely defensive actions. The British warlord alone seems to have recognized the point of von Lettow's needling, attrition-style warfare. The best way to combat someone spoiling for a fight is not to fight them at all: "You are entirely mistaken," Kitchener wrote to General Wapshare in February, "that offensive operations are necessary. The experience at Jasin shows you are not well informed of the strength of your enemy. You should concentrate your forces and give up risky expeditions in East Africa, where we cannot reinforce you sufficiently to be sure of success." A few months later he called yet another reinforcement proposal for BEA part of "a dangerous project in the present state of the war, when we require to concentrate all our efforts to defeat the Germans in Europe." Kitchener got it. Fortunately for the success of von Lettow's strategy, he was the only one.

Using hit-and-run guerrilla tactics, von Lettow managed to terrorize the Uganda Railway through the end of the year. His Schutztruppe blew up a dozen bridges and at least one dam, tore up hundreds of miles of track, wiped out remote outposts. Thirty-two trains were destroyed by guerrilla patrols; in July, they took five trains in one week. At the same time, other patrols blew up nine bridges and ransacked several British encampments in the bush. On one of these raids, they captured enough horses to double the strength of Schutztruppe mounted units. Also, as the Kilimanjaro sector of the Uganda Railway received some of its heaviest traffic, disruptions of service there expanded, accordion-like, down the entire length of the line all the way to the sea. As the *Official History* put it: "The practical effects of the German raids were far greater than the actual damage to the line."

In attacking trains, von Lettow's guerrilla foot patrols used tactics recalling those employed by the legendary bandits of the American West. First, they "listened" for an approaching locomotive—not by pressing their ears to the rails as in Western films, but by tapping in to telegraph lines with British phone equipment abandoned on the beach at Tanga. Dynamite, laid under the tracks and set to go off with a pressure switch, would detonate as a locomotive passed overtop. The explosion derailed the train; *askaris* immediately opened up with Maxims or volley fire. Resistance extinguished, the guerrillas swarmed over the wreck, scavenging what they could carry. Then they disappeared into the trackless bush, to strike elsewhere in a few hours or a few days.

Mounted patrols employed similar tactics. Over sections of track through difficult, undulating country, locomotive engineers were forced to slow to fifteen miles per hour. Guerrillas on horseback, appearing out of nowhere, would overtake the crawling locomotive, shoot the hapless engineer and fireman, and jump aboard to stop the train. Others would emerge from the bush and press home the attack. Only a smoldering wreck—and the bodies of anyone who resisted—remained when they rode off into the scrub. Raids at night, like the one experienced by Meinertzhagen and Tighe, held their own particular terror: the chattering flashes of machine-gun fire in the black night, the unseen enemy, and afterward a darkness alive with the roar and bellow of dangerous wild animals.

Thus, a few hundred men might absorb the efforts of an army of thousands.

This kind of warfare had bedeviled the Germans in South West Africa. Now it enraged the British, who found they could not combat it efficiently without a major campaign and a massive injection of fresh troops. But fighting in such a harsh environment also took its toll on the Germans. Guerrilla patrols marched hundreds of miles across inhospitable waterless country, mostly unmapped and uninhabitable; many got lost in the wilderness. True, Kilimanjaro's snowy peak hovered over every *askari* shoulder, the single fixed point on any map. But given climatic conditions and clouds of dust obscuring the horizon, the entire mountain often disappeared from view for days.

The Germans called this region the *Dursteppe*, a place where thirst and starvation were constant companions. Exotic wildlife—lions, rhinos, zebras, giraffes, ostriches, elephants—abounded so thickly in some areas that one trooper likened it to "fighting in a zoo"—but the Germans could not shoot them for fear of alerting the British patrols of the East African Mounted Rifles (EAMR), aided by native Masai guides, always on the lookout for German saboteurs. To avoid detection, von Lettow's guerrillas often went without fires, which meant no hot food or warmth after sunset. Only vigilance kept marauding lions away in the dark hours.

Water, however, remained the single most pressing need. The men hauled what they could on their backs. When supplies dried up, von Lettow advised them to drink their own urine or the blood of snared birds—both tricks he had learned from the Hottentots. This hard country forced other, equally hard choices on the men fighting in it: "It was a bad business," von Lettow wrote, "when anyone fell ill or wounded. With the best will in the world, it was impossible to bring him along. To carry a severely wounded man from the Uganda Railway to the German camps, as was occasionally done, was a tremendous feat." Hardly practical and a waste of military energy, he might have added—but the men, reluctant to abandon their wounded comrades in the bush, kept trying. At last, von Lettow reluctantly gave the order that those badly wounded must not be saved. Good-byes said, they were stripped of their arms and clothing and shot in the head, their bodies left behind unburied as a feast for carrion.

But the unsentimental *Oberstleutnant* could not expose his men to hardships he would not himself endure, and personally commanded several raids against the railway: "The influence of these expeditions on both Europeans and natives was so great that it would be difficult to find a force imbued with a stronger fighting spirit," he later wrote. From a military standpoint, however, von Lettow's personal involvement was foolish, if not dangerous to the German war effort. His loss or capture might easily have meant the end of German resistance in East Africa. He makes the excuse of morale, but one has the feeling he simply couldn't resist getting in on the cowboy-and-Indian-style action.

In May 1915 he led a guerrilla patrol consisting of three German NCOs, eight *askaris*, and a dozen porters. The march to the railway took six days through rough country and ended with a night attack on a train using powerful dynamite sourced from one of the coastal plantations and—luxury item—an electric detonator. The explosion blew the locomotive off the tracks as an outrageous booming resounded across the desert. The resulting concussion so frightened the African porters that they dropped the precious water skins in their charge and ran for the hills. At first light they returned, sheepishly; unfortunately, by this time, the water skins lay on the ground deflated in dark puddles of moisture that might as well have been blood.

The march back to base camp proved nearly fatal for von Lettow and his patrol. They found no water along the way and no sustenance. The patches of edible berries occasionally encountered were not there this time. Then one of the German sergeants accidentally shot himself in the leg. Here von Lettow couldn't bear to follow his own dictates. He ordered the *askaris* to carry the wounded man as far as they could. Traveling at night, guided by the stars, von Lettow led his patrol across many miles of waterless desert until, quite by accident—or with the necessary luck of a born soldier—he came across a German outpost and all were saved.

This kind of hairbreadth escape from destruction repeated itself time and again in the audacious yearlong antirailway guerrilla campaign. A few Germans were captured by the enemy, a score died, but more often than not, the raiders prevailed, rarely failing to meet their military objectives.

———

Meanwhile, the British, under the vacillating Wapshare, tried several countermeasures against German attacks—all failures: The obvious expedient of armoring the trains with bulletproof iron plates six feet high only made them more cumbersome and thus more vulnerable. Also, the plating turned train cars into rolling ovens: Open to sky and burning sun, the thick iron walls drew cinders from the locomotive onto the heads of British troops already roasting within. They dozed over their rifles, stupefied by the heat—only to be woken abruptly by the familiar chatter of ambushing *askari* machine-gun fire.

Another British stratagem involved running the locomotives behind two freight cars, weighed down with stones: These were supposed to act as minesweepers, detonating any charges in time to spare the locomotive and its engineers—both in short supply in East Africa at the moment, thanks to von Lettow's guerrilla strikes. But the Germans quickly adapted themselves to this clumsy expedient by installing time-delay fuses on their undertrack explosive devices: The minesweepers would pass over the dynamite unharmed; only when the locomotive crossed would the device detonate.

The few Indian troops now stationed by Wapshare in remote outposts to guard the railway proved less than effective against Schutztruppe raiders. These were drawn from the same forlorn personnel of the Imperial Service Brigade who had performed so poorly at Tanga—sepoys from Jhind, Kapurthala, Faridkot, Gwalior, and Zanpur, all generally despised by their counterparts in the regular army, even by other Indians.

Tales of Imperial Service Brigade incompetence and cowardice under fire soon attained the status of a dark legend: An Indian detachment, picketed in the bush near an area of heavy Schutztruppe guerrilla activity, heard the enemy rummaging around in the darkness at the edge of their campfires one night. They were surrounded! Rifles in hand and back to back, they stood trembling with fear until dawn. First light plainly revealed the enemy insurgents—a family of baboons!

In April, a detachment of the 98th Indian Infantry, protecting a crucial railway bridge at Milepost 218, near Voi, chose to stand guard without their weapons. These lay stacked in neat tripods, just beyond reach. A Schutz-truppe company attacked—that is, they strolled into camp unopposed, took the Indians' rifles and the Indians themselves prisoner, drank their water and ate their food, and only then set about blowing up the bridge. When they strolled out again, they left the Indians behind, weaponless but un-harmed, figuring troops of such vast incompetence actually *helped* the Ger-man cause. In another incident, a contingent of sepoys mistook a young female rhinoceros and her calf for charging German cavalry. About to be overwhelmed by the enemy, so they thought, they ran, abandoning their post to the rhinos.

Meinertzhagen, now an intelligence officer in Nairobi, by his own account made repeated trips into the bush in 1915. On these personal safaris, he says he did a bit of his own counterguerrilla work and along the way in-spected a few of the Indian outposts guarding the railway. At one of these he found the troops lolling about inside a hastily constructed zariba enclos-ing a pool afloat with dead hippos. The poor lumbering beasts had been shot by the Indian officer for target practice. Meinertzhagen found the man responsible bathing in the fetid pool, now rendered nonpotable in a region where the availability of water might mean the difference between life and death.

International agreements signed by the belligerent parties before the war forbade the poisoning of water holes. British HQ in Nairobi would not countenance the use of poison—equally reprehensible to their German counterparts. But a scattered handful of water holes allowed Schutztruppe guerrilla patrols to operate freely along the most arid sections of track. No water, no guerrilla attacks. While Meinertzhagen could not "legally" poison these water sources, he came up with what was perhaps his antiguerrilla masterstroke: He shot a few animals and birds and placed their carcasses around a water hole near Kasigau. He then put up signs labeled POISON!

decorated with the requisite skull and crossbones. The water of the non-poisoned-poisoned water hole was, of course, perfectly drinkable. But the effect of Meinertzhagen's signs was exactly the same as if it had been actually poisoned.

"At least eighty miles of track were rendered absolutely secure from attack," Meinertzhagen wrote in his diary. "We know that the first German patrol to visit the well turned back without drinking, and as they relied on the water, one member of the patrol perished of thirst on the homeward journey. We had an official complaint about international usage respecting poisoned water to which we have not replied. . . . It may be an offense to poison water, but surely there is nothing wrong in labeling water as poisoned when it is not so treated?"

Indeed, von Lettow lodged an official protest with British officials in Nairobi. Poisoned water holes, he asserted, were "ungentlemanly." But the ruse kept the line from Kasigau to Voi free of attacks for weeks.

The "Poisoned Water Hole Caper," offers an example of a brilliantly devious mind at work. Brian Garfield, in his earnest and exhaustive takedown of Meinertzhagen's double life, pooh-poohs nearly all his subject's tales regarding intelligence work in East Africa. Meinertzhagen, Garfield insists, merely sat behind a desk in Nairobi composing intelligence reports culled from other reports sent in by field agents. But the poisoned water hole fraud is exactly the sort of thing a first-class fraudster like Meinertzhagen would concoct. It has about it the ring of truth, as do several of the other stratagems Meinertzhagen describes in his diary.

Around this time, he assembled what has been called "unquestionably the best intelligence apparatus in the East African theater," a spy ring comprising Swahili Muslims, East African Indians, the occasional Masai tribesman, Greeks, Portuguese, and sundry others. They were called the "DPM," an acronym for "Dirty Paper Method." One of their most effective intelligence-gathering techniques explains this sobriquet: DPM agents would infiltrate German latrines and outhouses in Dar es Salaam and elsewhere and filch any papers found stuck to the piles of excrement. Given the severe wartime shortage of toilet paper all over Africa, German soldiers used discarded personal letters, military orders, official reports, and other papers as a substitute. Information gleaned from this unsanitary ephemera enabled Meinertzhagen to forestall several German raids against the railway. From them he also created a valuable intelligence document—extant today—giving examples of the signatures of all the top German military commanders, including von Lettow's.

"I found that the contents of German officers' latrines were a constant source of filthy though accurate information," Meinertzhagen wrote, "as odd pieces of paper containing messages, notes on enciphering and decoding, and private letters were often used where lavatory paper did not exist."

But Meinertzhagen himself might have unintentionally contributed to ending—or at least ameliorating—the toilet paper shortage in German East Africa. One of his more ambitious stratagems involved counterfeiting GEA twenty-*rupien* bills, to be passed by his agents in the German colony. He hoped to flood the market with these fake bills, thus destabilizing the precarious German economy, already hit hard by the blockade. Meinertzhagen, a talented artist and mapmaker, engraved the bills himself. Then he commandeered a letter press, printing up by his account "several millions" of bills. The scheme failed. The counterfeit bills, marked with different serial numbers front and back and printed on stiffer paper than the originals, fooled no one. A few survive today and command high prices among currency collectors. The bills are rare because most, undoubtedly, ended up as toilet paper in the very latrines Meinertzhagen's DPM agents hoped to find their "dirty paper" documents.

But trickery and intelligence gathering comprised only a part of the DPM's duties. "Action, that is what we want here, action!" Oft repeated, the phrase became Meinertzhagen's favorite exhortation. Accordingly, he armed his best and most aggressive DPM agents and led them into the bush on contraguerrilla raids—so he writes in his diaries. Here experience with the KAR in 1905–07 and his background as an amateur naturalist served him well. Always at home in wild places, he could read a landscape with the squinty-eyed accuracy of an Apache scout.

On one contraguerrilla raid, the animals themselves alerted him to the presence of an enemy patrol: Approaching the glittering ribbon of the Uganda Railway through the thorn scrub, Meinertzhagen suddenly realized all the animals in the vicinity (giraffes, ostriches, impala, zebra) were looking anxiously in a single direction. Crawling along on hands and knees, Meinertzhagen and his men soon came across a twelve-man Schutztruppe patrol resting in the ample shade of a baobab. Taking careful aim with his .303 Enfield, Meinertzhagen shot five of them at 150 yards. Three more, taking cover behind the tree, were shot from the rear by flanking DPM agents. The rest surrendered, delivering up weapons and the explosive kit they were about to use against the railway.

Meinertzhagen's mad schemes and contraguerrilla forays—and the larger expeditions of the East African Mounted Rifles—made bright spots in what remained a crepuscular period for the British in the East African war. To the nervous civilians of Nairobi, and to the coffee farmers of the outlying districts (like Karen von Blixen and her husband, Bror), who resented the irruption of the war into their lives, the British could do nothing right. To them, the army was led by incompetents and fools. Mightn't it be best to seek a separate peace with the Germans on the African continent rather than fight them? Many in the military thought BEA's governor Belfield a halfhearted patriot whom the Colonial Office ought to "place in front of a firing squad," for pursuing a "hands-off policy" against the Germans. Nonetheless, Belfield's neutral-leaning attitude found support among a majority of colonists.

According to Meinertzhagen, "Many . . . have been too willing to take their cue from Belfield and have preferred to sit on their farms whilst others protected them. It has been a disgrace to the British name and a considerable anxiety to us."

Snobbish aristocrats among the colonists resented the military presence in their clubs, especially the tony Muthaiga. One colonist complained that Indian Army officers "ostentatiously decorated with tabs of various hues and full of their own importance were pouring into Nairobi. They filled the clubs where they groused at the absence of pukka sahibs [*pukka* being Anglo-Indian slang for "excellent" or "socially acceptable"], pukka golf, pukka polo, pukka bearers, pukka clubs, and all the other pukkas they had left behind in India."

A sarcastic song making the rounds in Nairobi club lounges in the weeks following the disaster at Tanga clearly illustrates the contempt in which the average British colonial held his *own* army:

See them shortly landing
*   At the chosen spot,*
Find the local climate
*   Just a trifle hot.*
Foes unsympathetic,
*   Maxims on them train*
Careful first by signal
*   Range to ascertain*

Ping, ping go the bullets,
*   Crash explode the shells,*
Major General's worried
*   Thinks it's just as well*
Not to move too rashly
*   While he's in the dark.*
What's the strength opposing?
*   Orders: Re-embark.*

Back to old Mombasa
*   Steams B Force again*
Are these generals ruffled?
*   Not the smallest grain.*
Martial regulations
*   Inform us day by day*
They may have foozled Tanga
*   But they've taken BEA!*

———————

By April 1915 General Wapshare—Aitken's successor—generally the butt of jokes, was already fading, more interested in big game hunting than fighting Germans. At last, the War Office transferred him to the Mesopotamian Front—a demotion, as he would not there have an independent command. True to form, on the train from Nairobi to Mombasa, he pulled the emergency stop and, while astonished passengers watched, shot a couple of ostriches running alongside; this in a country consistently plagued by Schutztruppe raiders—which also happened to be a game reserve.

"Some twenty passengers assisted him in dragging the two huge birds back to the train," Meinertzhagen reported, "where they were loaded into the goods van, where Wappy sat for the rest of the trip, plucking them."

Tighe followed Wapshare as supreme commander but, once installed, began to drink even more heavily than before: "Alas and alack," Meinertzhagen confided to his diary, "Tighe has been drinking much more than is good for him, with the result that he is now fast in the clutches of gout and liver. . . . I gave him some quite good advice, begging him for the sake of the campaign to pull himself together . . . but it is difficult for a junior staff officer to really take his general and shake him into sobriety." Tighe's assumption of overall command left the odious Malleson in charge of the coastal districts, an appointment deemed disastrous by many. Malleson seemed to lack a basic understanding of offensive strategy and quavered under fire.

Meanwhile, as the daring Schutztruppe raids on the Uganda Railway continued, all sorts of wild rumors circulated regarding the apparently undefeatable von Lettow, who was rapidly attaining the status of legend in the British Colony.

In the gin mills of Mombasa they said he had built a homemade U-boat to spearhead a sneak invasion of the city. The town guard was called out on the night of the supposed submarine invasion and put to digging entrenchments to defend against an attack that never came. In the Nairobi clubs they told weird tales of a bloodthirsty female warrior, Bibi Sakharani, widow of the redoubtable Tom von Prince, killed at Tanga. Sister to one of Siegfried's Valkyries in terms of sheer ferocity, Bibi sought to castrate as many British soldiers as she could get her hands on. Lieutenant Lord Cranworth, of the EAMR, remarks in his *Kenya Chronicles* that the existence of Bibi Sakharani was firmly believed by the troops; all outgoing EAMR patrols were warned to be on the lookout for her. Supposedly, she commanded "a German *askari* patrol determined to avenge her husband by taking no prisoners, and indeed, by mutilating any white person she took." Her presence was further evidenced by "small, booted footprints found in the vicinity of her outrages."

To von Lettow, these rumors pointed neatly to the crumbling state of enemy morale—confirmed by the British themselves in confidential reports: "The morale of our men," remarked Brigadier General J. H. V. Crowe in 1915, "was none the best, partly owing to the state of health, partly to their previous lack of success, and in measure to the defensive attitude adopted." But Lord Kitchener's decision not to reinforce the army in British East Africa had just been doubly reinforced by his brother's hasty conclusions on the feasibility of recruiting more native troops for the KAR—which, the latter insisted, could not be justified by the expense of training them. Never mind that native African fighters knew their own country as no one else and were immune to the violent strains of malaria just then wreaking havoc on the army. Meanwhile, Lord Cranworth's own recommendations regarding an increase in African troops were disregarded; his careful report on the matter "speedily found its way into the official wastepaper basket."

Still, a few stray detachments made it through to join the fight in East Africa: In March, 500 rifles of the 2nd Rhodesian Regiment came down from the distant highlands of Rhodesia to offer their services to Tighe. And in April, the famous Legion of Frontiersmen disembarked at Mombasa after a stormy voyage from England. This curious, colorful regiment, a kind of Boy Scouts with Guns for grown men, founded in 1906 as a force of "colonial territorials . . . of good character who have trained in wild countries, at sea, or in war," had just been subsumed into the British Army as the 25th Royal Fusiliers.

Mockingly known as the "Old and the Bold"—a swipe at the relatively advanced average age of early recruits—the Frontiersmen boasted fighters from all over the world and from all walks of life: Among their ranks were to be found more than one former circus clown; bartenders; failed Arctic explorers; American cowboys; disgraced Russian aristocrats escaped from penal colonies in Siberia; musicians; deserters from the French Foreign Legion; an opera singer; an American planter as large as a linebacker who wore a sixty-four-inch sword belt and tipped the scale at 336 pounds; a lighthouse keeper; a general from the Army of Honduras who now served as a sergeant; Moroccan bandits; at least one member of Parliament; several boxers; and a member of the prewar vaudeville team called Six Brothers Luck, who could climb stairs on his head.

But perhaps the Frontiersmen's most famous recruit was Frederick Courteney Selous, the English big game hunter, writer, celebrity, conservationist, and personal friend of Theodore Roosevelt, who had once remarked that "there was never a more welcome guest at the White House than Selous." Commissioned a lieutenant in the Frontiersmen at sixty-four, Selous became the oldest serving British soldier in any regiment in the war. Still sleek and sinewy and utterly fit, he had the piercing blue eyes of a natural-born hunter. If the Legion of Frontiersmen seemed to have sprung fully formed from the brain of a novelist, perhaps it had: Its general council included Arthur Conan Doyle and H. Rider Haggard; the latter had used Selous as the model for Allan Quartermain in *King Solomon's Mines*—yet another example of life mimicking art mimicking life.

Selous had known the continent in the waning golden days before the European scramble for colonies changed things forever. Like Meinertzhagen, he hailed from an upper-class family of English bankers. There must be something about the banking life in England that drives its sons to the remote corners of the earth: In the early 1870s, at the age of nineteen, Selous fled civilized life and made his way to Africa, where he joined the last of the elephant hunters in their assault on the great herds roaming the savannah, thick as buffalo in the American West. He used a black-powder muzzle-loading rifle weighing 14 pounds, firing a quarter-pound bullet propelled by 540 grains of powder with a monster recoil that once dislocated his shoulder. Using this antiquated hand cannon, Selous bagged over 500 elephants; his hunting grounds encompassed thousands of square miles of the unexplored interior of the continent, which he roamed on foot, with few provisions and accompanied by a single native guide.

Accounts of Selous's youth in Africa's pristine wilderness enthralled the Victorian reading public. His books *A Hunter's Wanderings in Africa* and *Travel and Adventure in South-East Africa* became bestsellers. Selous had a way with native peoples; he spoke their languages, accepted their traditions and customs; like von Lettow, he took them on their own terms. Lobengula, the fractious, despotic king of Matabeleland, treated the hunter like an adopted son and gave him the run of the country, generally closed to other white hunters. Selous grew to manhood in the African wilderness, amassed a modest fortune trading ivory, married, fought in the Matabele Wars of the 1890s, and helped found Rhodesia alongside Cecil Rhodes—perhaps the greatest imperialist of them all.

But these adventures were more than a generation gone by 1915. Just before the outbreak of the First World War, Selous lived the life of a country gentleman on a small estate in England with his wife and two sons. He continued to write and gave passionate lectures on conservationism to appreciative crowds. And though he had spent years killing elephants, Selous came to regret the wholesale slaughter of these proud, intelligent beasts and now worked to set aside game preserves and hunting quotas.

But retirement didn't come easy for a man of Selous's restless temperament. When the Universal Conflict came to Africa, he could not help getting involved. Too old for a regular army commission, he applied to Colonel Patrick Driscoll of the Frontiersmen. Driscoll, at first skeptical, soon set aside his reservations: Selous could outmarch, outrun, and out-soldier kids a quarter his age. He didn't drink, didn't eat much, was abstemious in all his habits, utterly reliable, and liked by everyone. Also, appropriately "seasoned" by his early years in Africa, he had built up a near-native resistance to the tropical diseases that would incapacitate so many. But there was something else: Selous radiated a moral authority that seemed to have vanished from the new world of mechanized warfare and the gas attack. In Africa, his fellow soldiers saw him as "a saint in a country where men are not saints," and refused to cheat him at cards, even though at cards everyone usually cheated everyone else. With the Legion of Frontiersmen and this greatest of Great White Hunters on their side, how could the British fail to beat the Germans?

Encouraged by the addition of these fresh troops to his army, Tighe now petitioned the War Office for permission to launch another offensive—a raid against the port of Bukoba on the German side of Lake Victoria. Here the last German wireless tower left standing in Africa still allowed the embattled von Lettow occasional contact with Berlin. Bukoba must be seized, the wireless station destroyed. The operation, though risky, was also critical:

Tighe's army had stagnated; idle men were more susceptible to diseases and dissipation. The Loyal North Lancs, one of the most hardworking units in East Africa, had just been removed from the active list, every officer and man down with fever. Any more of this waiting and British forces would rot to nothing.

Surprising everyone, Lord Kitchener yielded to Tighe's request. Bukoba it would be, with the untested Legion of Frontiersmen leading the way.

On June 20, 1915, a small British army commanded by General Stewart, formerly of Expeditionary Force C, embarked at Kisumu, terminus of the Uganda Railway, on the western shore of Lake Victoria for Bukoba on the German side. The operation, called "a glorified commando raid," nevertheless mobilized nearly 2,000 officers and men. These were armed with two field guns of the crack 28th Mountain Battery, a machine gun section from the East Africa Regiment, and four additional machine guns of the Colonial Volunteer Maxim Force. Regiments participating included the Legion of Frontiersmen—Selous and Driscoll present—the 3rd KAR, the 29th Punjabs, and a detachment of Loyal North Lancs who had risen from their feverous beds for the occasion—stricken more by inactivity, it would seem, than disease. Meinertzhagen went along as the eyes and ears of General Tighe.

A mini armada of ancient steamers transported the men across the lake: the *Kavirondo*, *Nyanza*, *Percy Anderson*, *Rusinge*, *Usofe*, and *Winifred*, each carrying outsize naval guns stripped from the hulk of the unfortunate HMS *Pegasus*, whose remains still lay stricken in the shallow waters of Zanzibar Harbor. Stewart and Tighe had planned a lightning attack. They would not occupy territory; they would destroy the radio tower, wreck the *boma* that housed it, and get out. The heterogeneous units of the Bukoba Force, poorly handled and clumsily maneuvered by Stewart, were slated for a secret night landing—shades of the Tanga disaster all over again. Stewart counted on surprising the Germans but had failed to black out his ships and a bright tropical half-moon illuminated his every move. Moments before the scheduled landing, the sky went bright with German rockets—they had been found out by spotters on Bushira Island in the lake opposite Bukoba.

With the element of surprise gone, Stewart decided not to risk the obvious hazards of a night landing. Just after dawn on the 21st, he selected what to everyone looked like the worst possible site—more shades of Tanga—a beach at the foot of a steep cliff about three and a half miles north of the town. The Bukoba *boma* lay at the center of a small, neat colonial settlement on Kiaya Bay, the town divided by the Kanoni River, itself the main feature of a marshy, reed-clogged diluvial plain. Grassy hills surrounded the town. Tall cliffs protected its flanks from waterborne assault. Rwanga Hill, the cliff Stewart had selected for his troops to climb, was 380 feet high and rather sheer, offering little purchase for men laden with weapons and ammunition. But the flotilla's naval guns bombarded the area relentlessly, lobbing more than 100 shells to cover the climb up the cliff face—somehow managed by the Loyal North Lancs and the Frontiersmen.

Fortunately for the British, the Germans themselves hadn't deemed such an ascent possible and had failed to fortify the promontory, and the invasion force gained the summit unscathed. From here to Bukoba, however, proved much more difficult. The British formed a skirmish line along a two-mile front, its objective a hill overlooking the town upon which they might install their artillery. Assembled by midday, they began to advance, supported by the guns of the 28th Mountain Battery.

The Germans garrisoning Bukoba—7 FK under Major Willibald von Stuemer—now absent on patrol with 150 *askaris*—at full strength amounted to no more than 200 rifles. Leutnant Eberhard Gudowinus, in temporary command of about eighty *askaris* and a few volunteers in the fort, replied to the Mountain Battery's bombardment with the three aging German 75mm field guns in his possession. Though vastly outnumbered, Gudowinus and his men occupied strong defensive positions, and the *askaris* of 7 FK danced from "rock to rock . . . and tree clumps" firing their smoky 71 Jagerbuch rifles with great accuracy.

The difficulty of the swampy terrain—often the men found themselves chest-high in muck—stalled the British advance until late afternoon, when they attained a ridge overlooking the town. By this time, precise fire from the 28th Mountain Battery had smashed two of the German guns, but with night falling rapidly, Stewart elected to wait till morning for the final assault. They were still at least a mile from Bukoba. The Frontiersmen at the center of the line had been advancing for twelve hours, fighting every step of the way. Also, they'd had no food since leaving the ships at dawn. Night descended rapidly, as it always does in the tropics, and with it an unexpected chill. The men, still wet from wading through the swamp, shivered, teeth chattering, so cold they could not sleep. Adding to their misery, it began to rain, sometimes heavily, and rained in fits all night long. Selous and Meinertzhagen, finding shelter beneath a rock, lay awake comparing notes on birds and other wildlife.

"Provisions were to have been sent on shore for us," Selous later wrote to a friend, "but if they were, we never got them. I had a hard biscuit and a lump of cheese in my pocket, but these were ruined in the swamp." Still, the lingering excitement of the previous day's battle and the anticipation of the next day's assault kept them alert, and—so the hardy Selous claimed—even after the day's exertions, he "was not really tired at all."

Just after dawn, with rain coming down in buckets, Stewart ordered the troops forward, under another artillery barrage from the lake. The Germans replied with the single remaining 75, while their sharpshooters, concealed in the swamp, did more damage than the occasional artillery shell. The Frontiersmen's much-respected sergeant major, a man named Bottomly, went down, hit by a sniper's bullet, bare inches from where Selous lay. Meanwhile, the British bombardment, raging overhead, made a stupendous clamor.

"Their shells came screaming and whistling over us," Selous wrote. "The machine-guns were going too with their wicked rattle, and bullets from snipers' rifles came with an unpleasant sound . . . within a few inches of our bodies, which were just then pressed as close to the ground as possible. I thought, as I lay there only a yard away from the blood-stained corpse of poor Sergeant-Major Bottomly, listening to the peculiar noise of each kind of projectile as it found its invisible course through the air above and around me, that I could recall various half-hours of my life passed amidst much pleasanter surroundings. And yet what a small and miserable thing this was, after all, in the way of a battle compared with the titanic combats which have been taking place in Europe."

For a while, a lone sniper kept the Frontiersmen pinned down from a choice firing position somewhere in the swamp. All efforts to take him out failed, artillery being too blunt an instrument for such fine surgery and the Maxims lacking a clear field of fire. At this point, Meinertzhagen grabbed a Mannlicher hunting rifle, waded into the swamp, scoped out the sniper's blind, and dropped him with a single shot to the back of the head—or so he reports in his diaries. Sniper gone, the advance continued.

Meanwhile, von Stuemer and his 150 *askari* reinforcements returned from patrol to find their *boma* under siege. But the British had advanced too far, and with greatly superior numbers; von Stuemer knew they could not now be stopped. He ordered the retreat, and the Germans quickly abandoned their positions and withdrew through the banana plantations at the edge of town to fight another day.

In the early afternoon, with the rain slowed to a drizzle, 3rd KAR and the Frontiersmen entered Bukoba. Lieutenant Dartnell, an Australian Frontiersman officer, pulled down the Imperial German flag from its pole and raised the Union Jack. The British had sustained 30 killed and wounded out of 2,000; von Stuemer had lost more than fifteen percent of his total force of around 300. Bukoba's wireless tower—Meinertzhagen thought it resembled a mini *Tour Eiffel*—the expedition's prime target, was then quickly mined by sappers. It fell with a hideous crash in the subsequent explosion. Moments later, the whole town quaked when the arsenal beneath the fort went up: Two tame pelicans who sauntered about the arsenal grounds had refused to be shooed away; these obstinate birds went up in a cloud of feathers and half-digested fish along with the munitions.

Thus far, the Bukoba Expedition might be called a success—somewhat clumsily managed, perhaps, but relatively light on British casualties. Then Colonel Driscoll of the Frontiersmen approached Stewart and asked permission for his men to loot the place. Bukoba's German residents had evacuated with the army, leaving their possessions behind, their houses locked and empty. Many African civilians had remained and were still hunkered in the native quarter; their numbers included women and children. To his discredit, Stewart agreed to Driscoll's request—though he stipulated that there be no drunkenness or violence while the town was sacked. To Meinertzhagen, this was like telling "a ferret that he can enter a rabbit hole and not touch the rabbits."

Naturally, a bacchanal of looting and rape ensued. Troops who had so

recently crawled through swamps, braved sniper fire, and risked annihilation cut loose and ransacked the place—though Meinertzhagen, Selous,
and the officers and men of the Loyal North Lancs refused to participate.
The German houses were smashed into and thoroughly looted. KAR and
Frontiersmen alike emerged from the shattered structures with booty of all
sorts. Meinertzhagen saw British soldiers in looted tuxedos wearing German officers' *Pickelhaube* dress helmets; African porters sashayed around
clothed in ladies' undergarments; KAR smoked looted Henry Clay cigars
half as long as their arms and drank champagne from bottles with broken
necks. Several of them spent an hour throwing stones at a huge portrait of
the Kaiser. A German parrot, trained to say *"Ach du Schwein!"* was liberated
by a Frontiersman with a debilitating stutter named Tanner who planned
to teach the bird imprecations against its former owners. Meinertzhagen
wondered if the bird would "reproduce the stuttering"—though whether a
stutterer stutters while communicating with his own parrot is a question
that remains unanswered.

Also among the spoils were some dirty photographs from the house of
Major von Stuemer. The Frontiersmen found a looted diptych especially
titillating: One side showed the commander resplendent in his best dress
uniform standing stiffly at attention beside his naked wife; its companion
piece showed the commandant completely naked and the wife resplen-
dently dressed. One can only speculate as to the sex games prevalent among
these Germans living on the frontier at the edge of the civilized world.

On the darker side, however, several native women were raped by KAR
troops. These the offending parties attempted to mollify with gifts of food
when British forces withdrew on the morning of the 24th. Thirty-two thousand rounds of ammunition, sixty-four rifles, and a German field gun comprised the only official loot from Bukoba—though the field gun, improperly
lashed to a raft for transport to the steamers, slipped its restraints and sank
irretrievably into the lake.

The British War Office and the International Press made much of the Bukoba Expedition. Lord Kitchener, though opposed to offensive operations
in East Africa, was not opposed to victory. He telegraphed his congratula-

tions to both Generals Tighe and Stewart; the expedition, he said, had been "a brilliant success." Even ex-President Roosevelt in the faraway United States sent his friend Selous a letter praising Bukoba as a "first-class little fight." But the reactions on the ground from civilians in British East Africa frustrated its participants. Perhaps word of the looting and rapes had spread to Nairobi; or perhaps the denizens of the clubs and other, less exalted civilians just didn't care: After nearly a year of war, the average civilian in BEA was still not invested in the war effort.

"One would have thought," Selous wrote, "that as our men had come out from England to fight for East Africa, and that as we had just returned from a successful attack on an enemy's stronghold, and as our time of arrival in Nairobi had been telegraphed on ahead, that something might have been done by the townspeople on behalf of our tired and hungry men. . . . But not a bite of food for man or officer was to be had on our arrival at Nairobi, and not even hot water could be obtained to make tea with."

Also, the British failed to follow up on their "first-class little fight." After Bukoba, a series of losses at the hands of the Schutztruppe in the latter half of 1915 knocked morale back down to the subterranean levels it had occupied directly after Jasin. General Malleson, deploying the KAR, the Loyal North Lancs, a battalion of Punjabis, and an irregular company of Somali cavalry raised and led by a prominent colonist, Berkeley Cole (one of Karen von Blixen's great friends in Africa), failed to dislodge an inferior number of *askaris* under Captain Vorberg and Leutnant Merensky at Mbuyuni, just east of the town of Taveta in the shadow of Kilimanjaro. In August, a strongly held British outpost at Voi fell to the surprise attack of a small German patrol. And of course guerrilla attacks on the Uganda Railway continued unabated.

"It is no longer a question of invading GEA," wrote Meinertzhagen in despair in late 1915, "or even undertaking minor operations. We have lost the initiative."

Presently, as if to drown his sorrows, Tighe began drinking even more heavily than usual: "The poor man," Meinertzhagen noted in his diaries, "I fear incipient delirium tremens. . . . He told me that he could not resist his liquor and knew it was going to kill him in the end."

Tighe's drinking produced more than the usual befuddlement and bad hangovers; it appeared for a time that he had begun to hallucinate: During a voyage on Lake Victoria, he became possessed by the idea that the ship was going backward. When Meinertzhagen informed him that this was not the case, he became nearly hysterical. "If I say the ship is going back, it's going back; send for the captain!" he screamed. Upon being assured by both captain and chief engineer that the ship was indeed going in the proper direction, he then decided it was on fire. When informed that the burning smell coming from the galley was merely the crew's dinner being prepared, he again began to rant and rave: "Who's the best judge as to whether the ship's on fire or not? I'm in command here and if I say the ship's on fire, it jolly well is and damn you all!" Tighe eventually saw the light of reason after being taken by the hand and shown the inept cook at work—but these sorts of lapses from reality did not bode well for the British Army's future in Africa.

Simply put, Tighe, a veteran of too many fights, had grown weary of a war fought without the proper resources against a commander as cool-headed and inventive as von Lettow. And the fall rainy season brought the various plagues indigenous to the tropics. Soon after Bukoba, the Loyal North Lancs really did collapse with disease: Their war diary asserts that "of the soldiers of the Battalion since the beginning of the war . . . 836 have been admitted to hospital; only 278 have not." The Indian troops suffered even more from malaria than soldiers of other nationalities; as it turned out, they had less natural immunity to the disease than Europeans and nearly ceased to exist as a fighting force. Their strength had been reduced three-quarters by the end of 1915.

Indeed, the war seemed lost just a year after it had begun. But one colonist, the handsome, resourceful Captain Ewart "Cape to Cairo" Grogan, the first man to walk the length of Africa between these two distant points, saw conscription as the only way the Germans could be beaten. He submitted a proposal on the matter to the lethargic Belfield, who rejected it immediately. Grogan then held a patriotic rally, with Tighe's blessing, at Nairobi's Theater Royal to a packed house on September 7, 1915. It was a memorable event, called "the greatest meeting in the history of British East Africa." The orchestra played for an hour; patriotic songs were sung so loud they shook the roof beams. Then Grogan stood and gave a stirring oration criticizing the

colony's war efforts thus far. Surprisingly, the audience greeted his chastisements with deafening roars of approval:

"When the history of the war comes to be written," Grogan thundered,
"and the children ask, 'What did your daddy do in the war?' let no man
shrink from having the question asked! When we pass on our account of
what we have done, let us be sure the answer from home will be 'Well done,
thou babe of Empire!'"

Meinertzhagen saw this moment as the decisive turning point in the
colony's war effort. At last, he wrote, "the colony had found itself." And yet
troops still did not materialize in sufficient numbers to take the war to the
Germans in GEA. They were simply unavailable, drained white on the killing fields of Europe. Only von Lettow, with typical prescience, guessed his
enemy's next move:

"The scanty wireless messages and other communications we received
about events in the outside world indicated our affairs in South West Africa
were going badly," he wrote. "And that the British troops employed there
would become available for other purposes in the immediate future."

In other words, the South Africans were coming to take charge of
the war.

Chapter 18

THE WRECK OF THE *KÖNIGSBERG*

A British policeman stopped Pieter J. Pretorius—the great Boer elephant hunter, wanderer, and scout—on the street of his native Nylstroom in the Transvaal in January 1915 with a preemptory order:

"You must come with me to the charge office!" (Nylstroom's police station) the policeman barked.

Pretorius hesitated.

He was a famous, perhaps notorious figure in South Africa, known to authorities and natives alike; in the tribal lands, in the jungles, and on the veldt, they called him *Mtanda Bantu*—Easy with People. There, in Africa's wild places, he had many friends, and not a few enemies. The authorities, meanwhile, knew he was not someone to be trifled with. One of those tough, sinewy men impossible to kill, his skin permanently stained a curious yellow ocher from frequent bouts of malaria, Pretorius had spent the past quarter century hunting and wandering the continent from Kisumu to the Cape in search of elephant ivory and adventure. His last name—as famous in his country as Washington in our own—marked him as a member of one of South Africa's First Families:

In 1838, P. J. Pretorius's great-great-grandfather, Andries Pretorius, had led the Voortrekkers (Boers attempting to escape oppressive British rule) across the Drakensberg Range to found a free, though slave-owning, republic in the as yet unsettled Transvaal. Its capital, Pretoria, is still South Africa's administrative seat. That same year, Andries led a commando of 420

Boers against the 30,000-strong impis of the Zulu king, Dingane, in the celebrated Battle of Blood River. The Boers took refuge behind a laager of their heavy wagons circled and chained together atop a ridge and beat back the Zulu onslaught. It was one of history's greatest lopsided victories: The Zulus lost at least a tenth of their forces to the rock-steady volley fire of the Boers, who escaped with a few minor injuries.

P. J. Pretorius had inherited a goodly portion of his ancestor's grit. He once single-handedly polished off forty-seven hostile tribesmen from an ambushing war party in German East Africa. The German authorities tracked him down and imprisoned him for two years following this slaughter, before deciding he had acted in self-defense. Pretorius spent his time in jail—cruel punishment for a man to whom Africa itself seemed small—learning German and coming to despise the race of Teutons for what he called their "forthright sins":

"I am convinced that no other race in the world would have acted as the authorities in German East Africa did," he later wrote. "The German thinks that whatever he does is proved right by his power to do it. His is the true law of the jungle which knows no morals, only might."

Pretorius was understandably bitter: German authorities had, via a pretext, already confiscated his farm in the Upper Rufiji Delta on behalf of a German officer, Hauptmann Blake, to whom Pretorius had earlier refused sale. To the latter, the farm was sacred ground: A few years before, Pretorius, temporarily retired from elephant hunting, had built a substantial farmhouse as a wedding present for his beautiful young wife on land he had cleared himself. Unfortunately, a few months after moving in, she died of fever; Pretorius went back to elephant hunting but kept the farm as a kind of shrine to the wife he had loved and lost.

Following the farm's confiscation, Pretorius revenged himself on the Germans—after duly informing them of his intentions in a letter—by poaching elephants from German territory without a license. And he would keep doing this, he wrote, until he had recouped the value in ivory of his stolen farm. The seasoned Pretorius knew the Rufiji intimately; he had hunted the district for years. The Germans chased him through the mangroves and the jungles, one step behind the trail of elephant carcasses—always minus their ivory. At last, Pretorius paid himself back for his farm, the Germans gave up, and the matter subsided, though he remained at the top of their Most Wanted list.

During the decade preceding 1914, Pretorius kept hunting, carefully staying on the Portuguese side of the Rovuma River, which marked the boundary between German and Portuguese East Africa. Working the deep bush, he knew nothing of events in the wider world. The morning of August 14, 1914, found him at his summer hunting camp on an island in the Rovuma, loafing around in his pajamas, when suddenly a column of 200 *askaris* appeared out of nowhere. They were led by the sinister Dr. Wolfgang Weck, the Schutztruppe's chief surgeon, a violent man who had recently violated Portuguese neutrality by attacking their *boma* at Maziua without provocation and killing its commander and a dozen native soldiers. Now Weck had taken it upon himself to capture or kill Pretorius—even though the elephant hunter's camp lay in Portuguese territory.

Weck's *askaris* overran Pretorius's camp, rifles blazing. They shot him through both legs and were closing in for the kill when he escaped by throwing himself in the river. Badly wounded, he floated to safety in the reeds. Thus began a four-month odyssey that saw Pretorius captured, escaped, captured again, escaped again. At one point, in horrible pain and barely able to walk, he kidnapped a quartet of village women on a trail at gunpoint to force their husbands to carry him in a litter to British territory. Along the way, the bullet wounds in his legs became seriously infected.

In one leg, "between the bullet wounds was a big lump," he wrote, "and all up to the knee was black. The only thing to do was to open the knee and let out the pus. . . . Otherwise, blood-poisoning and death would result." Pretorius then plunged a blunt knife into the lump, releasing an explosion of infected matter. He passed out from the pain but somehow survived the ordeal. At last he gained the English mission station at Malindi, Nyasaland. In his thoroughly depleted and very yellow state—he was also again suffering from malaria—an old friend there, a Catholic priest, failed to recognize him. Eventually, Pretorius, now burning for revenge on the Germans, made his way to South Africa and volunteered for the British Army. The recruiting officer, however, turned him down. British authorities didn't believe his fantastic tale of escape from Weck on the Rovuma, took him for a spy, and put him under surveillance.

Disgruntled, Pretorius returned home to Nylstroom and his family, whom he hadn't seen in twenty-five years. Two weeks later, the policeman accosted him on the street: "Come with me," the policeman repeated. Pretorius went, immune, he says, to any thoughts of the future indignities in store for him at the hands of fate and officialdom, German or English. What awaited him at the police station was a mysterious command from the British War Office disguised as a polite request: Would P. J. Pretorius kindly "accept service" with the imperial government? Pretorius accepted. "And from that moment," he says, "I lived in a whirl of suspense." A special train whisked him through the night toward Durban, on the coast, halting only to take on a telegram from another train coming in the opposite direction: WITH COMPLIMENTS FROM ADMIRAL KING-HALL. ON ARRIVAL IN DURBAN PROCEED IMMEDIATELY TO C. SHED POINT. Apparently, the British Royal Navy had just recruited an elephant hunter to bring down a battleship.

More than three months had passed since the unlucky aviator Cutler spotted the *Königsberg* hidden in an elbow of the Simba-Uranga, near the hamlet of Salale—and since he had crash-landed into the Rufiji and the mists of history. No one in the British Navy could now say whether *Königsberg* remained where she had last been seen, or whether the German battle cruiser had steamed to another hideout in the swampy morass of the delta. Or indeed, if she might have escaped one night, unseen, down the channel and into the open sea—though this last possibility seemed unlikely.

Twenty-four British warships now patrolled the shallow waters off the Rufiji mouths, from the massive, antiquated HMS *Goliath*—now Admiral King-Hall's flagship, *Hyacinth* having been sent off to duty elsewhere—to the tiny HMS *Pickle*, little more than a speedboat with an abbreviated crew. All these, large and small, wasted away on the Rufiji Station, where conditions aboard ship were among the worst anywhere in the navy: Shore leave nonexistent, the crews languished in a tropical floating hell. Temperatures topside never descended below 85° F; in engine rooms they often surpassed

125°; most of the ships, badly outdated, had not been fitted with refrigeration units. Food spoiled; cockroaches of incredible size swarmed everywhere. Worst of all, supplies of rum quickly reached the bottom of the barrel. Even these decrepit ships might have better served Great Britain's war in other theaters—but the destruction of the *Königsberg* had become a consuming passion at the Admiralty. Churchill, worst of the *Königsberg* obsessives, attempted to micromanage the campaign against her via radio signals and coded messages from London. The First Sea Lord dictated; King-Hall resisted—a battle of wills conducted over the ether from half a world away.

King-Hall, mulling things over on the quarterdeck of *Goliath*, found himself in need of more accurate information regarding *Königsberg*. He had been promised more seaplanes for reconnaissance; they were supposedly on their way from various points in the empire. But he also needed to know things that could not be discovered from the air. He had heard about the famous P. J. Pretorius from connections in South Africa and, because the elephant hunter was already under official surveillance, knew exactly where to lay hands on him. King-Hall also knew the sad story of Pretorius's lost farm on the Rufiji and the latter's personal war against the German colony: Here was more than an old Africa hand; here was someone with a grudge against Germany to whom the Rufiji had literally been his own backyard.

The first meeting between the admiral and the elephant hunter aboard *Goliath* went well: The "ugliest man in the British Navy" (a diminutive, bearded homunculus) and perhaps the ugliest man in Africa (a yellow-skinned, chicken-scrawny, sun-withered beanpole), both far tougher than they looked, took to each other immediately:

"King-Hall was a charming man," Pretorius wrote (possibly the only man in Africa to think so), ". . . red complexioned and [with] the bushiest eyebrows I have ever seen. . . . From the first, I instinctively liked him. He shook hands with me and signalled me to sit down."

Pretorius sat; the admiral laid out his plans. Before he could launch his final assault on *Königsberg*, King-Hall said, he needed several absolutely vital pieces of information: First—of course—where was *Königsberg*? Second, was she fit and capable? Third, did her guns still work? Fourth, did she still possess all her torpedoes? Or had they been parceled out to torpedo launches along the river where they might be fired at invading British riverine craft? Fifth, did a passage exist up the Simba-Uranga or the Kikunja Channels—the widest of the Rufiji's mouths—that might allow entry of a British warship of shallow draft? Finally, since the Rufiji remained essentially uncharted, the British Navy required a tidal chart showing high and low tides in the channels every day for a month.

Fortunately, Pretorius need not come up with this information immediately or all at once, King-Hall continued. The elephant hunter would have until spring, as the two essential components of the admiral's new strategy had yet to arrive from England: Reconnaissance airplanes able to carry bombs—so he had been assured—were definitely on their way; but the real work of destruction would be accomplished by the monitors.

———————

In 1913, the Brazilian Navy, eager to dominate the upper reaches of the Amazon, had ordered three curious, old-fashioned gunboats from the Scottish shipyards at Barrow-in-Furness. These vessels, called monitors because of their resemblance to the original ironclad warship (that "cheesebox on a raft," the USS *Monitor* of the American Civil War), were little more than floating gun platforms. An unusually shallow draft of about six feet allowed the monitors to work close inshore and navigate rivers impassible to deeper-hulled warships. Their heavy armaments—two 6-inch and two 4.7-inch guns—made them formidable opponents. Indeed, these guns were as large as anything carried aboard German battle cruisers like *Königsberg*.

The monitors, 256 feet long and 1,256 tons unloaded, sported a single prominent funnel and an 80-foot central mainmast. Projected top speed of a painfully slow twelve knots proved much slower in practice. Each carried a minimal coal supply and so could not manage long voyages, which was just as well: Waves crashed over their narrow freeboard at stem and stern; with a direct wind from either port or starboard they wallowed and threatened to swamp—all obvious liabilities for any oceangoing vessel. But for river wars, they were just the thing.

Brazilian Navy officials eagerly awaited delivery of their new warships. They had already been christened *Solomos*, *Madeira*, and *Javery* and were undergoing acceptance trials when war broke out in August 1914. An ocean voyage being impossible under their own steam, the monitors would soon be towed across the Atlantic to the Amazon by oceangoing tugs. Suddenly, the Admiralty stepped in and confiscated the three ungainly vessels; their use was immediately required for Great Britain's war against Germany and the Central Powers. The Brazilians' reaction to this seizure must have been utter dismay: They had spent freely on lavish interior fittings and other cosmetic niceties. Indeed, the Brazilian monitors were perhaps the most luxurious naval vessels anywhere in the world.

When British officials came aboard for an inspection tour, they looked around aghast: Behind the monitors' steel bulkheads, painted a jaunty Coast Guard white, the interiors resembled a posh gentleman's club—or a high-class bordello: Captain's cabin and officers' quarters, ready room and gun room were done up in glossy oak paneling agleam with brass touches. Persian carpets decorated the decks. Blue linen tablecloths flecked with white embroidered anchors, monogrammed china, and chairs with interchangeable seats (wicker for hot weather, velvet for cold) had been specially made for the officers' mess. Chandeliers hung from the ceilings. The British Navy inspectors allowed themselves a moment of envious awe, then took to the interior with crowbars and sledgehammers. The monitors' gleaming white hulls—calculated to dazzle any Amazonian Indian approaching in a canoe—were immediately covered in wartime gray; any remaining brass fittings ended up a tarry black. All the luxurious accoutrements—carpets, tablecloths, interchangeable chairs—ripped out and discarded, ended up in a heap on the docks. Renamed *Humber*, *Severn*, and *Mersey*, the squat little ships were made ready for war.

Now dubbed the "Inshore Flotilla and Squadron," they engaged in early action along the Belgian coast in 1914 and 1915 and played an appreciable part in the "Race to the Sea" campaign of the first weeks of the war: As trenches were dug in a frantic burst all the way across Flanders to the English Channel, the monitors lying just offshore supported the action on land with their big guns. Coming under fire from German field artillery, they sustained damage and casualties, but played their role well. Churchill credited them with preventing the fall of Calais, Dunkirk, and Boulogne and saving what was left of the Belgian Army.

"The Inshore Flotilla and Squadron," he intoned, "have played an appreciable part in the great battle now proceeding. You have shown the Germans that, in this case, there is a flank they cannot turn."

Flotilla officers, an odd mix of merchant marine and naval reservists, suited their curious ships. Most, getting on in years, had already pursued a variety of nonmilitary careers—including the stage and the teaching of German to high school students—before being recalled to service in August. Captain E. J. A. Fullerton, first of *Mersey*, then *Severn*, the flotilla's commander, had been a gym instructor at the Royal Naval College, Osborne, and had served aboard King Edward VII's yacht, HMY *Victoria and Albert*, in the last days of the Belle Epoque. When promoted to captain in January 1915, he provided a pint of beer to every sailor in the flotilla for a toast to his health.

Following action in Belgian waters, the Admiralty ordered the monitors to the Dardanelles to take part in the ill-fated Gallipoli Campaign. There, along with several of the most obsolete vessels in the British Navy, they were to help force the straits—the goal of the campaign being the capture of Constantinople from the Turks by naval action alone. Made as seaworthy as possible, with topmast stowed and hatches battened, the monitors wallowed down the European coasts and through the Straits of Gibraltar in heavy seas, towed by their tugs at the punishingly slow speed of six knots. They arrived at Malta in March, next stop Turkey. All officers and men of the Inshore Flotilla and Squadron had been sent ahead as passengers aboard the HMS *Trent*.

But by this time, the Turks under the famous Mustapha Kemal—later Ataturk—with German help had sunk three British battleships off the Dardanelles and disabled three more. British Admiral John de Robeck, in charge of naval operations, abruptly called off his battered fleet, in favor of an amphibious invasion force. Now, suddenly, the monitors had become redundant. They languished in the fortified harbor at Valetta for weeks—until Admiral King-Hall, from his watch on the far-off Rufiji Station, got wind of their presence in the Mediterranean. These clumsy, powerfully armed, shallow-draft vessels might have been made expressly for his ongoing battle against *Königsberg*.

After some wrangling with the Admiralty, King-Hall secured the use of *Mersey* and *Severn* and their officers and crews, though not *Humber*. The pair of monitors, again fixed to their oceangoing tugs via steel cables, began another long journey—this time 5,000 miles across the Mediterranean, through the Suez Canal, down the Red Sea to the Indian Ocean, and to the clotted, crocodile-infested channels of the Rufiji Delta.

The German garrison on Mafia Island had surrendered to a British invasion force consisting of 1st KAR and a company of the 101st Grenadiers not long after *Königsberg* sought refuge up the Rufiji. Invading British troops had met slight resistance from thirty *askaris* commanded by Leutnant Eric Schiller, who, after a two-hour engagement, gave up and lowered the Imperial German flag at the village of Ngombeni. Kilindome, the island's capital, quickly followed suit. This small island—once a pirates' nest, now home to 1,000 or so natives, a couple of dozen square miles of nutmeg plantations, and five or six Germans—had just rejoined the British Empire, to whom it had once belonged. (Mafia had been traded to the Germans for an equally insignificant though even less habitable part of the African interior called the "Caprivi Finger" back in 1890.)

Colonel Mackay, the former Force B intelligence chief officer, was given charge of the place. Mackay now suffered from an apparently incurable malaria; General Tighe thought the sea air would do him good. Unfortunately, insalubrious, mosquito-ridden Mafia Island, "a sweltering hellhole," proved even more malarial than Mackay's former posting in Mombasa, and his condition worsened.

A single scrawny company of the 63rd Palamcottahs made up Mackay's command; for them, Mafia was punishment duty, meted out for their miserable performance at Tanga. But Mafia would soon assume an importance in the history of African aviation all out of proportion to its size and discomforts. The first naval air station in Africa quickly materialized on Mafia's southeastern flank: It consisted of a couple of thatched huts, a field on which to park any planes that might (hopefully) arrive soon, and an airstrip—a narrow 200-yard-long stretch of packed earth, ending in a bog.

Meanwhile, P. J. Pretorius had already set up a base for his intelligence-gathering operation on nearby Komo, a minuscule islet two miles off the Rufiji Delta. As the first phase of his mission would require some muscle, the elephant hunter recruited six stout fellows from the coastal settlements—

these, according to Colonel Mackay, "the biggest rogues on the entire east coast," nevertheless "made up in courage what they lacked in morals."

With his hooligan commandos assembled in two dugouts, Pretorius approached the Rufiji in the dark hours just past 2 a.m. one night in late February 1915. They landed on a secluded beach, hid the dugouts in the mangroves, and crept inland, often passing within a few feet of German patrols. At dawn, they came to a new road, a raw red scar in the deep green jungle; the Germans had cleared it to move ammunition and reinforcements from Dar es Salaam to Delta Force rifle pits and gun emplacements in the Rufiji. Pretorius and his hooligans waited in the underbrush as a German patrol went by unawares. When, after a while, two African youths passed, he ordered his men to pounce. The youths, taken hostage, were forced at gunpoint back to their village. There Pretorius swapped them for the village *jumbee*—an office, it would seem, for which being taken hostage ought to have been part of the job description.

Pretorius informed the captive *jumbee* that he was now a prisoner of the British Navy—at a salary of five pounds per month!—as long as he agreed to help find the *Königsberg*. The *jumbee* happily accepted the position of paid prisoner and acquiesced to the elephant hunter's terms. Like that other *jumbee* kidnapped by Drury-Lowe's men months before, he bore no special love for the Germans who ran his country, nor for the British— but in this case, the latter paid nicely.

The *jumbee* quickly led Pretorius to a rise crowned with a grove of tall trees overlooking the Simba-Uranga Channel, and instructed the wiry elephant hunter to climb. Pretorius clambered to the top of the tallest palm and scanned the delta through high-powered binoculars. Below, he saw nothing, only an endless forest. Then, suddenly—as with the lookout on *Hyacinth*—one of the trees moved. And there she was, SMS *Königsberg*, just a few hundred yards away, anchored in the Simba-Uranga and so well camouflaged as to be practically indistinguishable from the surrounding greenery. Pretorius watched for a long while. The German battle cruiser seemed in good working order: Polished decking showed from beneath her camouflaged awnings. Presently, a puff of smoke issued from one of her funnels. The elephant hunter shimmied down, exultant—he had found the *Königsberg* on his first foray into the delta!

After reminding the *jumbee* of his new status as a civilian employee/ prisoner of the Royal Navy, Pretorius and his bravos returned to their lair on Komo. The next morning, he paddled out to HMS *Goliath* for a meeting with King-Hall. The admiral was pleased. At least *Königsberg*'s location no longer remained a mystery. But—as planned—the intelligence-gathering operation had only just begun; the most difficult parts lay ahead. A few days later, the elephant hunter returned to the Rufiji, this time without his commandos. The next phase required finesse, not muscle: Pretorius needed to get as close to the *Königsberg* as possible, if not actually inside the cruiser's hold.

Meanwhile, Captain Loof, having just lost half his crew to the Schutz-truppe, had been recruiting temporary stokers from the local native population; one of these was the *jumbee*'s son. Confined to *Königsberg* for the sake of secrecy, the son was, oddly, allowed to receive visitors. Pretorius disguised himself as a Swahili-Arab trader, a part he played with ease— given his command of both Swahili and Arabic and his permanently ma-larial yellow complexion further darkened by years spent in the wild. Accompanied by the *jumbee*, posing as his "boy," the pair visited the *Königsberg* under the guise of paying a paternal call.

On the *jumbee*'s advice, Pretorius brought along a basket of live chick-ens. These he offered to the German sentry on duty—a gift happily ac-cepted. The *jumbee* then asked to see his son. The boy, summoned, appeared; the two embraced. The *jumbee*, carefully rehearsed by Pretorius to appear casual, now asked a few quick, pertinent questions in Swahili disguised with the inflections of harmless banter. Were the ship's big guns working properly? Yes, the son replied. And what of the torpedoes, the "long bullets that swim in the water"? These had been removed and parceled out to smaller boats downriver, the son said—a vital piece of intelligence: One of the *Königsberg* torpedoes might easily sink a British warship attempting to force the channel. And what of the condition of the crew? Not good—many were sick with malaria and other diseases.

Information thus obtained, the Arab trader and his "boy" disappeared into the bush.

Pretorius's role-playing now progressed to its second act. In his next guise as a native fisherman, wearing only a loincloth, he trolled up and down the channels of both the Simba-Uranga and Kikunja in a native dugout every day for weeks. Catching fish as necessary to support his disguise—often within sight of Delta Force rifle pits—Pretorius still managed to make careful soundings of channel depths using a specially prepared notched pole. The main channel averaged six to seven feet, he discovered; just deep enough to allow a shallow-draft, monitor-class vessel into its upper reaches—but only so far: *Königsberg's* current anchorage lay on the other side of an impassable sandbar.

Unable to progress any farther by water, Pretorius hid his dugout along the riverbank and walked, counting each step as he followed the channel's wild meanderings all the way to the German battle cruiser. She lay, so he finally figured, well within the reach of a monitor's guns—if the vessel could reach the sandbar.

Pretorius's next and last mission in the Rufiji was "a simply ghastly job." He fixed his notched pole in a secluded spot near the mouth of the Simba-Uranga to measure the rise and fall of the tides, and measured them several times a day for a month: Unable to catch more than a few hours' sleep at a time, surrounded by crocodiles and enveloped in clouds of vicious mosquitoes, the elephant hunter nevertheless managed to produce an accurate tidal chart—though, he allowed, "I was glad the day I placed the chart in the Admiral's hands." This statement was as close as the leathery Pretorius ever got to a complaint.

With the completion of this last work, P. J. Pretorius's intelligence-gathering mission in the Rufiji came to an end. His worth as the most capable intelligence resource in the British forces in Africa—and probably any other theater of the war—had been proven without a doubt. He later accepted a commission as chief of scouts, would be promoted major and receive the DSO—but we get ahead of our story.

Now in full possession of *Königsberg's* vital statistics, Admiral King-Hall awaited only the arrival of his secret weapons to begin the final assault. After much anticipation, an entire "air wing" of the newly created Royal Naval Air Service commanded by Flight Lieutenant John Tullock Cull arrived at Mafia aboard the *Kinfauns Castle*. Also aboard came two new

Sopwith hydroplanes and eighteen RNAS officers and mechanics. Cull would pick up where the captured Cutler had left off; he and his men would find the *Königsberg* and destroy her. For this purpose, each Sopwith came outfitted with racks for sixteen- and fifty-pound bombs. With these, they planned to blow the German battle cruiser out of the water from the air, thus rendering any possible action by monitors unnecessary.

But the Sopwiths proved utterly unreliable, unsuited to the sweltering climate of the Rufiji Delta: Their hollow pontoons exploded in the heat and had to be hastily vented with an ax; their propellers, constructed from glued layers of laminated hardwood, came unglued and spun themselves to pieces; worst of all, the engines seized after just an hour in the air: Air supply to the Sopwith's engine entered through an exhaust valve that closed unpredictably in hot weather, thus choking internal combustion. Cull discovered this peccadillo the hard way: On Sopwith one's second flight, its engine quit in midair, dropping the aviator into the drink. Cull survived the crash; the Sopwith did not. It sank to the bottom of the Indian Ocean, its carcass rendered unsalvageable by salt water.

RNAS mechanics jerry-rigged a solution to the engine issue on the second Sopwith, but even with that gremlin slain, the plane remained basically unserviceable. It could not lift off the water loaded down with bombs, pilot, and observer; with all but the pilot removed, it could only rise a few feet above the reefs, making an easy target for German small-arms fire. Eventually, the idea of bombing *Königsberg* from the air was given up. The remaining Sopwith, withdrawn from service, made way for another shipment of planes—two Caudron biplanes and two "pusher"-model Henry Farnum seaplanes. Both of these makes, relative anachronisms compared to the Sopwiths, could nonetheless hold the air with ease.

For a month or so, Cull and his RNAS aviators made regular reconnaissance flights over the delta in their new-old planes; the most important took place on the morning of April 25, 1915. Cull and his observer, Sublieutenant Arnold, powered over the tree line at about 800 feet at the Farnum's poky top speed of sixty miles per hour. Delta Force immediately put up a barrage of rifle fire and a few 47mm shells, but somehow the Farnum droned through the mushrooming clouds of flak and flew on. Over the upper Kikunja Channel larger explosions darkened the sky; then Cull tilted his wing and caught sight of his quarry below: There lay *Königsberg*, firing her big guns at peak elevation—at him. An explosion not yards behind the Farnum's tail made itself felt as a shock wave in the air; the Farnum sputtered. Cull descended to 700 feet, exposing himself and his observer to more accurate fire, but getting a closer view of the trapped battle cruiser. She had moved on from the place where last seen by Pretorius. Now she anchored in a tight angle of the Kikunja, her bow facing downriver, readying herself, perhaps, for a quick sprint to freedom. Her deck awnings furled, her deck now painted a seagoing gray, no longer camouflaged, she made no effort to conceal herself.

Cull circled twice. For a bit of sport, he and Arnold let fly with the pistols they had brought aboard, but what use are pistols against a battleship? Cull laid his pistol aside, took up his Brownie box camera, and snapped several pictures before turning back, again running through clouds of Delta Force fire. This time, though, the Farnum was hit. The frail plane made open water, coughed, lost altitude; then the engine quit. Cull landed hard a mile or two off the Mafia aerodrome. Mechanics in steam launches towed the seaplane ashore; later, they found a German bullet in the main oil-feeder pipe and several holes in the fuselage. It had been a close call, but the exact position of *Königsberg*'s final anchorage could now be fixed on the charts—augmented by Pretorius's careful tide marks. And Cull's box Brownie had taken the first photograph from an airplane of a warship under siege in the history of naval warfare. Arguably the first step—via a wire and wood flying machine and photographic plates coated with silver nitrate—in a direct line that has led us to eye-in-the-sky spy satellites surveilling fleet maneuvers, and just about everything else, from the depths of space.

Cull completed several more such flights over the next several weeks. But the loss of another Farnum in May—its rudder shot off by accurate German ground fire—caused King-Hall to cancel all further RNAS reconnaissance missions. The two remaining planes (one Farnum and one Caudron) would be needed as spotters for the real-world game of Battleship, to be played out when the monitors arrived. They were on their way and overdue. They had been battling heavy currents and rough seas in the Indian Ocean for weeks, wallowing along, their few feet of freeboard plunging into the troughs of the waves, nearly sinking several times and making only a few knots per hour toward their ultimate destination in the Rufiji Delta.

Belying her shipshape appearance from the air, conditions aboard *Königsberg* had deteriorated. More than six months had passed since the German cruiser found refuge up the Rufiji, and the ship's larder had now run out of all dietary staples. Hard-pressed by the British blockade, von Lettow couldn't send supplies; *Königsberg*'s officers and crew now subsisted on what they could forage in the surrounding jungle. Theirs was an unhealthy diet of maize flour, cassava, and pawpaw fruit, occasionally augmented by a basket of chickens brought by native traders—the probable reason behind Pretorius's successful impersonation. It is a military maxim that a hungry sentry, in need of chicken, will often look the other way.

But Korvettenkapitan Loof, also facing a critical shortage of coal, refused to allow the galley mate enough of the stuff for proper cooking of what food they had—leading in turn to more cases of dysentery. Still, had Loof the necessary fuel and manpower and the exact right high tide at the dark of the moon, it is doubtful that *Königsberg* could have now made her escape: the German battle cruiser was rotting away. A pernicious green mold grew nightly on all her metal surfaces—on the guns and the railings and bulkheads—and had to be scraped off each morning. Worst of all, no mail from home—a crucial morale builder—had arrived in months. Radio communication from Germany had ceased following the destruction of the Telefunken wireless tower in Windhoek on the other side of the continent.

It seemed *Königsberg* had been forgotten. The spring rainy season, just upon them, made it all worse. Loof had waited too long.

In the bright gloaming of June 3, 1915, at seven p.m., the monitors *Severn* and *Mersey*, towed by their tugs, finally reached Mafia Island. Battered, shipping water, their engines cold for three months, these riverine vessels had barely survived the long ocean voyage from Scotland via Malta and the Suez Canal. Monitor crews recently disembarked from HMS *Trent* began refitment work immediately and continued without stopping for nearly a month. Leaky seams were reinforced; heavy steel plating—ironically stripped off the hulk of the *Pegasus* at Zanzibar and laid over the thin metal of the monitors' decks— would protect against high-trajectory fire from German guns. Both vessels got yet another coat of paint, now a Rufiji-appropriate mangrove green. Walls of sandbags rose along the low-riding decks; the wheelhouses and three-pound gun emplacements received more steel plating, now hung with hammocks to deflect German shrapnel. Blacksmiths lengthened the monitors' rudders to improve turning radius in the Rufiji's twisty estuaries. Finally, 10,000 kerosene tins filled with air were jammed into the holds to prevent sinking in the event of a hit below the waterline. All of this a far cry from the interchangeable velvet seats and monogrammed tablecloths of the Brazilian Navy.

Sea trials began upon completion of the major work. For days, the monitors took blind potshots at a dhow moored behind a small islet 8,000 yards away. This gunnery was directed by yet another batch of newly arrived RNAS airplanes—two more Henry Farnums and two Caudrons. The latter, fitted with wheels rather than pontoons, actually made use of the primitive airstrip on Mafia Island, another African aviation first. The new Henry Farnums, a more powerful model than their predecessors, managed to maintain a respectable altitude of 4,000 feet over the delta. One of the Caudrons quickly crashed and Squadron Leader Gordon grounded the other one, but the Farnums, newly fitted with wireless sets, kept the air. Pilots— or, as Churchill called them, "chauffeurs of aeroplanes"—had now become artillery spotters and were able to radio accurate information to gunners aboard the monitors.

At last, the squat little ships vaporized the unseen dhow, and King-Hall deemed them ready for action. On the morning of July 5, the admiral sent a message to the monitors' anxiously waiting crews: "The commander in chief desires to wish the captains, officers, and crew of the monitors every success for tomorrow. He is confident that all ranks will uphold the honor of the British flag for King and Country."

Remaining ephemera—doors, beds, oil, and most of the coal—hauled off the monitors that afternoon now made way for more ammunition and food. Baskets of oranges, bottles of fresh water, and buckets of oatmeal came aboard, supplemented by meat sandwiches, four per man.

German spotters had been watching the monitors lumbering down the coast for weeks. Loof, aware of their approach, thought it best not to inform his crew—their nerves already wrecked by the long months of waiting in a malarial backwater. Thus the low-riding vessels took one Delta Force officer by surprise when he caught sight of them steaming through the dawn mists towards the Kikunja Channel on July 6. He saw, as he later reported, "two shadowy-looking ships coming rapidly up the channel. . . . They advanced . . . 7,000, 6,000 yards as if they were coming home," and prepared himself and his men as best he could for the onslaught of a fresh horror.

Severn, Captain Fullerton commanding, led the way. *Mersey* followed. Both, after a momentary lull, came under intense fire from Delta Force 47mm guns. Months earlier, Commander Werner Schönfeld—the same brilliant reserve officer who had supervised the removal and transportation of *Königsberg*'s furry boilers to Dar es Salaam—had begged Loof to release his biggest naval guns to Delta Force for shore defense. Loof had refused, then still hoping to break out of the Rufiji, fully armed and ready to join the Kreuzerkrieg. With the benefit of hindsight, this decision seems an error in judgment—only *Königsberg*'s 105mm guns could have sunk the monitors now surging up the Kikunja Channel. As the monitors passed the German batteries, on cue, every British warship on the Rufiji Station launched a coordinated barrage, designed to destabilize Delta Force, already hard-pressed by return fire from Fullerton and his men. Suddenly, the river exploded; bloody bits of crocodile and other animals, fish, and tree trunks flew into the air with each impacting shell.

Hit a couple of times by German ground fire, the monitors kept moving forward. Two hours after forcing the Kikunja, at six twenty-three a.m., they reached their anchorage—beyond the harassments of Delta Force and within range of *Königsberg*, about 11,000 yards away, according to Fullerton's estimate. Meanwhile, Lieutenants Cull and Arnold, aloft 4,000 feet up in one of the Farnums, ascertained the positions of both the German battle cruiser and the British monitors and radioed their readiness to direct fire. At six forty-five a.m., *Severn* let loose the opening salvo with her six-inch guns.

Aboard the *Königsberg*, the sailors of the first watch had just settled down to their breakfasts in the mess hall, a distasteful meal of cassava porridge, hippopotamus tongue, and other from-hunger concoctions, when "suddenly the cry rang out, 'Clear ships for action!' " as Signalman Ritter later remembered: "The alarm gongs sounded and in a second all were at their battle stations. . . . Our guns opened fire on two airmen who were approaching the *Königsberg*. Shortly afterwards the signal arrived that the monitors *Mersey* and *Severn* had run up the mouth . . . keeping both banks under sharp machine gun and rifle fire."

The battle was on. A release from monotony perhaps, long anticipated by *Königsberg*'s trapped crew; though weirdly, at the sound of the first of *Severn*'s shells Leutnant Joseph Jaeger shot himself in the head in a botched suicide attempt and died painfully at the end of the day. He had been an officer aboard a cushy Deutsche Ost-Afrika Liner before the war and perhaps couldn't handle the stress of the coming battle, deciding to die by his own hand rather than British shrapnel. But another version of his motivations also made the rounds: Some said he was a British spy and knew he had been found out; how else to explain enemy foreknowledge of their booby-trap torpedo boats, several of which had already been carefully targeted and destroyed by the British? Of course Pretorius's intelligence-gathering operation, unknown to the Germans, had supplied the requisite information regarding the "long bullets that swim in water." Not the doomed, despairing *Leutnant*, who must have been a sort of Jonah to his fellow officers.

The actual author of the security leaks now watched the unfolding naval battle, the first he had ever seen, with awe from the deck of *Hyacinth*:

"We fired in salvos, all previous noises fading into insignificance as salvo after salvo belched out," Pretorius wrote. "It was terrific . . . and I gaped in wonderment at the nonchalance of the English sailors. One group, not engaged in the firing, were calmly sitting on the deck mending their boots; others were stitching canvas just as if nothing untoward was happening. They did not even trouble to watch the bombardment."

Less than an hour after the monitors made their anchorage up the Kikunja, guided by the airborne artillery spotters, Cull and Arnold, the *Severn* scored its first hit. The game of Battleship had commenced: *Severn*'s shell hit the *Königsberg*'s upper deck and dug into the officers' galley, where it vaporized one of the cooks. A second shell killed two more sailors; one of these had been impressed off the *Zieten*, boarded back in July 1914. Metal spray from the same shell flayed Seaman Richard Wenig's left foot—his existential musings about the meaning of it all temporarily silenced by pain. A third hit smashed the signal bridge and took out another sailor.

The *Königsberg* responded immediately, though hampered by her inability to maneuver and limited to the use of starboard batteries by her position in the channel. Still, Chief Gunner Leutnant Hans Apel directed more or less accurate fire with the help of spotters on a platform concealed in the trees not far from the monitors' anchorage, and more spotters atop Pemba Hill, a local promontory a couple of miles away. Apel managed to hit *Mersey* twice in the first hour. The second shell bored through steel plates and hammocks and disabled the forward six-inch gun, killing two British sailors. Several shots thereafter straddled the monitor; it seemed only a matter of moments before a direct hit. Captain Fullerton, aboard *Severn*, ordered *Mersey*'s Commander Wilson to loose her moorings and vacate the anchorage—fortunately, Wilson immediately complied. Moments later, a German shell hit the water exactly where *Mersey* had been; the strike exactly amidships would have been a kill shot.

The duel of the big naval guns continued for hours. Cull flew his Farnum back to Mafia and turned it over to Squadron Leader Gordon, who volunteered the air wing's assistant paymaster as his spotter. The monitors, eminently maneuverable, changed their positions twice again to evade incoming German fire. On the second move, *Severn*'s lookout caught sight of the German spotting platform in the trees; this was quickly taken out with a six-inch shell. Unwittingly, by moving, the monitors had rendered themselves invisible to the remaining spotters on Pemba Hill. The Germans now fired blind. Meanwhile, the British airmen circling above had gotten their signals crossed: 4,000 feet up they confused *Severn* for *Mersey* and vice versa—it was difficult to say which one was shooting, rendering each shot, whether hit or miss, impervious to signaled adjustments.

By late afternoon, the monitors had lobbed 635 shells at the stranded German battle cruiser. Out of these, they had scored a meager six hits, none of them fatal. *Königsberg* herself had fired far fewer shells—her ordnance supply being severely limited—but had managed to eliminate nearly a third of *Mersey*'s crew. The day had also taken a toll on the British airmen. They had logged fifteen hours of flying time in their marginally airworthy crates, so stiff with cold when they reached the Mafia airfield they had to be lifted out of the cockpits by ground crews.

At last, as the tide ebbed, the monitors withdrew, once again running

the gauntlet of Delta Force. The first day's battle had been inconclusive—
worse, according to Cull: "From all points, discouraging," he wrote. The
bedraggled monitors trailed through the waiting fleet in the dying light at
dusk, belching smoke, their engines laboring—so loud, "the ever increasing
volume of sound" as they approached remained in Lieutenant Charlewood's memory for years afterward as a dictionary-perfect example of "in-
fernal din."

Night settled on the Rufiji Delta.

Aboard *Königsberg*, the Germans assessed their casualties. Besides Jaeger's suicide, the enemy had accounted for five dead with thirty-five more
wounded—including Gunner Apel and Korvettenkapitan Loof himself, cut by
a piece of shrapnel. Richard Wenig's left foot would need amputating; to make
matters worse, he now felt the alternating chills and fever of incipient malaria.
Those sailors who remained unhurt drew a deep breath of relief; a few offered
prayers of thanks. Loof nursed his injury on the bridge and ordered a ration
of schnapps for the men. Everyone knew the battle, as yet neither won nor lost,
was not over. Everyone knew the monitors would be back.

Over the next few days, a patched-up Loof organized repair parties. All
flammable materials were set ashore; a hole below the waterline was hastily
repaired. New observer platforms rose in the trees and on Pemba Hill—
now connected to *Königsberg* by newly strung telephone lines. The seriously
wounded, transported five miles upstream on a paddleboat, would recuperate at a field hospital on the Neustieten Plantation. Loof also directed the
installation of aiming stakes along the banks of the Kikunja—this time he
planned to blow the monitors out of the water with more accurate fire.

Two more days passed. The crocodiles floating like logs in the shallows
awaited the next rain of bloody human meat. At last, on Sunday, July 11,
1915, at ten thirty a.m., the monitors again advanced up the Kikunja Channel into the Rufiji, past the guns of Delta Force. They'd been scrubbed free
of blood, patched, and reloaded with thousands of shells. This time they
meant to sink the *Königsberg* or get sunk trying. Leutnant Paul Khool of the
German battle cruiser later noted that, while the barrage of July 6 had been
"very sharp and damaging," it was "but child's play compared with the

second on July 11.... The dispiriting effect was so great as to make one ill to think of it, trying with two or three men and rifles to stand up against such a bombardment, knowing one can do nothing."

Cull, again circling overhead, directed *Severn's* fire—the confusion of July 6 now remedied by using *Mersey* as bait for *Königsberg's* guns while *Severn* did the dirty work. Almost immediately, *Mersey* took a direct hit, then another. The second shell smashed into the captain's cabin and knocked out two more sailors. Meanwhile, *Severn*, once more straddled by German fire, rocked back and forth, apparently idling in the bloody brown water. But Captain Fullerton, choosing to ignore the possibility that the next bracketing shot might catch him amidships, calmly readied *Severn* for her first salvo of the day. At last, *Severn* let fly, firing again and again as Cull buzzed overhead, signaling the accuracy of each shot. The eighth salvo scored a direct hit on *Königsberg*—a lucky strike, it nevertheless fixed the German battleship's position exactly. From 4,000 feet up, Cull radioed the hit: More like it! In the next ten minutes, *Severn* scored seven more hits.

The *Königsberg* continued to return fire but could not make her target. Gradually, her guns, struck by British shells one by one, fell into silence—though there remained a small victory for the Germans: *Königsberg's* final shot ended the flight of Cull's Farnum. As Wenig remembered it, "The plane banked, remained motionless for a second, then went down like an arrow. Blackened with powder and blood, our gunners' faces lit up ... only momentarily! They had triumphed, then they disappeared, shreds of their flesh sticking to the bulkhead and deck." The gun and its crew of three, found by a British shell, had suddenly ceased to exist.

For his part, Cull dropped to the Rufiji in a controlled spin. At twelve forty-nine p.m., his spotter, Lieutenant Arnold, radioed, "We are hit, send a boat." The rest comes from Cull's memoirs: "I started to glide towards the *Mersey*, as, though *Severn* was nearest, I did not want to interfere with her fire.... On our way down, my observer, with great coolness, gave a correction by wireless to the *Severn*, bringing her hits from forward on the *Königsberg* to amidships."

Cull, making what Fullerton called "a magnificent landing," managed to land the Farnum in the Rufiji, though at the last moment its pontoons hit something in the water and the plane flipped. Arnold was flung free; Cull found himself trapped in the cockpit. "I had . . . foolishly forgotten to un-strap my belt and I went down with the machine. My feet were also entan-gled, and I had great difficulty freeing myself, tearing off my boots and the legs of my trousers in so doing. When I came to the surface, my observer was hunting through the wreckage for me. . . . We both swam for the *Mersey*, whose motorboat picked us up."

Meanwhile, aboard *Königsberg*, Korvettenkapitan Loof had refused to quit the bridge during the bombardment, believing his presence there would inspire his men. Hit twice by shrapnel, his naval whites stained a gory red, he at last handed command of the sinking battle cruiser to his first officer, Commander Koch. A flying shard had sliced open Loof's stomach; he was carried to sick bay, where it seemed he wouldn't have long to live.

Now that *Königsberg*'s range had been found by the British guns, she took repeated shell-fire—twenty-eight hits in the next hour. Aboard, all was chaos and blood: "Blood flowed all over the deck," wrote the wounded Wenig. "Only shovelfuls of sand made it passable. Corpses lay in heaps near the forecastle. Two torn-off heads rested side by side beneath a locker."

Then, miraculously, the captain reappeared, carried by orderlies to the bridge and laid on a bloody mattress. The wound in his stomach, though critical, was not fatal—the shrapnel had been stopped millimeters from the abdominal wall by his large pocket watch and gold cigarette case. He took command again and prepared for the end: He ordered sailors below to flood the magazine; the blocks of the guns removed by Apel were cast into the brown water. The walking wounded went ashore, Loof with them, under protest. Only Koch remained aboard to execute the captain's last order: to scuttle the ship with its single remaining torpedo, hidden below. At two p.m. Loof watched from his bloody mattress laid among the wounded as the torpedo went off and the last German battle cruiser below the equator sank into the muck of the Rufiji. But the river was not deep enough. The wreck of the *Königsberg* shuddered and settled, slightly cocked to one side and only up to her quarterdeck in water. The Imperial German flag still flew from her highest mast. At dusk, a sailor climbed back aboard and hauled it down to loud cheering of "God save the Kaiser!" from the watching wounded.

Then they set about burying the dead. These included radio officer

Neimyer—who had plucked the first reports of the war out of the ether—
and thirty-two others. They were laid in the soggy ground of the delta far
from Germany beneath thirty-three wooden crosses and a plaque made out
of a steam pipe marked with their names.

Returning from the shooting gallery of the Rufiji late in the afternoon, the
monitors ran the fleet to cheering from the officers and men assembled
topside. Admiral King-Hall, now aboard *Weymouth*, hung signal flags
spelling out WELL DONE MONITORS, and everyone celebrated the victory
that night with extra rations of rum and champagne.

It had been the longest single naval engagement in history (and remains
so), officially lasting 252 days, beginning October 30, 1914, and ending July
11, 1915, with a British victory. But was it such a victory? To Loof, the
Königsberg remained undefeated. Her guns, raised from the Rufiji's muddy
waters within the week, were hauled to the same Dar es Salaam workshops
that had repaired her boilers. There, fitted to rolling gun carriages, they
gave von Lettow the most powerful artillery of the land war, an indispensable asset in the coming years of hard campaigning.

That tough old sea dog Loof recovered completely from his wounds.
Despite ongoing friction between himself and von Lettow, he became one
of the Schutztruppe's ablest commanders. He was later awarded the Pour le
Mérite by the Kaiser and promoted to *Kapitan zur See*, in which rank he
technically outranked his commanding general. Though, when the crafty
Governor Schnee then suggested he take overall command of the colony
from von Lettow, Loof refused.

But to the British Navy, nothing failed like success: King-Hall, whose
imperious, eccentric ways had slowly earned him the enmity of his fleet
officers, came under much criticism following the sinking of *Königsberg*.
"Had we served under more inspired leadership than we had from King-
Hall," later remarked a junior officer, "I am sure we would have left with a
different feeling, for we had taken part in a campaign that was to say the
least unusual."

King-Hall found himself blamed for tremendous cost overruns, for not
using a more aggressive, land-based strategy against the *Königsberg*, and for

tarrying too long on the Rufiji Station—though a land attack had been rejected by Wapshare early on, and the strategy he came up with (monitors, spotter planes) was extremely innovative. But, in truth, the cost of the *Königsberg* campaign had been tremendous: King-Hall's determination to destroy the German battle cruiser—*Königsberg* obsessive Winston Churchill stood firmly behind him in this matter—had occupied twenty-seven British fighting ships for nearly a year, pissed off the Brazilian Navy, burned up 38,000 tons of coal, and cost the equivalent of many millions of pounds in today's money. Yes, the *Königsberg* had been sunk at last with relatively few British casualties; even so, a sour taste remained.

King-Hall, denied transfer to another fleet command by the Admiralty, ended his war as a deskbound sailor, the frustrated commandant of the Royal Naval Base at Scapa Flow in the Outer Hebrides. Churchill himself, out of favor for the *Königsberg* affair and for his support of the disastrous Gallipoli Campaign, resigned from the Admiralty and immediately proposed himself for the governorship of British East Africa. When this suggestion was refused, he offered to serve as the commander of an armored car detachment in the African theater. This too was refused, and he ended up as the humble major of a yeomanry regiment stationed behind the lines in France for the remainder of the war.

As for SMS *Königsberg*, she lay where she had settled in the green hell of the Rufiji, gently rusting away for the next fifty years. At last, in the early 1960s her shot-up, rusted-out remains were cut up and destroyed. Only fifteen members of the original crew of 355, shipped out for the Colonial Exhibition at Dar es Salaam in September 1914, lived to see Germany again.

Chapter 19

BATTLE FOR KILIMANJARO

Kilimanjaro's summit, the local tribes believed, wore a silver crown. They said God (*munga*) lived there as well as many evil spirits, and also that the mountain cursed anyone who tried to climb it by causing the hands and feet of the offending party to "stiffen" and fall off. Living at the equator, in a land of perpetual heat and warm torrential rains, the natives didn't suspect the existence of ice or snow or frostbite; climbing the mountain had long been thought forbidden by *munga*: "Who are you that you should ascend the mighty Kilima Njaro?" they said to British missionary Charles New, the first European to reach the snow line in 1871. "Didn't the last Mzungu [white man] that came here try it, and wasn't he driven back?"

But New persisted, hired local guides at exorbitant rates, and began his climb. Most fell away the higher they went; the few who made it to the frozen zone above 14,000 feet gleefully chipped away at the ice, believing it to be a powerful magic that would make them great men in their home villages. When New explained that it was only water and would melt as they descended, they laughed and refused to believe him: How could a stone melt?

The same incredulity—though from learned men who should have known better—had greeted the German missionary-explorers Johann Krapf and Johannes Rebmann, the first Europeans to catch sight of Kilimanjaro in 1848: "This morning we discerned the mountains . . . more distinctly than ever. . . . About ten o'clock, I fancied I saw the summit of one of them covered with a dazzlingly white cloud. My guide called the white which I saw merely 'Beredi,' cold; it was perfectly clear to me, however, that it could be nothing else but snow."

When news of their discovery reached the wider world, eminent geographers called Rebmann's tale another example of African mythologizing: "Statements such as these," said William Desbrough Cooley, a fellow of the Royal Geographic Society in London, "betraying weak powers of observation, strong fancy, an eager craving for wonders, and childish reasoning, could not fail to awaken mistrust by their intrinsic demerits. . . . Those eternal snows . . . have so little of shape and substance, and appear so severed from realities, that they take quite a spectral character."

But the snow-peaked equatorial mountain, no ghost, *was* there—rising improbably above a vast, baking plain teeming with wildlife.

Eventually, others found it, as they had since ancient times: Kilimanjaro was probably the "Silver Mountain" mentioned by Aristotle, from which he believed the Nile flowed. It had also probably inspired tales of the Mountains of the Moon, spread by Ptolemy and the medieval Arab geographers— that persistent chimera the eminent Victorian explorers Burton and Speke sought as the Nile's source in the 1850s.

The first person to summit Kilimanjaro's highest peak (19,302 feet) was a German, Dr. Hans Meyer, without oxygen or modern climbing equipment, in 1889, the year before the Border Commission added it to the Kaiser's empire. Meyer wrote a book about his exploit with the excellent title of *Across East African Glaciers*, a bestseller in both England and Germany.

We now know that the Nile flows from the capacious inland reservoir of Lake Victoria, a discovery brought at the expense of much blood and—as it turns out—not a little spit: When in 1848 Rebmann and Krapf beheld Kilimanjaro, following mysterious rumors brought to Mombasa by Arab slavers, each step of their hard journey through Chaggaland to the mountain had been preceded by gallons of the stuff. Every time they left one native village for another, "the usual ceremony of expectorating upon the departing stranger and repeating the words 'Go in Peace' had first to be endured." Covered by the "saliva of peace," the explorers turned their faces toward the snowcapped mountain.

But peace was not what either the British, still commanded by the now-dipsomaniacal Tighe, or the Germans, under the resolute von Lettow, expected from Kilimanjaro in January 1916.

Only more war and more blood.

Von Lettow's guerrilla raiders had made their home on Kilimanjaro's thickly forested lower slopes since early spring 1915. Their successful months-long hit-and-run campaign against the Uganda Railway originated there, in secret Schutztruppe encampments reached via elephant tracks hidden in the bush. From their tents and lean-tos, they looked out over a beautiful, difficult landscape: This was the Africa that defined the word, a country of hills, swamp, and river, alternately well watered and arid, thick with wildlife and hardship. To the south lay the Northern Pare Mountain with Lake Jipe spread along its base. Out of this liver-shaped body of water issued the Ruvu, Nguru, and Lumi rivers—all home to many crocodiles and hippopotamuses. Here the air hung heavy with rolling clouds of mosquitoes; the wetlands extending along the banks of the rivers became a vast, shallow lake during the season of heavy rains from March to May.

Between Kilimanjaro in German East and the Pare foothills in British East Africa lay the border town of Taveta, seized by Tom von Prince in 1914. Taveta guarded the eastern end of the Nguru Valley, a twenty-mile-wide gap through which lay the natural gateway to the German colony. To defeat the Germans and drive the troublesome von Lettow into the sea, the British would have to take Taveta and pass through this gap. In their way stood twenty-five miles of waterless thorn scrub *pori* and several field companies of Schutztruppe *askaris* led by Major Georg Kraut, now von Lettow's second-in-command. Kraut was artfully entrenched on the hill of Salaita, a low mountain almost exactly at the center of the valley, blocking any enemy advance.

Whenever the British—or anyone else fighting a war during the colonial era—needed to reach a military objective in a region with no roads, they built a railroad. Motor transport, just coming into its own in Europe, was as yet generally unsuited to conditions in Africa. In mid-1915, while under continual attack from von Lettow's guerrilla raiders, British military engineers began a narrow-gauge spur from Voi on the Uganda line aiming toward Taveta. They hoped to take von Lettow in his Kilimanjaro stronghold with a mass mobilization of troops and raced along, laying miles of track each day without bothering to clear obstacles, simply going around quirks of landscape peacetime engineers would have taken time to blast away: hillocks and thick clumps of acacia trees, ponds. The sooner the British could get the line finished and their troops to Taveta and through the Nguru Gap, they thought, the sooner the war would end.

The machinery of the military mind moves slowly, but when it does moves with the inevitability of tectonic plates. A year of enforced inactivity on the British side, 1915, had come to an end. Lord Kitchener—described as cold, unreachable, and unknowable even by those with whom he had close association—nevertheless hotly deplored the loss of British lives in what he saw as futile adventures in Africa. He understood what von Lettow was up to. Others at the War Office couldn't see it or, more conventional in their military outlook, deemed another victory essential for British prestige in the region.

"Victory was necessary," as Lieutenant General Sir Archibald Murray put it in a report to the Imperial General Staff, expressing the majority opinion, "in order to render our position permanently secure and to restore our damaged reputation in that theater of war."

Murray recommended an infusion of 10,000 fresh troops, massive amounts of rifles, field guns, transport—including airplanes and armored cars—topped off with a fresh command structure. He would eventually get three times the number of troops he asked for and all the bells and whistles. In short, exactly what von Lettow wanted: that is, for the British to make ever-greater commitments to the war in Africa. He greeted the first air attacks by British BE2c biplanes on his headquarters at Neu Moshi in January 1916 with undisguised joy. Here were warplanes taken directly from the Western Front where his brother had died.

Schutztruppe *askari*, however, who had never seen a flying machine of any kind—or indeed heard of such a thing—reacted to this first air assault with primordial panic. It seemed the sky itself had gone to war with them, that these evil birds dropping bombs were the wrath of *munga* incarnate. Gun crews off the *Königsberg*—including Richard Wenig, recovered from his wounds and sporting a wooden foot—immediately went into action.

They had fixed an ancient 1873 vintage Hotchkiss gun to a swiveling platform made from wagon wheels; its highest elevation brought the Hotchkiss's lethal explosive rounds into contact with one of the British planes.
The fragile BE2c shattered in midair and fell to earth; the pilot lay crushed
amid a heap of canvas, wood, and wire.

The *askaris* approached fearfully but soon saw this was not the work of
munga—so their German officers pointed out—but the work of the English.
Still unsure, the *askaris* stood at a safe distance as the dead pilot was buried
in the ground like any other man, but they would never stand in awe of an
airplane again: A few months later during the fight over the Latema-Reata
Ridgeline, they mocked the BE2c's inefficiently dropped fifty-pound bombs
with cries of *"Ndege fanya mayai!"*—The bird is laying her eggs!

In the last days of 1915, the British government had, upon the recommendation of the subcommittee for the Committee of Imperial Defense, officially resolved to expand the African war. Most of the additional troops
would come from South Africa, as von Lettow had predicted.

General Sir Horace Smith-Dorrien, commander at the brutal First Battle
of Ypres on the Western Front, who had quarreled with his superior Sir John
French and been removed (reportedly with the words "'Orace, yer fer 'ome!"),
would lead the assault against the German colony. In distant London, Smith-
Dorrien pored over maps of East Africa and sought the advice of those
members of the General Staff who had actually been there. Smith-Dorrien
had seen action in South Africa years before, during the Zulu War. In 1879,
he'd been one of five officers to survive the massacre at Isandlwana—perhaps
the greatest defeat inflicted upon a British army by tribal warriors.

Lord Kitchener, enraged by the resolution for more troops, fulminated
against this "dangerous project in the present state of the war"—to no avail.
He was being edged out of the top spot in the War Office and living on
borrowed time: On June 5, 1916, on a diplomatic mission to Russia, his ship,
the HMS *Hampshire*, struck a mine laid by a German U-boat off the
Orkneys. Gale-force winds raged; the ship went down with 600 lives lost,
among the drowned, Kitchener. His body was never recovered—though,
bizarrely, in 1926, a hoaxer who convinced everyone he had discovered the

warlord's waterlogged remains buried in a fishermen's cemetery in Norway was unmasked on the eve of their reinterment in St. Paul's Cathedral: The coffin, opened, was found to contain only a man-shaped quantity of tar— one last golem from the age of empire.

Smith-Dorrien's new East African invasion plan, perhaps appropriate to a European campaign, envisioned massive injections of supplies and men, many motorized vehicles and fieldpieces, and also called for rapid movements of troops across terrain he had never seen. The German forces around Kilimanjaro would be assaulted, the Nguru Gap quickly forced, and British divisions would pour down into German East Africa. At the same time, the Royal Navy would coordinate a landing of more divisions at Dar es Salaam, to be taken after a punishing bombardment. These would advance up the Central Railway, take a sharp right across the Masai Steppe, and attack German positions from behind. A classic encircling maneuver that took into account none of East Africa's realities: the extended rainy season, the impassible jungles and rivers, the swamps and deserts, the horrific diseases, the wild animals.

The new commander departed for South Africa to confer with General Botha in January 1916. Botha, it had been decided, would oversee the recruitment of troops for the renewed war effort. On the voyage out, however, Smith-Dorrien came down with severe pneumonia. His health improved in the dry, sunny climate of Cape Town, but he insisted on sailing for Mombasa too soon and again took ill. For a while his life hung in the balance; at last he improved enough to sail back to England, where he would recover and finish out his war in semiretirement as warden of the Tower of London. There his command consisted of a few halberd-bearing Beefeaters and the tower's traditional clipped-wing, tame ravens—without whose presence there, so legend has it, England will fall.

With Smith-Dorrien suddenly out of the picture, Aitken disgraced, Wapshare banished, and Tighe too often drunk, the War Office cast about for yet another replacement. As the new army would consist mostly of South African troops, counterintuitively, they didn't want a South African for the job: Too many in the War Office remembered the vicious Boer War, less than thirteen years past. General Botha and his second-in-command, General Jan Smuts, had once ranked among Britain's most determined enemies; a South African commander of a largely South African army seemed a dangerous thing, not easily handled from London.

But with the fall of Windhoek, Botha had recently concluded the successful campaign against Franke in German South West Africa. The entire campaign took only six months—a record so far in the World War. This, after neatly suppressing the anti-British rebellion fomented by a disgruntled contingent of his fellow Boers, some of whom had been his personal friends. He had become, he insisted, one of Great Britain's firmest allies and now believed South Africa's fate lay within the embrace of the British Empire. Despite misgivings, the War Office offered Botha the East African command. He declined—citing political obligations and poor health—but recommended the younger Jan Smuts for the job. The brilliant Smuts, a former Boer cavalry general, academic, lawyer, legislator, and poetry lover, accepted the assignment on February 6, 1916. Meanwhile, the first South African Troops, a mounted brigade under Jaap van Deventer, another Boer cavalry commander, had already arrived in Mombasa on December 30.

Van Deventer was a block of granite of a man, well over six feet tall and thick as an oak; in photographs, he towers over other members of the General Staff. His vocal cords damaged by a British bullet in 1901, he spoke in a loud whisper and usually in Afrikaans. Though he understood English well, he communicated in Afrikaans through an interpreter. British officers in Nairobi mistrusted him, but among his own men he inspired unquestioning devotion. One of his troopers, who, like many, had sworn an oath during the Boer War to "fight against the *verdomde rooinekkes*" (damned redneck English) in perpetuity, had now become another enthusiastic servant of the empire. If "Jaapie" van Deventer fought for the English now, he said, it was good enough for him.

The newly arrived South African troops—whose ranks did include a couple of purely English battalions—would soon have the opportunity to prove their loyalty: Tighe, while waiting for Smuts to arrive, and eager to salvage his battered reputation after defeats at Tanga and Jasin, petitioned the War Office to open an offensive against Salaita Hill on the Kilimanjaro Front. With Salaita taken, he argued, the way would lie open through the Nguru Gap for Smuts's new army. Also, the fighting abilities of van Deventer's South Africans might thus be tested.

The next arrivals in theater came from India by way of Flanders. These, the 129th and 130th Baluchis, had been the first subcontinental troops to engage the Germans, at Hollebeke in 1914. One of their number, Sepoy Khudadad Khan, won the war's first Victoria Cross. On the Western Front, the Baluchis earned a reputation as a hard-fighting but troublesome lot. They hailed from the northwest borderlands of the Afghan frontier—in what is now Pakistan—and liked to fight, but had been nearly destroyed as a coherent force in the first two months of the war.

At Givenchy on December 19, 1914, the Germans blasted a pair of massive mines under the Baluchi trenches; the explosion routed the entire regiment and spread panic to other Indian troops. By this time all the Baluchis' British officers had been killed. A replacement officer, ordering them back to the trenches, was murdered by a disgruntled trooper and mutiny spread: Somehow the Baluchis, who were Muslims, became convinced that the Germans too were Muslims and so refused to fight against their coreligionists. A captured supply of German pork sausage eventually disabused the Baluchis of this notion but did not stop the War Office from withdrawing them from the line in disgrace.

After a period of punishment duty, the Baluchis were sent on to East Africa, where, it was hoped, they would recover their fighting spirit and lethal efficiency: They had used, as a rule, less ammunition to produce more enemy dead than any other imperial regiment. Dr. Francis Brett Young, the British novelist and medical officer serving with the Loyal North Lancs in the East African campaign, described them as "lean and lithe," and excellent fighters. You couldn't be "in a tight corner with better men," he wrote in *Marching on Tanga*, his memoir of the East African campaign. Though, at first, the contrast in deployments disoriented the Baluchis. As their regimental history put it: "No greater contrast climatically and otherwise existed than that between Flanders and Nairobi. In Flanders the men had suffered from too much rain, in Nairobi and on the *pori*, where they were headed, they experienced an excess of drought and dust."

Still, excepting the color of their skin, they bore no resemblance to those demoralized troops of the Imperial Service Brigade who had foundered at Tanga and were now perishing from malaria at various desultory encampments around BEA.

Surprisingly, the War Office immediately granted Tighe's request for a new offensive and approved his plan for an attack on Salaita Hill. Tighe unfortunately nominated the ineffectual Malleson to coordinate this assault, along with a reckless Boer brigadier general P. J. Beves commanding the 5th, 6th, 7th, and 8th Brigades of South African Infantry.

Beves had earned a solid military reputation in German South West Africa, where he had marched his battalion 230 miles from Karibib to Otavifontein in the record time of sixteen days, fighting all the way. But that was open country; of the obstructed thorn scrub *pori* of East Africa he had no experience. His South African Infantrymen were a cocky bunch, hardy young men who approached war as if they were off to a soccer match. Fresh from their whirlwind victory in GSWA, they regarded von Lettow's *askaris* with open contempt—calling them "damned kaffirs"—a derogatory term for blacks—and their own allied Indian troops "coolies." Limited by their prejudices, certain of an easy victory, they had no idea of the hard, miserable fighting awaiting them.

"I discussed the matter with van Deventer," Meinertzhagen wrote. "He was not very talkative but has implicit confidence in his men. I asked him what his plans were. 'Let them attack,' said the taciturn Dutchman. . . . 'For God's sake, do not despise the enemy,' I said. 'Damned kaffirs,' he replied."

At daybreak on February 12, 1916, Malleson ordered the South Africans and other troops assembled at Serengeti Camp at the end of the Voi-Taveta Military Spur to engage the "damned kaffirs," and dislodge them and their German masters from their fortified positions on Salaita Hill.

They would perform what he called "a reconnaissance in force," one of Malleson's bloodless euphemisms for the bloody realities of battle. The South Africans, supported by the 1st East African Brigade—which included the Baluchis and Loyal North Lancs, among others—made up a force of about 6,000 men with nearly 50 machine guns and the 18 field guns of the 28th Mountain Battery. They could not fail to dislodge the Germans on Salaita, who numbered fewer than 1,000—though these were solidly dug in and possessed two artillery pieces and twelve machine guns, and cleverly concealed in a bushy landscape dug with dummy trenches, fixed with sniper blinds and punctuated by booby-trapped pits full of elephant spikes and barbed wire.

In position by six forty-five on the morning of the 12th, British guns opened the battle with a barrage against the German trenches cut into the hillside about halfway up, picked out by RNAS spotter planes. A German *boma* flying the Imperial German flag and the Islamic banner together at the crown of the hill came in for a severe pummeling. The barrage lasted an hour and fifteen minutes; then Malleson ordered the men forward. The South Africans, supported by two RNAS armored cars—a new addition to the British arsenal—and Berkeley Cole's fearsome Somali Scouts, moved against the flank of the German entrenchments. At the same time, assorted units of the East African Brigade also moved against the front: Malleson was hoping for a quick pincer movement that would undoubtedly lead to a clean British victory.

This was not the way things shook out.

As the South Africans advanced, kicking up telltale clouds of chalky volcanic dust, they outdistanced their water wagons. Hacking through the thorn scrub, ordered to stay together in "massed battalions" by Beves (shades of Tanga), afflicted by increasing thirst and the sun, they found the going increasingly difficult. When they reached the denuded patch of ground—cleared by the Germans for an open field of fire—1,000 yards from the base of Salaita Hill, they paused.

The sun climbing overhead toward noon added the dry, scorching heat of the days immediately preceding the rainy season. The South Africans, very thirsty, tired, and cut up by thorns, quavered at the sight of all that open ground, but the British guns opened up again as if to urge them on. They went on, advancing into the teeth of furious German machine-gun fire; the artillery barrage on the German trenches seemed to have had none of the expected "softening" effect. At last, the German fusillade became too hot and the South Africans fell back to the scrub, where they regrouped to push forward again. This time, one of the South African officers, Colonel Freeth, advanced to a place within 600 feet of the hill, where he could clearly make out the German trenches above. Now he could see that these positions stood empty. They had always been empty—dug as decoys to draw enemy artillery fire. The real trenches had been dug in at the foot of the hill, carefully camouflaged with brush and just now merciless fire poured out of them.

At the same moment, Captain Collas of the Loyal North Lancs, attacking the frontal position, also discovered the empty trenches. It was now nine forty-five a.m. Collas managed to relay a message back to the artillery, but they could not redirect their fire; the attackers had worked their way too close to the front lines. Any shell lobbed at the Germans might well explode among British troops. So the artillery, needing a target, kept blasting away uselessly at the empty trenches and the *boma* at the top of the mountain, without, however, dislodging the Imperial German flag.

Meanwhile, the South Africans began to fall back. Major Kraut—given the nod by von Lettow, who had raced to the front from Neu Moshi HQ in a car—ordered a counterattack. Wave after wave of *askaris*, bayonets fixed and screaming *"Piga! Piga!"* (Fire! Fire!) crashed out of their trenches into the faltering line of South Africans. Attacked from three sides, the South Africans buckled, broke, and bolted for the thorn scrub they'd just hacked through, followed by the sound of *askari* jeering. Their abandoned machine guns and discarded rifles littered the field, along with 132 dead.

The frontal attack pushed forward by the Loyal North Lancs, the 130th Baluchis, and the Rhodesian Regiment, while not advancing, had not yet begun to retreat. The Baluchis and the Rhodesians held their ground in the face of another determined *askari* bayonet charge, but the flight of the South Africans left their flank dangerously exposed. At last they were forced to retire, which they did in good order. With the support of the RNAS armored cars, they backed away, firing as they went, and managed it without a single killed in action.

The newfangled armored cars took von Lettow's *askaris* by surprise. They called them *kifaru*—rhinos—because of their steely gray color and the speed with which they moved. Though von Lettow, who had not been able to see them from his observation post on the hill, later denied they had been present at the battle: "Fantastic reports came in," he wrote, "about hostile armored cars which were alleged to be moving through the thorn-bush desert. The imagination of the natives, to whom these armored cars were something altogether new and surprising, had made them see ghosts."

In the morning, the British tallied up the dead and licked their wounds. It had been another disaster, another victory for von Lettow and his *askaris* against heavy odds. Meanwhile, the Baluchis returned to the battlefield to retrieve abandoned South African weaponry, while exposing themselves to more German fire. That evening, the South Africans received several mule loads of their own rifles and Maxim guns, with a note from the Baluchis attached:

> *With the compliments of the 130th Baluchis. May we request that you do not any longer refer to our sepoys as coolies.*

To the Rhodesians, who had stood firm beside them in the bungled attack on Salaita, they sent a note of a different kind:

> *We the officers rank and file of the 130th Baluchis, having come to know this morning . . . that all the officers rank and file of your regiment requested heartily for leave to come to our aid when we were surrounded by the enemy, pay our best and hearty thanks for this sympathetic kindness and militarism. We hope for the future that we will all fight side by side. We pray to our Heavenly Father for the victory of our Government.*

The Baluchis had, with their first action in Africa, reclaimed their reputation, temporarily lost in the mud of Flanders, as a hard-fighting and patriotic Imperial regiment.

Salaita Hill had been another Tanga for the British. Not quite in terms of casualties but in terms of lost prestige and lost confidence on the part of the newly bloodied South Africans. A stunned Tighe held back news of the disaster for days. Upon at last hearing of the defeat, Kitchener, still months away from his death in the icy waters north of the Orkneys, responded with lofty Kitchenerian disgust: "I hope that the necessity of not undertaking premature operations, unless circumstances *absolutely* compel you, is realized by you."

Tighe's response to this humiliating cable is not recorded, but he probably cracked another bottle of bonded. He had hoped to greet the arriving Smuts with a fait accompli: The gateway to German East Africa kicked open for the new commander to push through. Nearly 30,000 troops backed by a substantial battery of 71 guns and 125 machine guns were now available for this purpose; perhaps Smuts would know how to make better use of these abundant resources.

Still aboard ship on his way to Mombasa, Smuts received news of the Salaita disaster via radio telegram. One can only imagine him crushing the blue square of paper in his gloved fist without a word and tossing it into the sea.

———————

Jan Christian Smuts, at forty-six the youngest lieutenant general in the British Army and the new commander in chief of Imperial forces in East Africa, wasn't a professional soldier. He was, in fact, a lawyer by profession, a politician by inclination, a botanist by avocation, and a soldier by chance. Francis Brett Young remarked upon Smuts's tremendous energy: Though his personality was "unsympathetic, cold, well-nigh inhuman," Brett Young wrote, it "impressed itself on the whole force as an incarnation of the will to conquer." Smuts feared, so the Bishop of Pretoria once said, "neither God nor man, and particularly the former."

Smuts, born on a remote farm near Riebeeck in the West Cape Colony, early on acquired a love of nature he retained for the rest of his life. Educated at home until age twelve, he went on to Victoria College in Stellenbosch, where he excelled; from there a scholarship sent him to Christ College, Cambridge, where he read the law and was among the few to obtain a double first in the tripos—a nearly unheard-of academic achievement. He also found time to write a learned study of Walt Whitman's Leaves of Grass, which he admired excessively. On first reading the book of poems, he later said, he felt struck blind, like St. Paul converted on the road to Damascus by the light of God. Admitted to practice law at the prestigious Inner Temple, Smuts nevertheless grew homesick for South Africa. He returned in 1895, just in time to be swept up in the bloody tumult of the Boer War.

During this savage internecine conflict, he led a commando raid 340 miles into British-held territory—one of the great cavalry exploits of the era.

Smuts was a compact, muscular man, redheaded, of middle height. He wore a neatly trimmed spade-shaped beard and possessed personal energies undreamed of by the sclerotic British generals who had mishandled the East African campaign so far. His men called him Slim Janny—*slim* being Afrikaans for "sly" or "clever." He had come to win the war in East Africa, so he said, before the rainy season inundated the country in late March. This gave him a month, give or take, to defeat and capture von Lettow, who had proven himself impervious to both.

Like von Lettow, Smuts believed in mobile tactics and rapid maneuvers; encirclements rather than the costly, inconclusive frontal assaults favored on the battlefields of Europe. Among the Boers back home, support for a war on behalf of the British in East Africa remained spotty. Smuts could not afford, he said, to be known as "the butcher of my people." The debacle of the "Salaita Show" had already soured many: In that single engagement, South Africa had lost nearly half the number of troops fallen during the entire six-month campaign to capture GSWA.

Within hours of disembarking at Mombasa, Smuts cabled the War Office for permission to initiate a major offensive; the War Office responded favorably and he began assembling troops on the Kilimanjaro Front. The new commander didn't have time to draw up a detailed battle plan entirely his own and so adapted the original plan proposed by Smith-Dorrien months before in London. This plan was shot through with not a few inherent defects—as usual, it envisioned rapid maneuvers over terrain through which it was impossible to maneuver rapidly. Smuts, like other South Africans, used to the endless veldts of his homeland, hadn't considered the difficulties imposed by East Africa's damnable *pori*, but he quickly brought nearly 30,000 men up the narrow-gauge, as-yet-uncompleted Voi–Neu Moshi Military Spur in the shadow of Kilimanjaro, and readied all units for the advance through the Nguru Gap. With him, as chief of scouts, now served that one-man army, P. J. Pretorius . Sent out to reconnoiter German positions in the darkness in the vicinity of Salaita on March 6, Pretorius worked his way—as always—to within inches of German patrols: "At sundown orders came from General Smuts for me to get around their lines," he wrote in *Jungle Man*, his entertaining account of his exploits. "That was the sort of life I led for many months—often taking part in a battle, and then haring off in the night to gauge effects."

He returned to Smuts in the morning bearing a couple of important pieces of intelligence: First, that Salaita lay in the middle of a little desert, utterly waterless. The Germans manning its defenses received this vital commodity via a mule train from Taveta eight miles distant once a day. Disrupt the mule train and the water supply and Salaita stood alone like a sore tooth in the dry mouth of the Nguru Gap. Subject to the sweltering temperatures of the *pori*, its fall would be measured in hours, no more than a day after the departure of the last water-bearing mule. Second, Pretorius discovered that the only German fortification guarding the Kilimanjaro encampments was an insignificant outpost on the banks of Lake Chala, an ancient volcanic crater.

Facing Smuts's new massive army from their strong positions on Salaita Hill and dug in around the captured town of Taveta and on the lower slopes of Kilimanjaro were, at best, 6,000 German troops led by von Lettow and Major Kraut. The British possessed big guns galore, armored cars, and that new deviltry, attack aircraft bearing bombs. The Germans, meanwhile, relied on their Maxim guns, on the bayonet, on massed rifle volleys, accurate sniper fire, antipersonnel mines, and a few desultory fieldpieces—later augmented by one of the big guns off the *Königsberg*, twelve of which had been carefully doled out to German forces around the colony. According to the Smuts/Smith-Dorrien Plan, described by the former in a confidential dispatch to the War Office, British forces would now:

". . . cross the thirty-five miles of waterless bush which lay between Longido and the Engare Nanjuki River, occupy the latter, and then advance between Meru and Kilimanjaro . . . thereafter to direct this division on Kahe, and cut the German line of communication by the Usambura [Northern] railway. The task of the First South African Mounted Brigade and of the Second Division was to advance through the gap between Kilimanjaro and the bare hills against the German main force . . . reported to be concentrated in the neighborhood of Taveta, with strong detachments at the head of Lake Jipe, in the bush, east of the river Lumi and at Salaita."

Without adequate numbers, the Germans would not be able to disrupt this concentrated advance. Encircled by vastly superior forces, they could only watch themselves being crushed, helpless as a bushbuck in the jaws of a lion. The 1st Division, including F. C. Selous and the Legion of Frontiersmen, under General Stewart—formerly of Expeditionary Force C and the Bukoba Fight—would complete the sixty-mile thrust toward Neu Moshi in three days. Generals Malleson and Tighe would advance to Salaita, take the mountain head-on in this second attempt, and drive on to dislodge the Germans from Taveta. General Stewart would continue his advance through the bush and cut off all possibility of German retreat. Meanwhile, van Deventer with his Mounted Brigade of South Africans would outflank everyone in a great sweeping maneuver around Lake Chala, across the Kilimanjaro foothills, and make for Kahe. The Germans would be caught in the midst of all this maneuvering and, after a major battle, soundly defeated—though details as to how exactly all this would work remained rather vague.

For his part, von Lettow knew his outnumbered and outgunned Schutztruppe, though superbly trained and fighting in familiar country and on interior lines, could not stand up to Smuts's massive, well-equipped assault for long. He had been expecting this day and had long planned for it. "From the outset it was very doubtful whether we could in succession defeat the two main hostile groups," he wrote. The ultimate German war goal in East Africa was to keep the Schutztruppe intact and fighting, and to bleed British resources as much as possible—not to defend territory, towns, railroads, bridges, and plantations he did not have enough men to defend in the first place: Smuts sought to bring the Schutztruppe to a decisive battle; von Lettow sought to avoid this encounter.

To the conventional military mind, armies took towns and capitals and railroads and won the war; von Lettow's mind was not conventional in any sense. The colony now existed to him less as a place than as a concept; his German East Africa could be found more in the imagination than on the map. Henceforth, fighting the Schutztruppe would be like beating a beanbag chair with a baseball bat. Beat away and the outer envelope might split, but the beans inside would remain intact; beat harder and they would spill everywhere.

The British offensive began on the morning of March 8, 1916, though Stewart had marched some of his more cumbersome elements from the town of Longido toward the Nguru Gap two days earlier. Von Lettow watched the opening moves from a commanding position near Taveta. The British columns threw up great, towering plumes of chalky dust that could be seen from miles away. Had he long-range guns at his disposal, von Lettow reflected ruefully, he might have knocked them out one by one; he was instead condemned "to look on quietly while the enemy executed unskillful maneuvers at no great distance from our front." Maneuvers that recalled other clumsy British troop movements he'd witnessed in China in 1900.

Some of the dust von Lettow saw was kicked up by the 4,000 South African horsemen commanded by van Deventer; watching them come along, he instantly divined Smuts's plan. Here was the encircling movement that was supposed to strangle the Schutztruppe like a python crushing its prey. Meanwhile, Tighe and Malleson could also be observed hesitating before Salaita—and it seemed, as von Lettow put it, "the enemy did not intend to get his head broken a second time on that mountain." In this assessment, he was soon proven wrong.

Down in the churning clouds of dust, marching men, driven half-mad by heat, choked on the thick chalky billows. Every hour, a number collapsed from exhaustion and thirst. General Stewart, whose advancing cloud could also be seen on the horizon, had the advantage of a road upon which to move forward, and only 800 *askaris* hidden in the bush to slow him down.

In a war of maneuvers, speed of movement is as important as the weight of the punch. Regarding speed, Stewart's push forward had already failed. His army moved with the alacrity of an inchworm: He had allowed a few minor Schutztruppe ambuscades to nearly stop his forward movement; he complained about the heat and the thornbushes and the dust. Obstacles thrown across the road stopped his columns for hours; at night, the roar of lions in the distance disturbed his sleep. A freak rainstorm—it being still too early for the seasonal deluge—seemed to completely derange him. His mind clearly set on an eventual retreat, he sent his sappers back to maintain the escape route, when they should have been pushing the way ahead, and he'd placed his big guns in the rear, guarded by cavalry better used in forward screening actions. Stewart also failed to string his telephone lines above the heads of passing giraffes; the result being the lanky animals knocked them down and he lost touch with Smuts at the Serengeti Camp HQ for two crucial days.

At last, at dusk on March 11, Stewart's front line reached the bridge crossing the Sanya River at *boma* Ngombe—which for some reason von Lettow had failed to destroy. Much to the disgust of General Smuts, Stewart had made barely twenty miles in three days. Now he came into contact with Schutztruppe elements under Major Erich Fischer, apparently one of the least able of von Lettow's officers. Fischer and Stewart engaged in confused fighting in the bush; neither bested the other and both withdrew: Stewart to angry recriminations from Smuts and a pending demotion; Fischer, upon his return to Schutztruppe HQ, to a suicide supposedly inspired by von Lettow's outrage. Maddened by Fischer's failure to destroy Stewart's poorly led force—so the rumors went—von Lettow handed the trembling officer his own pistol, saying, "Let me hear something interesting about you in a few days." Then he left Fischer alone with the weapon and a few minutes later a fatal shot rang out. Military records state only that Fischer shot himself. That von Lettow commanded him to do so seems highly unlikely. A German officer, even one who had just committed a military blunder, was worth more to the dwindling Schutztruppe alive than dead and could have been deployed elsewhere in a logistical capacity. Fischer's suicide was most likely the result of shell-shock and exhaustion, not an uncharacteristic order from his commanding officer.

Meanwhile, Malleson and Tighe began their frontal advance on Salaita. Tighe pressed the assault on this previously impregnable bastion by unleashing a "hurricane of artillery fire" on Salaita Hill on the morning of the 9th. For hours his fieldpieces blasted away, this time at the "real" trenches at the base of the hill.

Then the guns stopped and Tighe's troops advanced into the swirling dust—only to find that the Germans had abandoned their positions. The trenches and the rifle pits stood empty; makeshift telephone lines with insulators made from broken beer bottles swayed gently in the wind. Tighe looked around, astonished. The German trenches, incredibly well made, with step positions and bomb-proof dugouts, he described as "truly formidable . . . and would have cost us 1,500 men." He might have added, 1,500 men that, applying the pitiless calculus of war, a British Army of 30,000 could afford to lose. But the 900 *askaris* holding the hill under Major Kraut were indispensable to the Germans, a sizable chunk of von Lettow's army. In the predawn hours they had evacuated the mountain; at the same time, his forces also withdrew from Taveta, that bit of British territory held by the Germans since September 1914.

Tighe and Malleson entered Taveta later that day to discover a ransacked town. The Germans had destroyed or taken everything of value. And German *askaris* had shat all over the floors in the public buildings and used British settlers' homes as urinals. The British generals, appalled by German lack of "sportsmanship," protested loudly—but this was a war in which even shit could be used as a weapon.

———

Where had the Germans gone?

They had almost certainly withdrawn to the wooded slopes of the *nek*, the narrow road running through the cleavage of two tall hills, Latema and Reata. This was the pass that led down into German territory and the town of Neu Moshi, the next goal of the British advance. Smuts knew these heights would have to be taken before the seizure of Neu Moshi might be accomplished—and the invasion of German East Africa begun.

The assault on the Latema and Reata hills, where Major Kraut had indeed installed his 1,000-man force, began on the morning of March 11. Inexplicably, Smuts had chosen Malleson to command, leading the 130th Baluchis, the 3rd KAR, the 2nd Rhodesians, and other units; Tighe would back him with the 2nd Division. But on the appointed day, just as the attack was scheduled to begin, Malleson suddenly came down with a bad case of "dysentery," handed his command over to Tighe, and fled the front lines.

Meinertzhagen claimed he spoke to Malleson right before the latter drove away, smoking a cigarette and "reclining on soft cushions in a car . . . and making good headway from the battlefield. He said he was feeling very ill and had handed over his brigade. I felt like shooting the cur. He did not look ill in the least."

Tighe, the old thruster, dead sober for once but probably trembling for a drink, took personal command of his troops and led a frontal attack on German positions dug into the crest of both hills. All vegetation had been cleared for field of fire by the Germans to 100 yards below the ridge. From that point down to the base of the hill grew the natural barbed wire of thorn scrub.

As the Baluchis and Rhodesians came into the thorns, the Germans, 1,000 feet above them, opened up with their machine guns. Facing a steel wall of .50-caliber Maxim rounds, the advancing troops hit the ground; they soon found themselves unable to move forward or back and lay there helplessly as lead rained down upon them. At last, Tighe brought up his guns and ordered a barrage on the German positions. This managed to clear a path through the scrub and the advance crawled forward again—but the attackers didn't make it far: The thorny underbrush on the middle slope stood chest high. Here, on Latema, the Baluchis hastily dug in and remained, though blasted by the sun and harassed by converging machine-gun fire.

On Reata, the Rhodesians and the KAR actually reached the ridgeline, fixed bayonets, and charged the German positions, only to be thrust back in disarray by a countercharge of screaming *askaris*. The KAR, driven back down the slope, had also lost a valued officer—Colonel B. R. Graham—to a German ploy: During the close fighting directly below the ridge, a German officer called to Graham in English; Graham, thinking himself addressed by one of his own men, put his head up, caught a German bullet in the throat, and rolled back dead.

Night fell. The Germans had not been dislodged from their entrenched positions on either hill. Most of the British troops, withdrawn by Tighe, had regrouped on the plain below. As the moon rose he began preparing them for a risky night attack. Meanwhile, from his new command HQ on the Neu Steglitz plantation, von Lettow kept close touch with the progress of the battle via field telephone, furiously smoking his cigarettes as usual and pushing pins around the battle map. Just before midnight, one of his scouts caught sight of van Deventer's cavalry column coming through the bush several miles to the west of Neu Moshi. It appeared they had outflanked German positions and would soon threaten the town. Von Lettow couldn't know that van Deventer and his men were in no shape to fight a battle, that they were exhausted and low on water and food. The men, forced to eat unripe bananas plucked from the trees, were mostly ill and torn up by hacking through the thorn scrub all day—and unable to advance any farther.

The darkness thickened, full of confusion and desultory fighting, and might as well have passed beneath a bloodred moon. Von Lettow spent the first hours trying to figure out where matters stood on the Latema-Reata line. Were his troops still in possession of the heights? And where was the bulk of the enemy? Communications had broken down; his telephone lines had been cut in the early evening; his runners had all been shot. In frustration, with no news from the front as midnight approached, he abandoned HQ to his staff and, over their strenuous objections, mounted his bicycle and pedaled off toward the contested hills. When he reached the Taveta road, a sudden artillery blast knocked him off his bike. He shook himself off, kicked the damaged bike aside, and stumbled on, reaching Kraut just before midnight. Convinced that van Deventer's men would soon make an attack on the German flank, he failed to order a counterattack against a fresh regiment of South Africans under General Beves now making a move on German positions. He had no way of knowing van Deventer was now completely stopped by the impassible terrain of the *pori* in the thorny darkness.

Beves's South Africans advanced against the heavy German fire—foolishly, before moonrise, as they couldn't see exactly where they were going. When the moon cleared the cleavage in the hills, determined to make up for their poor performance at the "First Salaita Show" weeks before, they charged up the remaining slope—straight into the barrels of the German machine guns. Kraut cut them down gleefully. His machine guns didn't cease their deadly chattering until the unfortunate South Africans fell back, a bloody ruin. About to re-form for a second assault, they were suddenly called off, under orders from Smuts, ever sensible to South African casualties and public opinion back home.

At this point, with the enemy scattered and demoralized, von Lettow might have made a devastating counterattack down the hill and smashed through Beves's and Tighe's loosely held positions on the plain below. He might even have halted the British advance into GEA. He could then have turned to van Deventer, lost with thirsty horses and men in the middle of the *pori*, defeated them, and achieved an overwhelming victory—great enough to stall the British war effort and return them to the demoralized, lethargic state they'd experienced following Tanga. But denied a clear picture of the action, lacking accurate intelligence and literally groping around in the darkness, he failed to order his forces to attack. Instead, still certain Kraut and his men were on the verge of being flanked by van Deventer's South African cavalry, he ordered the retreat from the Latema-Reata Ridge and the immediate evacuation of Neu Moshi. Above all, he reasoned, he must save the Schutztruppe from encirclement and annihilation.

Dawn broke over the bloody hills. Cool morning air resounded with the sharp report of rifle fire, gasping bugle calls, and the screams of wounded men. First light revealed an astonishing sight: A few of Beves's South Africans and elements of the 130th Baluchis had remained on the slopes above; well dug in, they held on for the night. They now rose out of their hastily made entrenchments and advanced to take the ridgeline, unopposed. The Germans had abandoned their positions in the last hours of darkness and disappeared somewhere to the south.

Just before dawn, von Lettow had realized his mistake in ordering the retreat, but it was too late—half his troops had already gone and the moment had been lost. Still, he had remained true to his strategy. For him, this wasn't a war of territory: German East Africa had become the idea of resistance.

"We face an overwhelming force," he reminded his men later that day, "and it is unlikely that we can secure anything more than local victories. . . . Our object is to inflict as much damage as possible against them, and rather to give up territory than risk envelopment. At all costs, we must avoid being either killed or captured, for we must live to fight another day."

Meinertzhagen agreed: "The enemy lives to fight another day," he echoed when the battle was over. "We score nothing but territory."

The Schutztruppe counted only 40 dead, against 270 on the British side. For a while, at least, they had held off an overwhelming force of many thousands. But despite von Lettow's insouciant shrug at the British seizure of Taveta and Moshi, they had lost something special indeed: the Kaiser's only mountain, now receding in the distance, mighty Kilimanjaro, with its silver crown and impossible snows.

Chapter 20

WAR IN THE RAINY SEASON

The skies above Kilimanjaro showed a mottled, pearlescent gray. Monumental cloud banks bloomed and darkened on the horizon. Every creature on the *pori*—animals and men—waited. A kind of atmospheric silence descended; the air, formerly dry as old bones, grew heavy with moisture. The insects felt it first, then the birds. Silver clouds of locusts rose into the air— kicked up by the boots of armies on the move—and turned and banked, flashing northward into the dampening wind. High above these noisome bugs, squadrons of storks, destined for chimney-top nests in Germany and the Netherlands, had just begun their heroic journey: One of these, the famous *Pfeilstorch* (arrow stork), had been caught in Bremen, Germany, in 1820, with an African tribal fowler's arrow in its neck—the first indication to European naturalists of the thousands of miles flown by migratory birds every year.

Meanwhile, in the fetid delta of the Rufiji, the natives knew enough to flee from a new army of invaders millions strong and more irresistible than any battalion of German *askaris* or King's African Riflemen: The soldier ants were on the move. Every year, just before the onset of heavy rains, they marched—followed by snakes and beetles and other chthonic creatures—to higher ground. The ants traveled in yards-wide columns, consuming everything in their path: plants, animals, men. The only recourse was to step aside, to retreat—and in this lies a neat metaphor for the war in East Africa spanning the two rainy seasons from March 1916 to June 1917.

Smuts, determined to capitalize on the British advance through the

Nguru Gap, had decided to press on, despite the coming rains—a three-month period during which, most agreed, the country would become impassible and absolutely pestilential for all Europeans. The South African general—though he refused to admit it to himself—had become obsessed with his German counterpart: More than just an enemy commander, for him von Lettow incarnated the war. Now Smuts sent self-congratulatory and puffed-up dispatches back to London: The "first phase" of the campaign was over, he declared; the enemy couldn't possibly last much longer. It merely remained to encircle the demoralized Schutztruppe and administer the final, crushing blow, etc.—spin for the red tabs at the War Office. But without von Lettow captured, Smuts knew the war would go on.

In the last few days before the rains, Smuts reviewed the performance of his generals during the fight for Kilimanjaro—and came to a difficult decision: For the invasion of German East Africa to proceed successfully, all the major British commanders had to go. He began with Malleson.

"Just imagine," Meinertzhagen continued to fulminate, "any general leaving his brigade in the middle of a fight and taking a car as fast as it would carry him back to the rear." Smuts agreed: "He mentioned the affair to me this evening," Meinertzhagen continued, "and said . . . the man was a coward. I had to agree, but I dislike a Dutchman calling an English general a coward."

Malleson was sacked, for—as Smuts put it—"defective leadership in the field," and returned to London, where he skulked about the lobby of the Naval and Military Club, waiting for a Court of Inquiry to convene before which he could plead his case. The process took more than a year, but at last the eely Malleson wriggled out from under the consequences of his own incompetence. Astonishingly, the War Office confirmed his promotion to major general and eventually rewarded him with another command: In October 1918, he led an expedition to the Transcaspia—there to deter Bolshevik penetration into Persia and Afghanistan. He generally succeeded in doing so, but at such great cost to the national war chest it caused a public scandal. This was his last significant command. Knighted, he retired from the army in 1920. He died in his eighties in 1946 at the end of another horrific war, full of honors, having risen to the top of his profession in a world that, as ever, rewards mediocrity and distrusts genuine talent.

Stewart's turn came next. Smuts dismissed him without ceremony, furious with his failure to advance fast enough through the *pori* on the approach to Neu Moshi and about all the subsequent delays that, in his view, had spoiled the carefully planned "pincer" maneuver to encircle and crush von Lettow. While no one cared much about Malleson, Stewart remained popular with his men and fellow officers. He had spent his life in the army, had commanded the highly regarded 5th Gurkha Rifles in India, and was a plodding, solid officer who clearly cared for his soldiers' welfare. But Smuts did not want solidity; rather, he demanded drive and speed. Stewart finished out his career plodding along as a garrison commander in Aden.

And while "Fighting" Mickey Tighe was swept out with the other two, Smuts wanted to reassure the old campaigner that his service had been valuable to the East African war effort. Tighe, given a decoration and heaped with—not entirely hollow—praise, went back to India, where he was made inspector of troops and, no doubt, continued to drink. He retired in 1920 and died running to catch a bus five years later—a fitting end, perhaps for an inveterate "thruster."

In place of these commanders, Smuts installed South Africans. Beves and van Deventer, promoted, became the prime executors of his strategy of maneuvers. Only Tighe's replacement remained English: General Reginald Hoskins of the King's African Rifles, whose experience leading black troops made him the unavoidable choice. This appointment also underscored Smuts's growing awareness that black African troops made excellent fighters—perhaps better fighters than white men, who lacked native resistance to the extreme climates and diseases of Equatorial Africa. Other South Africans in Smuts's new chain of command included *Oom*—"Uncle"—Coenraad Brits. Another giant, blustery Boer, over six and a half feet tall, he carried a rhino-hide *sjambok* (a kind of swagger stick) with him wherever he went, whacking people with it as a sort of friendly greeting. The more he liked a person, the harder he whacked him. But, a sentimentalist at heart, Brits's general's red collar tabs had been embroidered with purple forget-me-nots by his wife—so that even on the battlefield he might be reminded of her love.

Though the British Army in East Africa rapidly assumed a thoroughly South African character, there remained a place in Smuts's command structure for men who liked to fight: One of these, British Brigadier General S. H. Sheppard, was "generally known by the sobriquet of 'Ha, Ha, Splendid,'" wrote Lord Cranworth in his *Kenya Chronicles*, "from his habit of turning up at a crisis and remarking 'Ha, ha, splendid! Lots of fighting and lots of fun!'"

———————

The rains came at last—a bit late—at the end of March 1916. A sensible commander would have suspended operations until the country dried up in June, but Smuts was not sensible: "He resolved accordingly," says the *Official History*, "while the greater part of his force would have to stand fast along the Ruvu River during the rains, to detach the new 2nd Division under Major-General van Deventer, which was to move southward towards Kondoa-Iragi and the Central Railway."

Smuts ordered van Deventer's Mounted Column to leave Neu Moshi and its environs—which they had occupied after the German evacuation—and advance to Kahe, strategically located on the Northern Railway. They would then move southwest to Kondoa-Irangi about 250 miles away, in the middle of the Masai Steppe. In the vicinity of this depot town, nestled in a bowl between blue hills, von Lettow had been massing his still-undefeated Schutztruppe.

Van Deventer's Mounted Brigade would pave the way for South African Infantry and artillery following close behind, their numbers inflated by recent recruits from the Cape. But Smuts had devised a new strategy, more sophisticated than just chase-and-fight: "Merely to follow the enemy in his very mobile retreat," he wrote in a prescient dispatch to the War Office, "might prove an endless game. . . . In view of the size of the country, it is therefore necessary to invade it from various points with columns strong enough to deal with any combination that could be brought against them." According to Smuts's plan as of March 1916, the colony would be simultaneously invaded from all quarters of the compass: Brigadier General Edward Northey, the tough new commander of British Rhodesian Forces, would push in from Rhodesia in the far southwest; Brigadier General Charles Crewe, a former newspaper editor and publisher of South Africa's *Daily Dispatch*, now in charge of British forces on Lake Tanganyika, would cooperate with Belgian forces under General Charles-Henri Tombeur. Together they would cross the lake to Kigoma and move down the Central Railway to take Tabora, German East Africa's new wartime capital, current home to Governor Schnee, who had recently relocated from Morogoro, and what remained of his civil administration. In the distant southeast, the Portuguese, who had officially declared war on Germany on March 9, would cross the Rovuma River and join the drive toward Kondoa-Irangi.

Smuts himself would advance down the Northern Railway from Moshi, taking on Major Kraut's Schutztruppe companies straddling the line. After defeating Kraut, he would make an abrupt right-hand turn, through the town of Mombo, and move down the Mombo-Handeni trolley line to seize Morogoro, nestled picturesquely in the gap between the Nguru and Uluguru Mountains. Clearly, von Lettow, encircled and soon to be facing nearly 100,000 men, would be forced to surrender.

"I ask you," von Lettow-Vorbeck said in a conversation with Leonard Mosley, "to imagine yourself in the position of a Commander, with insufficient means, exposed to attack by superior numbers, who has continually to ask himself what he must do in order to retain freedom of movement and hope?" Answer: He would rely on luck, fighting spirit, and the terrible rains, which would stick all the enemy's brilliant plans in thick, East African muck.

Smuts, infamous for disregarding most intelligence reports, nonetheless placed complete confidence in the advice of a group of Boer farmers who had fled South Africa during the Boer War and established themselves on farms in the fertile area around Bismarckburg near Lake Tanganyika. For some reason, Smuts chose to overlook the possibility that these East African Boers, having fled English domination in South Africa, might oppose his cause. Unbeknownst to Smuts, it was from this population that von Lettow had drawn Pretorius's opposite number, his chief scout, a master tracker named Piet Nieuwenhuizen.

To the consternation of Smuts's intelligence staff in Nairobi, he now chose to consult these suspect Boers in all matters requiring specialized local knowledge, and especially regarding the weather: While the rainy season might reduce the vicinity of Kilimanjaro to a swampy mess, the Boers reported to Smuts confidently, this was not the case elsewhere in the colony. The farther south you went, they said, the drier it got.

In fact, the opposite proved true. Smuts marched his armies into a soggy quagmire that would eventually claim many, many more lives than German bullets. Of course, the rains fell on Germans, South Africans, and Englishmen all alike; during the rainy season, rain was general all over East Africa. But von Lettow, accurately informed and better prepared for the climate, took it in stride on his fighting retreat toward Kondoa-Irangi.

"The rain came down harder and harder," von Lettow wrote in his *East African Campaigns*, "and the roads became deeper and deeper. At first there were only a few bad places, and twenty or more carriers managed to get us through by pulling and pushing. The *Niempara* [carrier leader] went ahead singing and dancing. The whole crowd joined in with '*Amsigo!*' and '*Kabubi, kabubi!*' and to the rhythm of these chants the work went on cheerily, and at first, easily enough. But on passing through Tulieni, we found that the rains had so swollen an otherwise quite shallow river, that during the morning its torrential waters had completely torn away the wagon bridge. We felled one of the big trees on the bank, but it was not tall enough for its branches to hold fast on the far side. Three feet thick, it was carried away like a match."

Leutnant Müller, von Lettow's adjutant, an excellent swimmer, stripped down and tried to swim across the raging Tulieni, carrying a rope between his teeth. The current swept him farther down the same bank. Another adjutant, Captain Tafel, reached the opposite side after great effort but had dropped his line and was stranded there, "without any clothes on the far side of the river." Meanwhile, von Lettow chafed, "the prospect of having to wait for the river to fall was not enticing. I couldn't afford to waste one minute reaching the head of the marching troops."

Later in the afternoon, a native guide found a ford farther downriver and von Lettow and his men were able to cross: "We continued our journey the whole night in pouring rain," he continued, "and had several times to ride for hours with water up to our saddles, or to wade with it up to our necks."

The rains kept pouring down. According to old Africa hands, it had quickly become one of the worst rainy seasons in living memory. The bushes on the *pori* split open and spilled a bloody red sap on the ground; rivers overflowed their banks and became torrents, deserts metamorphosed overnight into shallow lakes. The men marching beneath the deluge were susceptible to fevers, waterborne bacteria, parasites, and just plain mildew:

"I have never in all my life dreamed that rain could fall as it does here," Smuts wrote to a friend. "The rivers are full, the country is one vast swamp."

"Horses, mules, and men are all suffering terribly from the climate," agreed Selous. "It is the constant unending damp, I think, that gets into men's stomachs and bowels and gives them dysentery." But another type of bowel complaint entirely would soon send the sixty-five-year-old elephant hunter home on medical leave: hemorrhoids in their most painful manifestation—piles— which required the kind of delicate anal surgery better done at a hospital in England.

Selous was by now one of the few remaining Frontiersmen left from the original eccentric bunch. Their numbers, reduced to fewer than 200 by disease and battle, had lately been augmented by new recruits, but the character of the regiment had changed. They were now the 25th Royal Fusiliers in more than just name; Colonel Driscoll's old Legion had been wiped away. Selous went home reluctantly, soon to return, so he swore to his comrades.

Von Lettow reached Kondoa-Irangi at last, before the main body of his troops, in the second week of March. His uniform in tatters, he dressed in a spare *askari* tunic and hurried to the garrison town of Kimamba, to meet Governor Schnee, who had come down from Tabora for an update on the status of the war. The two men still detested each other. Their antipathy had only grown over the months since their last meeting, though Schnee, ever the politician, had made overtures of reconciliation following von Lettow's military successes: On January 27, 1915, the Kaiser's birthday, he'd gone down to Dar es Salaam to deliver a speech to the assembled populace.

The Schutztruppe, he said, "had shown themselves in no way inferior to their German brothers at home. In heroic struggles at Tanga, Jasin, and the Rufiji Delta, and at many places along the frontiers of our colony, they have not only prevented the enemy from setting foot in our protectorate but have also caused him serious losses in his own territory, especially by frequent mining of the Uganda Railway. . . ." Etc.

Schnee sent a copy of this speech to von Lettow, then preparing for the defense of Kilimanjaro—to a resounding silence. Von Lettow's private reaction, recorded by a subordinate, was anything but silent: "Good," he exclaimed. "At least he has accepted the fact that we are at war! I hope he speaks as resolutely in six weeks, when the military situation may not be so healthy for us."

Von Lettow had long ago learned not to trust politicians, and he never trusted Schnee. In the last days of 1915, the governor had interfered with von Lettow's troop deployments by insisting a Schutztruppe company heading for the front be kept in peaceful Lindi, an Indian Ocean port in the far south of the colony. In Lindi, Schnee said, they could continue to protect German inhabitants from native uprisings—always his greatest fear. Von Lettow immediately countermanded this order, insisting military matters must remain in the hands of the military commander. Schnee refused to budge, and for the moment the field companies remained in Lindi, his point made: He was *still* the governor.

During this disagreement both men wrote irate letters to the Kaiser, in which each complained about the other. To von Lettow, Schnee was attempting to tamper with the successful defense of the colony; for his part, Schnee believed that by moving all troops to the front, von Lettow jeopardized the safety of German settlers. But, in truth, Schnee's nightmares regarding rampaging natives had failed to materialize. The majority of African subjects in the German colony supported the Kaiser's war effort—perhaps as a result of von Lettow's egalitarian, race-blind treatment of his *askaris*. Or perhaps because they still preferred the devil they knew (Germany) over the devil they didn't (Great Britain).

In the British colonies, however, episodes of local unrest occurred—most notably the 1915 Chilembwe Rebellion in British Nyasaland (modern Malawi): John Chilembwe, a mission-educated Christian convert who'd been sent to the Virginia Theological College in Lynchburg, Virginia, returned radicalized in 1901 to agitate for an expulsion of all whites from Africa. With the advent of the World War, it seemed his opportunity had arrived: Chilembwe, now an extremist John Brown–style "millenarian Christian" pastor, had been collecting weapons for years and slowly radicalizing his flock; the millenarians, a neo-Baptist sect, preached universal egalitarianism and armed rebellion against all colonial powers in Africa.

On the night of January 22, 1915, Chilembwe's millenarian Christian soldiers armed for the race war, dispersed, and killed a few whites on local plantations. They soon besieged the British outpost of Mlanje; most of the men of the town were off fighting von Lettow in East Africa and the situation looked dire. But a German POW, Leutnant Weltheim, held in the *boma* there, volunteered to organize the defense in exchange for his freedom. Released, he commanded the garrison and staved off Chilembwe's marauders until KAR units arrived to relieve the siege. Apparently, the war of nations had been temporarily forgotten in the face of what European whites saw as a darker threat.

Chilembwe's rebellion, poorly planned and executed, soon petered out. The African population of Nyasaland wasn't ready for insurrection. The British executed forty of Chilembwe's millenarian soldiers, "their bodies left hanging from sunup to sundown as a warning to others of the penalty of a rebellion." Another 300 were imprisoned. Chilembwe himself, shot while trying to escape across the border into Portuguese East Africa, was later mythologized as the "first Malawian martyr in the cause of African freedom." His face decorates Malawian currency to this day.

"Despite the serious uprisings of the past," Schnee wrote in his letter of complaint to the Kaiser, "which proved exceedingly difficult to suppress using the whole Schutztruppe, the Commander seems to leave this danger out of his considerations altogether. . . . I shall allow the Commander . . . a free hand in the conduct of the war, so long as political factors or native problems do not compel me to take appropriate measures." Then he finished on a particularly underhanded note: "I should also like to point out, most respectfully, that my views regarding the present situation are fully shared by the *senior* officer of the East Africa Corps, Naval Korvettenkapitan Loof, commander *Königsberg*."

Schnee's letter was nothing less than an attempted palace coup, aimed at removing von Lettow and replacing him with Loof. Fortunately, thanks to the British blockade, neither Schnee's nor von Lettow's letter reached Berlin for more than a year, by which time the military situation had entirely changed. And neither letter ever reached the Kaiser himself. The German government's response, eventually written by officials in the Kolonialamt, came down firmly on the side of von Lettow: "The correctness of Colonel von Lettow's views has been confirmed by the success at Tanga. . . . We may add that playing off a naval captain against the Commander of the Schutztruppe appears highly inappropriate."

Neither von Lettow nor Schnee ever saw this last letter, which remained buried in the files at the Kolonialamt until after the war. When they met at Kimamba in March 1916, their disagreement, still unresolved, rankled. Because of what he interpreted as the "disasters at Kilimanjaro," Schnee assumed he now had the upper hand; he was wrong. A recent development had strengthened von Lettow's position enormously:

A second blockade runner, the 4,000-ton *Marie von Stettin*, had penetrated the British Naval cordon and landed her cargo safely at Sudi Bay near Lindi. This desperately needed shipment included a portable pontoon bridge, four field howitzers, 5,000,000 rounds of rifle ammunition, 10.5cm shells for *Königsberg*'s retooled naval guns—all ingeniously divided into thousands of carrier-sized bundles of sixty to sixty-five pounds each. One of these bundles contained new dress uniforms and decorations for both German officers and *askaris*. Von Lettow himself received two Iron Crosses, both first and second class. These high honors meant only one thing: the Kaiser and his government approved of von Lettow's conduct of the war so far. The Iron Crosses alone were enough to silence any opposition the governor might offer.

Von Lettow probably didn't wear the new medals on his rumpled *askari* tunic to the meeting at Kimamba, but he certainly knew about them, and it gave his ongoing argument with the governor the weight of Imperial authority. The minutes of the meeting, while not recorded, are not beyond speculation: Perhaps von Lettow quietly explained his strategy once more to the recalcitrant politician. The British had now fielded 45,000 fighting troops against the Schutztruppe, with many more coming, released by the combined Allied victories in GSWA, the Cameroons, and Togoland. The Belgians were coming too and, though not greatly to be feared, the Portuguese. As well as British battalions from Nigeria and the West Indies. No telling how many hundreds of thousands he'd be fighting before long.

Schutztruppe strength now stood at around 10,000, including both officers and men—a nice little army, but not enough to resist a juggernaut. Therefore German strategy must be one of continual retreat. After resisting the British at Kondoa-Irangi, von Lettow planned to consolidate and retire fighting across the Rufiji to the remote Mahenge country in the far south. There food was relatively plentiful and his army could live off the land if necessary. From Mahenge, von Lettow concluded, he would be able to continue the war indefinitely.

No doubt Governor Schnee expressed astonishment at what must have sounded like a bizarre military strategy. He probably suggested that, since victory remained impossible, better to surrender and spare the civilian populations further suffering and the infrastructure of the colony further damage. One can imagine von Lettow's response, his voice angry but controlled: The Fatherland didn't exist to serve the colony, but the colony the Fatherland! German East Africa, already transformed into a literal quagmire by the rains, would now become a giant trap for the Allied armies: The anopheles mosquito, the tse-tse fly, and a variety of other pests and parasites would do the work of 100 batteries of German artillery. The Schutztruppe would fight on until victory in Europe or until it had been entirely destroyed!

The meeting at Kimamba, described by Mosley as a "short sharp, not altogether diplomatic lecture by the Commander of the Schutztruppe," was the last time von Lettow and the governor met on what might be called equal footing. Schnee returned to his wife in Tabora, tail between his legs, with instructions from von Lettow to wait there for the signal to evacuate the town. When Crewe and the Belgians advanced to within artillery distance, it would be time to join von Lettow's force on the long march south.

No doubt, German East Africa's commander—for such he had become, though still a humble *Oberstleutnant*—did not relish the prospect of traveling with Schnee at his side. But it couldn't be helped. The governor's propaganda value as a British captive far outweighed the inconvenience of having to listen to the man's whining and prevarications for the remainder of the war.

The rains continued to pour down. Kahe fell into the hands of the British without a fight. Kraut retreated as instructed down the Northern Railway toward Tanga, drawing the enemy farther into the colony. Skirmishing continued all along the line, but Kraut, always moving off, refused to make a stand.

"The fighting consisted of the enemy receiving our advanced guard with one of several ambushes," complained van Deventer in a report to Smuts, "then falling back on a well-prepared position, and retiring from that on to further well-selected ambush places and positions. All the time our less-advanced troops were subjected to vigorous shelling by means of long-range naval guns."

The *Königsberg* guns, now beginning to make themselves felt, brought the spirit of the battleship to the deep interior. Had von Lettow several batteries of them, he might have—even given the numbers against him—won the war. As it was, the guns plastered advancing British troops daily from as far as eight miles away. On the receiving end, van Deventer's men called these regular barrages the "Daily Hate," a negative substitution for the mail from home they weren't receiving because of the rains. The Germans usually began their barrage in the late afternoon, as the sun set. Darkness would soon make the crash and boom of the shells that much more terrifying.

The torrential rains had by now rendered most of the country impassible. Smuts, again faced with pausing his campaign until late May, again decided against it. He confirmed his order to send van Deventer's 1,200 mounted South Africans, immediately followed by 8,600 infantry and artillery, on to Kondoa-Irangi and the Central Railway, which he assumed von Lettow would vigorously defend. His dubious Boer weathermen had repeatedly assured him that the rains, negligible farther south, wouldn't impede this advance. Again, he chose to believe them.

With the order of *"Opsaal!"* (Saddle up!), van Deventer's South African Division left the environs of Kahe in the first week of April for the Kondoa-Irangi District, roughly 250 miles away across broken, flooded country and beneath ferocious downpours. His mounted brigade, at first in good spirits despite the rain, laughed and joked and did a little hunting on the side—returning from woodland jaunts with bushbucks hanging from their saddlebags. They fought a few inconsequential skirmishes with von Lettow's rearguard positioned along the way to harass them and cheered triumphantly when the Germans disappeared into the rain. But all the while, they were riding into an ambush of a different kind, and far more terrible: In this country, the tse-tse fly ruled.

Glossinidae glossina, the gray or brown tse-tse fly—of which there are over thirty species and subspecies—carry the parasite *Trypanosoma*, which causes a fatal blood infection in large mammals, including humans, horses, and cattle. The flies inhabit specific "fly belts," of which the Masai Steppe is one. In these territories from which they cannot be extirpated, they will attack any large moving object indiscriminately, including trains and automobiles, looking for blood. Unusually, the females gestate one embryo at a time, nurtured on a rich, milky mucus distilled from the blood of her victims. The larval tse-tse is then released into the soil, from where it emerges to find its new home on woody surfaces, hence the high rate of infection in jungled areas. While the tse-tse does produce fatal sleeping sickness in humans—a 1904 epidemic in Uganda killed more than 200,000—horses and cows are its chief source of food and destruction. German scientists working out of the Amani labs near Morogoro before the war had produced maps depicting the major fly belts; the British had copies of these maps in their possession but do not seem to have consulted them.

As the South African Mounted Division advanced farther into the kingdom of *Glossina morsitans* (the subspecies of tse-tse fatal to horses and cattle), their horses began to die. On April 6, at the start of his long ride, van Deventer commanded more than 1,000 cavalrymen; six days later that number had been reduced to 800; in another week, as his forces penetrated the Kondoa-Irangi District, 800 had become 300.

The dead animals could not be buried or burned in the torrential downpours and so were left in wet, putrefying heaps by the side of the trail. Dead horseflesh marked the army's progress like cairns. To the infantry slogging along behind, these stinking piles were "van Deventer's milestones"—but one artillery officer, Captain F. H. Autt, pointed out the inaccuracy of this appellation: "The average interval between stinking dead carcasses," he wrote, "was 100 yards." Too many "of these dumb gentle brutes died here," commented Colonel Deneys Reitz, a Johannesburg lawyer and politician now serving with van Deventer's forces. "And that part of me which loved and understood horses . . . died too."

The presence of so much rotting animal flesh brought on other diseases. Amoebic dysentery advanced with van Deventer's army, and the sick could not be cared for properly in the rain: The road back to the nearest hospital facility that might merit the name had become a morass. Compelled to lie where they had fallen and protected from the weather only by leaky tents and makeshift lean-tos, sick men suffered and perished along with their animals: "We lay there in the mud and retched from the stench of the dead animals and watched the rats crawl over us," a despairing South African trooper wrote home.

Many who remained ambulatory lost their boots to the "sucking black mud" or traded them to the locals for food and so marched barefoot, exposing themselves to other parasites and to tetanus and septicemia. Even small abrasions became dangerously infected in such weather, especially given the half-starved condition of van Deventer's troops: The ration wagons bearing food and supplies simply couldn't keep up, stuck to their axles on the muddy roads, their oxen dropping in the yoke, felled by *Glossina morsitans* as if by an ax. As the march progressed, the men added starvation to their diet of disease. Clouds of mosquitoes fogged their path, even in the rain. And at night, as they tried to sleep, the roaring of lions rent the darkness.

But, as all good things must come to an end, so must all bad things, including suffering. Forward elements of van Deventer's South African Mounted Division reached Kondoa-Irangi on April 20. The German settlement, in a narrow valley surrounded by low hills, possessed a wireless station and warehouses once filled with grain and other comestibles—all now carefully destroyed. Von Lettow's *askaris* had evacuated the night before, setting the town on fire as they withdrew. Now dying flames sputtered and sizzled in the rain; the buildings would be of no use to the invading armies. Infantry and artillery units began to trickle in ten days later—exhausted and decimated before they had fought a single action. Of van Deventer's original combined strength of about 10,000, there remained perhaps 3,000 effective. Nearly half of the roughly 3,000 horses and mules had died on the march. Still, given the terrible rains and impassible country, it had been an achievement, later cited by historians as "one of the outstanding cavalry actions of the World War."

"Our capture of Kondoa took the Germans by surprise," Meinertzhagen later wrote. "They never suspected that we could move so quickly over bad roads in the rains. Neither did they credit Smuts with so bold a move. I doubt whether any British general with British troops could have planned and carried out the move in tropical Africa during the rains. Only South Africans born and bred to long distances and living on the country could have accomplished it."

But dysentery, malaria, and infected wounds, all made worse by the unrelenting damp, continued to torture the men: The 129th Baluchis who had advanced with the South African Infantry were down to 158 troopers; the 1st and 2nd Rhodesians had been reduced by more than ninety percent. Brett Young reported that the Rhodesians' "machine guns had been turned in to Ordnance for want of gunners, and pestilence had swept away the lives of all transport animals." On May 3, van Deventer sent a dire message to Smuts. The situation at Kondoa-Irangi, almost as bad as it had been on the march out, remained critical:

"Today 711 sick in hospital and 320 in convalescent camp. Lack of strengthening foods such as oatmeal, bacon, jam, cheese, milk, etc., renders it almost hopeless to expect convalescents to get fit for active duty. . . . The majority of our men are lying on the ground in tent hospitals as there are no stretchers available. Infantry regiments for the most part arrived here without blankets—dearth of boots, clothing, soap—the very poor rations are the cause of the heavy sick rate. . . . If immediate steps are not taken, the situation will daily become worse. . . . The animals are weak, arrangements will collapse."

Meanwhile, just ahead of the South African advance, von Lettow had established his Schutztruppe in the hills cupping the town. He set about strengthening his positions in anticipation of a major fight—as soon as a break in the rains made such a thing possible. In carefully selected emplacements he mounted two *Königsberg* guns, with which to shell the gathering South Africans. A copy of van Deventer's bleak note to Smuts soon fell into his hands, but he was not quite ready to strike. He wanted to inflict a smashing blow before moving south to the Mahenge country. At last, he began shelling the cantonment below with his *Königsberg* guns; this barrage answered, ironically, by guns salvaged from HMS *Pegasus*—it seemed the battle between the remnants of these two sunken warships would never end.

By May 7, von Lettow could count over 4,000 rifles assembled in the hills, more effectives than van Deventer had in the waterlogged cantonments below. For the first time in the course of the war, his forces outnumbered the enemies. Fever now ravaged the ranks of the South Africans who, without proper rations, survived on pawpaws and bananas and whatever they could scrounge from the surrounding countryside. Their hospital tents, the canvas black with continual rain, stood crammed to the flaps with sickened men. This was hardly an army that might resist a sudden onslaught of screaming *askaris* from the hills.

And yet the commander waited—though skirmishing continued. Von Lettow's *askaris* probed South African defenses and vice versa; the Germans seemed to get the best of these small actions: A Schutztruppe sharpshooter named Juma Murjal polished off a patrol of six mounted South African troopers from his carefully camouflaged position commanding a water hole much used by the surviving horses—and this with a smoky Model 71. Though the billowing clouds gave him away almost immediately, the South Africans went down before they could return fire.

Also, in addition to their *Königsberg* guns, the Germans mounted several smaller fieldpieces with which to bedevil the enemy. One of these, a mobile six-pounder on a portable wooden frame, caused particular annoyance, if not much damage, from any one of several emplacements on a hill above the South African camp. The South Africans, suffering beneath the accurate fire, mockingly called the small gun "Big Bertha." Deneys Reitz came to hate Big Bertha, though he acknowledged it was "daringly handled." Its German officer he came to "know by sight, so often did he appear from behind border or thicket, with his field-piece carried on a wooden frame by its *askari* crew. In a moment, half a dozen rounds would come screeching at us, after which the gun was taken off to reappear at some other spot."

At last, Reitz led an impulsive charge up a hill to take the gun's latest emplacement, but arrived minutes too late. The gun was gone. On the ground, the Germans had scattered a handful of Indian coins and tossed a hastily scrawled note: *15 RUPEES FOR THE BLUDDY ENGLISCH.*

"After our long crawl in the heat," Reitz remarked grimly, "we were not amused."

But the Germans *were* amused. And overly fond of such sardonic little jokes throughout the war both in Africa and in Europe. During the Zeppelin blitz of London, for example, similar provocations had rained down on the city along with the bombs. These included taunting messages and mocking caricatures of British officials. A bag attached to a small parachute found on the grass of a park in North London on the morning after a massive Zeppelin raid in 1915 contained a scrimshawed ham bone, engraved with a cartoon rendering of a tiny Zeppelin dropping a bomb on a crudely rendered Englishman in a top hat and high collar, labeled "Edwart Gray"—probably a depiction of Sir Edward Grey, the British foreign secretary, whose younger brother would lose an arm in the East Africa campaign. Scratched beneath this image: "A memento from Starved-Out Germany," and in a cartoon bubble from Mr. Grey himself, his eyes comically tilted toward the falling bomb: "What should I, poor devil, do?"

A question van Deventer no doubt asked himself as his men and horses dropped by the dozens in the rain and he waited for the Germans to launch their attack.

At last, in the second week of May, the rains ceased and the sky above Kondoa-Irangi gradually brightened from deep gray to vivid blue. A week or so, not more, remained before the big heat took hold of the country— good time for a fight.

Von Lettow chose the morning of May 10 for his attack. He had by now carefully planned the sequence of events, conferring repeatedly with his command staff: Captain von Kornatzki (one of his favorite young officers), Oberstleutnant von Bock, Captain Paul von Stemmermann, Major Willibald von Stuemer—in whose Bukoba home those naughty photographs had been found by Meinertzhagen. Now these men went over last-minute details. An accurate map of Kondoa-Irangi, drawn up before the war and left with a local *jumbee* for safekeeping, was retrieved and consulted. This would be a set-piece battle. The Schutztruppe would strike a shattering blow against a disease-ridden army and perhaps drive them, reeling, all the way back to Kilimanjaro and across the border. Von Lettow knew this couldn't be done with available forces, though he occasionally indulged himself in a military pipe dream. On May 9, he spent an exhausting day visiting the front lines on his bicycle and on foot, talking and joking with company commanders and *askaris* alike, improving morale and seeing to last-minute details. He returned to his headquarters camp after dark, exhausted, feeling the onset of fever. He was, so his medical officers told him, "malaria-prone and shouldn't be living in Africa at all."

"I tried to relieve my exhaustion with a cup of coffee and a little rum," he wrote, "but knowing I had no more orders to issue, soon fell fast asleep. . . . I was awakened by Leutnant Wunderlich. He could not make out the frequent flashes he saw in the direction of the enemy. Neither could I, at first. But soon there could be no doubt that these flashes, which became more and more frequent, were caused by rifles and machine guns. . . . Contrary to all our expectations a stiff fight was taking place on our front. But owing to the great distance and the bushy and rocky country, I didn't think I could engage the reserves. . . . For better or worse I had to let the fight take its course."

In defiance of all von Lettow's well-laid plans, the Battle of Kondoa-Irangi had begun without him and confusion reigned. Here's what had happened: Oberstleutnant von Bock's company, advancing to take up their positions in the first hours after dark, had run into an enemy patrol, with von Bock soon knocked out of the fight with a bullet to the throat. At that point, a junior officer—perhaps Kornatzki—took charge and, finding South African resistance crumbling, advanced into Kondoa. Unfortunately, once in the town, the officer had inadvertently come up against the strongest point of van Deventer's defensive line of trenches. A confused night battle ensued, the sky above the town rent by star shells and shattered by the booming of the *Königsberg* guns. There was nothing for it; sometimes, battles, like babies, come when they will.

Von Lettow now ordered the Schutztruppe to engage all along the line. *Askaris* charged in waves against the South African trenches and were each time hurled back. He then ordered a flank attack; this failed too. Observing the concentrated muzzle-flash of South African riflemen from a point seemingly to the rear of their trenches, von Lettow at last realized he'd been deceived. The new maps of Kondoa-Irangi examined so avidly back at HQ had failed to indicate a rise of low hills behind South African forward positions. These hills concealed a secondary line—the "real" trenches—and the main bulk of the South African army. A trick they'd apparently learned from Major Kraut's dummy fortifications at the First Battle of Salaita.

Too late to redirect the flow of the battle, von Lettow hoped his *askaris* might pull it off—but night battles were not their strong suit. Fighting finally petered out in a stalemate around three fifteen a.m. The South African trenches in Kondoa-Irangi held firm, but their forces weren't strong enough to mount a counterattack and the Germans maintained their commanding position in the hills.

Before dawn, von Lettow, now shaking with fever, paused to consider casualties. The damage inflicted on his small army had been too great— many wounded and fifty dead, though the South Africans later counted 128 German dead. But either number included two of von Lettow's most trusted officers, Kornatzki and von Bock. Another attack, von Lettow realized, and the Schutztruppe "was bound to suffer considerable and irreplaceable losses." Without sufficient artillery to "soften up" the South African defenses, another attack would rack up more pointless casualties. Also, according to intelligence reports, Smuts had already sent reinforcements. With these factors in mind, von Lettow made the difficult decision to withdraw immediately.

At dawn, the battle-weary South Africans looked up to find the blue hills above Kondoa-Irangi devoid of enemy troops. Hazy sunlight shone down on abandoned German gun emplacements and empty trenches. A murmur of astonishment passed along the line, followed by cheering, rising triumphantly as the sun rose. It seemed a major victory to van Deventer until he too counted his losses and tallied up the cost of his drive through the rain. Also, he knew the Schutztruppe hadn't been defeated; they had merely disappeared. Again. And they had let the country itself do most of their fighting for them.

In the weeks since the advance from Kahe, his original force of 10,000 had been reduced to a little more than 300 disease free and fully able to fight. The whole place stank like rotting horseflesh in the rising heat sure to bring on fresh epidemics. Both his doctors had died treating diseases they could not cure. No one had enough food to eat, though starvation-level rations were bumped up a little—one cup of flour, one cup of rice, a little sugar, tea, and salt per man—after the first carrier caravans reached the area on May 14.

The Battle of Kondoa-Irangi, while "a tactical setback" for the Schutz-truppe, cannot be described as a defeat. Von Lettow and his *askari* field companies, more or less intact, now moved off to meet up with Major Kraut, still straddling the Northern Railway. There they would meet Smuts bearing down with fresh battalions in his drive south toward Morogoro.

Kondoa-Irangi, however, did provide one of its participants with an-other opportunity to inflate his personal mythology: Meinertzhagen, pres-ent at the battle, later claimed he led a South African counterattack against a German machine gun nest not thirty yards from the lines, as artillery fire burst above his head. In the phosphorescent darkness, occasionally illumi-nated by explosions, he took refuge in a nullah (gully), where he bumped against someone he could not see. Taking this person to be one of his own KAR troopers, he called in Swahili, "Who are you?" and was then dealt a painful blow on the shoulder with a heavy fighting stick—an African tribal cudgel called a knobkerrie.

A miniature battle ensued—hand-to-hand, fists flying, in total darkness—as the main battle flashed and raged around them. At last, Meinertzhagen wrenched the knobkerrie from the hands of his attacker, "got my knee well into his stomach, and then set to on his head with the knobkerry until he was silent." At first light, with the Germans gone and battlefield cleanup begun, Meinertzhagen returned to the scene of his deadly fight to find Captain Kor-natzki lying dead, his head bashed in:

"My God," he announced to anyone who would listen, "I should have liked to have caught old von Lettow instead of poor Kornatzky."

Whether true or not, this tale only added to Meinertzhagen's brutal glamour and explained the African knobkerrie he carried with him every-where he went for the rest of his life.

Chapter 21

THE LONG RETREAT

The country dried up. The rains that had turned all terrain into swampland went wherever rain goes, and in the place of mud, the chalky dust that had bedeviled the advancing columns at Salaita returned in billowing clouds to choke the marching men of all armies.

After the Battle of Kondoa-Irangi, van Deventer realized his exhausted South Africans could advance no farther. Weakened by starvation and disease, their ranks further winnowed by battlefield casualties, they hunkered down and waited for medical supplies and provisions to reach them down the long, roundabout route from Mombasa to Taveta by train and thence through the Nguru Pass and down the rutted tracks to Kondoa-Irangi in ox wagons, with most of the oxen dying on the way. More often than not, before these stubborn, lumbering animals reached the needy troops with their load of provisions, trypanosome bacteria, invading their bloodstream, caused a massive swelling in the chest and enlarged the jugular. At that point, so a veterinary officer with van Deventer's division acknowledged, there was nothing to be done: "One may say with truth," he wrote, "that the commonest and most frequently prescribed veterinary medicine is the revolver."

That van Deventer's men still hung on to Kondoa-Irangi Meinertzhagen attributed to sheer luck and the confusion of night fighting. Perhaps led by the precipitous Kornatzki, the Germans had attacked at exactly the wrong spot, at the wrong time: "Van Deventer is a very lucky man and I told him so," Meinertzhagen confided to his diaries. Had the Germans followed von Lettow's battle plan, he believed, "we should all be prisoners of war," though he went on to tip his hat to the South African fighting spirit: "It is the first real knock von Lettow has had . . . all credit to old van Deventer and his South Africans."

Meanwhile, the German commander withdrew into the blue hills a safe distance away, there to await developments—and for the moment, the pendulum of the war swung to the Northern Railway, still held by Major Kraut and 2,000 *askaris*. Smuts was determined to capture Kraut, eliminate his command, and then capture Mombo and the trolley spur to Handeni. From Handeni, he would advance across open country to Morogoro, a major stop on the Central Railway, something of a resort town and one of the colony's chief adornments. With Morogoro taken, he hoped von Lettow might be persuaded to surrender.

Ever the fan of complex maneuvers, Smuts now divided his 1st Division under General Hoskins into three columns that would advance in tandem and along parallel lines toward Mombo: The first column, composed of KAR units under Hoskins, would follow the wooded slopes of the Pare Mountain Range; the second under Hannyngton, who had led the Baluchis in France on the Western Front, would head straight down the railway line; "Ha, Ha, Splendid" Sheppard would push along the banks of the Pagani River. These fast-moving columns, converging, would catch Kraut and his men on the sharp points of their bayonets; they were like the triple tines of an oyster fork, with Kraut as the oyster—unless he chose to retreat, yielding the pearl of Mombo-Handeni without a major battle. This, of course, was exactly what von Lettow had ordered his subordinate to do: Kraut would harass the British advance within the limits of his abilities, rip up tracks, destroy rolling stock, burn everything that might succor the invaders. But he would retreat all the while and keep retreating and, most important, not get caught.

On May 22, 1916, Smuts launched his big push. His armies advanced without serious opposition, making 180 miles under the hot African sun in two weeks. But the brightness and the dusty tracks and the equatorial heat, while preferable to torrential rain, conjured another host of horrors from the microscopic world.

Chief among these was blackwater fever, a particularly virulent form of malaria characterized by excessively high fevers and subzero chills. Violent vomiting and black urine followed, with death resulting in more than fifty percent of the cases. The high doses of morphine administered to ease those suffering from blackwater (as a side effect, morphine suppresses vomiting, thus reducing chances of dehydration) often led to unintended addictions in the few survivors. Captain Robert Dolbey, a medical officer attached to Sheppard's column, also recommended champagne as a reliable treatment for vomiting, though to him as to others, "blessed morphia" remained the "priceless boon."

Smuts's South Africans took pride in their hairy-chested ability to ac-climatize, often refused both quinine and mosquito netting, and, conse-quently, dropped by the hundreds. Army doctors disagreed on proper quinine dosages—whether five grams should be administered on a daily basis as some had it, or the "twenty grams on Saturday night and thirty the next," prescribed by one of the South African force's chief medical officers. The latter treatment held sway until medical staff discovered quinine ad-ministered in such high dosages could overwhelm the liver and actually worsen cases of malaria.

Meanwhile, the Germans—both European officers and native *askaris*—suffered far less from tropical diseases than the British during the East Af-rican war. In his *Sketches of the East Africa Campaign*, Captain Dolbey wrote that to him, "it has been a source of surprise that the German, who consistently drinks beer in huge quantities, takes little or no exercise, and cohabits with the black women of the country extensively, should have per-formed such prodigies of endurance on trek in this campaign. One would have thought that the Englishman, who keeps his body fitter for games, eschews beer for his liver's sake, and finds that intimacy with the native population lowers his prestige, would have done far better in this war than the German. That, in all fairness, he has not done so."

Part of this German resistance to disease must be attributed to the sim-ple matter of uniforms. In the field, the Germans wore high-collared tunics, long-sleeved shirts, long pants, and puttees or high boots, thus exposing less of their skin to noxious insect bites than the British, who dressed for comfort in shorts and open-neck, short-sleeved shirts. The "huge quantities of beer" Dolbey found so offensive also helped; liquid-borne microbes gen-erally cannot survive in the frothy, acidic medium of a good bottle of lager.

Fleas, perhaps humanity's greatest enemy after the mosquito, accounted for two of the most horrible afflictions experienced by the combatants in East Africa. Dracunculiasis, called Guinea worm, still endemic to the region, is a disease caused by a microscopic parasite, *Dracunculus medinensis*, carried in the bellies of the *Cyclops* species of water fleas. These tiny fleas, drunk down in unpurified water by thirsty troops on the march, release the larval parasites they carry into the human digestive tract. The parasites quickly bore into the intestinal wall and, growing into adult worms barely two millimeters wide but over a meter long, mate in the body cavity and eventually migrate to the subcutaneous layer of tissue just below the skin. After sex, the male immediately dies, while the female gestates for months, sometimes years, finally digging her way to the surface of the skin, usually through the legs or scrotum of the human host. The female will then release her eggs over a period of weeks only onto wet skin or into water (her amniotic sac often contains 3,000,000 eggs), where they will be ingested by the *Cyclops* water fleas, beginning the horrific cycle all over again.

At the point where the female Guinea worm breaches the skin, a painful round ulcer forms. Here a wooden needle can be attached to the worm's hindquarters as it appears; the worm can then be wound out, very carefully, a millimeter at a time, over a period of hours or days. Tearing the worm will cause it to die and rot, causing a painful abscess, fevers, and sometimes death from sepsis. Occasionally, the female worm, unable to reach the surface on time to release her eggs, will expel them into the body cavity of the human host. The growing worms can then migrate to the lungs, eyes, and heart, wrapping themselves around veins and entire organs—leading to a person becoming genuinely worm infested. As many as sixty pregnant female worms have been extracted from a single human body at one time. Victims often describe the sensation of being "on fire" as the worms emerge from the skin ulcers. First mentioned in ancient Egyptian medical texts, circa 1500 BC, the Guinea worm is probably the basis for a biblical scourge: the "fiery serpents" of Numbers 21:6, sent by God to punish the kvetching Israelites after they crossed the Red Sea and set up camp in areas now known to harbor dracunculiasis.

Another flea, the chigger or sand flea, *Tunga penetrans*, also attacked the troops of both sides in East Africa. These miniature monsters burrow beneath the toenails of poorly shod marching men, causing rot and infection. Once beneath the toenails, female chiggers ovulate and secrete a substance that decomposes human flesh into a digestible mulch upon which to nurture her brood. Not only do they attack the soles of the feet and toes, but also occasionally the scrotum and penis. Chigger egg sacs, about as large as a pea, must be removed carefully; once they're broken, poisonous abscesses often result. Captain Dolbey again:

"At least five percent of our army, both white and native, are constantly incapacitated. Hundreds of toenails have I removed for this cause alone." A corporal in the Twenty-fifth Fusiliers wrote in his diary: 'I took twelve jiggers out this morning—I think that is about the average each day!' One officer endured at a sitting the extraction of forty from one foot. Lieutenant W. S. Thatcher said, 'It is extremely painful. . . . I have seen cases where all the toes have been eaten away, while the rest of the foot resembled a mass of dirty putrefying rags.'"

Von Lettow attempted to emulate his *askaris* and march without boots, in anticipation of the day when his own would wear out with replacements unavailable. He came to regret this decision: Every night, Baba, his treasured native cook and batman, carefully cut the chiggers out of his feet, now pulpy and festering. Eventually, Schutztruppe medical orderlies removed two of von Lettow's toenails; he continued the long retreat in constant pain, barely able to hobble along. Still, he refused to give up the idea of marching barefoot:

"It was remarkable how soon the foot became inured to the ground and hardened up," he later said. "For scaling mountains and slithering over rocks, there was no doubt that the unshod foot gave the surest footing. It was also possible to march over trodden paths without shoes, but never through the bush—for there spines and spikes bit into the flesh and caused grievously painful sores." For the latter kind of marching, he took to wearing light sandals, then boots with the toes cut away, both of which did nothing to protect his feet from the depredations of the baleful chigger.

Tick-bite fever, resembling malaria but unresponsive to quinine treatments; botfly bites, quickly infested with large maggot larvae; sand fly bites, causing fever and ceaseless itching—these rounded out the calendar of natural afflictions in a war where those who died from disease outnumbered those who died in battle at the rate of thirty-one to one! Given the multiplicity of deadly natural afflictions in Africa, it's not difficult to understand why, after arising there, a goodly portion of the human species decided to seek its fortunes elsewhere.

British forces marching on Kraut in May down the Northern Railway, subject to daily bombardments from the *Königsberg* guns and carefully planned *askari* ambushes, also felt assaulted by the sheer physical beauty of the country through which they passed. Brett Young describes it best in his novel *Jim Redlake*, drawn from personal experience, much of which takes place during the campaign:

"The background, ever changing yet ever the same, of golden grasslands and silvery bush; of a winding impetuous river, now near, now far, yet ever present to the parched imagination in a vision of greener trees in whose shadow temptation and death were always lurking . . . of suns that rose on new landscapes of incredible, golden calm . . . a calm which, like as not, would be suddenly broken by the boom of the invisible enemy's naval guns and the shriek of shells that ripped the blue tissue of sky like tearing silk, or the whip-crack of snipers' bullets snapping in the air, or a rattle of Maxim-fire simultaneous with shots that smote like a sudden hailstorm launched from the cloudless heaven."

Meanwhile, Kraut mounted his *Königsberg* gun on a railway carriage and ran it up and down the line, firing furiously; *askari* snipers roosted in the trees; Schutztruppe ordnance experts fabricated thousands of land mines and booby-trap bombs—all to impede the British advance.

The best of the bomb-makers, the Danish sailor Nis Kock off the blockade runner *Rubens*, wrote a vivid account of his experience making antipersonnel bombs and land mines in *Blockade and Jungle*: These vicious booby traps, fabricated from artillery shells, discarded tins of bully beef, biscuit boxes, and anything Kock could get his hands on, fixed with simple pressure fuses and lightly buried or triggered by a trip wire, could not be easily detected by advancing troops: "So far as I could see," complained a British scout, "the only way to find a mine was to walk into it and be blown up." Advancing South Africans occasionally drove cattle down suspect trails; resulting explosions caused a bloody rain of instantly butchered cow and saved human lives.

But Schutztruppe machine gun units remained the greatest hazard. The Germans carefully cleared sight lines through the bush, staked and marked the ranges, camouflaged their Maxims, and waited for the enemy to come lumbering into the trap: "Even in this bush warfare," Brett Young wrote in a letter home, "where man, one would think, is matched against single man, the machine-gun has become the most important weapon. That is partly the reason why the Germans in this campaign have been able to put up so splendid a resistance."

And yet all these adversaries, both natural and man-made, failed to slow Smuts's advance significantly. His central column reached Buiko, halfway to Mombo and the Handeni trolley line, on May 30. Here Kraut had positioned artillery spotters on the crests of the lower hills and began shelling the approaching columns, visible for miles on account of the usual clouds of white dust rising above them like evil ghosts. Kraut lobbed shell after shell at the approaching British, destroying creaking supply wagons and wreaking havoc on both beasts and men. At last, Sheppard ordered an attack on the main German positions at a spot near Buiko where the Pagani River doglegged to the east. The Rhodesians pushed up through heavy scrub, drawing such an intensity of fire they were forced to drop and crawl along the ground. Major Kraut, faced with overwhelming numbers and ever mindful of von Lettow's orders to avoid encirclement at all costs, now initiated a textbook fighting retreat. As the Schutztruppe began to pull back, the Rhodesians rose out of the underbrush, fixed bayonets, and prepared to charge—only to be called off at the last possible second via heliograph by Smuts, chary of incurring heavy casualties across ground most assuredly booby-trapped. The Rhodesians threw down their rifles in disgust, pulled out their entrenching tools, and dug in as Kraut and his *askaris* escaped unharmed down the line.

Smuts paused at Buiko for nearly a month. His advance had again outpaced his supply line. The South Africans who had been marching and fighting almost continuously since breaking through the Nguru Gap could go no farther. Hunger and disease prevented the immediate seizure of Handeni, though elements of Sheppard's column penetrated the Usambara

Highlands—the most healthy and cultivated district in the entire colony, favored by the Germans for their summer homes.

The famous research labs at Amani, not far away, remained in German hands. Here German scientists, indispensible to von Lettow's war effort, were still hard at work devising a miraculous variety of substitute medications and other necessities impossible to obtain because of the blockade. They had, for example, distilled, to date, 15,000 bottles of their moonshine "whiskey," all eagerly consumed by the Schutztruppe. But von Lettow, who had begun his withdrawal from Kondoa-Irangi and hoped to join forces with Kraut on the Central Railway, could not be deflected to defend the labs—which were, in any case, undefendable.

In mid-June, a former British missionary named Pearce, now an officer with Sheppard's column, took it upon himself to march on Amani. He had been part of an Anglican mission in the district before the war and still counted many of the local tribesmen as his friends. Under orders to warn the researchers at Amani of approaching enemy soldiers, the tribesmen, however, did nothing when Pearce walked up from the direction of British-held Monga, at the head of half a dozen Baluchis. Pearce stopped, greeted his former parishioners, shook hands, kissed babies, and was cheered along the way. Everyone seemed happy to see him and apparently considered the six sepoys armed with Lee-Enfields trailing along behind him as a sort of honor guard thoughtfully provided by the British.

At dusk, Pearce and his men wound up the long drive to the research institute. They soon came upon the well-known German scientist Arthur Zimmerman taking his ease on a bench in the garden by the hothouses, smoking and oblivious to the existence of a war beyond his peaceful foothills.

"Professor Zimmerman, I assume?" offered Pearce, appearing out of nowhere. The German looked up, puzzled at this intrusion—though less so as the Baluchis marched out of the gloom, unlimbering their rifles.

"Yes," Zimmerman replied at last, "but how in the devil did you get here?"

"I walked from Monga." Pearce grinned. "And now I take possession in the name of His Britannic Majesty."

Thus one of von Lettow's irreplaceable assets fell into the enemy's hands, soft as one of the ripe plums falling from Amani's hothouse trees.

Handeni, undefended, also fell softly on June 19. Sheppard's column, unopposed, had seized the Mombo-Handeni trolley line the day before and now rolled into town to find the usual smoldering, shit-smeared buildings and booby traps and the Germans gone. Only the 3rd FK under Captain Robert Doring had been left by Kraut near the bridge over the Lukigura River to guard his retreat.

Here, on June 24, Sheppard deployed a heavy column consisting of the newly reinforced Loyal North Lancs, the 25th Royal Fusiliers, and the Gurkhas, backed by two fearsome Rolls-Royce Silver Ghost armored cars. The Rolls-Royces crashed along the rutted track toward the bridge, impervious to German machine-gun fire, their own .50-caliber Maxim firing furiously from a central turret. But the Germans had dug a hasty trench across the road; this and a shell into the radiator of the forward car stopped the column. The Rolls-Royces pulled up short; drivers and gunners spilled out with shovels to fill the trench under hostile fire, then got back in their cars and drove on, spitting fire to clear a path for the infantry.

The Lancs and the Gurkhas came up eagerly enough behind the cars, but were slowed by the usual accuracy of German fire. The much-reduced Frontiersmen, bedraggled, exhausted, and bedeviled by sickness, now surprised everyone. As described in the *Official History*:

"The Kashmiri Rifles (Gurkhas) . . . pushed to close range, preparing to charge. The companies extended into the bush were somewhat difficult to control, and the assault had not been launched when three companies of the 25/Royal Fusiliers . . . in all perhaps 150 strong, came up on the left flank, grasped the situation instantly, fixed bayonets, and rushed forward, cheering. The Gurkhas . . . took up the cheering and charged in alongside the Fusiliers, sweeping over all opposition. . . .

"For once—rarest of occurrences in this particular campaign—the assault got home with the bayonet. The German machine guns and a field gun . . . were carried, their detachments bayoneted and the weapons captured undamaged. The defending force was driven in utter rout from the ridge . . . and its remnants scattered in the bush."

The British lost ten men with thirty-six wounded; the Germans lost four European officers and thirty *askaris*, with twenty-one Germans and thirty-two captured of all ranks. A blow to von Lettow's shrinking forces, but ultimately a failure: Sheppard's action had been intended as one of the arms of an encircling maneuver to catch the bulk of Kraut's forces; now the trap closed shut on an unpeopled bush. Kraut had escaped and was racing toward Morogoro to join forces with von Lettow.

In July, Smuts's columns once again outran their supply lines and he called a general halt to the precipitous advance into German East Africa. Photographs of South African troops, emaciated and dressed in tatters, had found their way to the newspapers back home and had caused a public outcry; caution was being urged upon him by Botha, who would soon make a visit to the front to investigate. For now, Smuts decided to dig in at a particularly insalubrious place called Msiha. Unfortunately situated on a damp piece of ground beneath Kanga Mountain, it lay in the sights of a pair of *Königsberg* guns positioned in the hills. German artillery fire, inaccurate at first, gradually found the range of the British encampment and soon the shells thundered in, adding to the casualty list of sick and dying men. Supplied with a hoard of new ammunition from the *Marie von Stettin*, Schutztruppe gunners kept up the barrage day and night—pausing only for an hour at dinnertime.

Smuts's command, reduced by poor rations, malaria, and other terrible ailments, could not summon the energy to mount an attack on the German hilltop—or indeed to move the encampment beyond the reach of German shells. Instead the troops languished at Msiha for a month, suffering from their illnesses and all the while enduring nearly continuous bombardment. Mini earthquakes caused by falling shells disturbed the sick and dying men cramming the hospital tents—but somehow had no effect on the imperturbable Smuts, who found the sojourn at Msiha pleasant enough to keep up his intellectual pursuits. A regular subscriber to *The Philosophical Review* and *The New Republic*, Smuts grew anxious only when these magazines failed to arrive on time by military post. He read Walter Lippmann's *Drift and Mastery*, Benedetto Croce's *Philosophy of the Practical*. He dipped into Hegel. A steady stream of German philosophical works acquired as spoils of war from the summer homes of the Usambara Highlands added to his growing library. "Some of my dear old German philosophers I have found in this country," he wrote to a friend, "and I can therefore reread them at odd times."

Von Lettow and the Germans, however, were disappointed in the quality of the literature they captured from their enemies from time to time during the war—mostly cheap detective fiction from the English; the Portuguese preferred the rankest pornography—though von Lettow could occasionally get his hands on a copy of something by Dickens, whom he read in English and admired.

———————

Meanwhile, on July 7, after a punishing naval bombardment, British troops finally entered Tanga. The destruction, so feared by Schnee, had occurred at last and the town—as he had long ago predicted—had been reduced to a smoldering ruin:

"Our bombproof shelter proved ineffective," wrote the officer in charge of Tanga's coast guard unit. "I with several other people found a drain for protection and the air was very stifling. Twelve-inch shells poured into the town for nine hours. All large and important buildings were wrecked. A shell fell right on my house, blowing all my belongings to glory. I last saw my bed go flying into the air, having been driven straight through two stone walls. Such a fine bed too! It was a good job I was not lying in it."

The capture of Tanga, nearly two years after their first attempt, now opened the entire length of the Northern Railway to the British all the way from Neu Moshi to the coast—though they inherited a waste of twisted ties, incinerated sleepers, derailed rolling stock, and blown-up engines. Retreating Germans had made sure the enemy would have to start from scratch. The British, inveterate railroad builders, did not shrink from the challenge: On its most basic level, imperialism was all about building railroads. Now they put battalions of coolies to work on the tracks with astonishing results; the first trains went through to Mombo in just a few weeks, at last opening the critical supply line that had plagued Smuts's advance.

By late July, the Schutztruppe had fallen back on the Central Railway, which bisected the country from Dar es Salaam to Kigoma on Lake Tanganyika. Now the entire northern half of the colony lay in enemy hands. Compared to the north—where German colonizers had focused the better part of their energies since the brutal, buccaneering days of Karl Peters—German East Africa's southern portion lay mostly wild and undeveloped, all the way from the Central Railway, across the Rufiji to the Rovuma River and the Portuguese border. This region, now relatively unpopulated, had borne the brunt of the Maji-Maji Rebellion and subsequent famines a decade before. Whole villages still stood deserted, their gardens untended; human bones lay strewn across the fallow fields. Here native carriers—essential to any army fighting in Africa—could not be found in sufficient numbers.

Smuts hoped that von Lettow would refuse to give up the Central Railway and that the German commander might be brought to a decisive battle at last somewhere in the vicinity of Morogoro. Surely, von Lettow must decide to defend this town and its numerous German merchants and their families. Also, how could any army survive in the colony's wild southern half? Quite simply, what would they *eat*? Smuts didn't know that von Lettow had seeded this region with supply dumps before the war and had ordered the planting of thousands of acres of maize, and that he had been planning this fighting retreat from the beginning. Still, the larger question as to why a man as "slim" as Smuts might think von Lettow would suddenly reverse himself and give battle to vastly superior British forces remains something of a mystery. Surely, the German strategy of retreat-ambush-retreat was clear to him by now.

Meanwhile, van Deventer's division, having recovered via an infusion of fresh troops and supplies, was advancing toward Morogoro and expected to unite with Smuts, thus creating an overwhelming force to crush the Schutztruppe and end the war. In an attempt to catch the Germans at Morogoro, Smuts again pushed his men to the breaking point, across some of the most difficult and gorgeous terrain in Africa. Like von Lettow, Smuts often fought in the midst of his men. Critical as ever, Meinertzhagen thought this willingness to bear the hardships of fighting and marching—no matter how laudable—a strategic weakness, as it obscured a tactical grasp of the battle at hand:

"Smuts has made a mistake," Meinertzhagen wrote in his diary, "in mixing himself up with local situations. . . . During an advance, he is usually with or in front of the advance guard. During an action, he is often in the firing line and loses control of the fight. His staff has often pointed this out but it falls on deaf ears."

For von Lettow, as the commander of a much smaller force, such personal involvement had always been an asset. He seemed to be everywhere at once during a battle, often on his bicycle, pedaling like mad up and down the line to coordinate the fire of his *askaris*: "He has lost 12 kilos in the past two weeks," his adjutant von Ruckteschell wrote during the retreat from Kondoa-Irangi, "and is yellow with fever, but he will not stop. He seems to live on coffee. But he steams with energy and never complains of the oppressive heat. I watched him coming back to camp today after twelve hours in the bush. He has climbed mountains, swum rivers, waded through quagmires, and been badly stung by bees, but he is indefatigable. He arrived dragging his horse behind him, both of them footsore, and I am not sure which one more resembled a skeleton. One thing is certain. The horse will not last the next 24 hours, but the colonel will."

Smuts and van Deventer, lumbering along through the bush, had hoped to encircle the Schutztruppe as they prepared for the defense of Morogoro—yet another example of the former's complex maneuverings over inhospitable country—and, not incidentally, an example of a kind of magical thinking. For his part, von Lettow found Smuts's tactics "never altogether intelligible." It would be madness, he wrote, for him "to await at this place the junction of the hostile columns . . . and then fight with our back to the steep and rocky mountains!"

At the end of August 1916, Smuts's columns at last converged on Morogoro. The night before the assault on the town, Lord Cranworth—first of the East African Mounted Rifles (disbanded and absorbed into other units), then with Cole's Scouts, and now serving on Smuts's staff—watched from the safe distance of the British lines as the Germans went about their usual acts of destruction. Flames painted the horizon red. The crack and boom of distant explosions sounded like the heavens caving in.

"We lay through the night," Cranworth wrote, "and heard the crashes and saw the flames as the Germans ran their engines and rolling stock from both sides of a destroyed bridge into a steep gorge."

Still, Smuts persisted in his belief, now unshakable, that the Germans were going to defend the place and that here, at last, he would have his set battle and the Schutztruppe would be destroyed. But during the dark hours before dawn on August 25, the Germans evacuated the town. African carriers had converged from all over the district, summoned by the beat of tribal drums. Assembled in long lines, they loaded up and moved out, to the refrain of one of their traditional marching songs:

Let all men stay home / Who are jealous of their wives . . .

Then Kraut ordered the destruction of the ammunition dump. Ordnance the carriers could not manage went up in a series of massive explosions: "Never in my wildest imaginings had I conceived such violence," Nis Kock wrote. "And it went on and on. . . . We pressed flat to the earth, as if under the heaviest shelling."

In the morning, the 130th Baluchis and the 2nd Rhodesians reached the town in advance of Smuts's main forces. Morogoro's African inhabitants, at least the ones who had not fled with the Germans, lined the sandy streets as if to watch a parade. Not a single German or *askari* could be found anywhere. A rank smell wafted from the Banhoff Hotel, the town's most impressive building. As usual, Schutztruppe *askaris* had shat and pissed everywhere, all over the lobby. "The troops had left under pressure," joked Cranworth, "and in a great hurry. But they had had time to issue their evacuation orders and on every piece of furniture was laid an exhibit of human excreta."

The poop was fresh. The pianola by the registration desk still played "*Deutschland Über Alles.*" The last departing trooper, after relieving himself, had pumped a couple of German coins into the slot and withdrawn, not minutes before.

From this period of the war dates two of its most treasured tales: First, an astonishing example of von Lettow's famously anachronistic sense of fair play. In August 1916, when presented with the perfect opportunity to assassinate the enemy commander in chief, he declined to give the order to shoot!

"Last week, General Smuts came forward on a reconnaissance ahead of his troops and rode into a *nullah* overlooked by one of our machine gun posts"—so von Lettow recounted to Frau Englemann at the Mgeta Mission station, shortly after the fall of Morogoro. "I had him in my sights and was about to fire when I recognized from his hat and red beard who he was. I decided that it was unsportsmanlike to shoot an enemy commander in such circumstances and I held my fire. . . . One of our *askaris* who was captured by the English—and subsequently escaped—recounted the incident to Smuts, who said: 'von Lettow is a fool—but a gentleman. But of course it was the only thing to do. There must be honour and chivalry even in war.'"

Sportsmanlike behavior, honor, chivalry—these old-fashioned concepts, rendered absurd by the vicious trench warfare of the Western Front—had survived somehow, like a rare hothouse flower, in the remote African bush.

Another old-fashioned concept—love—also blossomed in the equatorial heat: A British officer shot in an ambush before Morogoro was captured by the Germans and sent to the hospital in Dar es Salaam for treatment. There he fell in love with the pretty young wife of the German officer who had shot him; she nursed him back to health. The German officer was himself killed during the long trek to the Mahenge country; after the war, the English officer and the nurse found each other again and married.

"In view of the concentric advance of the enemy from all directions," von Lettow mused in his *East African Campaigns*, regarding the difficult period following the fall of Morogoro, "the question now arose what should be done with the main body of my protective force. . . . For an attack, the situation was altogether too unfavorable. The problem, therefore, was what should be the general direction of our retreat? I had already decided on the Mahenge Plateau. By moving there, we should avoid being surrounded, it was fertile, and suitable for guerrilla warfare. From there, also, it would be possible to withdraw further to the south and continue the war for a long time to come."

Now the Schutztruppe began a fighting retreat toward the Rufiji—the first stage of von Lettow's relocation farther south. For once, Smuts seems to have guessed von Lettow's plans: He wrote to his wife that he intended to beat the Germans to the river and there destroy them before the torrential spring rains once again churned the war into a bloody swamp, and more South Africans died unnecessarily of disease and malnutrition.

"You cannot imagine how dangerous the rains become in this country," Smuts complained. "An old missionary informs me that the forty-mile plain between Kissaki and the Rufiji River becomes one continuous sea of water in the rainy season. How am I to pursue the enemy thence? And if I do so and the rain comes, how do we get food and water and what will become of us, cut off from the world on the Rufiji?"

In other theaters of the war, however, Smuts could point to more encouraging developments:

On September 4, Dar es Salaam fell after being subjected to a naval bombardment from a British flotilla consisting of HMS *Challenger*, HMS *Vengeance*, the much-patched-up monitors *Severn* and *Mersey*, and a grab bag of smaller vessels, including the ubiquitous HMS *Pickle*. Korvettenkapitan Loof, fully recovered from his dangerous abdominal wounds, had ably served as the capital's military governor since shortly after the battle in the delta. Loof knew the British were gullible—"always easily taken in by the simplest ruses," as he put it—and sought to delay them as he evacuated the town and destroyed what was left of its infrastructure.

He put Richard Wenig in charge of the two *Königsberg* guns allotted for the defense of the town. Wenig, now hopping around on his wooden foot, vigorously directed his gun crews as they hustled the heavy 10.5cm naval guns from place to place. They fired, moved on, fired again—making the British think they were facing an entire shore battery. A lucky shot from *Challenger* eventually destroyed one of the guns; Wenig managed to escape with the other.

To Nis Kock, now in Dar es Salaam assisting in the evacuation of remaining ordnance, the town "was like a whole community in dissolution. Troops on the march passed through, hardly making a pause. The white soldiers flung themselves on the hotels' good food like starving beasts, and often they were utterly played out. Long columns of bearers also passed through, going north or south, and white women and children poured in from every point of the compass. The good old days in Dar es Salaam were over," he concluded sadly. And now "the whole country was finally up against it." Though he does not say so explicitly, by "it" he meant the end of the era of German rule in East Africa.

Lieutenant Commander (formerly Lieutenant) Charlewood—once of the captured tug *Helmuth*, who had first spotted *Königsberg* bearing down on HMS *Pegasus* through the morning mists in Zanzibar harbor in July 1914 and had participated in just about every naval action since then—was now chosen to accept the capital's official capitulation. Entering the town with a party of marines, he observed, not surprisingly, that many of the "female citizens were in tears, and the majority sulky and sullen." The men, however, wisely kept out of sight. But not much was left of Dar es Salaam to surrender. Dock facilities and railway terminal had been destroyed, roads blown up and more than sixty bridges smashed down the Central Line between Dar and Dodoma. Only 300 male German civilians remained in town, including the sick and wounded in the hospital.

Next came Tabora's turn.

The colony's "summer capital," where Governor Schnee and his wife, Ada, had been holed up since the beginning of the war, fell to the Belgian Force Publique under General Tombeur on September 19—just steps ahead of a British column led by the South African general Charles Crewe.

The Belgians, vividly anti-British—an outrage, since Britain's entry into the war had been precipitated by the German invasion of their country— had done everything possible to hinder Crewe's advance and claim the laurel of Tabora's fall for themselves. Also, they had taken the easier route: Crewe came around the lake, fighting through thick bush, where he had the dubious distinction of becoming the only British officer in the entire World War wounded by an arrow, probably shot by a "Ruga-Ruga" tribal irregular. These primitive warriors, often dressed in nothing more than feathers, sometimes fought with Schutztruppe patrols.

Meanwhile, Tombeur crossed Lake Tanganyika on a steamer in touristic comfort, disembarked at Kigoma, and marched down the railway. His native troops had a reputation for cannibalism; some hailed from tribes who filed their teeth to a point. Only with difficulty did General Whale, Schutztruppe commander in charge of the Tabora District, convince his trembling *askaris* that the wild men from the Congo would probably not eat them.

Nonetheless, "Dig, O Bin Makoma, trenches in Tabora / Others will arrive, the Belgians / who eat men . . ." his men sang, as they excavated rifle pits and gun emplacements in anticipation of the feared arrival of battalions of Belgian cannibals.

That the Belgians crossed Lake Tanganyika at all, they owed to the wildly eccentric British naval officer Lieutenant Commander Geoffrey Spicer-Simon, who had cleared it of German vessels the year before. Covered with tattoos acquired in places like Brighton and Portsmouth, a self-dramatizer and a bit thick, Spicer-Simon regaled anyone who would listen with tales of his Meinertzhagen-like imaginary exploits: He had killed tigers in Africa (tigers exist only on the Indian subcontinent); he had bested pirates and rescued damsels in distress and sunk enemy cruisers. None of it was true.

Relegated to do-nothing desk jobs at the Admiralty, Spicer-Simon had been tapped to lead the Lake Tanganyika Expedition because every other sailor worth the name had either refused the dubious honor or was already at sea.

The assault on Lake Tanganyika, originally dreamed up by an English big game hunter named John Lee and denounced by everyone else as an "impossible adventure," was certainly one of the most harebrained undertakings of the entire war: With the Admiralty's approval, Lee located two forty-foot-long, 100-horsepower mahogany motor launches—under construction as seaplane tenders for the Greek Air Force—and had them confiscated by the Royal Navy (shades of *Severn* and *Mersey*) and outfitted with three-pounders and Maxim guns.

The armed motor launches, accompanied by Spicer-Simon and a detachment of sailors and various oddballs, went by ship to Cape Town, then to Elizabethville in the Belgian Congo, and by train to the end of the line at Fungurumue. From there circus-style tractor engines and hundreds of Africans with ropes pulled the launches over the Mitumba Mountain Ranges and through the trackless jungles of Central Africa to the western shore of Lake Tanganyika. Refloated, the launches, commanded by Spicer-Simon, would now engage the much larger German gunboats that controlled the lake. Spicer-Simon designed his own opéra comique uniform for this bizarre campaign. It consisted of a cap covered with gold braid, a bright blue flannel shirt, and an attractive khaki skirt, made for him by his wife, that showed off the brightly colored tattoos on his legs. Shorts or pants were not for him: In the event of dysentery, he reasoned, wearing a skirt would make it that much easier to relieve himself. He named his motor launches HMS *Mimi* and HMS *Toutou* after *Dog* and *Cat* had been nixed by the Admiralty board.

Against all odds, the Lake Tanganyika mission succeeded. *Mimi* and *Toutou* took the Germans by surprise, captured the German gunboat *Kingani*, sank the 800-ton steamer *Hedwig von Wissmann*, and generally rid the lake of the enemy. Spicer-Simon's adventures make for amusing reading—an exploit straight off the pages of Joyce Cary or, perhaps, Noel Coward: The Baholo-holo Tribe, primitive hunter-gatherers indigenous to the deep forests of the Belgian Congo, intrigued by Spicer-Simon's tattoos, daily calisthenics, and public bathing—as much as by his tractor engines and steam launches—claimed him for their new god and made clay idols in his likeness, complete with gold-braided hat, skirt, and tattoos. These same tribesmen broke and ran wildly into the jungle, utterly terrified by the first seaplanes to appear over the lake:

"Suddenly, the seaplanes shot into view out of the clouds, describing circles and going through sundry evolutions over the camp," wrote Frank Magee, an American journalist who, along with Josephine, his pet monkey, had accompanied the Spicer-Simon expedition. "The natives stood spellbound, gazing upward with arms extended, eyes bulging and mouths agape. . . . The airmen then made a sudden dive downward that broke the spell. The savages bounded off into the bush, terror lending wings to their progress. Mothers snatched up their pickaninnies and dived for the shelter of kraals, shrieking at the top of their voices. It was real pandemonium."

In other words, Civilization had come to the Belgian Congo.

Captain Max Wintgens, one of von Lettow's best officers, and a genius at guerrilla fighting in his own right, managed to delay the Belgian advance on Tabora as Governor Schnee cleared the town of government files and mountainous bundles of newly printed paper money—the GEA Treasury—and marched off to spend the rest of the war at the side of von Lettow. Schnee's wife, Ada, however, was left behind to care for 140 German women and children who would not survive a trek through the jungle. Ada remained in the summer capital as the unofficial spokeswoman for the captured Germans. General Tombeur, impressed by her forthright character, allowed her to retain the governor's mansion, which she turned into a sort of nursery and schoolhouse for the children.

Tombeur then released the 2,000 Allied prisoners incarcerated in a prisoner of war camp on the outskirts of town—among them Cutler, the intrepid aviator of the Rufiji. Certain English civilians now made accusations of maltreatment against their German jailers. Repeated to the *London Times*, these charges caused national outrage in Britain. A certain Dr. Holtom complained that the pillow he had been given in camp "was very thin and lumpy and not conducive to slumber." Also, he was not immediately issued a proper "sleeping suit." And the German woman who cooked for him and a few others served too-small potatoes, tough meat, and never any rice pudding; also, tea was rarely ready promptly at four p.m. More seriously, some European men had been forced to collect dung for fuel, and to drag a wagon, so said the *Times*, "loaded with government stores through the streets, and were halted in the native market to afford opportunity for the Negroes to come and jeer at them while they were doing the work of oxen." Unpleasant perhaps, even extremely so, but hardly Auschwitz.

In response to similar reports regarding the mistreatment of German prisoners in Dar es Salaam after the fall of the city, Governor Schnee sent an irate letter citing violations of the Geneva convention through the lines to Smuts, for the moment comfortably ensconced at Morogoro. Smuts thought it over for a while, and used the opportunity of his response to ask for the surrender of the colony:

> *May I make use of the present opportunity to raise a different and far more important issue with Your Excellency? The present campaign has . . . now reached a stage which must make it clear to your Excellency, as indeed to every observer, that the end cannot be either far off or uncertain. In spite of the conspicuous ability and bravery with which the defense has been conducted, it has not been possible for the German force to withstand the superior forces under my command, nor will it be possible for them by any continued resistance to do more than prolong the campaign for a very short while longer at the cost of terrible losses and suffering to the population of this Colony . . .*
>
> *A continuation of the campaign for even a short time longer at this season of the year and in the deadly country to which your forces are now confined must mean untold suffering and complete*

ruin for them and at the end, there will be no alternative but an
unconditional surrender. Under these circumstances, I would im-
press on Your Excellency that the time has come for you and Col-
onel von Lettow to consider very seriously whether this useless
resistance should now cease in a manner honorable to your-
selves. . . .

Given that all the major cities, both railways, and nearly the entire
coastline now lay in the hands of the British, Smuts's request for an honorable surrender certainly seemed reasonable. Schnee, of course, embraced
the idea immediately. But whether to surrender or not remained a military
matter over which von Lettow now exercised complete authority. Needless
to say, the commander met Schnee's enthusiasm for capitulation with a
derisive snort. He saw Smuts's letter for what it was: a desperate attempt to
end a war costing British forces far too much in blood and treasure. Exactly
his aim in the first place.

"General Smuts realized that his blow had failed," von Lettow commented drily. "He sent me a letter calling upon me to surrender, by which
he showed that, as far as his force was concerned, he had reached the end of
his resources." Von Lettow's assessment of the situation was correct; he
didn't bother to honor Smuts's letter with a reply.

The Schutztruppe retired across the Rufiji in October just as the "short
rains" began. Smuts's pursuit of the Germans presently ground to a halt. It
would rain for a few weeks—nothing like the torrents of spring, but drench-
ing enough—until the onset of winter. A substantial percentage of Smuts's
army now nearly 80,000 strong couldn't go any farther, laid low by disease,
parasites, and lack of adequate food. Brigadier General Crowe, on Smuts's
operational staff, put it this way:

"The area before us was notoriously more unhealthy than any through
which we had previously passed. It was obviously useless to take men who
were constantly down with malaria into this country; they would only
prove an encumbrance." Smuts now convened a board of medical officers
to report, says Crowe, "on the fitness or otherwise of all white troops for
further service in the country. . . . The result of the medical examinations
was that some 12,000 white troops were sent to South Africa as unfit to

stand the hardships of further campaigning in this region till they had regained their normal strength by a period of rest in a healthy climate."

When the 12,000 demobbed South African troops disembarked in Cape Town—a number exceeding the Schutztruppe's full fighting strength—the South African Union gave out a collective gasp. It was not an army but a rabble of malaria-ridden walking skeletons who had returned to their temperate homeland. Irate editorials again appeared in the *Natal Mercury*, the *Johannesburg Star*, and elsewhere, calling for immediate official inquiries and decrying the human cost inherent in any imperial undertaking.

Bitter fighting—especially around the Kibata *boma*, a large German fort near the coastal town of Kilwa—continued through the short rains and over Christmas 1916. Smuts, now utterly desperate to end the campaign, briefly considered using poison gas against the Schutztruppe. He gave up on the idea when experts in the War Office advised him that the terrain and humidity of German East Africa would make the use of gas impractical—and also, perhaps, because his conscience militated against such an attack. Offered 3,000 fifty-pound cylinders, enough to envelop a 1,400-yard front in a poisonous cloud—and ruin his reputation forever—he wisely declined.

Then, on January 17, 1917, the war stopped for a day. White flags popped up along the lines hard against the Rufiji River and Smuts's emissary paddled across the swollen brown flow in a collapsible boat bearing a special message from the British major general to the German commander, Oberstleutnant von Lettow-Vorbeck. Hippos, spouting water like whales, wallowed in herds in the shallows. They had been known to swamp light craft attempting the crossing and were better off avoided. The procedure for a parley, well understood in what both sides had tried to maintain as a "Gentleman's War," followed the usual pattern:

An emissary approached under a flag of truce; advance scouts from the opposing side stepped out of the bush and led him blindfolded to the main encampment and the officer in charge. Then the parley began—during which the adversaries organized prisoner exchanges, made arrangements for the sick and wounded, tendered official communiqués, offered holiday greetings, traded cigarettes and booze. Once, a captured English veterinary officer was swapped by the Germans for two bottles of whiskey. All very civil and polite, an example of the chivalric mode of warfare still surviving in East Africa but, like everything in wartime, freighted with ulterior motives: These humanitarian visits doubled as intelligence-gathering operations. The emissary, usually attached in some capacity to the intelligence staff of one side or another, would afterward report to his superiors. A quick visit to an enemy encampment and a brief look around might yield a satchel full of information regarding enemy fighting capabilities.

At this stage of the campaign, per Smuts's obsession, British emissaries always sought to ascertain von Lettow's whereabouts. Notoriously difficult to pin down, the German commander had taken on the quality of myth; he was a jungle ghost, an elemental force more than a man, and everywhere at once. If the British could determine von Lettow's exact location, they might be able to capture him; once they captured him, Smuts believed, the war would end. For this reason, von Lettow purposely faded into the background when British emissaries arrived. He now wore a nondescript *askari* tunic stripped of all insignia, grew a beard so as not to be recognized, and let his subordinates handle the negotiations. Now cut off from the outside world, radio transmitters gone, the Germans received news of the wider war only through captured British newspapers or via one of these emissaries, allowed by Smuts to drop a tantalizing tidbit or two. This time, though, the British emissary brought two pieces of startling news which von Lettow felt compelled to recognize personally: One, a cause for celebration, the other for regret.

First, the Kaiser had awarded Paul von Lettow-Vorbeck Germany's highest military honor, the famous Pour le Mérite. This same medal, established by Frederick the Great in 1740, had been awarded to his great-great-granduncle, General Heinrich Wilhelm, in 1771. Von Lettow now joined the ranks of the German heroes he had studied as a cadet at Kassel. His name could be inscribed on the list beside those of Feldmarschall Alexander von Kleist; the great Blücher who had been so instrumental in the victory over Napoleon at Waterloo; von Moltke, architect of the victory over the French in 1870; and of course Otto von Bismarck, the great Iron Chancellor. Originally a Prussian royal "order"—distinct from a "decoration" or medal in that, like the British OBE (Order of the British Empire), it admits the recipient into a military fraternity of other winners—the Pour le Mérite, after German unification, assumed the character of an imperial honor. Only the Kaiser might bestow it upon serving military personnel. According to the original criteria, those awarded the order must have successfully defended a fortress against siege, taken a fortress from the enemy, or been responsible for a significant German victory.

World War One recipients included U-boat commanders Lothar von Arnauld de la Perière, who sank 200,000 tons of Allied shipping in 1916, and Walther Schwieger of U-20, whose carefully aimed torpedo sank the *Lusitania*; Korvettenkapitan Peter Strasser, who led the Zeppelin blitz against London; Erwin Rommel, later one of Hitler's most famous soldiers, whose actions helped defeat the Italians at Caporetto; and the flying aces Manfred von Richthofen (the Red Baron) and Max Immelmann—from whom the medal had acquired its nickname the "Blue Max." The medal itself, a Maltese cross enameled in vivid blue with gold eagles between the arms and the words *Pour le Mérite* and the cipher of the Prussian royal house inlaid in gold, was worn around the neck at all times while in uniform. The imperial order went extinct with the abdication of the Kaiser in 1918. Infantry officer/novelist/acid-dropping existentialist Ernst Junger, author of *Storm of Steel*, was its last living recipient. He died in 1998 at the age of 104.

Along with news of the Pour le Mérite, Smuts's emissary brought von Lettow the Kaiser's personal congratulations—plucked from the airwaves and decoded, as always, by the eggheads in Room 40. For the German warlord, the continued existence of the Schutztruppe in Africa remained a solace in a wider war that now seemed to be going badly for Germany:

> *I cannot allow the opening of a new year of war to go by without again expressing to you, my dear colonel, and your gallant troops, my boundless recognition for your heroic conduct. Strengthened by the spirit of loyalty, you have displayed undaunted and confident courage in the unequal fight and for three years you have defended East Africa with never-tiring energy. Your many victories have shown me that in a fateful hour, the right man is in the right place. . . . Never, never did the world expect what your iron strength of will has rendered possible. In faith and with proud astonishment, today, on the threshold of a*

new year of war, the thankful Fatherland is mindful with me of
its distant heroes and their victorious leader, whose quiet perfor-
mance of his duty will ever form a brilliant example of the his-
tory of the war. May God further bless your arms.

Smuts added his own congratulations in an appended notation: "May I hope that, though we are unfortunately compelled to oppose each other, an expression of my sincere congratulations on you richly deserved distinction may not be distasteful to you."

More than the medal itself, these words of encouragement from the Kaiser—and Smuts—cannot have failed to cheer von Lettow, now in poor health and suffering from his fourth consecutive bout of malaria in as many months:

"I was peculiarly vulnerable to the African mosquito," the commander acknowledged in a conversation with Mosley. "He bit right into my bones. I had long since abandoned a bed or even a hammock and slept most of the time on the ground, but my bearers always draped a mosquito net over me. The mosquitoes always found a way through. If you have not experienced a night in the heart of an African swamp, you can have no conception of how many insects descend upon you in the hours of darkness. They gather in clouds and they plunge down upon pink skin like a shower of needles, and so sharply do they bite and so maddening are their stings, that I have known my officers to sleep in swamp waters, preferring leeches and the possibility of attack by crocodiles and water snakes to their tortures."

In addition to the malaria, the chiggers continued to eat away at his feet, making it difficult for him to walk. He had been mercilessly bitten by sand flies, and—worst of all—his precious right eye had been cut across the iris by a whipping blade of sawgrass. He had also lost his reading glasses, which after the fall of Dar es Salaam could not be replaced. Given the injuries to his left eye acquired in the Hottentot War, he was, for the moment, nearly blind. He could not read maps or reports, though somehow, instinct perhaps, his shooting skills remained unaffected: He could still drop a hippo at fifty yards with a single shot.

The second bit of news brought by Smuts's emissary, however, tempered any celebration occasioned by the Pour le Mérite. Another brave soldier—like von Lettow, a legend to both sides—had been killed in action: Frederick Courteney Selous, the elephant hunter, conservationist, author, and oldest field officer serving in the British Army, had been shot through the head by a Schutztruppe sniper near the village of Behobeho just south of the Rufiji on January 4. Selous, recovered from anal surgery in England, had returned to active duty in East Africa on December 16, leading 150 fresh volunteers. He had been chasing a retreating Schutztruppe company, his men pinned down:

"We were on a crest line at the time, with the Germans in front and on both flanks," wrote one of the Fusiliers present, for the British magazine *Field*. "We were subjected to heavy enfilade fire, and could not locate the enemy properly owing to the wooded nature of their positions. . . . Selous went forward down the slope about 15 yards, and was just raising his glasses in order to see . . . where certain snipers were, when he received his first wound in the side. He was half turning towards us when he was shot through the side of the head. He died immediately."

In the moment after Selous received the fatal shot, his gun bearer and friend, an East African named Ramizani, who had been with him since Bukoba, now overcome with grief and rage, seized a rifle, charged the enemy, and accounted for several German soldiers and *askaris*—including the sniper who had killed his master.

Von Lettow, a great admirer of Selous's books on big game hunting, had recognized a kindred spirit in the man and was saddened by this news of his death. In a letter to Smuts, sent back with the emissary, he expressed his regrets and mentioned that the elephant hunter had been "well liked among the Germans on account of his charming manner and excellent stories."

Selous was buried where he fell, beneath a simple wooden cross later replaced by a concrete slab bearing the words *Captain F. C. Selous DSO 25 Royal Fusiliers, killed in action 4.1.17.* Six other Fusiliers fell in the Behobeho fight. Buried beside him, their bodies were moved after the war. Only Selous's bones remained untouched, left beneath the crest of a hill in Africa, in the midst of the game reserve that now bears his name.

In the months leading up to the spring rains, increasingly desperate fighting occurred on both sides of the Rufiji—fighting characterized by the usual precipitous advances made by exhausted British troops and carefully orchestrated fighting retreats on the part of the Schutztruppe.

Smuts saw this rump campaign before the rains as his last chance to catch von Lettow, end the war, and burnish his record—somewhat tarnished after the return of the emaciated thousands of South African troops in November. But his original orders from the War Office did not take him any farther than the Rufiji; the possibility remained that he might be recalled. Now he drove his men without mercy through the fecund, deadly landscape, plagued by the usual lack of supplies and pestilential climate. Africa is a land of physical wonders haunted by death: The country through which the armies now fought struck the men of both sides as some of the most beautiful—and the deadliest—they had seen over the course of the war: "It seemed absurd," wrote Brett Young of this phase of the fighting, "in this meadow, on this sunny day." Von Lettow was also quite moved by so much natural beauty in the midst of so much death.

"One stood on the edge of a river gorge at dawn, looking down across the thick vegetation, amazed at the richness and vividness of the scene," he wrote. "A few feet away, the tiny hyrax, or rock rabbits, would be whistling happily to each other, while across the gorge one of their giant relatives, an old bull elephant, would be trumpeting to his herd and flapping his great ears like sails in the morning breeze.

"There were birds of every color and size—goshawks, eagles, red-billed shrike, crowned hornbills—and clouds of Urania moths, fluttering past like emerald rain-showers. Whenever there were elephants there were elephants' turds, and around them whirled beetles and butterflies of every color. We grew quite fond of the scarab beetles and the *askaris* used to run races with them and gamble on which ones would be first to reach a turd."

By now Punjabi and Nigerian troops had stepped in to fill the gaps in the line opened by the departing fever-ridden South Africans. The Nigerians, soon bloodied, lost 400 men in the fighting around Kilossa in September 1916 and 500 more to a virulent strain of pneumonia—a new arrival to the regiment of diseases fighting the troops of both armies—over the next few months. The Nigerians had also been treated with the usual lack of logistical tact by the War Office. Their home battalions, scrambled and stripped of well-liked and seasoned officers, had been assigned new officers from

England—most of whom had never served with black troops. Also, they had been outfitted with new, unfamiliar weapons: Their comfortable old "long" Lee-Enfield rifles were replaced by the new "short" model, and the Nigerian troops struggled to find space aboard the ships to drill properly.

Fortunately, the new commander, General F. H. B. Cunliffe, immediately made efforts to ameliorate these setbacks. Mindful of the debilitated ship-bound Indian soldiers at Tanga in 1914, he disembarked the entire Nigerian contingent at Durban for a little R and R. He marched them around for exercise, arranged trips to the Durban Zoo, and, according to Captain W. D. Downes in his *With the Nigerians in German East Africa*, took them to a "picture palace" to see a Charlie Chaplin and Fatty Arbuckle film. Cinema was a new experience for the Nigerians, and they went wild as the first black-and-white images flickered onto the screen: "The men stood up in their place," Downes wrote, "and shouted at the top of their voices when that wonderful little man managed simultaneously to hook by the neck and kick in the stomach a fat rival who aspired to the company of a charming, though rather eccentric, young lady."

Smuts counted on these newcomers and on an ever-increasing availability of supplies—now that the British Navy controlled the entire coast from Jasin to Lindi—to help him catch von Lettow. Lindi had fallen to a flotilla consisting of HMS *Vengeance*, HMS *Talbot*, and HMS *Challenger* on September 18, taking with it any hope the Germans might have for another blockade runner to reach the Schutztruppe. Still, despite an ever-expanding war chest and his usual rapid maneuvering, Smuts had thus far failed to trap his quarry—though, as always, the next maneuver might do the trick: "I have a month to trap him," Smuts acknowledged in a very Smutsian pronouncement in early January. "At all cost we must move with dispatch to ensure he must not get away."

To Smuts's biographer, W. K. Hancock, his subject had failed to come to grips with a burgeoning fixation on the wily German adversary: "Perhaps he had allowed his personal duel with von Lettow to become something of an obsession," Hancock acknowledges in *Smuts: The Sanguine Years*. "He still looked forward to catching him within a few months and thus making a clean finish of the campaign." More magical thinking on the part of the South African general—particularly, since von Lettow seemed to be recovering his health and spirits, buoyed, perhaps, by the Pour le Mérite and the Kaiser's words of praise. Whatever the reason, von Lettow's feet, now scraped free of chiggers, were toughening; his right eye had recovered from its scrape and he could read maps again; his skin glowed slightly less yellow. Another message from the Kaiser on the occasion of the Imperial Birthday only strengthened his resolve to fight on:

"Whatever fate the Lord Almighty has reserved for your little band of heroes, the Fatherland remembers with pride its sons fighting in distant Africa," the Kaiser gushed. "I wish to convey to the corps my Imperial gratitude and my high esteem for its heroic stand in the unequal struggle. . . ."

Etc.

A herd of hungry hippos—there's no other way to put it—overturned a company of Punjabis trying to cross the Rufiji in small boats and catch the Schutztruppe unawares in February 1917. Many drowned. It seemed nature herself had been recruited on the side of the Germans. After this incident, a lull in the fighting allowed von Lettow a momentary respite, during which he sought to cull his diminishing army of the sick and the superfluous: This meant the wounded who could not be cared for properly and the many camp followers and German evacuees—mostly women and children—who had attached themselves to the army since Morogoro and who represented only more mouths to feed. Now he made the hard decision to leave all noncombatants in the path of the British advance, confident, in this Gentleman's War, that they would be well treated and sent back to Dar es Salaam.

Many among the Germans resented von Lettow's decision. Others, including Schnee, felt the Schutztruppe had fought long enough, that the war had ended with the fall of Morogoro and Dar es Salaam, and they ought to surrender. German civilians congregating around the field hospital at Kungiolu now criticized the commander in loud voices. They formed a kind of loosely associated "peace party" and at their first meeting at the hospital agitated against the evacuation of the women and children and for an immediate surrender of the entire force to the British. That is, until one of the German nurses mounted the soapbox:

"In one of the wards this morning," she said, "I heard a civilian patient

criticizing the wisdom of our glorious von Lettow for his insistence on carrying on the war. One of the Schutztruppe, lying in the bed next to him and
badly wounded, leaned over and said: 'Anyone who is not for the Commander now is a traitor to Germany and should be shot for it. If you were
not a sick man, I would shoot you myself. How dare you attack such a man?
Von Lettow is the brains of this campaign; you sound to me very much like
its asshole!'"

The nurse's speech elicited a shocked murmur and not a little laughter
from the congregated malcontents—but with it, the mood changed and all
the German camp followers agreed to stay behind and let themselves fall
into the hands of advancing British forces. But the *bibis*—native wives of
askaris, usually accompanied by children born on the march—refused
evacuation. Rounded up, given three days' provisions, they were sent north
under the guard of a single Schutztruppe sergeant. This arrangement
proved untenable: Half a day in, the *bibis* settled down for a picnic. They
quickly ate all their provisions with gusto, then surrounded the sergeant,
beat him senseless, and with the bloodied man in tow, returned to von
Lettow's camp. The commander thought it best to leave such Amazons
alone. He let them stay and they accompanied their men to the Mahenge
country.

Meanwhile, Smuts, ever more determined to follow von Lettow into the
depths of hell if necessary, worked furiously to prepare his men for a final
ambitious encircling maneuver before the spring rains made any further
advance impossible. Then, suddenly, on January 20, 1917, he resigned his
command. Handing his forces over to Major General Hoskins of the 1st
Division, he left the country for good. He had been recalled by Botha—but
in such a way that it seemed like a promotion. Botha, aware of Smuts's von
Lettow fixation, concerned that "Janny will take root in those African
swamps," engineered his friend's appointment as South Africa's representative to the Imperial Conference in London. This was an honor Smuts
could not refuse. At first he felt downcast. Since von Lettow remained undefeated, his tenure in East Africa, he felt, had been a failure. And indeed
he had left his men behind in a tough spot, mired on the Rufiji Front:

According to one of Smuts's artillery officers, it was "the most deadly
place we have yet stuck. Mosquitoes, tse-tse flies, and other crawling insects

are here by the million. At night the yelping and howling of wild beasts keep us awake. We are having a bad time with fever. The gun can only be fired with the help of two cooks and a servant."

But by the time Smuts arrived in London for the conference, he had reversed his self-assessment. In a stopover in South Africa, crowds hailing him as a conquering hero met his ship. Had he not, after all, pushed the marauding Germans off the British border and out of their major cities, including Dar es Salaam? Smuts rose to the occasion: With von Lettow all but defeated, he told the crowd, what fighting remained was no more than a mopping-up operation. This version of a war practically won, and of himself as a soldier of genius, heartily presented to the Imperial War Cabinet a few weeks later, carried the day. On March 20, as heavy rains threatened to inundate the Rufiji, and the voracious columns of army ants began their annual pilgrimage to higher ground, British Prime Minister Lloyd George introduced Smuts to his ministers as "one of the most brilliant generals of the war."

But Smuts, a bold leader of irregular cavalry during the Boer War, had never really been a professional soldier. In East Africa he had expended great resources and uncounted lives in pursuit of an enemy he failed to capture. Essentially a political animal, he now basked in the generous praise of a cabal of soft-handed English politicians and diplomats who stood in awe of what they saw as his rough-and-ready soldiering. His reputation grew. But the man who actually merited Lloyd George's praise was just now in good spirits and preparing to fight on from the Mahenge heartland—and had even allowed himself to imagine victory.

"I regarded the military situation in the Colony as remarkably favorable," von Lettow later wrote. "I knew that the South African troops were for the most part worn out with battle casualties and sickness, while a large portion of the remainder were returning to South Africa. Prisoners had repeatedly assured us they'd had enough of the 'picnic' in East Africa . . . and we could calmly contemplate the continuation of the war for a considerable time. I still believe that we would have succeeded in beating the enemy if he had not enjoyed the power of continually filling up his reduced units and bringing in new ones."

Schutztruppe numbers as of March 1917, including General Whale's column still moving across the colony from Tabora to von Lettow on the Rufiji, now stood well below 10,000. This number included all German officers, underofficers, and *askaris*—down from its peak strength of 3,000 Germans and 12,000 *askaris* a year earlier. Attrition in the German ranks over the long, bloody months of 1916—battlefield casualties, disease, some desertion—had accounted for more than a few. But von Lettow's remaining forces, an undefeated battle-hardened phalanx, would stand against tens of thousands of Allied troops in the year and a half of fighting still to come.

Chapter 22

A ZEPPELIN OVER AFRICA

Though *streng geheim*, the secret purpose of the super Zeppelins being built in the cavernous sheds at Friedrichshafen, the Luftschiff mother base, in September 1917, had long been known to every urchin on the streets of the town. And to Central Power allies as far away as Constantinople. And of course to the Room 40 code breakers, and to the intelligence staff of the British War Office—perhaps alerted, as Woodhall claimed in his *Spies of the Great War*, by his mysterious Bulgarian/American agent.

An officer of the Kaiserlich Marine's Airship Service on a train from Friedrichshafen to Berlin was approached by a random passenger with questions about the new Zeppelins: Were they really going to Africa? And would the officer have the honor of going with them? Having been sworn to silence, having even signed very serious papers to this effect, the officer feigned ignorance. But perhaps silence lacked pertinence to a morale-boosting mission everyone in Germany—and elsewhere—already seemed to know about.

By May 1917, von Lettow had become a national hero. Valiantly fighting to preserve German honor in a lost colony, completely isolated by the enemies of the Fatherland, he now lacked nearly everything, even the most basic supplies. His Schutztruppe lived off the land at the edges of the Makonde Plateau in the Mahenge country; most of his *askaris* fought with rifles and ammunition captured from the British. To the Kaiser and to others in the High Command, von Lettow's long struggle in an African backwater had become a matter of great strategic importance: Both the Allies and the

Central Powers expected the war to end in a negotiated settlement; at the peace talks it would help the German cause if Germany could claim her forces still held the field in Africa, fighting for possession of at least one of her overseas colonies. Unfortunately, von Lettow's situation now seemed more desperate than ever. How long could he continue the struggle without material aid from the Fatherland?

Professor Dr. Max Zupitza, zoologist and medical doctor, came up with a singular answer to this question. Zupitza, an old Africa hand from the Karl Peters era, had survived both the Maji-Maji Rebellion and the Herero-Hottentot War, and at the outbreak of the Universal Conflict in 1914 was the chief medical officer of German South West Africa. Captured by the British after the fall of Windhoek, he spent a year cooling his heels in a POW camp in Togo, where he heard tales of von Lettow-Vorbeck's impressive victories in GEA. Exchanged in 1916, he returned to Germany, determined to help the Oberstleutnant in his unequal struggle—but how? Then, in July 1917, Zupitza read in the *Wilnaer Zeitung* about the endurance flight of LZ 120, which had recently spent more than 100 hours circling the Baltic. Fired with enthusiasm that "an airship could remain aloft to accomplish a voyage to Africa," he petitioned the Kolonialamt with a wild scheme to outfit a Zeppelin to resupply the beleaguered Schutztruppe.

In desperate times, government officials are often willing to listen to wild schemes; the wilder the better. Zupitza's proposal, forwarded by the Colonial Office to the navy, found favor with naval chief of staff Admiral von Holtzendorff, who passed it on to the Kaiser. The German emperor, nearly as obsessed with von Lettow as Smuts had been, readily gave his imperial blessings. Construction of the first of the super Zeppelins, the ill-fated *L57*, began in October 1917. Zupitza immediately proposed himself as medical officer for the expedition and was accepted. It seemed fitting that the originator of the Zeppelin-Schutztruppe resupply mission, now code-named "China Show," should share its fate.

They chose Bockholt for his boldness and also because he was expendable. But following the disastrous incineration of *L57* at the forward Luftschiff base in Jamboli, Bulgaria, on October 7, 1917, Korvettenkapitan Peter

Strasser, the steel-souled mastermind of the Zeppelin blitz on London and commander of the Naval Airship Division, had wanted Bockholt removed from command of China Show. The floundering, storm-racked airship, Strasser believed, had been mishandled by her commander. An inquiry had revealed that, at the height of the gale, with the ground crew still clinging desperately to *L57*'s mooring ropes, Bockholt had ordered riflemen to shoot holes in the Zeppelin's hydrogen cells, hoping to release enough gas to bring her down. Not only did this gesture show a poor understanding of basic Zeppelin mechanics (a few bullet-sized puncture wounds wouldn't make much difference), the bullets probably ignited the volatile hydrogen/oxygen mixture, causing the blaze that destroyed her.

But forces higher up the command structure of the German Navy intervened. Some saw the Kaiser's hand in it, as Bockholt was not popular with his immediate superiors or his fellow officers—many of whom thought him a selfish careerist who put personal advancement above the good of the service—though all agreed he did not lack courage. Had he not captured the schooner *Royal* by Zeppelin at sea, an event unique in the war? Still, "Every commander wanted to make the African flight," so said Emil Hoff, elevator man aboard Zeppelin *L42*, "and matches were drawn," selecting another. To no avail; Bockholt kept his job.

"A fine airship commander and a skillful flyer," Strasser allowed at last, bowing to the Imperial Will. Though he added, "He has not enough experience of the capabilities of airships."

The same lack of experience characterized *L59*'s crew—not the best men available, but adequate—and also, like Bockholt, because of their inexperience, expendable. Most, fairly new to the airship service, had been chosen because the mission didn't come with a return ticket. Once its payload of armaments, ammunition, and supplies had been delivered to von Lettow, *L59* would be disassembled on the ground in East Africa and all her parts cannibalized to aid the war effort there, captain and crew included: Like the men of the *Königsberg* before them, they would join the Schutztruppe and fight alongside von Lettow's *askaris* in the jungle until the end.

Strasser privately saw the African mission as little more than a morale-boosting stunt in a military backwater and, though popular with command staff, of secondary importance. All his fearsome energies were directed toward the destruction of England, all his best captains and crews reserved for this imperative. He still believed—as he had written in a memo to Vizeadmiral Reinhard Scheer, commander of Germany's High Seas Fleet— that "England can be overcome by means of airships, inasmuch as the country will be deprived of the means of existence through the increasingly extensive destruction of cities, factory complexes, dockyards, harbor works with war and merchant ships lying therein, railroads, etc. . . . The airships offer certain means of victoriously ending the war."

Ironically, in the end, Strasser came to agree with the Kaiser's choice of Bockholt for China Show. It saved better men for the real Zeppelin war, which to him belonged to the darkened skies over London, to the bombs falling on the Theater District and perhaps on Buckingham Palace itself.

———————

L59, pushed by a tailwind from the direction of the German Reich, rumbled south from Jamboli in the freezing dawn of November 21, 1917, at speeds in excess of fifty miles per hour. The great lumbering airship cast her shadow over Adrianople in Turkey at nine forty-five a.m., and over the Sea of Marmara's chop a short time later. At Pandena, on the southern shore, she picked up the railroad tracks to Smyrna, a steel ribbon barely visible after sunset. At seven forty p.m., *L59* pulled free of the Turkish coast at the Lipsas Straits. Now the Greek Dodecanese Islands—Kos, Patmos, Rhodes—passed below, nestled like dark jewels in the black Mediterranean waters, notoriously stormy this time of year. But tonight, the Zeppelin surged forward beneath a clear sky and brilliant stars. Bockholt, who had made his life in the navy, had long ago learned to steer by them when necessary.

L59's crew of twenty—excluding Bockholt and Zupitza—included twelve mechanics to service the five Maybach 240-horsepower engines (one in the forward control car, two opposed on the belly one-third of the way back, and two aft, each driving a single, massive twenty-foot propeller); two "elevator operators" (the elevators, movable flaps at the tail, controlled the upward or downward incline of the nose cone); a radio operator; and a sailmaker, whose job it was to sew up tears in the muslin envelopes affixed within the belly filled with the flammable hydrogen/oxygen mixture that kept the massive airship afloat.

As in the seaborne navy, watches divided the day into four-hour incre-
ments. As *L59* approached the island of Crete at eight thirty p.m., a quarter
of the crew just gone off watch opened their dinnertime cans of *Kaloritkon*,
a bizarre sort of self-heating MRE. These undigestible, oversalted tubes of
potted meat literally cooked themselves via a chemical reaction when exposed to air—heating food over open flame and smoking being strictly verboten aboard the flammable airship. The *Kaloritkons*, which everyone
hated, took much water to wash down, and water was scarce, with barely 14
liters allotted per man for the duration of the voyage.

At ten fifteen p.m., *L59* passed above Cape Sidero at Crete's eastern ex-
tremity at 3,000 feet. Then the stars by which Bockholt had been guiding the
Zeppelin to Africa suddenly disappeared, blotted out by a solid mass of black,
churning clouds, shot through with bright veins of lightning. The Zeppelin
headed into this cloud bank and, buffeted by thunderclaps and driving rain,
was also suddenly consumed by a strange, vivid flame, cool to the touch, that
seemed to dance across every surface of the doped canvas envelope.

"The ship's burning!" called the top lookout—alarming, but no cause for
alarm: This was St. Elmo's fire, named after Erasmus of Formia, the patron
saint of sailors. Technically a luminous plasma generated by coronal discharge
in an atmospheric electrical field, it burned a vivid violet-blue and, in nontech-
nical terms, was entirely beautiful. For uncounted centuries the phenomenon
had been interpreted as a sign—of what, exactly, no one could say—of God's
blessing, or God's curse: It had been seen dancing above the obelisks of the
Hippodrome just before the Fall of Constantinople to the Turks in 1453; it
would be seen later, curling along the cockpit and around the spinning props
of the B-29 *Bockscar* as she dropped Fat Boy on Nagasaki in 1945.

Not a quiet phenomenon, St. Elmo's fire now hissed and sizzled and
popped as *L59* passed through the storm, fading at last as the super Zeppelin broke into clear air and dazzling moonlight. Now Africa glowed faintly
dead ahead, the pirate seaports of the northern coast. For the duration of
the storm, *L59*'s radio antennae, three long delicate wires trailing below her
vast belly, had been wound in. Muffled in radio silence, the Zeppelin had
been unreachable by any communication from Germany.

As it happened, three and a half hours into the flight, officials at the
Kolonialamt having been informed somehow—how, exactly, will become a

critical question—of British advances into the Makonde Highlands, last known gathering place of the Schutztruppe, decided to recall the mission. The Kolonialamt relayed this decision to Admiral von Holtzendorff, who broke the news to a crestfallen Kaiser. The Zeppelin handlers at Jamboli, soon informed of the recall, attempted to contact *L59* but could not; she had passed beyond the limits of their frail transmitter. Jamboli called this failure back to Berlin: "*L59* can no longer be reached from here, request recall through Nauen." The radio transmitter at Nauen, near Berlin, the most powerful in Germany, then took up the recall message and continued to broadcast it all night long. But with her antenna wound in, deaf to these entreaties, *L59* kept on her course for East Africa.

At five fifteen a.m., the sun cracked the rim of earth and the huge airship passed over the African continent at Ras Bulair on the Libyan coast. Miles of desert lay ahead; no Zeppelin had flown across such a landscape before. Now the level wastes of sand and rock stretched monotonously below *L59*'s keel, from horizon to horizon. Soon, the sun, blazing down, began to dry her canvas skin, still drenched and heavy from the storm. The airship grew lighter as the watery sheen evaporated; lighter still as fuel consumption continued apace. Then the gas in her envelopes, expanding with the heat, blew out the automatic valves into the atmosphere and soon, *L59* became dangerously light and increasingly difficult to handle. To compensate, Bockholt flew her "nose down" throughout the day, shifting 1,650 pounds of ballast aft as a counterbalance.

In the late morning, hot desert air rose in bubbles of buoyancy, alternating with heavy downdrafts of cooler air. This caused a roller-coaster effect that made most of the crew violently airsick. Even the hardened navy veterans among them, used to storms at sea, were not immune to the stomach-churning sensation of weightlessness as *L59* plunged into the downdrafts and precipitously rose again. Despite all this, *L59* plowed ahead and made the Farafra Oasis around noon. This incandescent patch of green slid by below, its date palms rustling in the hot wind. The Bedouin tribesmen gathered there looked up in wild surmise, shading their eyes as the massive Zeppelin slid by overhead, still watching as she disappeared toward the west, the grumbling of her five Maybach engines audible long after she had vanished into the clouds.

Three hours later, the airship reached another oasis, at Dakhla. In this remote place, at the very heart of the desert, many of the tribesmen gathered with their camels around the murky spring had not heard of the war, or been aware that men could take to the air in flying machines. The sight of L59 looming above them like a visitation from a strange new god filled them with fear. (Years later, in 1933, a German aviator passing through the Dakhla Oasis saw crude images of a Zeppelin scrawled on the walls and doors of native huts. Questioning a Bedouin sheikh as to the meaning of these renderings, he was told the scrawl represented the shape of a "powerful sign from the heavens," which had appeared twenty years before, and that it was worshipped as "a herald of Holy Grace." Even now, he said, his people watched the skies for its return.)

From Dakhla, where apparently L59 had just inspired its own cargo cult, Bockholt aimed for the Nile. Flying across the endless desert, some of the men in this last era before the ubiquity of sunglasses had gone half-blind from the dazzling glare of sun on sand. Others had been visited with splitting headaches. A few, mesmerized by the persistent drone and the featureless monotony passing below, had become prey to hallucinations: Mirages rose out of the desert, ancient cities, half as old as time, full of jinn out of the *Arabian Nights*.

Meanwhile, the prosaic Bockholt in the forward gondola used the ship's shadow crawling along the desert floor as a navigational tool. L59's exact length, known to the millimeter and factored into a preset equation, measured both ground speed and drift. The Zeppelin sailed through the hot afternoon toward the Nile at sixty miles per hour, functioning perfectly until four twenty p.m. when a juddering sensation preceded the failure of her forward engine. Presently, the big propeller spun to a stop. Mechanics soon determined the reduction gear housing had cracked; they repaired it as best they could but took the engine out of service for the remainder of the journey. Now L59's radio could not send messages, as this engine drove the radio generator—though radio signals could still be received.

Just before dusk, a flock of flamingos, vividly pink in the setting sun, flapped below L59's nose cone; a moment later the marshes of the Nile came into view and the airship flew over mile after mile of verdant wetlands. Bockholt made for the great river, crossing over it at Wadi Halfa. Here he turned south, skirting the Nile's broad flow and droning onward toward Khartoum and the Sudan beyond the last cataract.

Flying a Zeppelin is a difficult undertaking under the best conditions: Gas expands and contracts according to changing temperatures; lift and buoyancy fluctuate; all must be counterbalanced ceaselessly by the release of ballast water, the measured shifting of cargo, the canting of nose or tail via clumsy elevator flaps—and all this becomes doubly difficult over the desert. Bockholt had lightened his airship by 4,400 pounds of ballast in the last full heat of day and had even tossed some boxes of supplies overboard. He knew the rapidly cooling temperatures of the desert at night would contract the gas, causing the Zeppelin to sink. To counterbalance this sinking effect, he had planned to fly the ship at four degrees "nose up" on her four remaining engines.

But he had not counted on the humid, dense air of the Nile Valley. Even at 3,000 feet, ambient temperatures had reached sixty-eight degrees by ten p.m.; they rose steadily after midnight and still L59's lift capacity gradually diminished. Finally, at three a.m., L59 began to lose altitude precipitously. The engines stalled. Forward thrust gone, the Zeppelin sank through the atmosphere from 3,100 feet to just under 1,300, not high enough to clear a looming desert escarpment; a minute later, her main radio antennae sheared off upon contact with an outcropping of red rock.

Now Bockholt ordered his crew to lighten the ship even further. With all engines stopped, 6,200 pounds of ballast and ammunition went overboard. The crew watched cases of ammunition, much needed by the Schutztruppe, shatter and explode on the ragged slopes below. But this sacrifice had its desired effect: Gradually, the sinking super Zeppelin stabilized; slowly, she rose into safer atmospheres:

"To fly steadily at 4 degrees heavy at night can easily be catastrophic, especially with sudden temperature changes in the Sudan, as at Jebel Ain," Bockholt later confided to L59's war diary, "particularly if the engines fail from overheating with warm outside temperatures. . . . Ship should have 3000 kg of 4 percent of her lift for each night to take care of cooling effect."

Clearly, it was a complicated business.

L59, now less than 125 miles west of Khartoum, had two-thirds of the perilous journey behind her. But presently, to the dismay of all aboard, Bockholt turned the great airship around and pointed her nose cone due north—a faint radio signal had just been received from the radio transmitter at Nauen: *Break off operation, return. Enemy has seized greater part of Makonde Highlands, already holds Kitangari. Portuguese are attacking remainder of Protectorate Forces from south.*

This is the message that Bockholt penciled into the ship's war diary. But the actual recall message received by *L59* has been variously reported, with both its exact wording and—more important—its source varying according to the account. Here *L59* sails from the dark cataracts of the Nile on the early morning of November 23, 1917, into the darker realm of historical conjecture:

"One of the many legends of the Naval Airship Division is that the British robbed Bockholt of success by sending a false recall message in captured German code," wrote Douglas H. Robinson in his exhaustive study of airship warfare, *The Zeppelin in Combat*. Robinson, one of the foremost scholars of Zeppelinia, pointedly does not delve into the whys and wherefores of this "legend," refusing to come down firmly on one side or the other.

Mosley, in his *Duel for Kilimanjaro*, written with the cooperation of von Lettow himself, reports the message as *Go back. Newale has been taken. The war is over and the Schutztruppe has been defeated*—and states flatly that "the message came from British sources which had set up their own radio station and were in possession of the German code." Meanwhile, Zeppelin expert Frank A. Contey calls the idea of the British being responsible "unlikely," stating that they probably couldn't have "known the code and wavelength of *L59*'s radio communication." But the British had possessed the German Naval Code, taken off the wreck of SMS *Magdeburg*, since the beginning of the war. The cipher masters of Room 40 had long since cracked it and, familiar with its intricacies, could both decipher captured messages and send messages of their own. Given Room 40's massed-egghead brainpower, that they knew *L59*'s particular radio wavelength on the night of November 23, 1917, is not implausible.

Meinertzhagen later claimed that he alone originated the false recall message sent to *L59*—and indeed its odor is redolent of the many subterfuges he and his DPM crew perpetrated upon the Germans during von Lettow's guerrilla campaign against the Uganda Railway in 1915. But Brian

Garfield, the great and vigorous Meinertzhagen debunker, deftly puts the lie to this assertion. Garfield points out that Meinertzhagen's account of his involvement in the *L59* caper occurs in the much-revised 1926 version of his infamous diaries and not in the contemporaneous 1917 diary, and that the great fabulist wasn't even in Africa during the time of *L59*'s clandestine flight. In fact, Meinertzhagen, suffering from a case of pernicious anemia, had been ordered out of theater by Smuts on November 10, 1916, and after a period of R and R at the luxurious Rift Hotel in Nairobi and an extended spell of home leave, had reported for duty in Cairo on May 24, 1917. By the end of the year, when *L59* made her journey, Meinertzhagen was serving in Palestine far from the campaign in East Africa, and could not have sighted the Zeppelin either entering or exiting African airspace at Solum, in Egypt, as he later stated in his diary.

Garfield further states that what actually turned *L59* back to Germany was "a signal relayed from one of Lettow's little transmitters. The frail signal was amplified and forwarded by neutral stations in a few towns friendly to Lettow, and after some hours it reached German Naval Command. The signal informed headquarters not that Lettow had surrendered . . . but that the Schutztruppe had been unable to hold the flatlands around Mahenge and had been forced by heavy blanket-fire from British artillery to retreat back into jagged mountains where the dirigible would have no chance of landing without risking explosion."

This version of events, however, is open to question: According to Mosley, via von Lettow, this message could not have originated from the Schutztruppe or any other German source in East Africa, as they had, by this time, no means of sending such a message:

"Lettow-Vorbeck's sole remaining radio transmitter in Africa was situated at Newale, three days' march north of the Rovuma River. Through this station he had, late in October, received news of his promotion to general and a message of personal congratulations from the Kaiser. He had assembled his Schutztruppe at Newale on November 17, 1917. . . . He was then informed that the radio station was in such a state of disrepair that it could only receive *but not send any messages*; a fact which could not, of course, be communicated to Berlin and does not seem to have been appreciated there."

Actually, von Lettow did not seem to have been aware of the Zeppelin mission at all: "It was just as well for [his] peace of mind," Mosley wrote, "that he did not know until after the war of what was happening in the skies over Africa. . . . On November 20," Mosley concludes, "he ordered the [Newale radio] station to be dismantled."

This was a full day before the departure of *L59* from Jamboli for Africa.

How, then, was Bockholt and *L59* supposed to reach the embattled Schutztruppe? His instructions in this regard were vague. According to Robinson: "On approaching the East African protectorate, [Bockholt] would endeavor to make radio contact with the troop headquarters, supposed to be southeast of Mahenge, and otherwise was to land northeast of Liwale." These, as Robinson says, "sketchy directions" were the best available—as there now existed no way to contact von Lettow.

On putting the accounts together, it now seems certain (a) that the recall message taken in by Bockholt aboard *L59* near Khartoum did indeed originate with the German transmitters at Nauen, but (b) that the message first informing Berlin of the Schutztruppe's defeat—or at the very least of von Lettow's retreat from the Makonde Plateau—did not come from von Lettow at all, and (c) that this message was a magnificent piece of disinformation, originating with British intelligence and sent out in German naval code via radio from London or Cairo or elsewhere and picked up by radio operators in Germany.

Indeed, the British knew all about the Zeppelin mission far in advance of *L59*'s departure—perhaps from Woodhall's mysterious Balkan agent or another source—and had a long time to plan their strategies against her. Van Deventer, now overall commander of British forces in East Africa, mentioned it in dispatches on November 10. (Hoskins, Smuts's replacement, had been dismissed for "dawdling" in May 1917.) Lord Cranworth complained that he was "awakened during the night to decode immensely long cypher dispatches as to the necessary steps to be taken on *L59*'s approach." The handful of creaky BE2cs that constituted van Deventer's East African Royal Flying Corps Squadron remained, props turning, in a state of readiness for days preceding the Zeppelin mission and "two mountain guns were dug in for *L59*'s reception" near the Makonde Plateau.

Captain Loof, by late 1917 a prisoner of the British, was thoroughly interrogated regarding the impending Zeppelin flight. They wanted to know where, exactly, it was going to land. Not only had Loof never heard of *L59*'s improbable mission, but he thought the proposition so fantastical that it had to have been some kind of ruse emanating from British intelligence—and decided to play along: "I can tell you in the strictest confidence," he said, with all the false seriousness he could muster, "that *two* Zeppelins are coming, one to bomb Lindi and the other Tabora."

Back in Germany, following the recall, they clearly believed von Lettow had been defeated. According to Mosley, "the false news of Lettow-Vorbeck's capitulation which Zeppelin *L59* brought back from its abortive journey to Africa filled the High Command with dismay." But three weeks later, German agents working out of Dar es Salaam were able to smuggle the truth to Berlin: von Lettow-Vorbeck and the East African Schutztruppe still fought on. The Kaiser, despondent since receiving the news of von Lettow's defeat, perked up enough to write out another effusive message, which he passed to Dr. Solf of the Kolonialamt, in hopes that it might be delivered, somehow, to von Lettow in Africa:

> *The Schutztruppe command has reported to me the most recent feat of arms of the remnant of our East African Army under the command of General von Lettow-Vorbeck. According to the latest news, there seemed to be no way out of their desperate situation and the merciless hounding-down seemed to be drawing to its end. We receive instead the joyous news that the strength of the band of heroes is unbroken, that they still uphold the German flag on the Black Continent, firmly hoping for the victory of German arms in Europe. Only a corps inspired by unreserved trust in their leader and a commander of General von Lettow-Vorbeck's energy are capable of such an accomplishment, which fills us with pride and admiration, and which is held in esteem even by the adversary. And should in the future the courageous band be overpowered by the enemy, the history of this war will pay tribute to General von Lettow and his troops. May God grant you His aid.*

After the destruction of the radio equipment at Newale, von Lettow had no way to receive this appreciation. The British themselves sent it through the lines under white flag, in these last days of the Gentleman's War.

But we have gotten ahead of our story. Whatever the source of the recall message received by Bockholt aboard *L59* at twelve forty-five p.m. on November 22, 1917, it caused a near mutiny among his crew. To a man, they insisted vociferously the recall message must be false, that the mission must continue. That Bockholt only with difficulty persuaded them to follow orders is shown by the delay of nearly two hours between receiving the recall and carrying it out. At two thirty a.m., the lumbering airship finally swung a wide loop over the Nile and headed north again toward Europe. The journey out, difficult enough with its heat bumps, airsickness, and noxious self-heating canned food, seemed like a pleasure cruise compared to the return trip. The crew, no longer buoyed by hope, adrenaline, and a belief in their mission, fell prey to strange fevers. Sleep became impossible in the narrow confines of their hammocks slung in the keel too close to a noisily flapping panel. Temperatures fluctuated from 82°F over the Libyan Desert to 14°F above the Anatolian Highlands. Nearly twenty-four hours after turning around, *L59* left Africa behind at the Gulf of Solum. Crossing the Mediterranean proved fraught with vicious storms, though this time no St. Elmo's fire appeared to guide them on their way.

At dawn on November 24, the weather cleared and *L59* soared to 10,000 feet over the Gulf of Adalia in northwest Turkey. By two p.m., she had crossed the Anatolian heartland, fishing vessels in the Gulf of Chalona riding the waves far below. Proceeding across Asia Minor after dark, she again lost headway and, as in the Sudan, nearly came to a disastrous end, sinking from 3,000 to 1,300 feet above the mountains north of Ushak. Her nose cone pointed six degrees up, the four remaining Maybach engines running at full power failed to stop the descent. A cold northern wind pushed her down and Bockholt ordered the dumping of 6,600 more pounds of ballast. Again, her antennae weights struck the slopes of the mountain; since they extended only a few hundred feet, here she came perilously close to crashing in the dark.

At last, at seven thirty a.m. on November 25, 1917, *L59* made her docking station at Jamboli. Her mooring ropes dropped, the ground crew drew her down and walked her into the long shed. China Show had ended in failure.

The twenty-two aeronauts, wobbly-legged, nearly deafened by the droning Maybachs at close quarters, stumbled down the ladders to the ground in the gray Balkan morning. They had been in the air for almost four days and had covered 4,200 air miles—the longest distance in the shortest time of any airship to date. And in truth, they might have gone farther: 19,900 pounds of fuel remained in *L59*'s tanks—enough to power the Zeppelin for sixty-four more hours of flight—though her hydrogen reserves, reduced by a third, and the lack of sufficient ballast wouldn't have permitted *L59* to reach her maxim range of—say—Chicago.

From here the elusive Professor Dr. Zupitza, medical doctor and professor of zoology, disappears from the pages of history. Kapitänleutnant Bockholt, awarded the Iron Cross, First Class, for his Africa exploit (had he succeeded, the Pour le Mérite would certainly have been his), remained in command of *L59*. His crew, now among the most experienced in terms of distance traveled, remained with him. But what to do with the moribund super Zeppelin? The hulking, unwieldy airship had not been expected to return from her suicide mission. Now she wallowed aimlessly in her shed in Jamboli, deflating slowly like a helium balloon after a birthday party.

For weeks her fate, debated between Strasser, Bockholt, naval chief of staff Admiral von Holtzendorff, and the Kaiser himself, floated between yea and nay. Bockholt wanted to try for Africa again, locate the still-undefeated Schutztruppe, and deliver his goods as intended. The Kaiser wanted to send her on a 2,300-mile journey to the coast of Yemen—there to deliver a load of gold and armaments to his Turkish ally, Enver Pasha, just then battling Lawrence of Arabia in the desert. The navy wanted to use her as a scout ship to search for mines in the Dardanelles. Strasser wanted to rebuild her as a bomb carrier, with which to attack England. The only purpose, he once more insisted, for which a Zeppelin was truly suited.

"England would be very pleased to have this airship kept away from her," he wrote in a heated letter to von Holtzendorff. "Airship operations have never been worthwhile and never will be worthwhile except in the North Sea, scouting for the Fleet and in raids on England."

Bockholt then drew up plans of his own that called for *L59* to be converted into an offensive weapon and used against Allied military targets in the Mediterranean—Malta, Port Said, and various Italian cities, including Brindisi and Naples—all hitherto inaccessible to German aircraft. He sent a letter outlining this plan to von Holtzendorff over Strasser's head, incurring the latter's ire: To Strasser, such a proposal routed outside the chain of command smelled of rank careerism. But on January 5, 1918, the Kaiser with the naval chief's recommendation decided in favor of Bockholt, and L59 was refitted as a bomb carrier at Jamboli.

Over the first three months of the new year, Bockholt made several sorties with L59. On March 10, 1918, after crossing the Adriatic from Scutari, he attacked Naples from 12,000 feet, dropping 14,000 tons of bombs on several military and industrial targets, including the naval base, the gasworks, and the Bagnoli Steel Plant. One can only imagine the pleasure-loving and excitable Neapolitans, hysterically running for cover as the yellow-gray sausage-shaped monster pierced the clouds over the Bay of Naples and the bombs began to fall. In the self-congratulatory telegram he later sent back to the Naval Airship Division HQ in Friedrichshafen, Bockholt complained about the bad food supplied to his crew (undoubtedly more foul, self-heating *Kaloritkon*) and made a lame joke: "If I ever get married, I won't go to Naples on my honeymoon!"

On March 20, Bockholt aimed L59 for Port Said on the Egyptian coast, but was driven back by powerful headwinds and returned to Jamboli, bombs still nestled in the keel like so many poisonous eggs. This time, Bockholt ordered a complete overhaul of her engines—they should have been able to deal with the headwind, no matter how strong. Eighteen days later, on April 7, 1918, ready to fly again, the super Zeppelin kicked off her mooring ropes and sailed above the dour Bulgarian landscape, nose cone pointed to the southeast. Bockholt had decided to attack the important British naval base at Malta, via a route that took him across the Balkans and the Straits of Otranto into the Mediterranean.

Later that day, at sea, in the vermillion dusk, U53, a U-boat assigned to the German Mediterranean Flotilla, surfaced in the Adriatic off the Apulian coast. Oberleutnant zur See Sprenger, in command, came topside and observed a giant airship flying low over the water, following in his wake. At first unsure of her nationality—the Italians and other Allies now also used airships—he made ready to fire at her with his deck guns. Then he saw the Knight's Cross emblazoned on her underbelly and the designation *L59* on her hull and recognized her for a friend. Sprenger and his gun crew now watched as the Zeppelin overtook them, floating along quite low at only 700 feet, and kept watching as she disappeared, an ominous presence in the Adriatic gloom, bound for parts unknown—though Sprenger figured she might be heading for Otranto, which the German Mediterranean Flotilla had just been ordered to subject to a naval bombardment.

Then, after about an hour and a half, Sprenger saw "two points of fire" in the sky on the horizon, which he took for shrapnel bursts: "Shortly thereafter," he saw, so he wrote in his ship's log, "a gigantic flame which lit the entire horizon bright as day for a short time and then slowly fell to the water, where it continued to burn over the horizon for twenty minutes longer. When the fire started, several heavy explosions were heard. From all appearances, the airship was shot at and fell burning. Searchlights in the direction where she fell made it appear that a search was being made. On passing the approximate spot three hours later, nothing was visible. Position about 41 degrees, 2' N, 18 degrees, 53' E."

Sprenger had witnessed the final end of the famous *Afrika-Schiff L59*, lost with all hands and all engines in the dark sea at the heel of Italy. Neither the British nor Italians claimed to have shot her down—though how to explain the searchlights? Later, an oil slick was found, a few enigmatic pieces of floating wood, a fuel drop tank; nothing more. The exact cause of her demise remains unknown, but members of her crew had complained of fuel-line leaks, so it is assumed an accident in which a fuel fire ignited the hydrogen and led to her destruction.

It would have been better for Bockholt and his ship had he ignored the recall message received five months earlier, despite all the odds against finding von Lettow, and continued his journey to East Africa. He turned back and perished. Though *L59*'s greatest mission was a failure, her record-making journey from Jamboli to Khartoum, the first truly intercontinental flight of any consequence, is still remembered by aviation historians as pointing the way to the future of modern air travel.

Chapter 23

MARCHING WITH THE SHROUD MAKER

Just before dawn on November 25, 1917, one day after *L59* returned to her dismal shed at Jamboli, von Lettow and the remainder of the Schutztruppe bivouacked in the bush at a place called Negomano, on the northern bank of the Rovuma River, just below the confluence of the Rovuma and the Ludgenda. The Rovuma marked the border between what was left of German East Africa—now only the ground upon which von Lettow stood *at that moment*—and Portuguese East Africa, the fat, fertile colony to the south, so far mostly untouched by the hardships of war.

Another rainy season, occurring much earlier this far south, would soon transform the Rovuma into a thick brown torrent and the low-lying area around it into floodplain. Now little more than a trickle, the river ran no more than waist-high. But the ants knew what was coming and already crackled through the bush in deep columns to the higher ground.

Portuguese East Africa was unknown to von Lettow. He didn't possess maps of its terrain or knowledge of its tribes. But a border being an artificial thing, an imaginary line drawn on a map by cartographers in Europe, its terrain probably wasn't much different from that through which he'd been marching since Kondoa-Irangi: The same thick bush and rivers large and small in bewildering array crisscrossing each other in a race to the sea—interspersed with a few areas of heavy cultivation (sisal, cotton, millet) and here and there, jagged mountains folded into the landscape like creases into the bedspread of a fever patient. And all of it horribly mismanaged by the Portuguese, whom, with the exception of the murderous Belgians of the

Congo, history records as perhaps the worst of the European colonial regimes in Africa.

Meinertzhagen, now safely ensconced in the Sinai and wielding his insults and fabrications against the Turks, nevertheless reserved some of his choicest rhetoric of the period for Britain's Portuguese "allies":

"The Portuguese . . . should have remained outside a war in which northern nations are involved," he wrote. "They certainly have no right to colonies. In fact, it is time such a miserable, effete, and decadent nation came under some form of control, for by themselves they can only do harm. . . . Their colonies are a scandal, the natives being much worse off than they ever were before. Except for introducing every European vice and withholding every European virtue, they have done nothing."

These were the adversaries von Lettow, with van Deventer's columns snapping at his heels, would now be facing. The British were "hunting us," he later said. "And we were hunting the Portuguese."

But even a shallow river is best forded in the daylight, and waiting for the sun to rise, von Lettow hesitated. As his men stirred around him in sleep, he contemplated the recent events in the war that had led him to this Rubicon moment—to the necessity of abandoning his own colony and crossing a river to invade an alien land.

The most recent phase of the war had been disastrous for the Schutztruppe: It had begun with the Battle of Mahiwa, a kind of equatorial Somme, occurring over the course of four bloody days, October 15–19, 1917. Captain W. D. Downes of the Nigerian Brigade called Mahiwa "the most savage fought battle in the history of African conflict—not excluding Omdurman or any engagement of the Boer War." A confused battle of trench warfare, barbed wire, hand grenades, sustained artillery barrages, futile bayonet charges against entrenched machine gun positions, it resembled the static contests of the Western Front more than the "War of Maneuvers" pursued in East Africa to that point.

Accounts of the action at Mahiwa set down by its participants differ widely from each other; no two agree in particulars and often do not seem to describe the same engagement. Unfortunately, von Lettow's war diaries covering the period were lost during the months of Portuguese exile. As most of the fighting occurred between the town of Mahiwa and the village of Nyangao, but closer to the latter, some feel the battle should rightly be associated with that name—but as Nyangao was obliterated from the map by the action, to its larger neighbor go the honors.

By mid-October 1917, von Lettow's forces—now joined by General Whale's column, which had hacked its way across the colony from Tabora—had been driven to the edge of the Makonde Plateau by concentrated advances of British columns under General Hannyngton, in charge of the freshly deployed Nigerian Brigade, and General Beves, the tempestuous South African—an avid butterfly collector—who had sacrificed so many of his men in frontal assaults on the Latema-Reata Ridge back in March 1916.

Fighting with Beves was Brigadier General Henry de Courcy-O'Grady, a coolheaded Anglo-Irishman, formerly of the Indian Army, whose first exposure to Africa had been at Tanga with the disastrous Expeditionary Force B. Wherever O'Grady went, there went also his West Highland terrier, O'Mara. This little dog, as oblivious to shell-fire and shot as the most hardened trooper, would trot along after his master during a battle, snuffling at the cordite-laden air and barking at the impact of each exploding shell.

Hoping as always to crush von Lettow in a pincer movement, Hannyngton divided his army into two massive heterogeneous columns: "Hanforce," consisting of British, Indian, and KAR battalions, advancing from north to south, commanded by Hannyngton himself, and "Linforce," composed largely of Nigerian troops advancing up the Lukuledi River Valley from the direction of the port of Lindi, under the command of Beves and O'Grady. Both these columns together outnumbered the Schutztruppe by more than five to one.

But von Lettow's *askaris* "shot steadily and with judgment," according to an admiring Nis Kock, now fighting at their side, rifle in hand. "They definitely knew their business." During one action defending the fortified town of Ruponda in September, he noted, "on each flank, small groups of *askaris* were beginning to crawl out towards the enemy, carefully making use of every unevenness in the ground, and every scrap of cover. . . . Less than a minute after entering the fight, they were threatening the English flanks; they acted without commands, simply on a gesture from their

NCO . . . and they carried out the most effective form of attack almost by instinct."

Ruponda fell eventually, overwhelmed by the inevitable superior numbers, and the Schutztruppe faded into the bush, but not before they had killed more of the enemy than their own strength.

During the weeks leading up to Mahiwa, van Deventer, determined to end the war before Christmas 1917, became as obsessed with capturing von Lettow as Smuts had ever been. Van Deventer had caught his former commander's fixation with the man like a bad tropical fever. Every officer on his intelligence staff received orders to devote all their energies to locating the elusive German. But von Lettow, now always half-disguised in *askari* khaki, a nondescript corduroy sun helmet pulled low to obscure his face, could not be easily identified by British scouts.

"Captured mails revealed the fact that in spite of his extensive intelligence and spy systems, the enemy was groping in the dark," von Lettow wrote in his *East African Campaigns*. "He did not know, for instance, where I was, though he seemed to place the greatest importance upon knowing. . . . While one letter-writer thought I was in the neighborhood of Lukuledi, another insisted that I was at Tunduru, and according to a third, I was at Mahenge. . . . It is difficult to understand how intelligent people can entrust to the mail important matters which must be kept from the enemy, knowing how unreliable the mail is, and that letters often fall into the enemy's hands."

Von Lettow encouraged this confusion by allowing the British to acquire misleading German dispatches—all of it a perfect illustration of Sun Tzu's dictum from *Art of War*: "When you are near, make them think you are far away; when far away, near." One can imagine the wily commander chuckling in hindsight as he composed the above quoted excerpt, but at that moment, in October 1917, any humor was strictly of the gallows variety.

Hanforce and Linforce, working together, had driven the Schutztruppe into a small wedge of the colony, no more than 100 miles square. General Whale, dug in along the Lukuledi between Mahiwa and Nyangao, hoped to hold the line. British Intelligence caught wind of Whale's presence there, and soon, both Hanforce and Linforce advanced against him from two directions at once: The Schutztruppe, van Deventer dared to imagine, would be smashed flat as a horseshoe between the hammer and anvil of his advancing armies, now numbering more than 5,000—mostly fresh, unblooded Nigerian troops. The British columns also included the 127th Baluchis, the Bharatpur Infantry, and the last remnant of Selous's 25th Royal Fusiliers, the "old and bold" Legion of Frontiersmen. This eccentric battalion, once 2,000 strong, now numbered fewer than 200. Nearly 1,800 of them had been killed in battle or died of disease.

Unfortunately for Beves and O'Grady, no one seemed to be able to locate von Lettow. Aware of this fact, the German commander moved his *askaris* stealthily up behind Whale, strengthening the center of the line. He remembered Beves well. The South African general's foolhardy assaults at Latema-Reata had stuck in his memory: "I had learned in that engagement," von Lettow wrote, "that General Beves threw his men into action regardless of loss of life. He pushed for victory not by skillful handling and low casualties, but rather by repeated frontal attacks which, if the defense had anything like adequate forces and held its ground, led to severe losses. I guessed that here at Mahiwa, Beves would prosecute the same tactics."

On the morning of October 15, 1917, von Lettow assumed his full regimentals—which is to say, put on his dress uniform with all medals and ribbons displayed—for the first time since 1914. This exchange of rough *askari* garb for the costume of an Imperial German general betokened two things, both detrimental to the success of British efforts: First, von Lettow, though now nearly driven from German East Africa entirely, was not prepared to surrender. Second, after two years of a skillfully wrought fighting retreat, von Lettow had at last decided to engage in the stand-up battle that Smuts had always sought and he had always avoided. Hard against the Portuguese border, what remained of GEA could be crossed on foot in a few hours. The Schutztruppe no longer had anything to lose: Time to make a stand.

Von Lettow's *askaris* who saw their general splendidly arrayed in his dress uniform with his medals glinting found themselves both inspired to fight and stricken with a kind of fearful awe. Now they gave him a new name: He was no longer the *Bwana Obersti*—or, given his recent promotion, the *Bwana*

General—but now the *Bwana Aliyefanya Saanda*: "the Shroud Maker." And they would follow him willingly, most of them, to their doom.

Whale's column, nearly 2,000 strong, dug in Western Front–style behind barbed wire and in deep trenches, received Beves's opening assault in the gray hour just after dawn on October 15. The first wave of Nigerians were quickly driven back by the efficient rattle of *askari* machine-gun fire. Wave after wave of punishing attacks proceeded over the course of the day, as the heat rose and iridescent insects chattered from the thickets. Beves lost many men, but spoiled by two years of Schutztruppe fighting retreats, he expected the Germans to fade with the dusk. No doubt morning light would reveal empty trenches as at Kondoa-Irangi. But as the sun sank below the tree line, Schutztruppe bugle calls didn't sound the expected call to disengage. Rather, they summoned von Lettow and the reserves to the center of the line:

"Wave after wave . . . broke on our front," von Lettow remembered, though the energy of the attackers began to dim as the afternoon wore on: "My own observation told me that the weight of the attacks here on the right wing was diminishing."

These costly frontal assaults continued in the waning light with the Nigerians absorbing the hardest blows: The last *Königsberg* gun, hauled from one end of Africa to the other for the last two years, now did tremendous damage. Exposed to this punishing fire in hastily dug, shallow trenches, the Nigerians suffered beneath a typhoon of massive 10.5 shells, big enough to sink a battleship. Most were blown to bits, their body parts flung into the branches of overhanging trees. For days afterward, Captain Downes observed, the trees, "dripped blood from the limbs and trunks of men who had been blown up and been wedged between the branches."

Meanwhile, in another part of the line, General O'Grady's little dog had disappeared. The distraught, dog-loving general, careful to hide his anxiety, walked calmly up and down the line, exposing himself to continual enemy fire, inquiring everywhere after O'Mara: Had anyone seen his dog? Whether the tenacious battle pooch ever returned to his owner is unfortunately not recorded.

Fighting ceased at last with the fall of a particularly dark tropical night, but immediately picked up again with first light. October 16, according to the British *Official History*, "was the most disastrous day for the Nigerians since the formation of the force." Many of the new Nigerian recruits, inadequately supplied, inexperienced and fighting on the inaccessible flanks of the German line, subsisted on a handful of rice and barely enough water to wet their tongues—the closest watering hole being covered by *askari* sharpshooters:

"We find ourselves literally besieged," signaled one of their British officers. "Ammunition is very scarce, and the men have eaten all their emergency rations. To add to all these troubles, the enemy have a machine gun and snipers posted along the water, so that our men are continuously getting hit whilst trying to obtain water. As our trenches are dug in sand, more or less out in the open, the heat is terrific, and the men are willing to do anything to quench their thirst. . . . There is no news of any reinforcements or of a relieving column. Matters are extremely critical, and if we are not relieved shortly, we shall meet with disaster."

But the fighting only got hotter throughout the day—especially at the center of the line where Beves, like an imbecile banging his head repeatedly against a brick wall, kept throwing his troops at the German trenches, as von Lettow had predicted. These assaults, turned back by machine guns and wire, were often followed by *askari* counterattacks that carried the fight all the way across no-man's-land to the British trenches. During one of these actions, the last of the Frontiersmen raced into a gap between two advancing columns. Schutztruppe machine guns cut them down; fewer than a dozen crawled back alive. The 25th Royal Fusiliers had ceased to exist as a unit of the British Army.

Again night fell, black and cloying with humidity and filled with the cries of the wounded and the dying. The next day, again, fighting started with first light. An unidentified Schutztruppe officer, apparently sick of the battle and sick of the war and sick of life itself, mounted a white horse—obtained who knows where—and led a suicidal charge against an entrenched British position. One British officer watched, astonished, as the German, with "no less than two machine guns and two score rifles aimed at him, disappeared in a storm of lead—never, I should think, to lead his troops on earth again." But perhaps, he might have added, in Valhalla.

As the battle wore into its third day, a kind of psychological fatigue set in and bizarre doings abounded: A company of Nigerians jumped out of their trenches, dropped their rifles, and performed a traditional tribal war dance, as *askari* bullets splattered the mud at their feet. Von Lettow himself now appeared in the forward German trench to direct the course of the day's action, his resplendent uniform disheveled and powder-burned from too close an association with the fighting. Drinking black coffee and smoking like a fiend, he deliberately exposed himself to enemy fire as an example to the troops.

His current supply of cigarettes—so critical to his military judgment—had come in the form of manna from heaven: During the retreat from the Rufiji, British planes had dropped tiny parachuted bundles on the German lines. The *askaris* had watched them fall softly to earth but hesitated to retrieve them—was this some kind of dastardly British trick? Did the bundles contain tiny bombs? No. Thousands of cigarettes, intended as a gift for British troops but blown by the German-leaning wind, had landed in von Lettow's lap. A miracle! Enough cigarettes to keep him supplied for the rest of the war.

The fighting at Mahiwa, by now both sanguine and pointless, continued for another two days. Not the "Gentleman's War" of the long retreat at all, but a vicious slugfest between mismatched brawlers complete with—rare in the East African campaign—accusations of atrocities on both sides. The British charged that their wounded had been indiscriminately bayonetted in bush fighting on the flanks of the battle lines. One of the Nigerian's British officers, Captain A. K. Stretton, kept a "small Nigerian boy," an orphan, as a servant; the boy himself kept a pet monkey, which had become the mascot of the 1st Battalion. Both were found shot and stabbed, bayonetted multiple times.

At last, by the evening of October 18, the machine guns stopped their chattering and the sharp crack of rifle fire drew down. Both the British and the Germans simply stopped fighting. The smoke cleared; the sound of insects and birds could be heard again. Row after row of wounded men of both sides lay on stretchers on the ground at nearby Nyangao in British-held territory. A photograph exists, showing this tragic scene; it's like the crane shot of the casualties lying in the dusty street after the Battle of Atlanta in *Gone with the Wind*.

The British had thrown themselves at von Lettow's entrenched positions in profligate numbers—"at least 4,000, but no less than 6,000 strong," he says in his *Campaigns*: "We had with our 1,500 men," he says, "completely defeated the enemy." True, British losses amounted to more than half their original number; they had also lost Beves, who following his disastrous frontal assaults experienced an acute attack of conscience manifested as a nervous breakdown, and had to be removed from command. Meanwhile, the Germans lost only 95 Europeans and 422 *askaris*. A victory, von Lettow declared, but this wasn't quite true. As at Jasin, the Schutztruppe couldn't afford any more such victories: Most of their ammunition had been expended, including all the shells for the last of the *Königsberg* guns. For them, Mahiwa, decidedly pyrrhic, only bought them a couple of weeks' breathing room.

While the British regrouped and buried their dead, von Lettow consolidated. He withdrew to a place called Chitawa; there he abandoned the first batch of walking wounded—98 Germans and 425 *askaris*—to the pursuing British columns. He continued to retreat toward the Rovuma through the last weeks of October and into November 1917. His little army was plagued by shortages of all sorts—only a few hundred thousand rounds of ammunition remained, all for the "old smokies," the much-loved, much-hated Jagerbuch 71 black-powder rifles. Barely enough firepower for a small engagement, certainly nothing on the scale of Mahiwa. Along the way, he left more sick and wounded—50 Germans and 600 *askaris* and carriers—at nameless jungle campsites for the British to find, feed, and cure.

On November 17–18, von Lettow paused for the final culling at Nambindinga, less than twenty miles from the Rovuma and Portuguese East Africa. Here he finalized his invasion plans, took stock of his supplies: Enough remained for maybe six weeks of self-sufficient marching. After that, the Schutztruppe would be forced to live off the land, an expedient open only to the healthy and the strong. Difficult decisions remained as to who would stay and who would go.

Captain Tafel, who with 1,000 *askaris* had remained behind on the Makonde Plateau, fighting a rearguard action against the British there, now struggled to reach the main body of the army. Encircled by enemy columns guided by the jungle man, Pretorius, and eventually starved out, Tafel surrendered at last in late November. Pretorius, now van Deventer's eyes and ears in the bush, watched gleefully from the top of a tall tree as Tafel's col-

umn, marching along blindly, missed von Lettow's advance guard by a single mile. Confused, Tafel turned right instead of left and marched into the
arms of the British. A pathetic, rambling note eventually reached von Lettow, by that time far into PEA, in which the officer, half-mad with hunger,
apologized to his commander for "having let you down."

Nis Kock, among the walking wounded at Nambindinga, made the list
for demobilization (his malaria had become chronic; he couldn't walk more
than a few feet without collapsing), as did a bitter Captain Loof, to whom
von Lettow assigned command of the wounded. After evacuating Dar es
Salaam, Loof had fought the Portuguese along the border, blasting them
with the *Königsberg* gun Leutnant Wenig had rescued from the fallen capital. Unfortunately for von Lettow, no excuse could be found to abandon
Governor Schnee, who remained with the Schutztruppe, still dragging his
supply of paper money via a dozen carriers—the colony's cash reserves, he
called them—though no colony now existed to guarantee their value.

Schnee again insisted, as he did periodically, that von Lettow must surrender. For the first time, the governor made a strong case: The Schutztruppe, cornered in the armpit of the colony, couldn't continue much
longer: Even down to its current low strength, the force could barely feed
itself and didn't have enough ammunition or medical supplies to fight another battle. Things looked bad indeed. Von Lettow paused and considered
Schnee's request, agreeing that "it would be madness to go on with fighting
that would not bring about a favorable decision." But sometimes the best of
us are mad. He had already decided to invade Portuguese East Africa
and there continue the war. Wherever he went, he knew the British would
follow, committing more and more troops and equipment that might otherwise go to the Western Front. He had never once deviated from his original plan, formulated back in 1913. His army, now trimmed of all but the
best and most healthy fighters, would continue its advance toward the
Rovuma in the morning—as it turned out, no more than two hours ahead
of pursuing British troops. His only strategic objective now was to remain
uncaught.

Nis Kock, both shivering and burning with the chills and fevers of malaria, woke from unpleasant dreams at midnight, just in time to watch the
pullout begin. Nambindinga, though little more than a clearing where once

had stood a town, became for him "a milestone in the history of the war in East Africa." He pushed aside his mosquito netting, raised himself on an elbow, "and stared . . . with wide-strained feverish eyes" at the Schutztruppe evacuation: "Swiftly, with hardly a sound, company followed company, grew out of the darkness, showed clear for an instant in the light of many fires, and were gone into the darkness again.

"This was the German East African Army, marching towards the frontier river, the Rovuma. The camp-fires gleamed on fantastic shapes, black and white, side by side, carrying rifles over their shoulders, butt pointing backwards. Some of the shapes were barefooted, some naked torsos had cartridge belts slung across them like bandoliers, some wore topis all askew, old felt hats, or uniform caps, and some were bareheaded. Rags of every kind of uniform sprang into sight in the firelight, and were gone into the blackness again. Camp-fire shone back from rifle barrels, or now and again from machine-guns carried between two men. More came by and still more. Some sections were very small, but there were many of them, perhaps the remnants of different companies. How many were there? I could not keep count, but there cannot have been more than 2,000. . . .

"Following the *askaris'* army of shadows came an endless stream of bearers and after them again, a long file of women and children, clinging to the rear of the army. It grew darker and darker, and I could see ever less of what went on around me. My fever grew worse; I had hardly any quinine. I lay down in my rugs, but still for a long time, I heard the sound of hundreds of feet leaving Nambindinga on the way to the Rovuma. They were going on, while I stayed behind."

Kock fell back into feverish sleep; it was as if he'd seen in a dream a vision of the retreat of the last army at the apocalypse.

Just after dawn, the vanguard of the British column arrived, drawn into the German camp by the sunlight. Abandoned men sat in clumps, thin as skeletons; others lay murmuring on pallets of leaves; a thin exhalation of gloom rose above them like a cloud. Hardy, well-fed men, rifles in hand, flooded the camp. These were, Kock noted, "Negro soldiers from the Cape in smart new uniforms and turned-up Boer hats. . . . They took no notice of the sick, they were looking for living, fighting troops."

At last, a South African officer appeared, angrily brandishing his Webley revolver: "Where's the general?" he shouted again and again, meaning von Lettow. "Where's the general?"

Silence, then laughter from one of the sick, then everyone, all the Germans laughing.

"The general?" someone shouted. "The general's gone to hell!"

Or Portuguese East Africa, whichever came first.

The final surrender of Nis Kock and the others at Nambindinga occurred on November 18, 1917. Eight days later, after marching through Newale and dismantling the radio transmitter there, and after the aborted mission of the *Afrika-Schiff L59*, and a few tight skirmishes, von Lettow stood on the banks of the Rovuma at Negomano at dawn, studying the unknown colony across the river's shallow flow. As the sun rose, he ordered the Schutztruppe—now reduced to about 200 German officers and underofficers and fewer than 2,000 *askaris*—to cross into Portuguese East Africa. Before noon, with half his force still waiting to cross to the other side, von Lettow engaged in his first battle against the Portuguese. The latter, informed by British Intelligence that the Schutztruppe might try to invade, had sent a sizable force to Negomano, fortified with tons of supplies and ammunition, to prevent the crossing. But the Portuguese troops—about 1,700 strong—behaved as if oblivious to the presence of the enemy they had been sent to fight. Unloading supplies in a leisurely fashion, halfheartedly digging trenches, their officers lounged about in clean white uniforms, thinking more about lunch than the military necessities at hand. Von Lettow watched them, both amazed and disgusted, through his field glasses. Meanwhile, the *askaris* of the Schutztruppe, as if to show their contempt for the Portuguese, made no attempt to conceal their crossing of the Rovuma.

"It was as if my men deliberately taunted the Portuguese to open fire upon them," recalled von Lettow. "We were in a filthy condition and we had our tattered uniforms to wash and our prickly heat to assuage, and it must be admitted that many of the troops flung off their clothes as soon as they got in the water and began to splash around in joyous bathing. When the enemy fired on them from the bank, they laughed at it, and I had considerable difficulty in making them take cover."

Fighting began in a desultory fashion, with the Portuguese taking a few poorly aimed and hesitant potshots at the Germans crossing the river; one could almost feel them trembling behind the sights of their rifles. Growing impatient with this penny-ante skirmishing, von Lettow brought up his single remaining piece of artillery, a mountain gun, and opened up on the Portuguese camp, while at the same time a column of *askaris*, mostly fresh from bathing in the river and still naked, moved in a neatly executed encircling movement around the Portuguese rear. The unfortunate Portuguese, it seemed, had never been in a real battle before. Von Lettow's *askaris*, armed only with their primitive smoky 71s, made good targets, each one of their shots sending up a telltale billow of smoke, but surprisingly none of them were hit.

"*Leo nafasi ya bunduki ya zamani!*" the *askaris* crowed—"It is the day of the old rifles!" But this fusillade, along with the artillery bombardment of the single German gun, quickly unmanned the Portuguese troops. Then the *askaris*, naked and screaming, attacked from the rear and sowed utter terror in their ranks. Many of the Portuguese native troops dropped their rifles and ran for it, only to end up on the point of *askari* bayonets. One officer threw up a white flag, which was ignored in the melee. Von Lettow's *askaris*, now driven by a kind of bloodlust, could not be restrained: Out-and-out slaughter ensued. The half-starved *askaris* massacred nearly 1,000 Portuguese over the course of the afternoon, some while trying to escape, others while trying to surrender. Von Lettow made every effort to stop the killing but at last threw up his hands.

"It was a moment when they needed to kill," he explained later, and made no attempt at an apology. In other words, bad things happen sometimes in war, especially when battle-hardened veterans driven by contempt and privation find themselves up against an overfed and unworthy enemy. After the general slaughter, the looting began. Von Lettow's sense of soldierly discipline, always offended by looting, prompted him to intervene perhaps more strenuously than he had during the killing. Also, the Portuguese supplies, critical to the Schutztruppe's survival, needed to be counted and conserved:

"Even the Portuguese *askari*, already taken prisoner, joined in the plunder of their own stores," he wrote. "To make an example, I dashed at least seven times at one bearer I knew, but each time he got away and immediately joined in the looting somewhere else." Still, von Lettow admitted, "with one blow we had freed ourselves of a great part of our difficulties." They had just acquired five tons of food, new Portuguese rifles in sufficient quantity to arm more than half the Schutztruppe, a quarter million rounds of ammunition, six machine guns, horses, medical supplies, and a 40mm fieldpiece. Not quite the fifteen tons carried in the belly of *L59*, but enough for immediate needs.

Now the rich colony with its fields and forests, plantations, and vast wilderness inhabited by compliant natives, so embittered by centuries of Portuguese misrule that they welcomed the invaders, lay before von Lettow and his men. But first the winter rains would inundate the landscape, and the Schutztruppe needed to find suitable quarters to wait them out.

Christmas 1917 found von Lettow and his army encamped around a lushly appointed plantation near Chirumba, in the heart of the Portuguese colony. Here they stayed for several weeks in a state of luxury unknown since the beginning of the war.

Von Ruckteschell, the artist and von Lettow's adjutant, had pushed his column through the bush and taken the place as a sort of Christmas present for his commander. On Christmas Eve, von Ruckteschell led him from a rough encampment in the bush to the plantation house, where he was shown a comfortably appointed bedroom. Finely woven mosquito netting hung from a four-poster bed spread with clean sheets, his first in at least two years. Von Lettow took off his new Portuguese boots—which he'd sliced open over the toes to accommodate his large feet—lay down, and fell deliciously asleep.

In the morning, his staff fixed up a breakfast of coffee, mangoes, and fresh eggs. Later, they all sat down to a Christmas dinner of roast pork with crackling, sauerkraut, and sweet potatoes, washed down with many bottles of Portuguese wine and a digestif of port. The highlight for von Lettow, however, was his Christmas gift: Von Ruckteschell handed him a nicely wrapped box that, when opened, contained a neat stack of excellent Portuguese cigars. The tobacco fiend was indeed pleased—and the attached card

provided a laugh: *For the Country Postman.* This peripatetic figure—mail
carriers in rural German often walked endless miles on their rounds—was
an indirect slam at Governor Schnee. "Still further?" Schnee had remarked
upon von Lettow's advance into PEA. "The fellow must come from a family
of country postmen!" The comment, an insult coming from Schnee (a striv-
ing son of the middle classes) aimed at von Lettow (a member of the rarefied
Junker aristocracy), had been turned on its maker.

December 1917 through January 1918—the weeks spent at Chirumba
Plantation—was a period remembered by all as an idyll in the midst of war.
Askari hunting parties went out into the bush in driving rain after hippos
and bagged scores of these helpless, ungainly creatures to feed the carriers:
A dozen hungry Africans, swarming over the massive carcass like ants,
could consume an entire hippo down to the bones in a single day. German
officers and underofficers preferred other offerings of the forest: the antelope or bushbuck and African catfish taken from the region's overflowing
rivers and fried in hippo lard—for which the taste, once acquired, becomes
something of an addiction; many of the German officers claimed they preferred hippo lard to butter on their bread. At night, the *bibis* danced in the
plantation's expansive outbuildings, while their children played in the mud.
Both black and white who had shared the hardships of war now shared its
spoils.

But all idylls are, by nature, brief. An army, even the small force the
Schutztruppe had become, can denude a well-stocked and fertile region in
a short time. A shortage of hippo meat coincided with the slackening of the
rains in late January 1918. But a more ominous sign that the war had found
them arrived at Chirumba early one morning toward the end of January:
Low-flying British aircraft dropped multicolored leaflets over the plantation house and fields. A warm wind blew them into the drying mud and
against the palings of the swine pens. Written in Swahili, the leaflets ex-
horted von Lettow's *askaris* to desert:

> *To the German askari. I greet you and bring you a message from
> the Bwana Mkubwa [Commander] of the English. The talks you
> have had from the Germans are full of lies. . . . Your commander
> has told you that by crossing over the Rovuma River you will be*

safe . . . but do you really believe we have given up the fight? Don't
we continue to search for you? Have you not heard our guns
sounding in the bush? There you are, without supplies and food
and you are getting no pay. Why do you continue to run away?
And why not instead run to us and bring this war which is of no
concern of yours to an end? . . . You will be given food and not
made to work . . . and you will be happy once again. We salaam,
Colonel Baxter.

In other words, after a delay of a few months because of the rains and
Portuguese shilly-shallying, the British under van Deventer had disembarked at Porto Amelia in PEA and were advancing now through poorly
charted country toward von Lettow. The Schutztruppe had not heard the
guns of the enemy, but they soon would. Again, von Lettow had forced
their hand: Britain would soon commit substantial forces—eight full
battalions!—to Portuguese East Africa, to finding him and catching him.
And even though the German colony had just been declared a British protectorate and fighting there had officially ended, to van Deventer and the
War Office in London, the war wouldn't be over until von Lettow had been
killed or captured.

Around this time, an official cable from England's King George V reached
van Deventer. The king saluted his South African subject for their total victory over the Germans: "I heartily congratulate you and the troops under
your command," the king wrote, "on having driven the remaining forces of
the enemy out of German East Africa." The text of this message—to use a
modern analogy—was akin to George W. Bush's infamous "Mission Accomplished" speech about the USS *Abraham Lincoln* in 2003. In other
words, many, many months of hard fighting remained; the enemy had not
been defeated at all.

Arnold Wienholt, an Australian soldier of fortune and a big game hunter
fighting with the British in East Africa, put it this way: "The retreat of von
Lettow's force into Portuguese territory was again the subject for further
and very premature congratulations in high quarters, and once more the

conquest of German East was hailed in the papers. The sale of the bear's skin had twice been concluded, though the animal himself, in the shape of von Lettow and his little army of picked men, was very much alive."

But for von Lettow, the certainty that his Schutztruppe remained a threat to the British arrived in the form of an official surrender offer sent through the German lines under white flag from van Deventer to von Lettow. Such requests always boosted the commander's fighting spirits. He operated under the principle that a surrender was never requested from an army that had already been beaten.

Van Deventer's message merely "strengthened my belief that our escape had taken him by surprise," von Lettow wrote, "and that our invasion of Portuguese territory had put him at a loss. Neither he nor General Smuts had ever thought of sending a summons to surrender when the situation was favorable to the English. Why should they do so in a situation like the present? . . . Only because they were at their wits' end."

True, a couple dozen or so of the German *askaris*, after digesting the information contained in the airborne British propaganda leaflets, deserted the Schutztruppe—but von Lettow, after swallowing his initial disappointment, was able to shrug philosophically over the loss: "Many of my troops were very war-weary," he said. "Added to this the feeling of uncertainty as to where the campaign was going to lead them. The great majority of black men cling to their homes and relations. They say to themselves: 'If we go further, we shall come into country we don't know. We can find our way back home from where we are now, but soon we won't be able to.'"

Von Lettow gathered his remaining forces and moved out of Chirumba Plantation in the first week of February 1918. Where was he going? Wherever the pickings offered the most bang for the bullet; wherever the British Army, now chasing him in earnest, would find it difficult to follow.

Chapter 24

THE ENGLISH MOTORCYCLE MESSENGER

Years later, looking back, von Lettow saw the last phase of the war, from February through November 1918—despite its myriad hardships—as one of the happiest periods of his military life. He was, in a sense, free to wage war on his own terms, unencumbered by supply lines or defensive strategies. The Schutztruppe marched and countermarched over unknown terrain, living off the land and on what they could capture from the enemy. They cut through any Portuguese units in their way like a bayonet through butter and were generally welcomed by the natives as liberators. At the same time they fought a continual rearguard action against pursuing British columns crashing about blindly in the bush. The rains had come and gone and von Lettow's little army marched in the blazing sun and through the lushness and fecundity of the tropics. His surviving war diaries give an accurate picture of the hard fighting endured in this last campaign of the war:

> **July 25, 1918.** Today we were able to bring into action our captured English trench mortar, which we seized from the King's African Rifles and have now turned against the Gold Coast Regiment. The first bombs landed in the center of the enemy's position and scattered both men and animals. Leutnant von Ruckteschell was hit in the leg by subsequent enemy fire. Captain Muller attacked the enemy from the hill on the other side, and there were few survivors. Most of the horses too were killed, and these were consumed by the troops.

August 1. We captured the settlement at Pekera, east of the Ligonja River, and drove out a Gold Coast mounted squadron, capturing some motor transport. These were used until we forsook the roads for bush paths, when they were destroyed.

August 5. Resting at Chalau. Captain Kruger, in charge of prisoners of war, died today from fever.

August 7. Enemy patrols came through today under the white flag, offering to exchange sick prisoners and asking for a rendezvous to bring over food and clothing for our English captives. We suspect this to be a pretext to gain information of our plans and have refused exchange. Our medical supplies are low. Our main diet now consists of millet bread, hippopotamus fat, and fungi.

August 24. We crossed the Likingo River and marched towards Numarroe. Two hours east of it, the advance guard was fired on. An enemy company has camped on our line of march and is retreating before our advance. Lieutenant Otto wounded in the chest. We cut through the bush and ravines around the enemy and took Numarroe from the flank. Before dark, our gun was brought into position and we fired on the boma and its entrenchments. Göring's detachment made a wider detour to the south in order, by using the ravine, to come up close to the boma in the rear. . . . When darkness fell, firing increased for a time, then died down. Göring's detachment surprised the enemy and stormed some strongly held trenches. The retreating enemy was, however, not recognized as the enemy by us, and allowed to pass through. Pouring rain and unpleasantly cold. . . .

Etc.

Always a genius of military logistics, von Lettow had by now divided the Schutztruppe into three columns, each made up of three companies, a field hospital, and a complement of carriers. Each column, moving along on its own initiative and commanded by von Lettow's most trusted subordinates (von Ruckteschell, Göring, Kraut), churned through over 2,000 miles of bush on foot, over the three months following the end of the rainy season of 1918. Often marching through regions where game was scarce, they survived on mushrooms, tubers, and other edibles scavenged from the forest floor.

Several of von Lettow's diminishing cadre of German officers didn't survive this punishing, serpentine trek—one of them, Leutnant Schaefer, had been a personal favorite: "I said good-bye to Leutnant Schaefer today," von Lettow wrote sadly in the war diary. "He had rendered such exemplary service in the preparation for the action at Jasin, and was now stricken with blackwater fever. This experienced 'African,' fully aware of his situation, but as cheerful as ever, faced his fast-approaching, inevitable end, with composure."

The columns groaned awake at three each morning, pulled themselves together, and advanced in parallel formation, each column separated by about a mile of bush but connected by an umbilical cord of German officers, all in turn connected to von Lettow. Scouts moved forward, on the lookout for enemy troops or game. Behind them came the *askaris*, rifles worn upside down over their shoulders; then the machine gun bearers, usually members of the Wanyamwezi Tribe. These were followed by the carriers, each bearing his sixty-five-pound burden on his head; behind them came the women and children, some born on the march. The marching *bibis*, now wrapped in blazingly colorful fabrics taken from Portuguese plantations, often singing and led by a Carrier Corps headman wearing a looted tuxedo and top hat, reminded von Lettow of a carnival parade.

"After the plunder of an enemy camp," he recalled, "which often yielded rich booty, cigarette smoke rose on all sides. . . . the *askaris* would call out their friendly '*Jambo Bwana Obao*,' or '*Jambo Bwana* General'. . . or a little signalman"—usually a child—"would express his hope of coming someday to Uleia (Europe) and Berlin," where he would "meet the Kaiser and look in the shop windows."

The endless marching through chest-high elephant grass and along jungle paths often became so monotonous that it induced a trancelike state.

According to the sole surviving Schutztruppe medical officer, Dr. Ludwig
Deppe, with Europeans, "this psychotic state had less than unpleasant symp-
toms. . . . The eternal marching, often for hours in the tall grass, which struck
boots and leggings as waves strike the hull of a ship, could make one so
drowsy that dreamlike visions of the Fatherland fluttered above us, and we
believed ourselves to be home. Thus, this curious form of homesickness
usually had a liberating effect." *Askaris* and carriers had their own way of
dealing with the monotony: tribal chants, German drinking songs in Swahili,
and always the official marching song of the Schutztruppe, "Haya Safari":

> Tunakwenda, tunashinda
> Tunafuata Bwana Obersti.
> Askari wanaendesha,
> Askari wanaendesha,
> Tunakwenda, tunashinda!

> *We're marching, we're winning,*
> *We're following the Lord Colonel.*
> *The askari are coming,*
> *The askari are coming,*
> *We're marching, we're winning!*

All this fighting and marching wore on into the fall of 1918. During one
particularly hot skirmish, the commanding officer of a KAR detachment,
Colonel Dickinson, fell into the hands of Leutnant Boell's *askaris*. When
Boell came upon Dickinson in the woods, the latter was in the middle of a
conversation with British HQ via field telephone:

"You're now a prisoner of the Kaiser," Boell said, leveling his newly captured Portuguese rifle at the Englishman.

"Mind if I finish my call?" Dickinson asked, possessed of the usual,
unflappable British sangfroid.

"Very good." Boell nodded.

"There's a German chap here says I'm caught," Dickinson said into the phone. "Thought you'd like to know. Well, got to dash." He hung up and was taken prisoner, along with his medical officer and adjutant.

Dickinson, a veteran of four years of bush fighting against the Schutztruppe, had never once set eyes on his great adversary, von Lettow. Marched back to the German camp, he walked past the commander—dressed down as usual in *askari* khaki—without recognizing him. Then it occurred to Dickinson that the frantically smoking German busily conducting the battle as if it were a complicated piece of music might be the man himself.

"Was that General Lettow-Vorbeck?" he asked Boell. "Or General Whale?"

Boell confirmed that it was von Lettow.

"Then please take me back to him. I should like to shake his hand."

Boell hesitated—it seemed a strange request from a prisoner of war—but he complied. Dickinson, ushered to the commander, put out his hand.

"I'd be proud to shake the hand of a valiant enemy," the Englishman said. "Been fighting you for four years."

Von Lettow, flattered, also remembered Dickinson as a veteran of many battles against the Schutztruppe.

"I am proud to shake your hand too," he said in his perfect English. "Sorry for your situation, but *à la guerre comme à la guerre.*"

They shook hands; Dickinson, as he joined the other prisoners, was heard to say, "A splendid man, a splendid man!"

Dickinson and von Lettow quickly became friends—a friendship engendered by the mutual respect of professional soldiers—and von Lettow later placed him in charge of all military prisoners. He was greatly distressed to hear of the affable English colonel's death from influenza in the hospital at Dar es Salaam in 1919.

———

The Schutztruppe moved along in their gaily bedecked, lethal columns, now closely pursued by tens of thousands of British troops—who were, however, seriously hampered by the problem of supply. Von Lettow's army, meanwhile, lived off the land. Like a herd of locusts, they would denude the region they came to and quickly move on—all the while fighting continual actions against British forward columns and plundering both British and Portuguese military supplies.

Their line of march cut a squiggle down the length of PEA, crossed back on itself, and kept its southward momentum, through Negomano, Chirumba, Korewa, Alto Moloque, Namacurra, and almost to the port town of Quelimane in the far south—from which the British were fearful the Schutztruppe would seize oceangoing vessels and escape from the African continent entirely. But they looped back across the Namirrue River to Numarroe, and turned abruptly north again through the Pere Hills until, after a period of months, they once again stood on the banks of the Rovuma, staring at German East Africa—now the British protectorate of Tanganyika—across the narrow brown flow.

Along the way, they fought 100 small engagements and a few major ones, most notably at Namacurra—and became experts in the nearly preternatural art of identifying the enemy by the sound of their guns:

"We had already learned to distinguish clearly between the dull, full detonation of our 71s," von Lettow wrote, "the sharp crack of our S-rifle, the double report of the English rifle, and the clear ring of the Portuguese 6mm." Though apparently the enemy had also mastered the same art: "Our askari had noticed . . . the speed with which their trench-mortars always got the range of our positions from [the sound of] our 71s, which threw up so much smoke they were impossible to conceal. On the other hand, when the 71s did hit their target, they made a very considerable hole."

Morale remained high. That von Lettow managed to instill such unit cohesion and fighting spirit among his men under the most difficult circumstances has been called "one of the major command achievements of the First World War." Now many of the carriers sought to enlist as full-fledged soldiers. Von Lettow's treasured cook and batman, Baba, though over seventy, was one of the first to volunteer to take up arms.

In July 1918, at Namacurra—the bloodiest battle of this period—the Schutztruppe scored one of the major hauls of the campaign. The town, little more than a supply depot for the British and Portuguese armies, contained vast warehouses stuffed full of arms and ammunition, food, wine, and whiskey. It was an abundance of the kind no one had seen in years and certainly more than they could carry—no less than two Zeppelins would have been required to haul away everything. Sugar, until now a rarity, abounded. The *bibis*, delighted, filled their mouths with handfuls of the stuff. And all the booze in great vats could not possibly be consumed, even by the assembled army:

"I explained that what we could not drink would have to be poured away," von Lettow said, and gave the go-ahead to try. "The risk of wholesale 'jollification' that involved was gladly taken," he noted, "and everyone was allowed to let go for once, after a long abstinence. We found some fine schnapps in a large number of casks . . . being stored for the English troops. With the best will in the world it was impossible to drink it all."

They also acquired 444 brand-new Portuguese and English rifles, 350,000 rounds of ammunition—enough to discard at last the remaining much-reviled but much-loved Jagerbuch 71s—and, most important, enough quinine to last out the war. But this incredible German windfall was dearly paid for in human life on the part of the British and Portuguese.

Early in the battle for control of the Namacurra warehouses, Schutztruppe gunners under Captain Erich Müller opened up with a captured 75 and another smaller gun, on Portuguese positions. As usual, the Portuguese panicked after a whiff of artillery fire and ran for it. Unusually, their flight set off a wave of hysteria across the entrenched KAR detachments guarding the Portuguese flanks. These reliably stalwart African soldiers abandoned their positions only to be shot down by Schutztruppe machine guns. Several hundred threw down their weapons and bolted for the Namacurra River, just then running at flood tide. Trying to swim for the other side but unable to resist the roiling current, most drowned—including their British officer, Major Gore-Browne, attempting to stem the flight of his men. Not a few were dragged under by crocodiles and eaten.

Had the Portuguese and the KAR merely surrendered, they would have survived, von Lettow noted ruefully. Over the course of the war, he had acquired a justly deserved reputation for humane treatment of captured enemy troops. A tale, perhaps apocryphal, circulated among the British: Von Lettow, they said, had promptly shot one of his own officers caught abusing a British prisoner. Certainly he would have offered the enemy at Namacurra the usual chance at parole—their freedom in exchange for a promise never to serve in Africa again. But the panicked men at Namacurra didn't think to take this chance and died horribly. Many limbless crocodile-munched torsos were found days later, bobbing in the fetid waters downstream.

At last, on September 28, 1918, the Schutztruppe crossed the Rovuma once more, reclaiming German East Africa for the Kaiser. *"Bwana Obersti anarudi!"* the *askaris* chanted joyfully as they stepped out of the river on the other side—"The Lord Colonel's come back!" Their first act back on German soil was to shoot eight hippos for the necessary supply of delicious lard. But after so much marching and countermarching in an alien bush, von Lettow and his men had reached their lowest ebb, physically. And the influenza, which would soon kill untold millions around the world, had already somehow reached the Schutztruppe in the remote reaches of the jungle. More deadly than enemy machine-gun fire, it promptly dispatched 250 *askaris*.

Presently, many of the German officers, too weak to walk, were hauled along in litters by the carriers. One officer could only shoot his rifle lying down; von Lettow had become so weak he leaned against Baba's shoulder when firing at the enemy. His feet once again infested with chiggers, he could barely walk. Indomitable, one-footed Richard Wenig of the *Königsberg*, apparently immune to the various microbes, parasites, and viruses attacking the Schutztruppe (chiggers, after all, can't find purchase in a wooden foot), though a junior officer, now commanded entire columns—all other available command personnel down with flu, malaria, or wounds.

But now they were home again. They left behind a colony devoid of sustenance—even for an army as small as the Schutztruppe had become: About 175 German officers and underofficers remained from the 3,000 or so who had joined up to fight in 1914–15 and 1,500 *askaris* (down from 11,000 at their peak strength) and 2,000 or so carriers. Living off the land without a supply line—the wolf strategy—is not an easy prospect and involves much hardship for both troops and inhabitants. An army becomes by necessity a band of marauders.

By September, von Lettow and his men, down to starvation rations, had run through all the provisions taken at Namacurra. Fortunately, fall 1918, the time of harvests, was a period of almost excessive fecundity in German East Africa. Maize, wheat, and fresh fruit grew along the base of the steep hills of the lush southeastern district bordering Lake Nyasa. The Livingstone Mountains, through which they marched, rolled down to the green banks of the lake, seemingly wide as an ocean and teeming with fish. Also, game abounded on the thickly wooded slopes. Amazingly, after a few weeks had passed, record time given the afflictions from which they suffered, the Schutztruppe recovered both strength and health.

With a new enthusiasm born of a full belly and healed wounds, von Lettow marched his men north in a parabola along the lake.

Miles behind them, huge British armies now struggled through the bush, hampered by size and attenuated supply lines: The closest one boasted 24,000 troops, supported by 17,000 service personnel and 124,000 carriers. Von Lettow knew van Deventer expected him to strike at Tabora, in whose general direction he seemed to be heading, and the British hoped to beat him there. But the commander had made a habit of confounding enemy expectations, and now prepared—against all odds, indeed, preposterously—to invade yet another British possession. This would be, technically, the fourth enemy colony invaded by the Schutztruppe over the course of the war: British East, Portuguese East, the British protectorate of Tanganyika, and now Rhodesia.

But before leaving German territory once again, von Lettow paused at a place called Ubena. Here he left an ailing General Whale for the British to find. Whale, now sixty-seven, worn-down and sick with flu, could barely lift his head. The Colonial Exhibition he had come to see in 1913 had been canceled by war; the son he had come to visit had been killed in battle in 1916. Now it seemed the father hadn't much longer to live, and that East Africa would hold both their bones.

On the last day of October 1918, the Schutztruppe crossed the Rhodesian border near the town of Fife, where, according to intelligence reports, a fat supply depot awaited. But a scrappy company of Rhodesian Mounted Police barred the way with entrenched machine guns. Here von Lettow found himself accidentally in the line of fire; he scrambled away, Maxim bullets exploding all around him. He had just come closer to dying in battle than at any other time during the entire conflict. How absurd it would have been, after four years of hard fighting and hundreds of battles, to be killed in a minor police action in the last month of the war!

A bit shaken by the experience, he turned his army toward Kasama, a market town well provided with food. An advance column under Leutnant Spangenberg took the town on November 9, 1918.

Here the carriers broke into the town liquor stores, and drunken chaos reigned for a few hours until Spangenberg with difficultly and a few well-placed rifle rounds restored order again. When von Lettow arrived to take possession at last on November 12, he found a lunch of fresh fruit, beer, and potted meat waiting for him on a table covered with a linen cloth and set with silverware at the district magistrate's house. This British official, now a prisoner of the Schutztruppe, bore the mellifluous name of Croad. A bit of a celebration followed. Kasama, after Taveta, had just become the second British town taken by the Germans in the entire course of the war in any theater.

Later that night, what remained of von Lettow's staff drank toasts to the commander and to the Kaiser and to the success of German arms in Europe—though a note of anxiety could be heard beneath the good cheer: Captured British newspapers had revealed the fall of Cambrai, St. Quentin, and Armientiers on the Western Front. Von Lettow insisted on viewing this troubling information in a positive light: "Positions could be given up for so many reasons," he shrugged. "I did not attribute any decisive importance to this news."

Over the next few days, as Schutztruppe columns arrived at Kasama—a slow-moving caterpillar, they straggled along a fifty-seven-mile front from Kilma to the Chambezi River—von Lettow and a few of his officers planned for the continuation of the war: As long as German forces fought on the Western Front, the Schutztruppe would keep up its end of the war in Africa; this much remained certain. And taking stock of his army, von Lettow found reasons for optimism.

"We were in a strong position," he wrote. "Our defenses were good. We had stores of food and ammunition. We had even captured enough quinine to supply us until June 1919. We also had 400 head of cattle to keep us supplied with fats and meat. Not for several months had the situation been more promising. It was probable that the pursuing enemy would continue to follow us, and that was what we wanted now—an opportunity to give battle."

But at what target would he aim the still-sharp arrow of the Schutz-truppe? Debate continued into the night on November 12: Perhaps they would march north to the Zambezi, where they could destroy Belgian copper mines, and from there west into Portuguese Angola, and perhaps thence clear across the continent to the Atlantic Ocean and West Africa. Von Lettow figured he might be able to fight on for another year—or until the situation in Europe had resolved itself and Germany had at last beaten the Allied armies, whichever came first. No one knew, of course, cut off in the deep interior of Africa, that the war had ended the day before.

At the 11th hour, on the 11th day, in the 11th month of 1918, the guns fell silent everywhere. Imperial Germany had surrendered, unconditionally, and the whole world that von Lettow had loved and fought for over the course of an astonishing military career was gone forever.

On the morning of November 13, 1918, von Lettow pedaled his bicycle along a soft Rhodesian track toward the forward Schutztruppe column already moving toward the Zambezi. He was overtaken by Captain Müller on another bicycle, pedaling hard and out of breath.

"Müller appeared before me . . . and reported that an armistice had been concluded," von Lettow wrote. "An English motorcyclist who was to have brought the news to British troops had apparently passed through Kasama and been captured there by Koehl's detachment. Thanks to the English telephone lines" (and the telephone equipment the Schutztruppe had captured on the beach at Tanga in 1914) "along which we were marching, we were soon able to understand each other, and thus did we get the news of the armistice."

The English motorcyclist had been carrying a telegram, which read:

12.11.18. TO BE FORWARDED VIA CABLE AND DISPATCH RIDER.
SEND FOLLOWING TO COLONEL VON LETTOW-VORBECK UNDER
WHITE FLAG: THE PRIME MINISTER OF ENGLAND HAS
ANNOUNCED THAT AN ARMISTICE WAS SIGNED AT 5 HOURS ON
NOV. 11TH, AND THAT HOSTILITIES ON ALL FRONTS CEASE AT
11 HOURS ON NOV. 11TH. I AM ORDERING MY TROOPS TO
CEASE HOSTILITIES FORTHWITH UNLESS ATTACKED, AND OF

COURSE I CONCLUDE THAT YOU WILL DO THE SAME. CONDITIONS
OF ARMISTICE WILL BE FORWARDED TO YOU IMMEDIATELY I
RECEIVE THEM. MEANWHILE I SUGGEST THAT YOU SHOULD
REMAIN IN YOUR PRESENT VICINITY IN ORDER TO FACILITATE
COMMUNICATION. GENERAL VAN DEVENTER.

"Our feelings were very mixed," von Lettow concluded in perhaps the
understatement of his life. But he persisted in believing that the "end of
hostilities must have been favorable, or at least not unfavorable to Germany." It wasn't until he received a second telegram from van Deventer that
he realized the full extent of the disaster that had befallen his country:

SEND FOLLOWING TO COLONEL VON LETTOW-VORBECK UNDER
WHITE FLAG: WAR OFFICE LONDON TELEGRAPHS THAT CLAUSE
SEVENTEEN OF THE ARMISTICE SIGNED BY THE GERMAN GOVT.
PROVIDES FOR UNCONDITIONAL SURRENDER OF ALL GERMAN
FORCES OPERATING IN EAST AFRICA WITHIN ONE MONTH FROM
NOV. 11TH. . . .

Von Lettow didn't know that this clause had been added specifically for
him—the British couldn't say exactly where he was at the time of the armistice and figured it would take at least a month to locate the Schutztruppe
and its elusive commander. Meanwhile, everyone else, in every other theater of the war, had surrendered by the eleventh hour on 11/11. But it was
the word *unconditional* that stuck in von Lettow's craw. Had the German
army simply stopped fighting and thrown itself on the mercy of the Allies?
To von Lettow—and to many other Germans later—this scenario seemed
unimaginable. "This was news enough," he wrote, "to show the desperate
situation of the Fatherland. Nothing else could account for the surrender of
a force still maintaining itself proudly and victoriously in the field."

Van Deventer's second telegram to von Lettow continued:

MY CONDITIONS ARE: FIRST: THAT YOU HAND OVER ALL ALLIED
PRISONERS IN YOUR HANDS, EUROPEANS AND NATIVES TO THE
NEAREST BODY OF BRITISH TROOPS FORTHWITH. SECOND: THAT

YOU BRING YOUR FORCES TO ABERCORN WITHOUT DELAY, AS
ABERCORN IS THE NEAREST PLACE AT WHICH I CAN SUPPLY YOU
WITH FOOD. THIRD: THAT YOU HAND OVER ALL ARMS AND
AMMUNITION TO MY REPRESENTATIVE AT ABERCORN. I WILL,
HOWEVER, ALLOW YOU AND YOUR OFFICERS AND EUROPEAN
RANKS TO RETAIN PERSONAL WEAPONS FOR THE PRESENT, IN
CONSIDERATION OF THE GALLANT FIGHT YOU HAVE MADE,
PROVIDED THAT YOU BRING YOUR FORCES INTO ABERCORN
WITHOUT DELAY. ARRANGEMENTS WILL BE MADE AT ABERCORN
TO SEND ALL GERMANS TO MOROGORO AND TO REPATRIATE
GERMAN ASKARI. KINDLY SEND AN EARLY ANSWER GIVING
PROBABLE DATE OF ARRIVAL AT ABERCORN AND NUMBERS OF
GERMAN OFFICERS AND MEN, ASKARI AND FOLLOWERS. . . .

Von Lettow met with District Commissioner Croad, now a free man, the next day and heard the rest of the bad news from home: The German fleet had mutinied; a revolution had broken out. The Kaiser had abdicated on November 10 and gone into exile in Switzerland. Von Lettow couldn't hide his dismay. He wrote a wild telegram to the Kaiser—even though the Kaiser was no longer his master, he couldn't imagine any other authority to whom he should be reporting—explaining that he would lay down his arms as requested, though reluctantly, and gave the telegram to Croad with a trembling hand. Then he got on his bike and pedaled to Kasama, where he addressed the assembled Schutztruppe, first in German, then in Swahili:

"The war in Europe is over," he said, trying to keep all emotion out of his voice and almost succeeding. "We have been told by the High Command in Berlin that it is over for us too and we have been ordered to cease fighting. As loyal Germans, we have no option but to obey. Someday, the achievements as well as the sufferings of all of you in Africa during these past four and a half years will be adequately recognized. For the moment, I ask you to accept your fate—loyally, bravely, and quietly—and to remember in your hearts that you are undefeated."

When the last words of his speech had settled in, the *bibis* began to wail and ululate, a horrible lament that went on for hours and broke out from time to time on the long march to Abercorn in the rain.

On November 25, 1918, two weeks after the armistice in Europe, the Imperial German East African Schutztruppe, the last German army in the field, still undefeated, laid down its arms in Abercorn, Rhodesia. Rain fell in torrents, soaking victor and vanquished alike. The 1/4 KAR under Major E. B. Hawkins formed a guard of honor as the Schutztruppe marched smartly through the mud into the center of town, where a flagpole had been erected on the square before Government House. From this the Union Jack hung limply, soaked through by the rain. Brigadier General Edwards had come in from Tabora to receive von Lettow's surrender on behalf of General van Deventer and King George V.

Certain elements of the Schutztruppe resisted the idea of laying down their arms; they wanted the commander to continue the fight. Von Lettow himself didn't think an undefeated army, which had freely surrendered itself, should also be required to surrender its arms. This particular stipulation he regarded as an insult to German honor. A moment of tension ensued between the commander and the British general until Edwards explained that each surrendered rifle, machine gun, ammunition box, and every other piece of military equipment would count toward the German war debt, already being tabulated in Europe. Major Hawkins, a witness to the events of the day, just then standing at attention with his men in the rain, later recorded his impression of von Lettow, who "turned out to be a very different man from what we expected. A little over medium height and wearing a short pointed beard, with fair hair turning grey, he is a fine-looking man of 49. In the bush, he invariably wore a rather battered sun helmet covered with corduroy, a bush shirt, corduroy shorts, grey puttees, and boots, but no badges of rank whatsoever. His boots, which presumably he had captured, were slit over the toes to make them fit, and this raggedness undoubtedly gave rise to the rumors that he wore sandals. Instead of the haughty Prussian one expected to meet, he turned out to be a most courteous and perfectly mannered man; his behavior throughout his captivity was a model to anyone in such a position. His men, both white and black, were in splendid condition in spite of their tremendous marching."

A reporter from the Rhodesian *Bulawayo Chronicle* picks up the account: "Von Lettow, whose striking presence is a good index of what must be a wonderful personality, came in at the head of his first detachment, which consisted of some Europeans, closely followed by some 400 *askaris*, with their machine guns, carriers, medical units, and women. After these troops had been quickly formed into three lines in a close formation, von Lettow advanced a few paces, saluted the flag, then, taking out a pocket book, read his formal statement of surrender in German. He repeated it in English, whereupon General Edwards replied, accepting his surrender on behalf of His Majesty King George V. Von Lettow was then presented to the officers present, and in turn introduced his own officers, among whom some of the more noticeable were Major Kraut, Lieuts Kempner, and Spangenberg. Ex-Governor Schnee was also there. Then followed the most dramatic moment of the proceedings when von Lettow called upon his troops to lay down their arms, the Europeans alone being allowed to retain theirs in recognition of the splendid fight which they had put up. The *askaris* laid down their rifles, took off and deposited their equipment, and were marched off by companies to the internment camp which had been prepared for them."

Night fell at last. A feeling of despair and then anger overwhelmed von Lettow's officers. As it turned out, the *askaris* had been crammed uncomfortably into a stark, undersize *boma*, surrounded by a thorn-scrub zareba. Von Lettow, checking on the circumstances of their captivity, found them in a state of near revolt, cursing and insulting their British-African guards on patrol outside the perimeter. Von Lettow, outraged, lodged a formal complaint with General Edwards, who promised to ameliorate the situation.

"We are not ordinary prisoners of war," von Lettow insisted. "You do not have to fear that we will escape. We gave ourselves into your hands voluntarily in the performance of an unpleasant duty. Our feelings, particularly the feelings of my *askaris*, should be respected."

But on the march to Tabora, where the *askaris* would be interned until repatriation, conditions worsened. Von Lettow now protested officially to van Deventer via telegraph; the oversize South African general replied coldly that the commander's complaints would be "duly forwarded to the War Office. Meanwhile, I am sure you will recognize that . . . I have no choice but to act in accordance with the orders of the War Office and treat your force as prisoners of war." He was clearly still angry over the drubbings administered by von Lettow's Schutztruppe to the thousands of South African troops under his command since 1915.

Van Deventer's response drew the special ire of von Lettow's second-in-command, Kraut, who, along with Spangenberg and Kempner, concocted a plot to continue the war: They had not been defeated in battle, but had voluntarily given themselves over to the enemy, in accordance with the terms of an armistice they couldn't quite believe. They still retained their sidearms; why not use them to hijack the KAR supply dump in a night raid and liberate their *askaris*? Then, fully armed with the latest weaponry, they could carry the war into the Congo and Angola as had been planned. And to hell with the British, who, given vast material superiority and a permanent supply of reinforcements, hadn't been able to inflict a single major defeat upon them in nearly half a decade of war.

Indeed, the military record of von Lettow and the Schutztruppe remains one of the most astonishing in modern warfare: By the commander's count, his little army—at its greatest strength no more than 15,000, had fought off, defeated, or confounded Allied forces totaling more than 300,000 led by 137 generals. They had inflicted casualties many times their own number, marched 10,000 miles on foot through impossibly rugged country, and had always managed to keep the respect of their enemy by fighting, as Lord Cranworth put it, "a campaign in which their conduct was as clean as it was efficient," and which, from von Lettow's perspective, had upheld the honor of the German Empire.

"I do not think that in the whole history of the war there has ever been a more striking character than General von Lettow-Vorbeck," wrote another admiring enemy, Captain Downes of the Nigeria Regiment. "He was a genius in the art of bush warfare, a man of indomitable spirit—a most remarkable leader of men, who did not know what it was to be beaten. To him, discomfort, hunger, heat, shortage of ammunition and supplies were all as nothing. He had one object in life only, and that was never to be taken by the British. He has at least earned for himself undying fame for being a brave man and a worthy enemy."

Though von Lettow's heart lay with the plotters ("I could only feel glad and proud of such a revelation of true soldierly spirit," he wrote, "a spirit which, even after we had handed over all our arms, did not shrink from storming an enemy camp and once more procuring for ourselves the means to continue the war"), he nevertheless refused to allow their plot to continue: What would they be fighting for? Without the Kaiser and the Imperial German cause behind them, he knew the Schutztruppe would devolve from an army into a company of brigands, reivers who disgraced the tattered German uniforms they still wore. Von Lettow expressed his disapproval in the severest terms. The plotters hung their heads and allowed themselves to be dissuaded.

The *askaris*, however, couldn't understand such niceties. They had given their loyalty to no cause but to a man. Perhaps the German Kaiser had ceased to fight, they said, but what about their own African Kaiser, the *Bwana Obersti*, von Lettow?

When the Schutztruppe reached Tabora at last, von Lettow assembled all forces on parade one last time, saluted them, made a small speech expressing his gratitude for their service, and, tears in his eyes, turned away and marched toward the train that would take him down the restored tracks of the Central Railway to Dar es Salaam and eventually a steamer back to the grim and defeated Germany of the Weimar years.

But at the last moment, one of his loyal *askaris* broke away from the rest and, with *bibi* and child in tow, clutched at the commander's sleeve.

"I have been asked to say this to you, *Bwana* General," he said. "Where do you go now? Where you go, we will go with you! And if this is not the time, then wait until my son grows up to be a warrior and he will take my place and go with you. We will go with the *Bwana* General, will we not?" he cried, loud enough to be heard by all.

To a man, the *askaris* stepped forward, cheering, ready to follow the commander to the ends of the earth. But von Lettow held them back with a gesture and kept on marching.

His war was over now.

Chapter 25

GYLIPPUS IN RETIREMENT

On the afternoon of March 2, 1919, with a winter chill in the air, the only undefeated general still commanding the armies of a defeated nation moved in a strange kind of victory parade through the Brandenburg Gate in Berlin, a city in the midst of brutal right-vs.-left revolutionary turmoil.

Von Lettow and the surviving Schutztruppe officers—including General Whale (who had miraculously recovered from the flu that had struck him down at Ubena, been captured by the British, and taken to the hospital at Dar es Salaam), Captain Loof, and Governor Schnee—all moved in regimental order through cheering crowds of Berliners. The officers were smartly mounted, with von Lettow astride a stunning black charger. Most wore the faded khakis and sun helmets they had worn in Africa, though the dandyish Loof sported a neatly arranged naval uniform.

"Berlin had experienced very different things," von Lettow later wrote in *Mein Leben*, "undisciplined troops with their cockades torn off and shrieking women sitting on cannons covered with flowers." What they got was the return of an army, much diminished, but undefeated, who moved "in strict military formation with bands playing through the Brandenburg Gate out into the Pariser Platz. . . . It was the first time in a long time that the citizens of Berlin had come out into the streets in crowds. Thousands cheered us. It was like an awakening from a stupor."

And what von Lettow and his men brought back with them from Africa—while not exactly victory—was a precious commodity in Germany at the moment: the aura of a war well fought.

"I believe it was the transparency of our aims," von Lettow later wrote in an attempt to explain his successes in Africa, "the love of our Fatherland, our strong sense of duty, and the spirit of self-sacrifice which animated our few Europeans—and was communicated, consciously or unconsciously, to our brave black soldiers—that gave our operations the impetus which they possessed to the end. In addition, we felt a soldierly pride, a firm feeling of mutual cooperation, and a spirit of enterprise without which, in the end, military achievement is impossible."

Perhaps these martial attributes, dancing around the heads of the vestigial Schutztruppe—only 114 German officers and underofficers had survived the war—communicated itself to the defeated city that day. Or at least most of the city: After the parade through the Brandenburg Gate, Berlin's mayor had planned a formal banquet to celebrate von Lettow's campaigns in Africa. This he canceled, fearing violent interruptions from gangs of anti-Imperialist, pro-Bolshevik revolutionaries.

———————

A kind of darkness had descended over Germany. The darkness of defeat, surely—but also a darkness wrought by bitterness and a bottomless rage over all the pointless deaths of the war, which would blossom into an evil flower with the advent of Hitler and the Nazis barely fifteen years later. The Germans have a word for this condition—*Wut*—the rage that rises from despair. This was not a Germany von Lettow recognized. He had been absent from the Fatherland for five and a half years, a period of enormous change, accelerated by war and suffering. Without the Kaiser and Prussian military traditions as his life's guiding star, von Lettow felt himself unmoored. And though he retained his commission in the new German army, the Reichswehr, it was no longer *his* army. He might as well have been a mercenary fighting for an alien cause.

He was now fifty years old. Trim and vigorous, the episodes of malaria, the dreadful African parasites, even the murderous Spanish flu behind him. He was, also for the moment, famous. When the ship bearing him back to Europe had called at Rotterdam, he'd been met by cheering Dutch crowds, presented with the keys to the city. There a beautiful woman insisted his was "the most famous name in the world!" Flattered but skeptical, von Lettow considered the matter philosophically and knew the moment wouldn't last. He had seen too much of life and its ironies and vicissitudes to trust in fame. Still, the fact remained that an unmarried man, both famous and brave, and successful in his field, is clearly in want of a wife.

In his autobiography, von Lettow is typically coy about his connection to Margarethe Wallrath, the woman he had met at Willemshaven in 1913. Then, she had been an unhappily married young wife, with three small children. They had communicated via letter until 1916, when mail from Germany became as rare as a good bottle of beer in East Africa. Now von Lettow heard the news that Frau Wallrath had divorced her husband and was a single woman once more. Shortly after his parade through the Brandenburg Gate, he fired off a quick telegram summoning her to Berlin. He then arranged a minister to marry them—without first informing her of his plans! He had been, he admitted later, perhaps too used to the privileges of command; it actually never occurred to him that she might refuse.

Margarethe arrived at the apartment of his aged parents—whom she had looked in on from time to time during the war—oblivious to von Lettow's arrangements. Upon hearing they were to be married the next day, she first laughed—he couldn't be serious! They hadn't seen each other since 1913! No, he said, he was absolutely serious; he wanted to start a family, and they didn't have much time to waste. Infuriated by his presumption, she demanded he call a taxi to take her back to the station immediately. Fortunately for von Lettow, postwar German chaos intervened. The taxi drivers of Berlin had just gone on strike; the streets were dangerous; rioting gripped half the city. Persuaded to stay until the morning, Margarethe unpacked her things in an empty flat in his parents' building. What transpired overnight, we shall never know. We may assume von Lettow used all his big guns—not the 10.5cm *Königsberg*'s, left behind in Africa, but all the blandishments, persuasions, eloquence, and outright willpower of which he was capable.

The next day, in his parents' apartment before a small group of friends who had thought they were coming to a "Welcome Home, Paul" party, Paul von Lettow-Vorbeck and Margarethe Wallrath were married by the minister. Food shortages still plagued the population of Berlin. Von Lettow remarked, with typical self-deprecation, that the guests had agreed to attend the party as much for the sake of the turkey acquired for the occasion as for the guest of honor.

As it turned out, von Lettow had married well. Margarethe proved to be an excellent wife, both loving and domestically talented—and with her he acquired a ready-made family of three children, to which they eventually added four of their own: two daughters and two sons. Like General d'Hubert, the grizzled old campaigner in Joseph Conrad's story of the Napoleonic Wars, *The Duel*, von Lettow had found happiness after many years of brutal conflict in the arms of a pretty and thoughtful young woman: Here was a soldier's dream incarnate—to find a home at last, after all the emperor's wars.

For von Lettow's life on the public stage, only a few brief acts remained. He commanded one of the Freikorps—heavily armed militias composed of veterans seeking to restore order in an increasingly disturbed Germany in 1919. With these men, and some of his old Schutztruppe comrades at his side, he put down a communistic "Spartacist" insurrection in Hamburg—such was his reputation as a fearsome warrior—without firing a shot. He remained a general in the Reichswehr until May 1920 when he was dismissed for his small part in a conservative-monarchist coup attempt known as the Kapp Putsch.

After this dismissal, desperately broke, with his general's pension canceled and a growing family to support, von Lettow took a succession of jobs in the import-export business in Bremen—where he made his home—and later in Hamburg, Germany's former colonial hub. In the mid 1920s, he tried his hand at politics and was elected to the Reichstag as a member of the Conservative Party. But whenever he rose to speak, elements of the radical left rose to their feet to shout him down. "Murderer!" they screamed. "Imperialist!" and—resurrecting an epithet from his days pushing for war in the club lounges of Dar es Salaam back in 1913—shouting "Mad Mullah! Mad Mullah!" like an *askari* chant, over and over again. Von Lettow, imperturbable as ever and graced with his indestructible sense of humor, liked the sound of the word and named his first daughter Mullah. She was, quite naturally, not consulted in the matter.

In 1929 von Lettow received an unexpected invitation from London. He was asked to attend the Tenth Anniversary Dinner of the British East African

Expeditionary Force, a veterans' organization formed by those who had fought in the African campaigns. When he walked into the ballroom prepared for the event, the assembled company rose to their feet, gave him a standing ovation, and sang "For He's a Jolly Good Fellow," the singing of which humbled the retired general in a way the British armies had not been able to do in Africa. It was the equivalent, he later said, "of being awarded the Victoria Cross." At the banquet, he sat beside General Smuts and near Meinertzhagen; swapping war stories, he quickly became friends with both these former enemies.

Meanwhile, the years raced toward new disasters for Germany. Frustrated with politics and disgusted by the emergence of Nazism, von Lettow withdrew from public life—though he became known, dangerously, for his opposition to Hitler, whom he despised as a low-class Austrian arriviste, murderer, and madman. Eventually, von Lettow's political offices in Hamburg were ransacked by Nazi SA thugs and his life was threatened.

Outraged, and perhaps believing the rule of law still held sway in Germany, von Lettow bravely took the train to Berlin to confront Hitler about the SA attack—the only time he met the dictator: "He did not make the outstanding impression on me that many claimed he did on them," von Lettow later wrote. "He soon revealed that he had no interest at all in my case, and lost himself in a tirade about all the party had endured, 400 deaths, 1,500 casualties, etc. Hitler had no interest at all in justice or injustice. I saw it was pointless to discuss the matter."

Shortly after this meeting came the bloody interregnum called the "Night of the Long Knives"—from June 30 to July 2, 1934—when the paranoid dictator set about purging everyone whom he saw as a political threat, both on the left and right. The vicious Ernst Röhm, Hitler's longtime supporter and founder of the SA, fell victim to the murder squads, as did prominent anti-Nazi conservatives, including the former chancellor Kurt von Schleicher. Rumors circulated that von Lettow's name had been added to the death list; Margarethe von Lettow overheard Nazi party members discussing the purges on the Bremen train: "General Lettow-Vorbeck is also to be shot," one of them said. She hurried home in a panic to find her husband uncaught—as usual—and still alive.

They did not shoot him; they could not. As the only undefeated German general of World War One and a recipient of the vaunted Pour le Mérite, von Lettow had earned an unassailable place among the German Heroes. But they killed many of his friends and acquaintances. He was particularly saddened by the murder of Gustav Ritter von Kahr, another conservative, who had been responsible for prosecuting Hitler after the Beer Hall Putsch in 1923. Though "long ago resigned from the Bavarian government and . . . living harmlessly in the mountains," von Lettow noted sadly, von Kahr "was surprised in his home and taken out and beaten to death with rifle butts." Von Lettow's fundamental decency made it hard for him to comprehend such behavior: "Surely, Hindenburg," he concluded, too generously—who had facilitated a monster's rise to power and who died of natural causes a few weeks after Kahr's murder—"never fully understood what was going on."

As the German nation embraced Hitler wholeheartedly, von Lettow persisted in his refusal to join the Nazi Party, though urged to do so by many of his more practical friends in Bremen. Meanwhile, ex-Governor Schnee, who had never ceased agitating for the return of the German colonies in Africa, became an enthusiastic Nazi and was declared "Governor of the Colonies in Absentia" by Hitler. At last, in 1937, the Führer tried to co-opt von Lettow's support, offering him the ambassadorship to the Court of St. James. The old soldier refused this gesture with what has been described by some as "frigid hauteur," and by others with a phrase that is the German equivalent of "Go fuck yourself."

As Germany entered the Second World War, von Lettow suffered for his rejection of the regime. Though both his sons, Arnd and Rüdiger, and his stepson, Peter, died fighting for Germany, Nazi propaganda slandered the retired general as a decadent aristocrat and disloyal German and the Gestapo kept him under constant surveillance. The death of his sons, von Lettow wrote, "extinguished the male line of my branch of the family. That was indescribably hard. . . . But many, many German families had to bear the same."

The end of World War Two found von Lettow reduced to making buttons out of the horns of his old hunting trophies. This small industry, along with care packages from Meinertzhagen and Smuts, enabled him to feed his wife and daughters during months of privation in 1945–46.

He lived on and on.

Born into the nascent German Empire of 1870, von Lettow lived through so many permutations of Germany—the vigorous Germany of the Iron Chancellor von Bismarck, the Germany of the Kaiser and his colonies, the artistic and political ferment of the Weimar Republic, the Götterdämmerung of Nazism—and into the divided Western Germany of the *Wirtschaftswunder*, the "Economic Miracle" of the 1950s and '60s. Meanwhile, his ancestral homeland of Pomerania had fallen to the Communists. His constitution wasn't iron, but tempered steel; his habits regular; his disposition, as ever, optimistic. Von Lettow continued to smoke every day, though not as much as he had smoked in Africa during battle. A few years before he died, the Beatles with Pete Best on drums played 48 nights at the scruffy Kaiserkeller in Hamburg, not so far from where the old general lived with his daughter in the respectable middle-class neighborhood of Hamburg-Altona.

A few admirers still came to see him. One of them, an old flame, Karen von Blixen, better known now under her pen name of Isak Dinesen, sent him kisses on his ninetieth birthday. She had visited him earlier, during the war, as the special correspondent for the Danish newspaper *Politiken*. Then, in defiance of her Nazi handlers, she had wandered around Bremen with von Lettow. He showed her the sights and they ended up at a park in which there stood a memorial to the African war, a huge elephant made of red bricks. On the elephant's foot was a medallion showing a man's head.

"Why, that's you!" Karen said.

"Yes, they put me there," von Lettow said, embarrassed.

Africa always remained close to his heart and in his thoughts. He never forgot his *askaris* and they never forgot him. During the ferment of the years of African Liberation, a few of the young leaders of the movement, all sons of his *askaris*, came to seek his advice—there had been, inevitably, anticolonialist, antiwhite violence in the former colony. To one of them, later a Tanzanian government official, he gave, as he told Leonard Mosley, "a good talking-to. I told him not to despise the white people and not to humiliate them for the mistakes they made. 'We only repudiate the small men, father,' he replied. 'When the white man is big enough, as you were big enough, we continue to respect him.'"

This pleased the old veteran. He laughed and slapped his knee at the memory of this encounter.

In 1953, when von Lettow was in his eighties, with his daughter by his side, he returned to Africa for the first time since the end of World War One. He came into the harbor at Dar es Salaam as a passenger aboard the *Rhodesia Castle*; the city revealed itself in the vivid tropical sunshine, much as he remembered it, the palms of the busy waterfront rustling in a warm wind, the sun reflecting off the spire of the Lutheran church the Germans had built before the war. In the middle of the channel, the floating dock, sunk since 1914, still lay in thick muck at the bottom. A red buoy marked its presence for passing ships.

About 400 of von Lettow's former *askaris* waited on the quay. Many had walked from the far interior to greet their returning commander—even though his visit had not been publicized. No one could say how the word got around, but there they were. A kind of grizzled roar went up as von Lettow stepped among them. Their names, the details of battles came quickly to his tongue; he shook everyone's hand, beaming. It was as if he had come home again after nearly half a century. A few curious street urchins appeared looking for *baksheesh*; these were quickly pushed away: "None of that!" the old *askaris* cried. "We have come to see our *Bwana Obersti!*" For them it was a dignified, almost sacred, occasion. They offered to pay von Lettow's hotel bill, pay the ship to stay longer so he could visit with them for days instead of hours. He declined, laughing. He was on his way to see his old enemy— now one of his greatest friends—Smuts, in South Africa.

The British commissioner soon arrived with local dignitaries and a new British car to transport von Lettow to an official reception, but his *askaris* wouldn't allow it. They hoisted him on their aged shoulders and bore him off like a king returned, toward the Governor's Palace.

Paul von Lettow-Vorbeck died a few days before his ninety-fifth birthday on March 9, 1964.

He had outlived almost everyone from his generation, including his wife, Margarethe. He had gone from obscurity to fame to obscurity to fame again, as the Germany of the Economic Miracle reached for an honorable past, back before the Nazi scourge. In the end, he came to question the colonialism for which he had fought so hard and so long: "It is neither politically nor humanly justifiable," he wrote before he died, "to bring civilization to the natives and at the same time try to keep them continually in a state of dependence." When he saw the pyramids at Giza for the first time in the 1950s, he could only think that they had been built by "a tyranny that placed no value on human life," enslaving "thousands of people driven ruthlessly with whips." He had become what he had always been—a humanist.

The technocratic Bundestag of Konrad Adenauer paused in its steady accumulation of profit and arranged an expensive state funeral for the general. A couple of aged *askaris* were found in Tanganyika and flown to Germany for the event to stand on guard beside the coffin; the German Defense Minister, Kai-Uwe von Hassel, son of Theodor von Hassel, who had been one of von Lettow's officers in the Schutztruppe, delivered the eulogy. When they buried the old soldier at last, beneath a gray German sky in the cemetery of the ancient round-towered *Vicelinkirche* in Pronstorf, Schleswig-Holstein, a military band played "Haya Safari," the old Schutztruppe marching song.

TANZANIA PARK

A few years ago, an American historian decided to visit the *askari* memorial in Hamburg. He took a fast train from Paris just to see it and arrived in Hamburg on a rainy day, half worried that, given the political climate, the memorial might disappear from public view before he got there. Designed by von Ruckteschell in 1938, the *askari* memorial is composed of two large terra-cotta bas-reliefs, about seven feet high; they were installed on either side of the gates of the von Lettow-Vorbeck *Kaserne* (military barracks) a few months before Hitler invaded Poland.

The left-hand bas-relief shows four carriers bearing bundles on their heads led by an *askari* NCO; the right-hand bas-relief shows a detachment of four *askaris*, each bearing their old Jagerbuch 71 rifles, led by a German officer. As originally installed, the bas-reliefs seemed to be marching toward each other, as if to a rendezvous in the bush. An inscription in Gothic lettering on the pedestal reads only SCHUTZTRUPPE, 1914–1918—DEUTSCH-OST-AFRIKA. The bas-reliefs are done in that heavy art-deco-meets-medieval-wood-carving style popular in Germany in the long gray years after World War One. They're well rendered and quite impressive. Von Ruckteschell was a good artist, equally competent in both sculpture and painting, perhaps unjustly neglected today.

The bas-reliefs remained where they had been placed on either side of the gates until 1992 when, in a spasm of historical revisionism, it was decided that von Lettow had been a racist and a brutal colonialist and that the era of German rule in East Africa should not be remembered with a statue of any kind, if at all. The *Kaserne*, which had been named for him after World War Two, was shut down and the memorial bas-reliefs moved to a forlorn spot inside the gates called Tanzania Park and the gates were themselves closed with a chain and padlocked. At the same time they changed the names of certain streets in several German cities that had been named in honor of von Lettow.

In Tanzania Park, the *askari* memorial keeps company with other disgraced monuments, most notably a statue of von Wissmann, which had been pulled down with ropes by rampaging students from its place in a public park in Hamburg in 1967; a bust of Lothar von Trotha, author of the infamous *Schrecklichkeit*; and a stele honoring the dead of Germany's colonial wars. Even sequestered as they are inside the *Kaserne*, and viewed only by special permission, these statues and memorials are accompanied with explanatory plaques in English, German, and Swahili that function like the warning labels on packs of cigarettes—lest they corrupt the viewer with their unalloyed colonialist and martial spirit. The warning label posted beside von Ruckteschell's *askari* memorial reads in part:

> These terra-cotta reliefs recall the campaign of the German colonial troops under General Paul von Lettow-Vorbeck during the First World War in the colony of German East Africa. The campaign was conducted between 1914 and 1918, with about half a million people, most of them African civilians, killed directly and indirectly by acts of war. It was viewed as an example of German "heroism" in the years following 1918.

> The reliefs were set up in order to cultivate the popular legend of the loyalty of African soldiers to the German colonial army, and to legitimize the call for the return of the former German colonies.

Etc.

The American historian had a difficult time seeing the monuments. He chased around Hamburg for a while in the rain—it rains a lot in Germany—took a couple of trams, found a receptionist at the *Rathaus*, the city hall, who sent him to a Christian Democratic Party official, who then referred him to an architect who belonged to the citizens' group that had been debating what should be done with the monuments. The architect had been given the keys to the gates of the *Kaserne* and hence control over Tanzania Park. The historian explained that he had come all the way from Paris and that he didn't have much time, that he had to be back to work in the morning.

The architect took pity on the historian's somewhat absurd quest and invited him over for tea. They waited in the architect's exquisitely neat apartment for the rain to end—it was raining heavily now, and the historian was treated to an impromptu lecture on the undeniable horrors of colonialism in general and the horrors of the First World War in Africa in particular:

The death toll of the war in Africa can never be accurately tabulated, the architect said. No one kept count of the carriers who died, not the Germans or the English—but all told, including the combatants of both sides, it was probably somewhere between 300,000 and 500,000, though no one could say for sure. In any case, big numbers like this got bandied about by the architect, though he admitted they probably included all those who died from tropical diseases and the flu, which the Europeans had brought to Africa unwittingly. Von Lettow was primarily responsible for all the deaths, the architect continued, because he insisted on prosecuting the war when he should have surrendered—which is exactly what the British said in 1914, 1915, 1916, 1917, and 1918.

Of course, von Lettow got blamed for many things by many different people after the war. He got blamed by the British for refusing to admit they would win; he got blamed by the Spartacists for being an imperial stooge; he got blamed by the Reichswehr generals for opposing the Republic; he got blamed by Hitler for not being a Nazi. He got blamed for the deaths of *askaris* and German soldiers and African carriers by historians as yet unborn, and also for the death of any native who died from the flu or starvation when their fields were stripped clean of yams by the invading Schutztruppe.

There is, no doubt, a lot of justice in these accusations. War is a terrible thing best avoided by reasonable people. Approximately 80,000 men died, for example, in one day at the Battle of the Somme in 1916, and about 1,200,000 over the course of the battle. But war is also a human constant; there are likely to be more wars soon. Given this sad certainty—and given von Lettow's level of expertise: for example, that he was an artist of logistics, strategy, tactics, artillery barrages, Maxim guns, maneuvers, and the handling of troops in impossible terrain; and given von Lettow's contempt for everything in life that was nasty, gaudy, and irresolute—in the next war you would probably want him there. You would want him on your side.

At last the rain stopped.

Though it was nearly dusk, the American historian and the German architect got into the latter's stylish and impeccably preserved 1967 NSU Ro80 and drove over to see the *askari* memorial. The padlock, rusty by now, took a little time to open but finally fell away, and the chains were removed, the gates thrust back with a metallic scrape. The historian and the architect entered and wandered around the dripping grounds of the *Kaserne* a bit before they found the forlorn statuary garden called Tanzania Park.

Von Ruckteschell's forbidden monument, set into concrete supports, stood in the middle of a weedy patch of brown, untended grass. Nobody had been there in a long time. The historian took out his camera but suddenly couldn't take a picture. The tall, dark terra-cotta figures of the *askaris* and carriers and their lone German officer, marching toward each other in an imaginary Africa long ago, gleamed in the day's last light.

Selected Bibliography

BOOKS

Abbott, Peter. *Armies in East Africa, 1914–1918.* Oxford: Osprey Publishing, 2002.

Amery, L. S. *The German Colonial Claim.* New York: Longmans, Green & Co., 1940.

Aronson, Theo. *The Fall of the Third Napoleon.* New York: Bobbs-Merrill & Co., 1970.

Aschan, Ulf. *The Man Whom Women Loved: The Life of Bror Blixen.* New York: St. Martin's Press, 1987.

Bartholomew, J. G. *A Literary and Historical Atlas of Africa and Australasia.* London: J. M. Dent & Sons, 1913.

Bodin, Lynn E. *The Boxer Rebellion.* London: Osprey Publishing, 1982.

Bridgeman, Jon M. *The Revolt of the Hereros.* Berkeley: University of California Press, 1981.

Buchanan, Capt. Angus. *Three Years of War in East Africa.* Uckfield, UK: Naval and Military Press, 2015. First published 1919.

Chatterton, E. Keble. *The Königsberg Adventure.* London: Hurst & Blackett, 1930.

———. *Severn's Saga.* London: Hurst & Blackett, 1938.

Christiansen, Eric. *The Northern Crusades.* New York: Macmillan, 1980.

Craig, Gordon. *The Germans.* New York: Putnam, 1982.

Cranworth, Lord. *Kenya Chronicles.* London: Macmillan, 1939.

Cross, Wilbur. *Zeppelins of World War I.* London: I. B. Tauris, 1991.

Dinesen, Isak. *Daguerreotypes and Other Essays.* Chicago: University of Chicago Press, 1979.

———. *Out of Africa.* New York: Random House, 1937.

Dolbey, Capt. Robert V. *Sketches of the East Africa Campaign.* London: John Murray, 1918.

Downes, Capt. W. D. *With the Nigerians in German East Africa.* London: Methuen & Co., 1919.

Evans, Charles M. *War of the Aeronauts*. Mechanicsburg, PA: Stackpole Books, 2002.

Eyck, Erich. *Bismarck and the German Empire*. New York: W. W. Norton & Co., 1964.

Farrar-Hockley, Anthony. *The Somme*. London: B. T. Batsford, 1964.

Farwell, Byron. *The Great War in Africa, 1914–1918*. New York: W. W. Norton & Co., 1986.

Fleming, Peter. *The Siege at Peking*. New York: Harper Bros., 1959.

Foden, Giles. *Mimi and Toutou's Big Adventure*. New York: Alfred A. Knopf, 2005.

Friedrich, Otto. *Before the Deluge: A Portrait of Berlin in the 1920s*. New York: Harper & Row, 1972.

Gardner, Brian. *On to Kilimanjaro*. Philadelphia: Macrae Smith, 1963.

Garfield, Brian. *The Meinertzhagen Mystery*. Dulles, VA: Potomac Books, 2007.

Hancock, W. K. *Smuts: The Sanguine Years, 1870–1919*. Cambridge: Cambridge University Press, 1962.

Hodges, Geoffrey. *The Carrier Corps*. New York: Greenwood Press, 1986.

Hoyt, Edwin P. *Guerilla*. New York: Macmillan, 1981.

———. *The Zeppelins*. New York: Lothrop, Lee & Shepard, 1969.

Huxley, Elspeth. *The Sorcerer's Apprentice: A Journey Through East Africa*. London: Chatto & Windus, 1948.

Ingham, Kenneth. *Jan Christian Smuts: The Conscience of a South African*. London: Weidenfeld & Nicolson, 1986.

James, Lawrence. *The Rise and Fall of the British Empire*. New York: Little, Brown & Co., 1994.

Junger, Ernst. *Copse 125*. New York: Howard Fertig, Inc., 1988.

Jurado, Carlos C. *The German Freikorps, 1918–1923*. Oxford, UK: Osprey Publishing, 2001.

Keegan, John. *The First World War*. New York: Vintage Books, 1998.

King-Hall, Admiral Sir Herbert. *Naval Memories and Traditions*. London: Hutchinson, 1926.

Kock, Nis. *Blockade and Jungle*. Nashville: Battery Press, 1986. First published 1940.

Lettow-Vorbeck, Paul von. *East African Campaigns*. New York: Robert Speller & Sons, 1957.

———. *Mein Leben*. Biberach an der Riss, West Germany: Koehlers Verlag, 1957.

Macintyre, Captain Donald. *Jutland*. London: Evans Bros. 1957.

Meinertzhagen, Richard. *Army Diary, 1899–1926*. London: Oliver & Boyd, 1960.

———. *Diary of a Black Sheep*. London: Oliver & Boyd, 1964.

————. *Kenya Diary, 1902–1906.* London: Oliver & Boyd, 1958.

Miller, Charles. *Battle for the Bundu.* New York: Macmillan, 1974.

————. *The Lunatic Express.* New York: Macmillan, 1971.

Morris, Ronald D. *The Washing of the Spears.* New York: Simon & Schuster, 1965.

Mosley, Leonard. *Duel for Kilimanjaro.* London: Weidenfeld & Nicolson, 1963.

O'Neill, H. C. *The Royal Fusiliers in the Great War.* London: Heinemann, 1932.

Paice, Edward. *World War I: The African Front.* New York: Pegasus Books, 2008.

Pakenham, Thomas. *The Boer War.* New York: Random House, 1979.

————. *The Scramble for Africa: White Man's Conquest of the Dark Continent from 1876 to 1912.* New York: HarperCollins, 1991.

Poolman, Kenneth. *Zeppelins over England.* London: Evans Bros., 1960.

Preston, Diana. *Besieged in Peking.* London: Constable & Co., 1999.

Pretorius, Major P. J. *Jungle Man.* New York: E. P. Dutton & Co., 1948.

Quesada, Alejandro de, and Chris Dale. *Imperial German Colonial and Overseas Troops, 1885–1918.* Oxford, UK: Osprey Publishing, 2014.

Reitz, Deneys. *Trekking On.* London: Faber & Faber, 1933.

Richthofen, Manfred von. *The Red Baron: My Life in the War.* New York: Ace Books, 1969.

Robinson, Douglas. *The Zeppelin in Combat.* London: G. T. Foulis & Co., 1962.

Shankland, Peter. *The Phantom Flotilla.* London: Collins, 1968.

Sibley, David J. *The Boxer Rebellion and the Great Game in China.* New York: Hill and Wang, 2012.

Stejskal, James. *The Horns of the Beast: World War I in South-West Africa, 1914–15.* Solihul, UK: Helion & Co., 2014.

Taylor, Stephen. *The Mighty Nimrod: A Life of Frederick Courteney Selous.* London: William Collins Sons & Co., 1989.

Thurman, Judith. *Isak Dinesen: The Life of a Storyteller.* New York: St. Martin's, 1982.

Townsend, Mary E. *The Rise and Fall of Germany's Colonial Empire, 1884–1918.* New York: Macmillan, 1930.

Waldman, Eric. *The Spartacist Uprising of 1919.* Milwaukee, WI: Marquette University Press, 1958.

Wenig, Richard. *In Monsun und Pori.* Berlin: Safari-Verlag, G.M.B.H., 1922.

Woodhall, Edwin T. *Spies of the Great War.* London: John Long, 1932.

Young, Francis Brett. *Jim Redlake.* London: William Heinemann, 1930.

————. *Marching on Tanga.* London: William Collins Sons & Co., 1917.

PERIODICALS

Contey, Frank A. "Zeppelin Mission to East Africa." *Aviation History Magazine,* Sept. 2002.

Gray, Edwyn. "Cruiser at Bay: The Story of the *Königsberg.*" *Military History Magazine,* Oct. 1990.

Index